INTERDISCIPLINARY GENERAL EDUCATION

QUESTIONING OUTSIDE THE LINES

MARCIA BUNDY SEABURY EDITOR

University of Hartford
All-University Curriculum

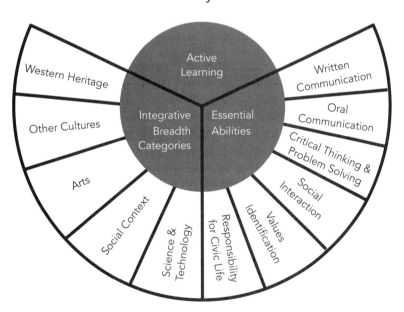

COLLEGE ENTRANCE EXAMINATION BOARD

NEW YORK

Editorial inquiries should be addressed to Publications Services, The College Board, 45 Columbus Avenue, New York, N.Y. 10023-6992.

Copies of this book may be ordered from College Board Publications, Box 886, New York, N.Y. 10101-0886, (800) 323-7155. The price of this book is $29.95 for hardcover, $22.95 for paperback.

Library of Congress Catalog Card Number: 99-074151

International Standard Book Number: 0-87447-640-2 hardcover
                                    0-87447-639-9 paperback

Printed in the United States of America.

CONTENTS

APPENDIX

References and sample syllabi follow each chapter.

ACKNOWLEDGMENTS

As editor I would like to acknowledge my appreciation for the conversations and collaboration with my colleagues at the University of Hartford who have participated in this project. I have learned a great deal from them along the way and thank them for their insights, as well as for their patience with deadlines, guidelines, and the multiple readings and revisions such a project entails. The process pushed both me and the individual contributors beyond our various initial conceptions of the whole and its parts. In this sense and others it has mirrored the process of collaborative interdisciplinary teaching, with its particular challenges, surprises, and rewards.

We all would like to thank the College Board, especially Robert Orrill, Director of the Office of Academic Affairs, for its sponsorship of this book and project manager Diane Foster for her expert advice and assistance over many months. We also appreciate the helpful feedback from the College Board's Advisory Panel on Interdisciplinary Studies (Julie Thompson Klein, William Newell, Beth Casey, Ben Ebersole, and Carl Zon), publishing consultant Joanne Daniels, and an anonymous outside reviewer. We are grateful to Bill Newell for sharing prepublication copies of *Interdisciplinarity: Essays from the Literature* (New York: College Entrance Examination Board, 1999), which contributors used to locate some of the articles referenced, and to Julie Klein for encouraging the project at its outset; we owe further thanks to these two for serving through their writings as such excellent guides to the issues and literatures of interdisciplinarity.

Appreciation goes to Neil Browne for adding his expert and eloquent voice to our efforts through his Foreword; to Karen Barrett, Elizabeth McDaniel, Marilyn Smith, and Rob Fried, as well as Jill Ghnassia, DeLois Traynum-Lindsey, and Marcia Moen, for reading and offering feedback on various parts of the volume; to Kim Farrington and her Interlibrary Loan Department at the University of Hartford for their extensive and patient assistance; and to the Vincent B. Coffin grant program at Hartford for help with expenses.

An Andrew W. Mellon Grant for General Education made possible the development of the interdisciplinary teams and courses that became the foundation for the interdisciplinary work described in this volume. Key members of the university's Board of Regents, in particular Donald W. Davis, retired chairman of the board and CEO, The Stanley Works, and Jon O. Newman, Judge, U.S. Court of Appeals for the Second Circuit, provided essential support for the successful adoption of Hartford's interdisciplinary curriculum.

Finally, we the contributors offer warm thanks to those with whom we live for their ongoing encouragement and forbearance as we broke from routines of both family and school to take on the open-ended challenges of interdisciplinary and collaborative work.

COURSES DISCUSSED

The chapters in this volume focus on issues of interdisciplinary teaching and learning arising out of particular courses that are offered in the All-University Curriculum at the University of Hartford within five categories (with the understanding that interdisciplinary courses cross these divisions as well). The courses discussed are listed below, followed by the names of the authors of the corresponding chapters.

Course	Authors
Living in a Cultural Context: Western Heritage	
• Discovering America I, II, and III	Grant; also Canedy
Living in a Cultural Context: Other Cultures	
• Hunger: Problems of Scarcity and Choice	Horvath, Dix, and den Ouden
• Literature and Film of Other Cultures	Hale
• The Caribbean Mosaic	Sandström and Duncan
• Cultures and Transnational Corporations	Sandström and Duncan
Living Responsively With the Arts	
• Romanticism in the Arts	Ghnassia; also Seabury
• Creativity: The Dynamics of Artistic Expression	Roderick
• Ethnic Roots and Urban Arts	Curtis, Rauche, and Weinswig
Living in a Social Context	
• Sources of Power	Horvath
• Sex, Society, and Selfhood	Edwards
• Ethics in the Professions	Smith, Gardow, and Reale-Foley
• What Is School?	Fried and DiBella-McCarthy
Living in a Scientific and Technological World	
• Reasoning in Science	Dix, Miller, Horn, and Brown
• Epidemics and AIDS	Aloisi, Barrett, Ciarcia, and Ghnassia
• Seeing Through Symmetry	Gould

An overview of the All-University Curriculum appears at the end of this volume.

CONTRIBUTORS

Ralph Aloisi (D.A. in Clinical Biochemistry, Catholic University of America) is Professor of Biology and Health Science, Chair of the Division of Health Professions, and Associate Dean of the College of Education, Nursing, and Health Professions at the University of Hartford. He has authored three books on clinical immunology and immunodiagnostics, and published numerous articles related to allied health education and clinical laboratory science.

Karen Barrett (M.S. in Allied Health Education and Evaluation, State University of New York at Buffalo) is Director of the All-University Curriculum (AUC), Associate Dean of Undergraduate Studies, Program Director of Medical Technology, and Director of Allied Health Education, Evaluation, and Accreditation at the University of Hartford. She is an American Society of Clinical Pathologists (ASCP) board-certified medical technologist and teaches courses in Hematology, Clinical Microbiology, and Management in the university's Clinical Laboratory Sciences program. She has published articles on interdisciplinary health and science education, and has recently presented workshops on outcomes assessment and problem-based learning.

Dale Brown (M.S. in Biology, University of Hartford) is adjunct instructor in the All-University Curriculum at the University of Hartford. He has taught courses in biology and environmental studies for many years, including the AUC's Living in the Environment course as well as Reasoning in Science, alongside his career in business.

M. Neil Browne (Ph.D. in Economics, University of Texas) is Distinguished Teaching Professor of Economics at Bowling Green State University. He is the coauthor of *Asking the Right Questions: A Guide to Critical Thinking* (5th ed., 1998), which has been translated into Chinese, Russian, Ukranian, and Korean. In addition, he is the coauthor of *Striving for Excellence in College: Tips for Active Learning* (2nd ed., 2000), *The Legal Environment of Business: A Critical Thinking Approach* (2nd ed., 2000), and over 100 refereed publications in law, economics, communication, and higher education journals. In addition, he has received numerous local, state, and national teaching awards. In 1994–95 he served as the University of Hartford's National Endowment for the Humanities/Harry Jack Gray Distinguished Visiting Humanist.

Charles R. Canedy, 3rd (M.B.A., Kent State; Ph.D. in History, Case Western Reserve) is Associate Professor in the Barney School of Business and Public Administration at the University of Hartford. He teaches graduate and undergraduate offerings in marketing and an All-University Curriculum course he designed on Understanding the Dynamics and Environment of the World of Business, as well as the Discovering America course. His particular interests are marketing management, product innovation and development, and case-method instruction. He is coauthor of articles on consumer satisfaction and product quality.

Margaret Ciarcia (M.S. in Biology, University of Hartford) is Health Science Program Director, Medical Technology Clinical Coordinator and Clinical Assistant Professor, and coordinator of Medical Technology Continuing Education at the University of Hartford. She is an American Society of Clinical Pathologists (ASCP)-certified medical technologist and an allied health educator. She has published and presented abstracts and papers on immunohematology as well as on AIDS, problem-based learning, and clinical laboratory science continuing education.

Guy C. Colarulli (Ph.D. in American Government, American University) is Associate Provost and Dean of Undergraduate Studies at the University of Hartford. He was director of the Mellon Grant for General Education that led to the development of the All-University Curriculum. His special interests include general education curriculum, higher education administration, and legislative and electoral politics.

A. Cheryl Curtis (Ed.D. in Reading Education, University of Massachusetts) is Assistant Professor of Secondary Education at the University of Hartford, where she teaches courses in secondary methods and introduction to education and human services. Previously she chaired and taught in the Reading and Academic Development Department of Hartford's Hillyer College. Her current research interests are in multicultural education, critical and feminist pedagogy, and culturally responsive curriculum.

Bernard den Ouden (Ph.D., Hartford Seminary) is Professor of Philosophy at the University of Hartford. He chairs three departments: Philosophy; Rhetoric, Language, and Culture; and International Languages and Cultures. He is the author of *Language & Creativity; Reason, Will, Creativity, and Time;* and *The Fusion of Naturalism and Humanism,* and has edited three other volumes. Den Ouden has worked as a consultant for Care International, the U.N. World Food Program, Environmental Quality International, World Share, and Catholic Relief Services, and has done fieldwork in India, Bangladesh, Egypt, Guatemala, and the Dominican Republic. He has given guest lectures at many universities across the United States, Europe, and Russia. Den Ouden has served as Distinguished Teaching Humanist at Hartford and received the university's Larsen Teaching Award.

Holly DiBella-McCarthy (M.Ed. in Special Education, University of Hartford; Sixth-Year Diploma in Educational Administration, University of Connecticut) is special education teacher in the Mansfield, Connecticut, public schools. Before assuming this position she taught in the Reading and Academic Development Department in Hillyer College at the University of Hartford and then served for several years as director of Educational Main Street, a grant-supported tutoring program linking university students with students in three neighboring Hartford public schools and including affiliate faculty, academic alliances, curriculum articulation, and parent education programming.

Doug Dix (B.S. in Chemistry and Ph.D. in Biochemistry, State University of New York at Buffalo) is Professor of Biology and Medical Technology at the University of Hartford. He is a Diplomate of the American Board of Clinical Chemistry and has published work in theoretical biology, cancer epidemiology, carcinogenesis, cancer chemotherapy, and clinical decision analysis.

Errol Duncan (M.A. in English and M.Sc. in Education, Central Connecticut) attended school, university, and law school in the Commonwealth West Indies, served as headmaster of an elementary school and as Director of Sports for the Jamaican government in the 1970s, and is now completing a Ph.D. in English. His dissertation focuses on Jamaican cultural icon Louise Bennett. His teaching experience as adjunct instructor in the All-University Curriculum, African American studies, history, and politics, and as a high school English teacher, reflect his interdisciplinary interests.

Jane Edwards (Ph.D. in Folklore and Folklife, University of Pennsylvania; B.A. in English, Cambridge University), interdisciplinarian by training and inclination, is Director of International Studies at Wesleyan University, where she is also an adjunct lecturer in the department of Romance Languages and Literatures. Prior to this appointment she taught for the departments of English and Sociology and for the All-University Curriculum at the University of Hartford. Author of *The World in the Curriculum* (with Humphrey Tonkin), she has published numerous articles on topics in international education.

Robert Fried (Ed.D. in Learning Environments, Harvard) is Visiting Associate Professor of Education at Northeastern University. Prior to this appointment he was Associate Professor of Education in the doctoral program of Educational Leadership at the University of Hartford. He has served as a field coordinator for the Coalition of Essential Schools and as a consultant with schools across the country. He is the author of *The Passionate Teacher* (Beacon, 1995).

Ernest Gardow (S.M., Massachusetts Institute of Technology; Ph.D. in Mechanical Engineering, State University of New York at Buffalo) is Professor of Mechanical Engineering at the University of Hartford. He is a former member of the Connecticut Board of Examiners for Professional Engineers and past Vice-President of the American Society of Mechanical Engineers (ASME) for Professional Practice and Ethics.

Jill Dix Ghnassia (Ph.D. in English, Duke University) is Associate Professor of English and Director of the Honors Program at the University of Hartford. She is author of *Metaphysical Rebellion in the Works of Emily Bronte* and coauthor of two AUC texts, and has published or lectured on subjects ranging from the Brontes, Mary Wollstonecraft, Edmund Burke, Percy Shelley, and Akutagawa, to Literature and Medicine.

Laurence I. Gould (Ph.D. in Physics, Temple University) is Professor of Physics at the University of Hartford. He also has taught math and interdisciplinary courses, including Astronomy, Linear Algebra, Musical Acoustics, and Reasoning in Science. His areas of specialization, mathematical physics and science education, have resulted in publication in such periodicals as the *International Journal of Theoretical Physics, American Journal of Physics,* and *Journal of College Science Teaching.* Honors include Yale Visiting Fellowships, listing in *Who's Who in Science and Engineering,* and membership in the Connecticut Academy of Arts and Sciences. He is also an avid amateur violinist.

Thomas Grant (Ph.D. in English, Rutgers) is Professor of English in the College of Arts and Sciences at the University of Hartford. He is the author of a book on Elizabethan comedy and many articles on American humorists, American drama, and western film. He has been a visiting professor at Yale University and a Senior Fulbright Lecturer in Germany and Portugal, as well as the recipient of four National Endowment for the Humanities fellowships.

Virginia Hale (Ph.D. in English, University of Connecticut) is Professor of English in Hartford's College of Arts and Sciences, specializing in medieval literature. Hale has taught in the All-University Curriculum since its inception and is a former director of the program. With Paul Stacy she edited the two-volume text *Literature and Film of Other Cultures.*

Anne Hendershott (Ph.D. in Sociology, Kent State University) is Chair of the Department of Sociology and coordinator of Urban Studies at the University of San Diego. Formerly the Director of the Center for Social Research at the University of Hartford, her research and publications focus upon inequality. She has taught in the areas of research methods, urban social problems, crime and delinquency, and work and the family. She has been the principal investigator for several grants that focus on urban areas and community service.

Mike Horn (M.S. in Mechanical Engineering, University of Miami) is Assistant Professor of Computer and Electronic Engineering Technology and Director of the Computer Applications Laboratory in Ward College of Technology at the University of Hartford. He serves on the AUC Committee.

Jane Horvath (B.A. in Economics and Sociology, and M.A. and Ph.D. in Economics with a concentration in economic development, University of Connecticut) is Associate Professor of Economics and Associate Dean for Academic Administration of Hillyer College at the University of Hartford. For several years she served as Associate Director of the All-University Curriculum. She is the author of *Small and Medium Scale Manufacturing in Mexican Development, 1954–1989* and has also published articles in the field of economic education. Her emerging research interest in the gay, lesbian, and queer movements stems from her work in the AUC course Sources of Power.

Elizabeth A. McDaniel (Ph.D. in Education, University of Miami) is currently serving as a Senior Fellow at the American Council on Education. Her special interests are teaching and learning in higher education, faculty efficacy, the new learning paradigm, and the integration of technology. Before moving to Florida to serve as Executive Provost and Vice President for Academic Affairs at Nova Southeastern University in Fort Lauderdale from 1995 to 1998, she taught for several years at the University of Hartford, served as the first director of the All-University Curriculum, and became Associate Vice President of Academic Affairs and Associate Dean of the Faculty.

Regina Miller (B.A. in Russian Language and Literature, M.A. in Child Development, and Ph.D. in Developmental and Child Psychology, University of Kansas) is Associate Professor of Early Childhood and Special Education, Director of the Early Childhood Center at the University of Hartford, and author of the book *The Developmentally Appropriate Inclusive Classroom in Early Education* (Delmar Publishers, 1996).

Anthony T. Rauche (Ph.D. in Musicology, University of Illinois) is Associate Professor of Ethnomusicology and Music Theory at the University of Hartford, where he has taught a wide range of undergraduate and graduate courses in western music and world music, as well as All-University Curriculum courses on Native American Cultures and Literature and Culture of Immigrant Groups in America. His research has focused on Italian American music, Hispanic music in northern New Mexico, and Native American music, and is published by UMI Research Press, the American Italian Historical Association, and Utah State University Press. He has presented papers at numerous national and international scholarly meetings, and is active as a professional pianist and organist.

Laura Reale-Foley (M.B.A. in Health Care Administration, University of Chicago School of Business; M.A. in Philosophy, Trinity College) is an adjunct instructor in the All-University Curriculum. She has 10 years of experience in business and is a member of the St. Francis Hospital Medical Ethics Committee.

John M. Roderick (Ph.D. in English, Brown University) has published fiction, creative nonfiction, journalism, and poetry in anthologies, magazines, newspapers, and journals nationally. He has been named Poet-of-the-Year by the New England Association of Teachers of English. A teacher of writing, literature, and journalism, Roderick received the University of Hartford's Larsen Award for Excellence in Teaching in 1996. He was also named 1996 Connecticut Professor of the Year by the Carnegie Foundation for the Advancement of Teaching and by the Council for Advancement and Support of Education.

Harald M. Sandström (Ph.D. in International Relations, University of Pennsylvania; M.Sc. in the same field, London School of Economics; postdoctoral work in Political Psychology, Yale) is Associate Professor of Politics and Government, Coordinator of Political Economy, and Director of African American Studies at the University of Hartford. Swedish born, he wrote his dissertation on the Jamaican Black Power movement and dependency theory. He teaches courses on Third World development and underdevelopment. He has coauthored and coedited a book on *The Caribbean After Grenada* and is completing a book on *The Third World After the Cold War: Continuing Dilemmas of Development.*

Marcia Bundy Seabury (Ph.D. in English, University of Illinois) is Associate Professor of English in Hillyer College, University of Hartford, and served as director of the All-University Curriculum from 1993–96. She teaches a variety of courses in composition, literature, and interdisciplinary arts. She has published articles on interdisciplinary teaching and learning in *Perspectives: The Journal of the Association for General and Liberal Studies* and *Humanities Education,* as well as on composition and literature pedagogy, contemporary fiction, and literary dystopias in such journals as *College Composition and Communication, Journal of General Education, Studies in Short Fiction,* and *Christianity and Literature.* (contact: *seabury@mail.hartford.edu*)

Marilyn S. Smith (B.A. in English Literature, Barnard; M.A., Columbia, and M.A., Union Theological Seminary, in the Philosophy of Religion) is Associate Professor Emerita in Philosophy. Her books include *Living Issues in Philosophy* and *The Range of Philosophy.* Her specialization is in biomedical ethical issues, American philosophy, and the Socratic dialogues of Plato.

S. Edward Weinswig (Ed.D., Boston University) is Professor of Curriculum and Instruction at the University of Hartford, where he teaches courses in educational issues and curriculum for both undergraduates and graduates. He has trained teachers and prospective teachers in the U.S. Virgin Islands, Puerto Rico, Holland, Israel, and England, and has developed curriculum for Upward Bound and Teacher Corps as well as many communities in the United States, emphasizing issues of diversity. He has been the recipient of the ACE Connecticut Professor of the Year, the Larsen Award for Excellence in Teaching, the Trachtenberg Award for University and Community Service, and the Greater Hartford Chamber of Commerce Renaissance Award for contributions to education. He has presented at many national conferences.

Sheila Phelan Wright (Ph.D. in Higher Education Administration, University of Connecticut) is Vice Provost for Undergraduate Studies, Wellness, and Campus Life at the University of Denver, where she is an Associate Professor in the School of Education. She is a former director of the All-University Curriculum at Hartford. She teaches courses in interdisciplinary humanities, leadership theory and development, and mentoring. Research and scholarship interests include interdisciplinary teaching and learning, as well as women and leadership.

FOREWORD:

LISTENING AND SPEAKING TO A LARGER AUDIENCE

M. Neil Browne

As a prospective graduate student, I studied the brochures touting the programs, talked to my undergraduate advisers, and considered the promised financial aid packages. While I knew myself well enough to realize that my curiosity would never be satisfied working within a single discipline, I knew I had to comply or feign compliance with uncommon devotion to one and only one discipline. Trying to find a match, I accepted the invitation of the economics program that promised to "provide students with a broad interdisciplinary understanding of economic questions." The brochure went on to mention multiple other disciplines that students would grow to appreciate as they moved through that Ph.D. program.

What I was seeking then is still a rare commodity, the exhilarating complexity and tension of interdisciplinary discourse. While in retrospect the economics program I completed was a tad more interdisciplinary than others I later encountered, the professors in the department correctly understood that their reputations and that of the department would be built on the strength of a disciplinary voice. Interdisciplinary work was a luxury they would not encourage for themselves or for their students, even when they personally saw its merits.

Scholars all know at one level that their brothers and sisters in other disciplines ask important questions and produce provocative output. The validity of this presumption is so clear that it appears to need no support. We appreciate that academics in other disciplines are intelligent, diligent, and driven to distinguish themselves by innovative contributions. Valuable insights are readily found beyond the comfortable seminars of our respective home disciplines. Anyone who dares to step outside that home discipline in search of interdisciplinary fertilizer soon encounters concepts and viewpoints that supplement disciplinary discourse. Thus it follows that every thoughtful academic should be busily mining multiple disciplines in search of remarkable gems that can bring new perspective to otherwise insular scholarship.

But something is wrong with that scenario. It is rarified; it does not ring true. Why are so few scholars developing productive careers designing models of interdisciplinary education? Why is interdisciplinary scholarship so frequently the preserve of aging scholars such as J. Kenneth Galbraith, Jerome Bruner, or Richard Posner who no longer feel the need to impress the mandarins within their own disciplines? Is the deluge of modern scholarship so overwhelming that no one but a dilettante would deign to make contributions to any domain other than a disciplinary subfield? Why is the logic of interdisciplinarity less than compelling? And what can *Interdisciplinary General Education* contribute to strengthening that logic?

THE AUTHORITY OF THE DISCIPLINE

As prelude to considering the demonstration of interdisciplinary prowess in this volume, we might remind ourselves of the strength of a disciplinary voice. First, and perhaps most important, a discipline provides a haven of identity. It serves as our very own village with all the comforting familiarity and potential provincialism implicit in that idea. An academic department is comprised of our people, people who are more or less familiar with the same canons and language on which we rely to make sense of the world. They see reality through a lens we too have used to good effect on many occasions.

Second, if we can judge from the large number of sneering comments about educational practice in "other" disciplines, our disciplinary voice offers a comforting sense of superiority. If only those in other disciplines understood what we understand in our discipline about methodology, rhetoric, and the world in general, we are convinced that they would make huge advances in their relatively enfeebled fields. Hence, we are quick to guard against interlopers from other disciplines who threaten to dirty the quality of our work by an adventurous foray into our territory. Even the use of one of our traditional nouns in the title of an essay or course sets our defense systems on ready alert. We wonder, what mischief might be afoot here?

The other sources of strength provided by a disciplinary voice are probably derivative from these psychological attributes. Disciplines give us comfort inside the community and serve as a boundary against potentially deficient pretenders who wish to garner the respect we cherish for ourselves. They give us a feeling of being special, and competent as well.

Many additional reasons for resistance to interdisciplinarity flow from the link between psychological comfort and identifiable membership in a particular disciplinary community. Mobility within the profession, awards of distinction, and professional reputation all ordinarily depend on achievement within a discipline. I hardly think mine is the only university in which the annual service record contains no special site of distinction for research output contributing to discourse in multiple disciplines. On the contrary, departmental colleagues assume that performances and publications will remain within the confines of the home discipline.

In place of numerous other rationales for resistance to interdisciplinarity, I offer one omnibus rationale: normal human laziness. I do not find any special problem among scholars in this regard. All of us know colleagues who could be poster people for diligence. Surveys suggest that most academics view themselves as busy and committed, but imagine how much more stressed their work would be were they to feel a need to read and question beyond their own disciplinary boundaries.

That task, broadly construed, is truly overwhelming. In the face of such a threat to inner peace, we are quick to lash out at the silliness implicit in interdisciplinary pretense. We speak, with much accuracy and compelling finality, of the Olympian effort required to keep up with developments even in our disciplinary subfields. Is the interdisciplinary vision, thus, just a manifestation of academic hubris?

THE DISCIPLINARY BASE
FOR INTERDISCIPLINARY PRACTICE

Those of us who embrace interdisciplinary general education have a responsibility to reason with our detractors. The previous section adumbrates some of the obstacles. How do we respond effectively?

Why not start by noting the strength of their reasoning? Interdisciplinary scholarship is audacious, as is any major human effort. It will always be plagued by a failure to appreciate certain nuances in the disciplines from which it borrows. It can never be accomplished with high distinction as long as the metaphor is mastery. These are not trivial difficulties; they haunt all of us who wish to listen and speak to larger audiences—those beyond our disciplinary enclaves.

Most readers of *Interdisciplinary General Education* are well aware of the counterarguments that sustain our vision. Those who contributed to this volume and their interdisciplinary colleagues have experienced the epiphanies of discovering patterns in the work of scholars in other fields. We know the words we want to say to those who shy away from the robustness of interdisciplinarity, but how can we be heard by our detractors? I have a suggestion. Explain that interdisciplinary scholarship depends on and is enriched by a solid grounding in the disciplines from which we draw. The hope here is that skeptics will welcome our efforts to ask the larger public to pay more respect to the various disciplines. Interdisciplinary work flatters specific disciplines by borrowing so much from them.

What I mean is that interdisciplinary general education depends on disciplinary perspectives. While interdisciplinary scholars may not pay reflexive allegiance to particular disciplinary approaches, they are reliant on disciplinary research. Synthesis, not just opposition, should be the theme of our efforts to champion interdisciplinarity. The sources of disagreement with some of our colleagues will remain, of course. But by telling as many of them as will listen how dependent we are on their understandings, we may create an opportunity to offer our standard arguments to more receptive ears.

Here is where the present volume can make an important contribution. Notice how the various models of interdisciplinarity presented relate to the disciplinary backgrounds and explorations of the authors. Developing integrative skills requires knowledge of at least two things to integrate. In the case of the essays in this volume, the substance for the integrative efforts often flows from disciplinary knowledge or process. Pointing out this reliance can serve as an anodyne, calming the often rancorous debates concerning the proper scope of interdisciplinarity in postsecondary education. Those of us who participate in these conversations and admire interdisciplinary scholarship need all the friends we can earn. The excellence of this volume and its celebration of multiple disciplines could well tempt numerous readers to join our mission.

If that rhetorical move is not effective, I suggest another based on a unifying theme that brings us all together as academics—the nurturing of learners. Our students do not and will not reside in disciplinary silos with thick concrete protecting them from enigmas and adventures that would profit from interdisciplinary insights. They need experience struggling with the broad integrative questions of purpose, epistemology, ethics, and aesthetics. Stimulated by the successful endeavors documented in this volume, readers can better articulate the manifest contributions of interdisciplinarity to cognitive development.

Focus on disciplinary questions, whatever its benefit to scholarship, can repress the broad curiosity of students that compels them to ask the larger questions. Interdisciplinary experiences encourage complex critical thinking that draws evidence and critique from every credible source, regardless of the discipline of origin. The resulting engagement with a rich panoply of perspectives and viewpoints can nurture a zeal for creative problem solving otherwise stunted by the strictures of disciplinary borders.

A unifying arc between both these suggestions for enlarging the interdisciplinary community is the belief that questions about human beings and society are not classified along disciplinary lines. On several occasions I have felt a certain shame and substantial humility when, after completing a research study from inside one or another discipline, I stumbled later on ideas and questions from other disciplines that would have either fertilized or, in some instances, debilitated my once-proud argument. Perhaps we can rightfully say that disciplinary work needs interdisciplinary work to achieve its full developmental promise.

INTEGRATIVE SKILLS AT WORK

Interdisciplinary work has a multitude of purposes. On display in this volume is one of the more important of those objectives: the development of integrative skills. Pattern creation and meaning construction are among the most enduring of human efforts. As readers of this book will surely note, this is where interdisciplinary skills and dispositions are especially enriching.

John Roderick's opening essay provides a framework for seeing the volume as a whole. Each author is trying to transcend the "mask" of the home discipline while at the same time using that perspective to free the creative process. When the students in Roderick's essay don their masks, they are able to express much more than without the masks. They have been liberated in a manner that is most difficult in a course in a particular discipline, in which disciplinary norms require a practitioner to deploy the accepted protocols and lexicons.

The next essay by Robert Fried and Holly DiBella McCarthy is especially thought provoking because it explicitly focuses on the role of the student in constructing the interdisciplinary classroom. The authors fairly characterize most published approaches to interdisciplinary education as focusing on the role of the teacher in *providing* an interdisciplinary perspective. They appropriately ask: Is the typically passive learning style of students compatible with interdisciplinary integration? Where is the constructivist engagement in such classrooms, they wonder.

Fried and DiBella McCarthy's essay, like so many others in this volume, has a tonal quality that I find especially valuable in interdisciplinary materials. The authors provoke and challenge but not with the domination motif that I notice at all too many academic conventions. If I am correct, this critical civility in the interdisciplinary community may occur because interdisciplinary scholars necessarily encounter multiple perspectives in their work. Hence they are unusually aware that commitment to a particular perspective should not preclude openness to those perspectives housed in other buildings on campus. As emphasized in the introduction to Part III, interdisciplinary conversations reveal mutual respect because participants have a heightened awareness that they need one another.

The broad scope of interdisciplinary learning requires special effort to wed the teacher's expectations to what the learner already possesses. The authors in this volume realize that interdisciplinary vision becomes a real possibility for students when we tie it to what they have already learned. For example, Jill Dix Ghnassia's use of Romanticism as an integrative device draws its strength from melding an understanding of Romanticism with the knowledge of music, art, and print that students bring into the classroom. The essays in the book are deeply respectful of disciplines as well as of the existing interests and appreciations of learners, as illustrated in the Ghnassia essay, which draws on experience inside the humanities to yield a broader perspective applicable far beyond the humanities.

Another illustration of this respect for who students are when they enter the interdisciplinary classroom can be seen in Marcia Seabury's thoughtful efforts to use an assortment of techniques to assist students in adjusting to the high level of abstraction and the multiple languages common in interdisciplinary courses. Similarly, Laurence Gould uses what students already know about order and art to introduce them to the power of symmetry for illuminating interconnections among disciplines. In Part III of the volume, Jane Edwards provides a further example when she explains the value of situating a gender course in the "gender issue of the day," a context that permits developmental growth by respecting the learner's current location. Cheryl Curtis, Anthony Rauche, and Edward Weinswig reflect a similar sensitivity to starting where the learner is when they initiate their students' engagement with ethnic identity by asking them to describe "the ethnic me."

The essay by Doug Dix, Regina Miller, Mike Horn, and Dale Brown openly searches for ways to make science education come alive. These teachers want their students to understand the various disciplines as helpful guides to common questions. Those who long for the relative security of their disciplinary territory have little to fear from this volume. It comes to assist, not undermine.

The promise of Part II for interdisciplinary educators is in the multiple portrayals of integrative tools applicable in any classroom. The reflective judgment model (Smith, Gardow, and Reale-Foley), the case method of analysis (Canedy), and the analysis of the forms and effects of power (Horvath) are all, with minor adjustments, powerful tools for constructing cognitive bridges among ideas and disciplines. The authors seem to recognize that their particular applications of the tools are less important than the potentially broad usefulness of those tools.

The essays in Part III describe another exciting interdisciplinary avenue for developing integrative skills. Because cultures are not constructed by academic departments but rather by the aspirations of and constraints on the participants in them, an interdisciplinary approach to studies of culture would seem natural. Instead, each discipline interested in a culture usually isolates a segment of cultural experience and studies it as an entity unto itself.

As I read the course descriptions and classroom achievements presented in Part III of *Interdisciplinary General Education,* I felt especially negligent as a teacher. I forced myself to review my own feeble efforts to address the same cultural understandings through the lens of my own discipline. This comparison with the quality of the efforts documented was as stimulating as it was uncomfortable.

GENUINE CLASSROOM PRACTICE

As a teacher, I want to stress the warmth I feel for these essays. They reveal high purpose. Moreover, they provide concrete discussions of efforts to develop integrative skills so that they will be read with appreciation by teachers at many levels of experience. When the authors discuss the problems they encounter, they are the familiar ones of inertia and confusion that all teachers must overcome when they go beyond the ordinary in their teaching practice.

In that regard, I particularly appreciate the narratives about tension and triumph in the classroom. For example, we know from Seabury's descriptions of common classroom dilemmas in interdisciplinary programs as well as from the quotations taped on the wall of Fried and McCarthy's classroom that student resistance is both predictable and remediable. Any experienced teacher will agonize with Dix and his coauthors when they wonder about the integrity of the grading process as a measure of engagement and achievement in a context that pressures students to jump through hoops to get high grades. Especially noteworthy is the frank exploration by Horvath and her colleagues of student attitudes toward their required role in a more interactive classroom. Such experiences remind us all of the dedication required to stimulate successful interdisciplinary class discussion.

As I read, I felt pride that these are my distant colleagues striving with me to develop and nurture responsible learners with hyperactive curiosities. Even on the rare occasions when I read descriptions of pedagogical practices that I have grown to mistrust, I found myself engaged in silent interchange with thoughtful teachers.

The next time we encounter someone skeptical of interdisciplinary education, we can confidently recommend *Interdisciplinary General Education* as illustrative of what is possible when the interdisciplinary perspective is applied by a talented community of learners. Here are classroom stories that, I know, informed my own teaching and promise to challenge the learning habits of all who will take their lessons seriously. Learning is so much more robust when its goal is to question without regard to artificial boundaries.

INTRODUCTION

Marcia Bundy Seabury

I. QUESTIONS FROM A DECADE OF ADVENTURE IN INTERDISCIPLINARY GENERAL EDUCATION

Driven in large part by concerns about lack of coherence in the under-graduate curriculum, during the 1980s over three-quarters of all U.S. colleges and universities revised their approach to what students must study outside their majors. One direction of change was toward more interdisciplinary study: for example, courses in which students and faculty come together to explore the environment through the multiple lenses of disciplines such as biology, philosophy, and economics. Meanwhile, widespread concerns about students' ability to think, write, speak, and act effectively led many colleges to give increased attention to the development of intellectual skills as part of general education. In some institutions, these changes evolved together; indeed, advocates of interdisciplinary study claim that interdisciplinary courses can be particularly effective in engaging students, coaching them to think well, and encouraging them to explore values. But while books on interdisciplinary studies often include discussion of general education and vice versa, we lack books focusing on interdisciplinary general education.[1]

A great many questions call for further attention. In particular, for the purposes of this volume, what differences do we make for students by bringing them into interdisciplinary courses early in their college careers? How in practice do these courses work to develop integrative skills? What are the processes of interdisciplinary teaching and learning? And what do faculty learn over time about interdisciplinary general education: what works, what doesn't, what should be done differently?

To such questions some would add doubts about both students and faculty. Don't students need a firm grounding in particular ways of knowing before they try to bring varied perspectives together, so that they have something to integrate? And can faculty, realistically, increase and exercise their expertise within their own corner of their discipline, know the wide-ranging territory of their changing discipline well enough to teach it in various forums, learn at least one or two other disciplines well enough to explore their connections, investigate current interdisciplinary theory in sufficient depth, plus teach intellectual skills in an informed manner (not even to mention committee responsibilities and all the rest)? Underlying all these questions is the issue of whether interdisciplinary general education curricula, course design, and teaching are simply worth the extra time and effort. Working within the usual structures, staying within one's own department, is safer and simpler.

One way to approach these various nationwide concerns and questions is to share local stories. The Association for Integrative Study, a national organization for the study of interdisciplinarity, reached in this direction in selecting for its 1997 conference focus "Tales of Transformation," inviting stories and case studies that "illuminate the process by which faculty and students are transformed through integrative work." Or are *not* transformed—we need to contemplate both advances and setbacks.

This volume offers a collection of such stories from a single institution with over a decade of experience with curricular reform. One of the universities that did not just shuffle around the pieces but dared significant change in the 1980s was the University of Hartford, in West Hartford, Connecticut. Its interdisciplinary general education program, the All-University Curriculum, brings together students, faculty, and ideas from across its nine diverse schools and colleges. Close to one hundred faculty regularly work together in team-designed and typically team-taught courses. Thirty-one of these faculty comment on their experiences in the following chapters. They explore intersections among their course topics, issues of interdisciplinary studies, and issues of student learning.

ORGANIZATION

The volume is organized into three parts (although as to be expected in a book on boundary crossing, various chapters and the courses they discuss could appear under more than one heading). Part I, "Asking Questions and Crossing Boundaries," focuses on classroom approaches to a series of fundamental "What is . . ." questions that lead students across disciplinary boundaries and encourage them to become active explorers, look more deeply, see things they have not seen before. Part II, "Framing Issues and Dealing With Problems," addresses approaches to problems such as hunger or AIDS that call for the combined insights of multiple disciplines and that demand responses from us as individuals that challenge the neat and relatively comfortable bounds of our understanding. Part III, "Exploring Cultures and Understanding Ourselves," examines interdisciplinary approaches to issues of culture that encourage students to explore others' values as well as their own.

The introduction to each part surveys intersections between issues of interdisciplinarity and issues of student learning, notes some of the attendant ironies and challenges encountered in classroom practice, and previews the chapters to follow. A lead chapter or two then focus in on a particular course, highlighting the various goals for student learning out of which it arose, strategies planned to accomplish those goals, and how those goals and strategies have worked out. In keeping with the theme of sharing stories, a variety of perspectives from other courses follow. References and sample syllabi accompany each chapter. Finally, the Afterword pulls back from these course-centered analyses to offer further detail on the history and current status of the general education curriculum at the University of Hartford and some thoughts about future directions.

CONTRIBUTORS

Readers of this volume will encounter a series of diverse voices,[2] accustomed to speaking within disciplines ranging from poetry to physics, from ethnomusicology to engineering or marketing, but here speaking of shared interdisciplinary concerns. Just as the interdisciplinary classroom can allow both students and faculty to bring their unique voices and areas of expertise to the common discussion, here too we attempt to create that space. The pedagogical approaches described vary widely as well.

Twenty-five of the contributors currently teach at the University of Hartford while six have left to assume positions elsewhere. We represent all faculty ranks, from adjunct and assistant professor to full professor. Thirteen of us are or have been department chairs, program directors, or senior administrators. Two of us teach full time in high schools, while three work regularly with high school faculty through graduate education programs. We represent about 19 different disciplines. The faculty teams for whom we speak are similarly diverse, with homes not only in the liberal arts and sciences but in various preprofessional programs. The inclusion of professional-school faculty in this volume and in the curriculum itself indicates our belief that disciplines such as business, engineering, and technology, while typically outside the purview of general education, shape the environment of our students' lives and should be incorporated into the processes of liberal learning and reflective judgment (cf. Grudin 1995).

DISCIPLINE-TRAINED FACULTY
IN INTERDISCIPLINARY COURSES

The hesitancy with which many faculty at our university, like their colleagues elsewhere, first approached the challenge of interdisciplinary teaching parallels the hesitancy with which some of us approached this volume. None of us has official interdisciplinary credentials or an interdisciplinary title. We are housed in separate departments and colleges within the university and typically publish and receive recognition within our disciplines. In this respect we may look much like our readers, for despite the gradual growth of interdisciplinary studies at both the undergraduate and graduate levels, most of us come to it through our disciplines. But as with faculty elsewhere, if you look beneath the surface you often find people who have been covert boundary crossers all along. A 25-year professor of marketing earned his Ph.D. in history; the general editor of this volume was the only nonmusic major in her college class to give a senior recital; another member of our program is a senior sociologist with an undergraduate major in chemistry. The complexity of many faculty's lives and interests continues to belie the relative linearity of their departmental careers.

Still, having learned to speak in forums where we have won some authority, many of this volume's contributors wondered about speaking where we can lay no such claim—in class and now in a public medium. Unlike working on a question within one's own discipline, in which the necessary background research may be fairly clearly defined, albeit extensive, in interdisciplinary studies one is always aware of something else one should read, should have read. Not a task for the timid—*or the* perfectionist. Further, in most cases university faculty do not have formal training in the literatures of student learning and skills building. In the development of our curriculum, while the interdisciplinary emphasis often generated humility or skepticism ("can you still keep depth?"), the emphasis on skills also generated some resistance in spite of its common sense. Some discipline-based faculty expressed concern about "education-ese." Gamson, speaking for the task force that wrote the widely circulated *Seven Principles for Good Practice in Undergraduate Education*, found this response nationwide: "we knew that college faculty are notoriously impatient with 'education talk'" (1991, 7). Here again we as authors perhaps resemble our readers, who may believe passionately in using their courses to encourage students to become more actively engaged, think within opposing frames of reference, and explore cultures and values—and who may indeed achieve such results in their teaching—but who often have not focused on such issues in their scholarly inquiry.

We present ourselves in this volume, then, not as experts and authorities but as seekers in the quest for student growth that we all share—occasionally overwhelmed by the magnitude of the tasks we have willingly taken on but more often buoyed by the sense that things do connect and should connect, that the divisions we set up, between departments and between content and skills courses, can divide what sometimes needs to be together. After all, effectively addressing issues such as world hunger or AIDS demands that people bring together insights from multiple disciplines as well as wide-ranging skills of engagement, thinking, and values clarification.

Our situation as authors may in fact help to account for the need, further documented below, for explorations of interdisciplinarity in the classroom, especially the general education classroom. Interdisciplinarity has become an area worth study in its own right, with its own concepts, methodologies, and professional community of practitioners—an additional tradition one feels one should master before adding another voice to the conversation. Further, specific areas of student learning and pedagogy have fully developed traditions and literatures of their own. Thus a scholarship of interdisciplinary teaching asks of faculty just what the teaching itself does: a willingness to be vulnerable, to allow ourselves to be explorers along with our students, bringing the rigors of our academic training to bear but aware that we may acclaim some discoveries while missing others.

INTERDISCIPLINARY TEAMS WITHIN A COMPREHENSIVE UNIVERSITY: THE ALL-UNIVERSITY CURRICULUM AT THE UNIVERSITY OF HARTFORD

The local context out of which we speak is an independent, comprehensive university of about 5,000 full- and part-time undergraduates and 1,800 graduate students that combines professional schools of engineering, technology, art, and music with colleges of arts and sciences, education and health professions, and business. A university-wide general education program in a comprehensive institution is no easy challenge to create or sustain, but one met with some degree of success at the University of Hartford. It was one of 17 institutions nationwide selected for the Association of American Colleges' (AAC) Strong Foundations for General Education project, described in a 1994 AAC book. In *Revitalizing General Education in a Time of Scarcity* (Kanter et al. 1997), Hartford is one of the case studies of institutions that have accomplished major reform. Hartford's acceptance for membership in the Associated New American Colleges,[3] a group of comprehensive colleges and universities creating a national dialogue, offers further evidence that its curricular ventures should be of interest to colleagues in academia.

Hartford's All-University Curriculum, or AUC, introduced in 1987, offers a unique crosshatch of disciplines and skills. Its roughly 25 interdisciplinary courses are divided into 5 categories: "Living in a Cultural Context: Western Heritage"; "Living in a Cultural Context: Other Cultures"; "Living Responsively With the Arts"; "Living in a Social Context"; and "Living in a Scientific and Technological World." Each course designates at least two essential abilities it explicitly works to develop: written and/or oral communication, critical thinking and problem solving, social interaction, values identification, and responsibility for civic life. And each course features opportunities for active learning. Students in all of the university's baccalaureate-granting schools and colleges are required to take at least four AUC courses, one from each of the four categories farthest from their major, although some elect to take more. A frequent pattern is one course per semester during the freshman and sophomore years, but basic requirements for some preprofessional majors plus student preferences bring juniors and seniors into these courses as well.

Most of the courses use the team-teaching approach discussed in the Appendix, a "dispersed-team model" in which two or three faculty members, each with 25 students, meet together for a joint session once a week and then in small sections the rest of the week. Thus team teaching is an important subtheme in many of the essays to follow. Exploring issues in teams allows us to learn from each other, to venture into new territory with others whose expertise complements our own—with the discovery, to use a different image, that the whole is greater than the sum of its parts, indeed something of the effect we hope this book will create. If interdisciplinarity consists of connections that faculty come to understand "before entering the classroom" and then "convey" to students (Richards 1996, 127), then we could have planned to move on to individually taught sections. But we continue to base our curriculum on a more interactive model, featuring interdisciplinary conversations among faculty and students, with students not as recipients of interdisciplinary knowledge but as participants in inter-disciplinary process.

AUDIENCE

The Hartford faculty who contributed to this volume seek to address colleagues across the boundaries of faculty and administration, colleges and secondary schools. Curricula at all levels are becoming increasingly inter-disciplinary. We offer our ideas and stories to others already engaged in interdisciplinary education and to those who may become so in the future, by their own choice or with external encouragement. Our reflections may stimulate others in their own curricular re-visionings as well as offer practical approaches that could be adapted at their institutions. We have posed and lived the questions of how and why teachers struggling with their daily classroom challenges might transform themselves from disciplinary experts to coexplorers with their students on interdisciplinary quests. We hope these discussions probing issues of interdisciplinarity encourage others to ask related questions and contribute their stories.

II. THE NATIONAL CONVERSATION

For those interested in further introduction to the subject matter of this volume, following are a few words about the ongoing national dialogue to which we add our voices. On what definitions, rationales, and resources does this volume build?

WHAT IS INTERDISCIPLINARY GENERAL EDUCATION?

Although scholars have debated the term *interdisciplinarity* for decades, we rely on the following widely accepted definition by Klein and Newell:

> *interdisciplinary studies* [IDS] may be defined as a process of answering a question, solving a problem, or addressing a topic that is too broad or complex to be dealt with adequately by a sin-

gle discipline or profession. . . . IDS draws on different disciplinary perspectives and integrates their insights through construction of a more comprehensive perspective. (1997, 393–94)

As Davis extends the definition, "If there is a key characteristic of interdisciplinary courses, it is 'integration,' scholars working together to pool their interests, insights, and methods, usually with the hope of gaining and presenting new understandings that could not be derived from working alone" (1995, 6). The contributors to this volume want to be sure that students are included in this formulation, as active agents in the process of working together and gaining and presenting new understandings.

The term *general education* also has been disputed, but a basic working definition will suffice: that component of the undergraduate curriculum, defined on an institution-wide or college-wide basis, which cultivates knowledge, intellectual skills, and attitudes useful throughout one's life (adapting wording from Levine 1978, 525, and Gaff and Ratcliff 1997, 710; also see Davis 1995, 157–60). Thus by interdisciplinary general education we mean courses outside a student's major that bring together disciplinary perspectives to address complex topics, an enterprise that has taken a wide variety of forms. While various curricular experiments have come and gone over the years, the move toward interdisciplinary general education has continued, as witnessed by a comparison of *Interdisciplinary Undergraduate Programs: A Directory* (Newell 1986) with the recently published second edition (Edwards 1996b). Both editions show general education to be by far the most common type of undergraduate interdisciplinary program, prominent at both public and private institutions (Edwards 1996a).

IS INTERDISCIPLINARY GENERAL EDUCATION WORTH THE BOTHER?

If we frame the question of the worth of interdisciplinary study within the context of upper-level university study in the major, a certain set of answers emerges. For example, an effective health care practitioner must be trained to attend to a patient's varied and interconnected physical, mental, and emotional needs. The interdisciplinary realities of the work place are reflected in accreditation guidelines for many college majors, which insist for example that future engineers have "an integrated experience" that relates their disciplinary expertise to issues in the humanities and social sciences (Accreditation Board for Engineering and Technology, Inc. 1996). The Association of American Colleges' (AAC) *The Challenge of Connecting Learning* stresses that students need to explore through their majors the "relationships between various ways of knowing, and between what [they] have learned and their lives beyond the academy" (1991, 6).

Framing the question in terms of general education has yielded a similar set of answers. The world's issues and problems, as so often stated, do not divide themselves into neat disciplinary boxes. But another question arises, and indeed arises literally and even loudly in curriculum discussions among faculty, as noted at the beginning of this introduction: Can students and faculty in lower-level courses handle the demands of interdisciplinary study? Some critics of the program at our own institution, who usually have not read Benson's presentation of similar arguments back in the early 1980s, continue to raise this issue.

Persuasive responses to the original question and this subsequent one have been abundant, from writers such as Kockelmans (1979), Newell (1983), Hursh, Haas, and Moore (1983), and Boyer (1987). The 1990s have seen an acceleration rather than a waning of advocacy for interdisciplinary general education. The AAC report cited above urges us to rethink the relationships between general education and the major: We need "the collegiate faculty as a whole working together to create courses of study that recognize difference, that bring multiple perspectives and crossdisciplinary dialogue to bear on common issues . . . and that foster the fashioning of connections" (1991, 6). The AAC's more recent *Strong Foundations* volume (1994) points to the emergence of consensus about the importance of integrative learning and the role of general education in that process. Klein (1990, also 1996), Gaff (1994), Davis (1995), and Newell and Klein (1996) survey the history of and rationale for interdisciplinary courses at a variety of levels including general education and argue the worth of integrative study at different levels of intellectual sophistication. The recent *Handbook of*

the Undergraduate Curriculum (Gaff and Ratcliff 1997), heralded as the
first major review of the undergraduate curriculum in 20 years, contains
multiple references to the need for students in general education to
address complex problems that cross disciplinary boundaries and to see
connections among ways of knowing.[4]

WHAT SKILLS DO STUDENTS GAIN?

Lists of the integrative skills claimed to be the goals and outcomes of interdisciplinary study have been variously framed. Kavaloski (1979), in what
is still one of the best available discussions of the importance of linking
interdisciplinary study with active learning, claims that interdisciplinary
education helps students to integrate knowledge, engage in free inquiry,
and break out of narrow thinking toward innovation. In 1987/1988 the
Association for Integrative Studies Task Force on the Description of Interdisciplinary Studies developed this more extended list:

- tolerance of ambiguity or paradox, receptivity to new ideas, celebration of diversity
- sensitivity to ethical dimensions of issues
- ability to synthesize or integrate
- enlarged perspectives or horizons, reduction of privatism, awareness of communal and public issues
- creativity, original insights, unconventional thinking
- critical thinking
- balance of subjective and objective thinking
- humility, listening skills
- sensitivity to bias—disciplinary, ideological, and religious (published in slightly different form in Field, Lee, and Field 1994)

In a more recent formulation, Newell asserts that interdisciplinary
courses are

> really about such matters as recognizing contrasting perspec-
> tives; learning how to synthesize, think critically, and reexam-
> ine the world that we take for granted; empowering students to
> tackle meaningful but complex issues; weaning students from

dependence on experts without dismissing expertise; and teaching students to value disciplines as powerful sources of insight while becoming aware of the nature of their various limitations. (1994, 43)

As we explore such large claims in action, focusing especially on active engagement, critical thinking, and cultural awareness, we do not intend to territorialize them within interdisciplinary studies or general education. We agree with the 1991 AAC report cited above that connected learning is the responsibility of the entire collegiate faculty and the entire curriculum.[5] But we do claim that interdisciplinary general education courses lend themselves well to encouraging the processes of growth described here. We also do not intend to territorialize these claims within the collegiate years. Such processes of growth are ongoing, from childhood through K–16 and beyond. As suggested in Part I of this volume, integrative thinking develops as part of our inheritance from our own childhood, before disciplined schooling taught us to compartmentalize. And in their readiness to discuss pedagogy and student learning, K–12 teachers often have gone before us. Of particular note are the analysis and wealth of examples from across the country in Clarke and Agne's *Interdisciplinary High School Teaching* (1997; also see Beane 1995). The authors in the present volume typically see their comments as applicable to precollege teaching and learning, and some of us have experience in secondary education. In the interest of maintaining focus and falling less easily into reductionism, however, we discuss our experiences in the context of higher education, with the hope that our readers from K–12 will interpret the possible connections within the rich context of their own experience.

THIS VOLUME JOINS THE CONVERSATION

Materials to assist with broad issues such as interdisciplinary program design, administration, and assessment are becoming more widely available (e.g., Klein and Doty 1994, Newell 1998). Davis (1995) explores a variety of issues in the design and delivery of interdisciplinary team-taught courses and offers page-length descriptions of a multitude of such courses nationwide, including three from the University of Hartford. But much remains to be said about the actual processes of teaching and learning in such courses, about the feel of these processes. Back in 1982, Benson highlighted a perceived "lack of reliable traditions and literature concerning interdisciplinary studies teaching" (41), and Newell agreed that faculty should "exchange information on individual interdisciplinary courses from a variety of institutions," exploring "the process of teaching itself, not just of curriculum development" (1983, 14). The need continues. Klein calls for "compiling narratives in order to understand how interdisciplinary work is actually done by individuals and teams" (1990, 195). And in particular, Klein and Newell cite the data beginning to emerge on how interdisciplinary study affects the development of students' skills and attitudes but note the need for further exploration of the processes by which this change takes place (1997, 411). To this challenge we contribute our perspectives.

Some useful guidelines to facilitate these processes appear in a recent "Guide to Interdisciplinary Syllabus Preparation" developed through the collaboration of faculty across the country. For example:

- Are the perspectives of disciplines or schools of thought explicit? Are their respective contributions to the issue explicit?
- Is integration on-going or does it appear only at the end of the course (following serial presentation of disciplinary perspectives, insight, or methods)?
- Is there collaboration between students and faculty in forging a synthesis/integration?
- Does the synthesis result in a larger, more holistic understanding of the issue? (Association for Integrative Studies and Institute in Integrative Studies 1996)

The authors in the present volume do not typically frame such questions in "yes-no" form but rather ask "to what extent" and "how." To what extent, and how in practice, can a particular course help students to examine the perspectives of multiple disciplines? To what extent, and how in practice, can faculty and students work together to integrate the insights of the disciplines?

Further, today's disciplines may not have *a* typical perspective or set of typical underlying assumptions, as suggested in the aforementioned "Guide," which obviously complicates these already challenging issues. Such wordings, using singular constructions, appear repeatedly in numerous sources, even when the writers are clearly aware of the complexity of today's disciplines. While it would be helpful for an interdisciplinarian to be "well-versed in how each discipline looks at the world, what questions it has asked or would ask in a given situation, and. . . what assumptions underlie its worldview" (Newell and Green 1982, 27), many faculty cannot claim such mastery even within their own rapidly evolving discipline. Today's "cross-field and cross-discipline peregrinations . . . redefine both their subject matter and the kinds of questions they put to it" (Gunn 1992, 240). The authors in this volume explore interdisciplinary processes in general education with the understanding that ongoing interdisciplinary processes outside those classrooms may make it no longer possible to talk about bringing together the "typical" perspectives of two or three particular disciplines.

It is fitting that Neil Browne offer the prefatory remarks to our comments on interdisciplinary general education, since it was over a dinner table with him and colleagues from the University of Hartford that a seed for the volume was sown. Neil had conducted a week of summer workshops bringing faculty from the university together with City of Hartford high school teachers, and then returned several times for follow-up workshops and public sessions. In one of those, entitled "The Rare Sound of Interdisciplinary Talk: Why It Is So Hard to Listen to THEM," he detailed reasons for the ongoing entrenched separation in the faculty cafeteria as well as in the curriculum of faculty members across the disciplinary divides. Afterward Neil commented that our experiences in interdisciplinary education were worth sharing. We knew how much good work in interdisciplinary general education was going on across the country. We had seen the statistics on the number of colleges revising their general education programs in the 1980s and had read box loads of articles about innovative program and course designs. But for reasons noted above we have followed Neil's nudge and are adding our voices to the rich national dialogue.

III. A POSTSCRIPT ON PROCESS

What are the teaching and learning processes of interdisciplinary general education like? For those interested in indulging in a more playful introduction to this question, following are some closing comments drawing on the play of figurative language.

Listening to experienced faculty talk about interdisciplinary teaching and learning reveals a wide variety of comparisons. An example overheard in the hallway from an overloaded professor: interdisciplinary teacher as Sherpa, guiding students over tricky terrain while carrying not just multiple perspectives but inordinate amounts of stuff—slide carousel, opera scores and CDs, boom box, books, and more. Faculty often refer to team teaching as marriage: some teams disband because of "irreconcilable differences" even though it seemed that those differences should complement each other, while other "arranged marriages" turn out just as well or better than ones born of common passion. Authors in this volume, unsolicited, describe their courses in terms ranging from struggling with a hydra to collaboratively constructing a quilt. In a faculty workshop at our university, experienced team teachers trying to describe their experience to others repeatedly invoked similes and metaphors to do what they do so well: get at the unfamiliar via the more familiar, send multiple messages along the wire simultaneously, and convey emotion as well as information. "When you walk into that classroom together it's like . . ." "No, it's more like . . ." The images create lively interplay and open up important issues for discussion.

Indeed, "a conversation about education cannot extend beyond two or three sentences before a metaphor is invoked"; "in a fundamental sense, all arguments about how education ought to be conducted are arguments about the validity of competing metaphors" (Postman 1979, 158, 157). But although these metaphors are powerful, they frequently remain hidden and unexplored. Educators who have brought them to light often have uncovered the assumption that education is some kind of a "filling" activity. Dewey, for example, objects that educators treat the student's mind "as if it were a cistern into which information is conducted" (1933, 261), while Freire argues that too often education becomes "an act of depositing," an oppressive "banking" model that stifles inquiry and inhibits the creative discovery of "ties which link one point to another and one problem to another" (1970, 58–60). As we pursue the exploration into the interdisciplinary classroom, where just such discovery should flourish, we would do well to take the lead from such analyses by looking beyond the notion of filling students' minds with important interdisciplinary connections.

The literature on interdisciplinarity likewise is often framed in terms of operative metaphors. Davis elaborates on Ralph Ross's metaphor of bread: integrative work looks at neither bits and pieces, the crumbs, nor at the whole loaf, and of course there are different ways you can slice it (1995, 208). Hursh, Haas, and Moore (1983) make a much-cited reference to fruit baskets. Exploring interdisciplinarity through metaphor, for example as an act of translating across disciplines, is a regular part of the summer workshops at the Institute in Integrative Studies at Miami University (St. Germain 1993). Klein (1990, ch. 4) surveys a series of metaphors emerging as dominant in the discourse of interdisciplinarity. The ways in which faculty talk about interdiscipli-nary teaching and learning, a subset of interdisciplinary activity, natu-rally draw on the major categories of metaphor for interdisciplinarity itself but with variations worth highlighting. Two examples follow.

GEOGRAPHY REVISITED

Klein notes the prominence in current scholarship of references to geopolitics: scholars have been remapping the territory, rethinking fields of knowledge, exploring disciplinary borders, crossing bound-aries, building bridges, meeting at the intersections. Her recent book *Crossing Boundaries* (1996) obviously continues to explore such metaphors, among others. Even those who object to some of these metaphors may choose geographical alternatives: Lyon for example pro-poses substituting images of river, current, flow, and confluence for those of territory to place less emphasis on "our standing position" than on the "process of coming to knowledge" (1992, 692). Geographical metaphors when used to describe interdisciplinary work often have connotations of adventure, exploration, discovery: we move to the "frontiers" of our discipline to discover new knowledge, and form new "alliances" to explore a research interest. But when faculty talk about the interdisciplinary classroom, they often refer not to "adventuring" but to "venturing" outside their usual territory: not just "undertaking a remarkable experience" but "undertaking at some risk," "daring in the face of possible danger or rebuff"—emotions many faculty indeed experience along with their students.

Faculty often do describe interdisciplinary general education programs through particular recurring geopolitical metaphors, with supporters suggesting liberation from artificial boundaries, overcoming the problem of "balkanized" departments and "departmental turf," and detractors suggesting instead imperialism—the interdisciplinary program "taking over territory" and "empire building." But when faculty describe their individual classes, the geographical metaphors become more idiosyncratic and suggestive. Adapting the protagonist's comment at the end of Voltaire's *Candide* on cultivating his own garden, a contributor to this volume once proposed that our faculty development series hold some workshops entitled "Trampling in Each Other's Gardens [for Fun and Profit]." When we enter an interdisciplinary course with our students we affirm the urge not to stay in our own garden. "Trampling" suggests awareness of our willfulness or gracelessness. Others have tended those disciplinary gardens carefully, then we move through them quickly for our own purposes, heedless of the carefully nurtured growth. We may find guilty pleasure in the act, yet perhaps we should not do it; we can cause harm—reductionism, not being up on developments in other fields. The metaphor suggests the challenge of crossing boundaries but not trampling too heavy-footedly across the well-tended complexities of the disciplines.

FROM WEBS TO MUSIC

If an interdisciplinary course is team taught, other metaphors arise, again with variations on the metaphors for interdisciplinarity in the literature. Klein explores images of networks, webs, and other such structures suggesting complexity and interdependence. Faculty often choose temporal rather than spatial metaphors to express these characteristics.

The recurring musical metaphors are particularly appropriate for teaching since music is experienced in time, with a rhythm of things that one has to feel, feel with; and interdisciplinarity itself, as so often emphasized by Klein, Newell, and others, is a *process*. Some faculty talk about an interdisciplinary class as if it were a symphony concert. Each member of the faculty team brings something different to the discussion and may take the lead at different times. The whole is definitely greater than the sum of its parts. Some teams comment on problems and challenges using this metaphor: "It takes extra time to orchestrate what will happen on Tuesday afternoon." A colleague claims that team members' "chiming in," if not "in the score" in advance, can disrupt the process—thus viewing the lead faculty member as a conductor with a well-laid-out score to follow, bringing both students and faculty team members (ideally with some charisma) along a defined path toward a worked-out conclusion by the end of the hour.

Other faculty have suggested the alternative musical metaphor of jazz: players begin together but improvise, play off each other, together create the unexpected. Although perhaps classically trained, they learn to go with the music, let go of control, of knowing how it will all come out, and allow something new to be created. Team members note the paradox of "learning to be spontaneous." Not everyone loves jazz and not all faculty members are willing to put themselves in this position. But faculty claim that the rewards rejuvenate their teaching as they learn to relinquish control, to other faculty and more important to students as well.

EXAMINING THE POSSIBILITIES AND LIMITATIONS OF OUR ASSUMPTIONS

Metaphors can open out our thinking, for example, helping a team to consider trying for jazz instead of symphonic mode, but they can also constrain: as Susan Sontag (1978) points out, they can oversimplify, prejudice our thinking, lock it into a set pattern. Both of the above musical metaphors can reinforce a faculty-oriented bias: faculty team as creators, students as audience. Granted each of these metaphors moves beyond the traditional model of solo teacher as virtuoso, and admittedly in some musical venues anyone in the room is welcome to join in a jam session. But even jazz can imply a performance mentality, and some of our teams, including the quite jazzy, have in practice had this limitation, getting so involved responding to each other that students remain too often as audience. Kavaloski warns against approaching interdisciplinary education with an overly objectivist epistemology that leads to an overly objectivist pedagogy, with teachers as "*active* counterpoints to the *reactive* students" (1979, 226, 231). Recognizing and exploring the metaphors at work can open up discussion and the possibility for change.

DO STUDENTS SHARE OUR ASSUMPTIONS?

Instructors' and students' metaphoric understandings of how a course is structured or what is going on in class at a given moment may differ, resulting in misunderstandings and missed connections. With three faculty, readings from diverse disciplines, and wide-ranging classroom discussions, students may feel they are encountering a set of puzzle pieces that they are somehow to put together to "get the picture." If faculty are sensing the freedom of jazz while students are imaging fragmentation, the effectiveness of the interdisciplinary class can be diminished.

Another example of conflicting metaphors involves the long-standing image of education as conversation. Oakeshott describes "the conversation of mankind" that we invite students to enter, with education as "an initiation into the skill and partnership of this conversation" (1991). His description of this conversation as "an unrehearsed intellectual adventure" brings together various metaphors discussed in this introduction. Klein, drawing on Jürgen Habermas, focuses on interdisciplinarity as "communicative action"; "interdisciplinary process is grounded in social learning" (1996, 221, 218; also see Cowan, Ewell, and McConnell 1995). In this case, comments from faculty accord well with the literature. As noted above, we intended for our program structure to embody this metaphor. Students in our team-taught courses would actually hear and engage in cross-disciplinary conversation instead of hearing a professor tell about it; faculty dialogue would move out of faculty offices and lunchrooms into the classroom, where students could join in an ongoing process of making meaning. But we may think we are operating within a metaphor and mode of open conversation, with students invited in, while students are watching the instructors as a Clash of the Titans. What are they to do? (Such combat is not for mere mortals, and it is not pretty.) Watch in awe, waiting for it all to be over, and see who wins?

Of course students are part of a long tradition themselves in this metaphorical understanding of argument as war, traced by Lakoff and Johnson (1980). When our team-teaching efforts first began, the question on the student evaluation form "Did the professors work well together?" yielded responses of "No, they sometimes disagreed with each other." "Wouldn't it be simpler to have just one teacher?" As noted above, simpler for them, simpler for us, but not always better. Davis's surveys reveal that "students don't have much grasp of or appreciation for the collaboration that has taken place behind the scenes" (1995, 126), which he attributes to their not seeing much collaborative teaching. But engaging in such teaching in itself may not alter the responses.

Many of us have learned to take a step back and talk with students about the process: for example, making explicit that we like each other, that an interdisciplinary course allows us all to experience the real-world challenge of integrating different, sometimes competing perspectives. Figurative language can help in this discussion, with a simple pause *in medias res* for "What are we doing here?" "This class is like . . ." Awareness of the similes and metaphors underlying their responses can help to liberate students from the unacknowledged domination of particular assumptions, from viewing teachers and classes within preconceived patterns that impede other kinds of responses. They can consider alternative metaphors and what those might imply. As Harris puts it, "If we think of the teachers who have influenced us most, over and over we are mindful of some example, some image, some use of a comparative metaphor that enabled us to see an entire area of reality" (1987, 49).

Robert Frost says he had always heard that "the teacher must teach the pupil to think. . . . but we seldom tell [students] what thinking means; we seldom tell them it is just putting this and that together; it is just saying one thing in terms of another. To tell them is to set their feet on the first rung of a ladder the top of which sticks through the sky" (1972, 335–36). Through such thinking students can learn not only to understand new classroom modes but to make connections across disciplines.[6] Putting this and that together, saying one thing in terms of another—such wordings suggest the interdisciplinary process itself. It is time to turn to some examples.

NOTES

1. For documentation of the changes noted above and analysis of their causes and effects, the reader might consult Ratcliff (1997), Kanter et al. (1997), and the further sources they cite. The only works focusing on interdisciplinary general education, other than a variety of articles, are not widely available: these include conference and workshop proceedings (Kelder 1994, Gager and Brownlee 1972), grant reports, theses, and a monograph (Winthrop 1971). Of particular note is Kelder, though not all of the papers there deal specifically with interdisciplinarity.

2. No formula or hidden agenda has dictated which of us speak here and for which courses, but rather the pragmatic criterion of who was interested and able to write during a particular window of time, amidst inevitable comings and goings and competing commitments.

3. The Associated New American Colleges (ANAC) define themselves in their mission statement as a group of independent

> small to mid-sized comprehensive colleges and universities dedicated to the integration of liberal and professional studies. These institutions share a commitment to teaching and learning, a collegial ethos that is student and value centered, a flexible professional model that emphasizes the faculty teacher scholar, and an integrative institutional model that blends highly personalized qualities of liberal arts colleges with the diversity of large universities. ANAC supports a national dialogue on educational issues and cooperative projects among New American Colleges, while enabling these institutions to serve as laboratories for models of excellence that have implications for all of higher education.

4. A recent Boyer Commission report (1998), released while this volume was in the publication process, serves as a still more recent example of this emphasis nationwide. The report criticizes the fragmentation at America's research universities and proposes 10 key changes in their education of undergraduates. One of these is to "remove barriers to interdisciplinary education," specifically including lower-division courses as well as study in the major. Advocacy of integrated and interdisciplinary study is prominent throughout the report, for example in its recommendation for a rethinking of the freshman year. Suggesting still further the timeliness of the present

volume, the Boyer report also urges that universities do more to "link communication skills with course work," a cornerstone of our program.

5. But after concurring with this stance, Association of American Colleges and Universities President Carol Schneider adds that "providing critical or multidisciplinary perspectives on the approaches of particular fields did not become a major theme in work undertaken within the AAC&U framework on the major, despite the prominence of this theme in the guidelines provided to the campuses." Perhaps, after all, general education has a particular role to play here (Schneider 1997, 259).

6. On the power of explicit comparisons to guide students through periods when "the student generally misconstrues what his teacher is doing, and both suffer," also see Perry (1970, 210–11). On approaching interdisciplinary thinking as metaphorical, see, e.g., Petrie (1976), Shin (1994), and Carlisle (1995).

REFERENCES

Accreditation Board for Engineering and Technology, Inc. [ABET]. 1996. *Criteria for Accrediting Programs in Engineering in the United States.* Baltimore: Engineering Accreditation Commission.

Association for Integrative Studies and Institute in Integrative Studies. 1996. "Guide to Interdisciplinary Syllabus Preparation." *Journal of General Education* 45 (2): 170–73.

Association of American Colleges [AAC]. 1991. *Liberal Learning and the Arts and Sciences Major.* Vol. 1: *The Challenge of Connecting Learning.* Washington, D.C.: Association of American Colleges.

Association of American Colleges. 1994. *Strong Foundations: Twelve Principles for Effective General Education Programs.* Washington, D.C.: Association of American Colleges.

Beane, James A., ed. 1995. *Toward a Coherent Curriculum. 1995 Yearbook of the Association for Supervision and Curriculum Development.* Alexandria, Va.: Association for Supervision and Curriculum Development.

Benson, Thomas. 1982. "Five Arguments against Interdisciplinary Studies." *Issues in Integrative Studies* 1: 38–48.

Boyer, Ernest L. 1987. *College: The Undergraduate Experience in America.* New York: Harper and Row.

Boyer Commission on Educating Undergraduates in the Research University. 1998. *Reinventing Undergraduate Education: A Blueprint for America's Research Universities.* 8 January 1999. <http://notes.cc.sunysb.edu/Pres/boyer.nsf>.

Carlisle, Barbara. 1995. "Music and Life." *American Music Teacher* 44 (June/July): 10–13.

Clarke, John H., and Russell M. Agne. 1997. *Interdisciplinary High School Teaching: Strategies for Integrated Learning.* Boston: Allyn and Bacon.

Cowan, Michael A., Barbara C. Ewell, and Peggy McConnell. 1995. *College Teaching* 43 (4): 127–31.

Davis, James R. 1995. *Interdisciplinary Courses and Team Teaching: New Arrangements for Learning.* Phoenix, Ariz.: American Council on Education and Oryx.

Dewey, John. 1933. *How We Think.* Lexington, Mass.: Heath.

Edwards, Alan F., Jr. 1996a. "Are Interdisciplinary Studies Still Alive and Well? Summary Findings from the New Undergraduate Interdisciplinary Studies Program Directory." *Association for Integrative Studies Newsletter* 18 (4): 1–3.

Edwards, Alan F., Jr. 1996b. *Interdisciplinary Undergraduate Programs: A Directory.* 2d ed. Acton, Mass.: Copley.

Field, Michael, Russell Lee, and Mary Lee Field. 1994. "Assessing Interdisciplinary Learning." In *Interdisciplinary Studies Today,* eds. Julie Thompson Klein and William G. Doty. San Francisco: Jossey-Bass.

Freire, Paulo. [1970] 1981. *Pedagogy of the Oppressed.* New York: Continuum.

Frost, Robert. 1972. "Education by Poetry: A Meditative Monologue." In *Robert Frost: Poetry and Prose,* ed. Edward Connery Lathem and Lawrance Thompson. New York: Holt, Rinehart and Winston.

Gaff, Jerry G. 1994. "Overcoming Barriers: Interdisciplinary Studies in Disciplinary Institutions." *Issues in Integrative Studies* 12: 169–80.

Gaff, Jerry G., and James L. Ratcliff, eds. 1997. *Handbook of the Undergraduate Curriculum.* San Francisco: Jossey-Bass.

Gager, William A., Jr., and Martha W. Brownlee, eds. 1972. *Perspectives on Interdisciplinary Education: Proceedings of a Workshop Sponsored by the National American Studies Faculty and the Florida Division of Community Colleges.* Tallahassee, Fla.: Department of Education.

Gamson, Zelda F. 1991. "A Brief History of the Seven Principles for Good Practice in Undergraduate Education." In *Applying the Seven Principles for Good Practice in Undergraduate Education,* eds. Arthur W. Chickering and Zelda F. Gamson. San Francisco: Jossey-Bass.

Grudin, Robert. 1995. "'Material Enterprise' Should Be at the Core of the Curriculum." *Chronicle of Higher Education* (24 February): A48.

Gunn, Giles. 1992. "Interdisciplinary Studies." In *Introduction to Scholarship in Modern Language and Literature,* ed. Joseph Gibaldi. New York: Modern Language Association.

Harris, Maria. 1987. *Teaching and Religious Imagination: An Essay in the Theology of Teaching.* San Francisco: Harper and Row.

Hursh, Barbara, Paul Haas, and Michael Moore. 1983. "An Interdisciplinary Model to Implement General Education." *Journal of Higher Education* 54 (1): 42–59.

Kanter, Sandra L., Zelda F. Gamson, and Howard B. London. 1997. *Revitalizing General Education in a Time of Scarcity: A Navigational Chart for Administrators and Faculty.* Boston: Allyn and Bacon.

Kavaloski, Vincent C. 1979. "Interdisciplinary Education and Humanistic Aspiration: A Critical Reflection." In *Interdisciplinarity and Higher Education,* ed. Joseph J. Kockelmans. University Park: Pennsylvania State University Press.

Kelder, Richard, ed. 1994. *Interdisciplinary Curricula, General Education, and Liberal Learning: Selected Papers from the Annual Conference of the Institute for the Study of Postsecondary Pedagogy.* New Paltz: State University of New York.

Klein, Julie Thompson. 1990. *Interdisciplinarity: History, Theory, and Practice.* Detroit, Mich.: Wayne State University Press.

Klein, Julie Thompson. 1996. *Crossing Boundaries: Knowledge, Disciplinarities, and Interdisciplinarities.* Charlottesville: University Press of Virginia.

Klein, Julie Thompson, and William G. Doty, eds. 1994. *Interdisciplinary Studies Today.* New Directions for Teaching and Learning 58. San Francisco: Jossey-Bass.

Klein, Julie Thompson, and William H. Newell. 1997. "Advancing Interdisciplinary Studies." In *Handbook of the Undergraduate Curriculum,* eds. Jerry G. Gaff and James L. Ratcliff. San Francisco: Jossey-Bass.

Kockelmans, Joseph J. 1979. "Why Interdisciplinarity?" In *Interdisciplinarity and Higher Education,* ed. Joseph J. Kockelmans. University Park: Pennsylvania State University Press.

Lakoff, George, and Mark Johnson. 1980. *Metaphors We Live By.* Chicago: University of Chicago Press.

Levine, Arthur. 1978. *Handbook on Undergraduate Curriculum.* San Francisco: Jossey-Bass.

Lyon, Arabella. 1992. "Interdisciplinarity: Giving up Territory." *College English* 54 (6): 681–93.

Newell, William H. 1983. "The Case for Interdisciplinary Studies: Response to Professor Benson's Five Arguments." *Issues in Integrative Studies* 2: 1–19.

Newell, William H. 1986. *Interdisciplinary Undergraduate Programs: A Directory.* Oxford, Ohio: Association for Integrative Studies.

Newell, William H. 1994. "Designing Interdisciplinary Courses." In *Interdisciplinary Studies Today,* eds. Julie Thompson Klein and William G. Doty. San Francisco: Jossey-Bass.

Newell, William H. 1998. *Interdisciplinarity: Essays from the Literature.* New York: College Entrance Examination Board.

Newell, William H., and William J. Green. 1982. "Defining and Teaching Interdisciplinary Studies." *Improving College and University Teaching* 30 (1): 23–30.

Newell, William H., and Julie Thompson Klein. 1996. "Interdisciplinary Studies into the 21st Century." *Journal of General Education* 45 (2): 152–69.

Oakeshott, Michael. 1991. "The Voice of Poetry in the Conversation of Mankind." In *Rationalism in Politics and Other Essays.* Indianapolis, Ind.: Liberty Press. First published as *The Voice of Poetry in the Conversation of Mankind* (Bowes and Bowes 1959).

Perry, W., Jr. [1968] 1970. *Forms of Intellectual and Ethical Development in the College Years.* New York: Holt, Rinehart and Winston.

Petrie, Hugh G. 1976. "Do You See What I See? The Epistemology of Interdisciplinary Inquiry." *Journal of Aesthetic Education* 10 (January): 29–43.

Postman, Neil. 1979. *Teaching as a Conserving Activity.* New York: Delacorte.

Ratcliff, James L. 1997. "Quality and Coherence in General Education." In *Handbook of the Undergraduate Curriculum,* eds. Jerry G. Gaff and James L. Ratcliff. San Francisco: Jossey-Bass.

Richards, Donald G. 1996. "The Meaning and Relevance of 'Synthesis' in Interdisciplinary Studies." *Journal of General Education* 45 (2): 114–28.

St. Germain, Sheryl. 1993. "Institute Journal." *Association for Integrative Studies Newsletter* 15 (3): 1–4.

Schneider, Carol Geary. 1997. "The Arts and Sciences Major." In *Handbook of the Undergraduate Curriculum,* eds. Jerry G. Gaff, James L. Ratcliff, and Associates. San Francisco: Jossey-Bass.

Shin, Un-Chol. 1994. "The Metaphorical Structure of Interdisciplinary Knowledge." *Association for Integrative Studies Newsletter* 16 (1–2): 8–12.

Sontag, Susan. 1978. *Illness as Metaphor.* New York: Farrar, Straus, and Giroux.

Winthrop, Henry. 1971. *Education and Culture in the Complex Society: Perspective on Interdisciplinary and General Education.* Tampa, Fla.: University of South Florida.

PART I

ASKING QUESTIONS AND CROSSING BOUNDARIES

ACTIVE ENGAGEMENT IN INTERDISCIPLINARY LEARNING

What differences can interdisciplinary courses make in students' learning? We see the natural intersections of interdisciplinarity and active engagement in learning when living with children or talking with creative adults. Big questions predate our awareness of disciplines and transcend particular disciplines once we recognize them. "Why do bad things happen?" "What is God like?" Or even, "Why do we go to school?" Children are famous for their perennial and persistent whats and whys that test the most educated adult's understandings. Children do not need to be taught to ask why, and their questions and processes of inquiry cross boundaries with a hop, skip, and a jump. These integrative learners busy themselves "doing things and thinking about the things they are doing," to use Bonwell and Eison's widely quoted definition of active learning (1991, 2): they go out to explore, get a bee sting, swat and dismember the bee, and question justice and God.

Unfortunately, in addition to helping students become aware of and use powerful tools for approaching their questions, schools often foster discipline-bound and passive learning. Students often see knowledge cut up into boxes—43-minute segments separated from each other by bells and hallways. They become passive in the face of disciplinary experts. They learn to fill in bubbles in answer to others' questions and to fit their thoughts onto short lines.

The essays in Part I of this volume discuss how interdisciplinary general education can encourage college students to become actively engaged in open-ended inquiry. The authors often explore a process analogous to the natural integrative learning of childhood. Children's questions draw or push us out of our immersion in the trivia of the day into a realm of wonder. Yet seemingly abstract questions—for example, about the nature of evil—often have quite concrete origins. "I got a bee sting *and* fell down the stairs *and* got yelled at all in one day." While the courses described here may pose abstract, wide-ranging questions about creativity, symmetry, or education, they bring students into direct encounters with the concrete even as they guide students to use new lenses through which to view it.

As noted in the introduction, Kavaloski's "Interdisciplinary Education and Humanistic Aspiration: A Critical Reflection" (1979) still offers one of the best available discussions of the promise of interdisciplinary study linked with pedagogies encouraging active engagement. Kavaloski argues that we do our students an injustice if we approach interdisciplinary courses with traditionalist assumptions. The essays in Part I share the implicit metaphor of venturing/adventuring discussed in the introduction. Faculty have developed certain skills of exploration and know part of the territory, but are not know-it-all guides talking down to the tourists; they become coadventurers, surprised as well by what is discovered along the way.

CHALLENGES

Various complications arise when this fine-sounding conceptualization of interdisciplinary general education meets the realities of classroom practice. To begin with, faculty are so used to professing that it can be hard to stop even in the face of our disciplinary limitations. We know that when students are engaged they learn better, whether or not we have read the supporting research (e.g., Pascarella and Terenzini 1991). But studies indicate that in spite of our belief in active learning, our classrooms are still dominated by "teacher talk" (Weimer 1996a, 1996b). Students describe themselves as being even less active than faculty report them to be (Fassinger 1995, 30). If we multiply these phenomena by the number of faculty in an interdisciplinary team-taught course, even one explicitly devoted to developing student skills through active learning, and add the temptation for faculty to enjoy exchanging ideas with each other, the result can be joint adventure transmuted into spectator sport.

Next is the sheer challenge of time. It is hard enough to help a student work with the methodologies and insights of three disciplines much less draw thoughtful connections among them. And of course the challenge is compounded if faculty are committed not just to lecturing about the integration of knowledge but to ensuring that students practice it. Sacrificing some course material can be difficult at first ("How can you possibly study Romanticism without Gericault?"). Even after a teaching team devises a manageable approach, the issue of time resurfaces each time a new member joins and inevitably wants to add this and that issue, this and that reading or assignment. But the arguments of active learning advocates (e.g., Weimer 1996a) apply well to interdisciplinary study: overvaluing "coverage" can be counterproductive for student learning, not to mention increasingly impossible in the face of the explosion of knowledge even within a single discipline. Such advocates have devised a wide variety of ways (even 101—see Silberman 1996) to help students explore ideas actively. The essays in Part I suggest that integrative learning can occur in a similarly wide variety of ways: in classes devoted to synthesis; in 10 minutes here, 10 minutes there; in asides; in journals, laboratory projects, and many other assignments asking students to do things and reflect on what they are doing.

A remaining issue is that faculty typically enter the interdisciplinary classroom because they want to do something they cannot easily do within their discipline. At the University of Hartford, for example, faculty in the health professions wanted to explore issues of AIDS with students across the university, while a philosopher wanted to discuss practical approaches to world hunger with students as he does in professional presentations worldwide. These are our questions, our quests. As *A New Vitality in General Education* asks, "How can the questions our courses raise become our student's own questions?" (Association of American Colleges 1988, 28). The authors in Part I probe this aspiration. Ideally, the core questions in our integrative courses are more organic to students' lives than the tradition-bound "What must one learn to gain an overview of this discipline?" But only ideally, given the continuing number of students who view any courses outside their major as irrelevant. How can we address such resistance and increase students' willingness to "tackle meaningful but complex issues" (Newell 1994)?

Juxtaposing interdisciplinary study and the expectation of active engagement can actually cause initial difficulties for some students because of the risks involved. Faculty not comfortable with the risks do not take the journey; those who do not want to be embarrassed by their lack of knowledge outside their discipline stay within it. But students are forced into the risks: general education requirements may demand the journey, albeit in the case of the All-University Curriculum (AUC) with some choice so that they may find an option they elect willingly. Students, too, fear being embarrassed. They, too, do not want to be wrong. Yet they must figure out a course with perhaps three professors plus reading materials from three disciplines. How can interdisciplinary courses encourage students to enter into the play of ideas, indeed with a playful spirit? For after all, part of the promise of interdisciplinary study is to introduce "more healthy play" into the curriculum, so that learners "do a little less marching and a little more dancing" (Halliburton 1981, 464).

OVERVIEW

"Creativity, original insights, unconventional thinking" are among the interdisciplinary outcomes cited by the Association for Integrative Studies Task Force. In the lead essay in Part I, John Roderick encourages us to honor "the creativity of interdisciplinarity and the interdisciplinarity of creativity." If students ever have the opportunity to examine creativity, it is typically within a particular discipline such as writing, without any attempt to explore the connections among creative individuals and among creative processes across the disciplines. And students often externalize the concept, as evidenced in early journal entries in Roderick's course: "I'm just not creative." Within a comprehensive university, it is too easy for engineering students never to set foot in the art or music school. Structures in the academy further divide one art from another and knowing from doing: "In liberal arts institutions, studio courses—*doing* courses of any kind—are barely recognized or, if recognized, are often not given full liberal arts standing" (Minnich 1990, 116–17). Roderick and his team developed a course that brings the riches of professional programs in the arts to nonmajors, offers hands-on experiments with creativity, and helps students break through resistances and inhibitions in ways that may increase their engagement and creativity in courses across the curriculum.

In the next essay, Robert Fried and Holly DiBella-McCarthy like-wise emphasize the importance of active student involvement in such inquiry. The unusual question mark in the title of their course *What Is School?* reflects the course's insistence on opening up fundamental questions, as did Peter Elbow's similarly titled volume *What Is English?* a few years back. Unless students are enrolled in a college of education, and sometimes not even then, nowhere in the curriculum do they typi-cally ask "what is school?" Universities allow what is by definition a uni-versal experience among students to remain unexamined. Fried and McCarthy have experimented with a team-taught interdisciplinary course that encourages students to explore rather than simply endure the process of schooling. (The course will move to permanent status upon gaining additional team members from such disciplines as psychology, sociology, history, and/or philosophy who will help to explore its inter-disciplinary potential.) The authors urge that students be treated as players rather than spectators in interdisciplinary education at large.[1]

Two pairs of follow-up essays, one based in the arts and the other in the sciences, complete Part I. The first essay within each pair high-lights a concept that crosses disciplines; the second, a related process that crosses disciplines. The arts essays both deal with a team-taught course on Romanticism in the Arts. How can faculty help students to understand an elusive concept that challenges scholars and relate it to themselves, their questions, their concerns? Jill Dix Ghnassia dis-cusses some of the complexities and pleasures involved. Students do not wait until they have a background in the Romantic period, the arts, and interart analysis before adding their voices. From the first meetings of the course they are comparing and contrasting works and actually singing their way into course materials and concepts.

Underlying students' encounters with "what is Romanticism?" may lurk another question: how on earth will they be able to learn multiple new disciplinary languages in a single course? In the next essay, based on my work on the Romanticism course team, I offer some thoughts about this process that may apply broadly to interdis-ciplinary courses. By learning to visualize one way that language works across the disciplines—movement among levels of abstraction and generalization—students gain confidence in using and combining the new languages. The dangers of getting stuck in specifics or generalities persist, but especially the latter; thus the importance of asking students not only to build but to debunk syntheses. Classroom experiences suggest the importance in interdisciplinary studies of moving not just toward holistic understanding and synthesis but away as well.

The next essays discuss science-based courses that become broadly interdisciplinary. Laurence Gould designed an innovative multimedia course called Seeing Through Symmetry in which students explore a "hub concept" important in both scientific and artistic worlds. Through it, students can see interrelations of mathematics and physics with art, music, poetry, and architecture. They not only learn about symmetry but experience it and experiment with it in a diverse series of labs that bring them through frustration to patience and even pleasure. Initiatives in interdisciplinary general education can influence the university at large. Gould and one of his colleagues obtained a substantial National Science Foundation equipment grant for his course that outfitted a new multimedia lab in which faculty and students in various programs work together on interactive computer-based projects.

All our interdisciplinary courses continue to evolve, but the final essay in Part I, like Fried and McCarthy's, focuses particularly on work in progress. Faculty on second-generation teams of Reasoning in Science, one of the first courses to become part of the AUC, are trying in different ways to increase student involvement in the process of experimentation. Doug Dix, Regina Miller, Mike Horn, and Dale Brown point out that students too often see science as a forced catechism into a faith divorced from their lives, a process quite different from the questioning, testing, and risk-taking characteristic of practicing scientists. They argue that engaged learning connects students with the child within as well as with the core of the academic areas of inquiry involved. Like Gould, they seek a two-way enrichment between students' experiences in their major and in general education.

Thus all of the following essays explore particular courses but address broader questions about how such sites can encourage students to practice integrative thinking.

NOTE

1. While this volume was in the publication process, we were pleased to learn that the Association for Integrative Studies, in accord with this emphasis, is planning to sponsor an anthology of essays tentatively titled *Innovative Teaching for Interdisciplinarians*. According to its editor, Carolyn Haynes of Miami University's School of Interdisciplinary Studies, it will "focus on various innovative pedagogical approaches and offer ideas about how those approaches might best be implemented in an interdisciplinary undergraduate context."

REFERENCES

Association of American Colleges. 1988. *A New Vitality in General Education.* Washington, D.C.: Association of American Colleges.

Bonwell, Charles C., and James A. Eison. 1991. *Active Learning: Creating Excitement in the Classroom.* ASHE-ERIC Higher Education Report No. 1. Washington, D.C.: George Washington University, School of Education and Human Development.

Fassinger, Polly A. 1995. "Professors' and Students' Perceptions of Why Students Participate in Class." *Teaching Sociology* 24 (1): 25–33.

Halliburton, David. 1981. "Interdisciplinary Studies." In *The Modern American College,* ed. Arthur Chickering. San Francisco: Jossey-Bass.

Kavaloski, Vincent C. 1979. "Interdisciplinary Education and Humanistic Aspiration: A Critical Reflection." In *Interdisciplinarity and Higher Education,* ed. Joseph J. Kockelmans. University Park: Pennsylvania State University Press.

Minnich, Elizabeth Kamarck. 1990. *Transforming Knowledge.* Philadelphia: Temple University Press.

Newell, William H. 1994. "Designing Interdisciplinary Courses." In *Interdisciplinary Studies Today,* eds. Julie Thompson Klein and William G. Doty. San Francisco: Jossey-Bass.

Pascarella, Ernest T., and Patrick T. Terenzini. 1991. *How College Affects Students: Findings and Insights from Twenty Years of Research.* San Francisco: Jossey-Bass.

Silberman, Mel. 1996. *Active Learning: 101 Strategies to Teach Any Subject.* Boston: Allyn and Bacon.

Weimer, Mary Ellen. 1996a. "Teaching for Change." Presentation at the Connecticut Consortium for Enhancing Learning and Teaching, 1 November, Gateway Community-Technical College, New Haven, Connecticut.

Weimer, Mary Ellen. 1996b. "Participation: Research and References." *Teaching Professor* 10 (7): 3.

THE CREATIVITY OF INTERDISCIPLINARITY AND THE INTERDISCIPLINARITY OF CREATIVITY

John M. Roderick

We tell ourselves and our students that the truly educated person is the one who sees the connections among the traditional disciplines. Yet it is human nature to categorize and thereby to institutionalize distinct boundary lines between, say, the study of history and the study of literature, or the study of biology and the study of chemistry. When the sometimes artificial walls that we construct to separate the disciplines in college and university curricula are viewed as transparent bridges to discover more about our understanding of humanity, we begin to approach what has become known as interdisciplinary studies.

Such an eclectic approach often meets institutional resistance because we tend to reward specialization, especially in higher education, even though the disciplines are, at times, difficult to separate neatly. Every literary scholar, for example, holds some value for the influence of historical factors on the evolution of a period's literature. All biologists agree that the study of the human body requires an understanding of the intricacies of its chemical makeup.

When a movement comes along that recognizes and highlights the innate connections, a perspective that respects the similarities or parallels as well as the differences among the disciplines, we as academicians may be skeptical and resistant at first. It does, after all, seem to threaten the sanctity of those disciplines we strove so hard to construct. Yet interdisciplinarity contributes a particular richness to our curricula. To justify adopting this approach, we have begun to follow a pattern of activity not too remote from our initial constructs for the traditional disciplines. We do what we as scholars do best: we gather data; we define terms; we draw conclusions based on our investigations; and we emerge, ultimately, with what could be called another discipline.

The ironic danger in this natural approach, of course, is that interdisciplinary study, evolving as it is with its own lexicography, its own "secret handshake," if you will, could move full circle and become the very mold for the principles we are trying to break down in our interdisciplinary approach to the study of the human condition. Yet that is perhaps the only way we know how to give value to what we perceive as important and worth knowing. We legitimize explorations by creating disciplines out of them.

Noteworthy efforts are being made nationwide to both institutionalize and legitimize the value of the interdisciplinary approach to curricula. Among the more germinal and, in some ways, groundbreaking work is Newell's *Interdisciplinarity: Essays from the Literature* (1998). As director of the Institute in Integrative Studies at Miami University in Ohio, Newell in this collection of essays explores interdisciplinary study without losing sight of its basic tenet to be expansive rather than reductive.

A further irony of a reductive approach is that in each of the traditional disciplines we can name, those practitioners or experts we identify as contributing most significantly have one basic thing in common: each is steeped in a multidisciplined eclecticism in which other disciplines contribute to better understanding of the discipline in question. In the field of literature, for example, the major critics over the years have been those scholars who bring a depth and breadth to the canon. The particular emphasis may change over time, but the overall similarity remains constant and is based on the simple premise that literature is influenced by every other discipline, that humankind does not write or read in a vacuum.

Literary study is enhanced by an exploration through the prisms of philosophy and history and psychology and sociology and the host of traditional disciplines that influence writer and reader alike. It is no accident that Sigmund Freud would find the works of William Shakespeare particularly useful in articulating some of his psychological theories. Nor, it might be added, should the rich psychological dimensions of Shakespeare's dramatic characters escape us. If we consider understanding humanity to be a worthwhile end, then surely the study that makes the best sense is interdisciplinary. Our handle on the traditional disciplines in this quest for understanding may be a useful starting point, but we soon reach a place where the scope of the human landscape is boundless and, yes, borderless.

Over the ages the better minds amongst us have been able to grasp the expanse of this vast landscape. Perhaps it is primarily with the compass of this or that discipline that they explore new territory, but the geography is as old as humankind itself. If the study of interdisciplinarity is anything, it has as its foundation that the whole is greater than the sum of its parts. And while each part may indeed have its place, without which the entire structure might collapse, the point is that the part is not the whole. It is through interdisciplinarity that we may hope to approach an understanding of this whole.

THIS THING WE CALL CREATIVITY

In some ways, the study of creativity is particularly useful in exploring the world beyond the walls of the disciplines. Each discipline clings to a kind of ownership of creative endeavors, but finding a commonality can thrust us into the heart of an interdisciplinary approach to learning, at least as it pertains to an area as potentially diverse as creativity. Particular disciplines have their own understandings of the concept of creativity, but perhaps a better working definition that is not discipline-specific can be derived from Csikszentmihalyi's germinal text, *Creativity.* The subtitle alone helps to define the interdisciplinary nature of creativity: *Flow and the Psychology of Discovery and Invention.* Csikszentmihalyi begins with the basic premise that creativity "arises from the synergy of many sources and not only from the mind of a single person" (1996, 1).

Even a narrow, discipline-specific definition of creativity can be fairly sweeping, as for the creativity in creative writing. Imagine the complexities when looking at creativity from a multiplicity of disciplines within the purview of a single course. What happens to our definition of creativity when it is broadened to encompass the multiple perspectives of multiple disciplines? Can the same things be said about what it means to be creative when moving from the area of written communication to the study of philosophy, or musical composition, or any of a number of disciplines in which the idea of creativity might come to bear in some integrative, essential way?

In developing the course Creativity: The Dynamics of Artistic Expression at the University of Hartford, the team leaders explored some of the specific disciplinary applications of the concept in an attempt to reach a broader understanding. And because the course was to focus not only on the breadth of disciplines but also on the breadth of the creative impulses within them, we were provided with a veritable living experiment in what it means to be creative. Students and instructors alike were confronted with the wider challenge of exploring issues of creativity in the specific arts and at the same time moving from these specific applications to greater syntheses, if they exist, to commonalities that indeed reach beyond the bounds of each discipline.

Herein was the greatest challenge but also the greatest possibility to advance beyond a single discipline and perhaps arrive at a higher understanding of the issues of creativity that overlap all disciplines. We were led to explore, among other things, whether the creative practice involved in specific art forms enjoys a spirit or dimension or quality that is larger than the discipline itself. Are there inherent interdisciplinary principles that we can extract from each artist, from whatever field, to arrive at a whole greater than its parts? The search has been intriguing, the answers even more so. The dynamics of this exploration provided some of the most important insights for students and instructors alike.

CREATIVITY: THE COURSE

Creativity: The Dynamics of Artistic Expression was designed to explore the landscape of imagination, providing students with an opportunity for original creation and responsive reaction to the creations of others. The focus of the course would be a series of approximately 10 to 12 workshops in various media presented by different artists, initially ranging from both planned and spontaneous musical events, to artistic interpretation through action, to expression in photography, to the muses of poetry, to creative listening and notation, to computer-generated art, and to visual presentation of the art of others.

Unlike many traditional offerings, the course of necessity would focus as much on the process as on the product of creation. This emphasis was particularly important because we could not expect students to become expert or even proficient in the 10 or 12 different disciplines they would be studying. For most students, it was the process that they could emulate, not execution of the practice of the art form. For example, mime and mask-maker Larry Hunt demonstrated in his workshop how hiding behind a mask allows individuals temporarily to lose their own identities in the persona represented by the mask. The implications for the arts of acting and dramatic presentation are clear, and while just a few students were selected to "act out" such presentation, most of the students, participants and non-participants, learned about a process that frees inhibitions and allows expression of truly creative role playing. Students learned the importance of the need to take risks, the freedom to make mistakes, and the willingness to take themselves less than seriously at times in the spirit of playful discovery. Some components would emphasize writing, but much of the course would develop less-refined aspects of the thought process such as visual thinking.

Einstein once said that "imagination is more important than knowledge." Perhaps he meant that with imagination, we have the resource for obtaining whatever knowledge we need. In developing the course, we believed that cultivating imagination enables students to use their knowledge to solve problems as they gain insights into their world. We wanted to encourage students to explore the relationship between what they know and how they express that knowledge in various art forms, thereby unlocking their own creativity.

More emphasis was placed on thematic content than on technique so that students could learn to appreciate art as a means of both self-expression and the communication of the ideas of others. We did not expect students to become expert in music, writing, or art; nor would they need a previous grounding in these forms. We sought, instead, to expose them to some of the rigors of the creative process in the various disciplines to embellish their roles as both creators and observers. The integrative content of the course was built in from the beginning. The disciplines explored were quite varied and, on the surface, almost appear to be unrelated to each other save the commonality they may share in tapping a creative force. Because each of the art forms possesses its own set of values, criteria, and technical and artistic skill, we felt that students might initially have difficulty integrating the diverse forms into a whole that made sense. Consequently, the course was set up on the basic premise that all art, regardless of its form or formlessness, is an attempt by the artist to posit an idea and that the essence of true creativity is the unique blending of imagination, emotion, and insight.

To encourage students to discover and express their individuality, we attempted to guide them toward perceiving new relationships and making startling connections. They were encouraged to use insight and imagination to fuse seemingly disparate fields of knowledge, thereby forging their own artistic vision, voice, and identity. The integrative objective of the course was to show that the relationship between art and civilization is codependent, that the interaction of art and life is crucial to the dynamic expansion of our cultural consciousness, and that art is not a separate field of endeavor restricted to specialists but an integral part of living fully as a well-educated individual. In short, we wanted our students to understand that creativity per se is not limited to the arts but is vital to every realm of human activity.

The course was designed so that the integration of knowledge and experience in the arts takes place spontaneously as students view and participate in the act of creating individual and collaborative works of art in several media. As noted, students were introduced to modes of artistic expression through workshops led by professional artists. Students gained valuable hands-on experience in a broad spectrum of creativity in the arts. Once they had been exposed to the fundamental differences between the disciplines, they were asked to make finer distinctions among them on the basis of the intrinsic limitations of each medium. From there we led them to the broader worldview that all creativity shares.

One of the first presenters in the course, Humbert Lucarelli, who spoke on Creativity and Learning, offers a good example of the sort of exposure students receive to the creative world. Lucarelli is a world-renowned oboe player. Students were surprised when he arrived without an instrument. Instead, he spoke to the class about how he managed to break new ground in his playing by getting away from music altogether for a while. He immersed himself in various other art forms, especially the visual arts. This immersion reminded him anew of the interconnectedness of all the arts. Lucarelli said that the very act of distancing himself from his music and moving toward a different form of artistic expression helped him embrace his own art more fully and expressively in the long run. With a renewed understanding and appreciation of disciplines seemingly quite remote from his own, he explained how his approach to his oboe music also changed dramatically, gaining a more complete dimension than it had heretofore had.

Students recorded their responses to each workshop in their journals, where they were asked to discuss what they learned from exposure to a particular artist or art form. All expressed surprise that a virtuoso of Lucarelli's stature would spend so much time and attention not just on his oboe playing but on developing his appreciation of other artistic endeavors as well. They were getting their first lesson on the premise that the creative spirit crosses the bounds of disciplines. Indeed, such excursions are mandatory broadening experiences that enhance the creative effort in any one area.

When it came to identifying specific abilities that the course would develop, the varied nature of the workshops led to a fourfold emphasis. Written communication underscored many of the sessions because students were asked to respond to each workshop with an extensive journal entry that became the basis for a portion of their evaluation. In workshops such as those in creative writing, students were asked to write an original short story. Oral communication was encouraged as a natural outgrowth of the workshops and journals. Students were expected to talk about each workshop experience in the follow-up sessions and to weigh the reactions recorded in their journals against those of their peers. Critical thinking and problem solving as well as values identification were fostered as students attempted to integrate the diverse experiences of the workshops with reference to specific themes. It was expected that values identification, specifically those generated within the particular discipline under study, would become a natural point of departure when we explored an artist's purpose in choosing this or that thematic element for his or her creative expression.

Another level of values identification emerged as students involved themselves in disciplines entirely new to their experience. Student understanding of and sensitivity to the role the arts play in our society was also emphasized in the course. While this was sometimes in the background of our discussions, it became a pervading element throughout the entire curriculum.

It was expected from the outset that students would participate directly in the various disciplines. This participatory or collaborative learning experience took place in small groups that created or critiqued works of art. Interaction among students was expected in the groups as students performed exercises designed to develop the imagination, stimulate new ways of seeing, and establish an atmosphere of trust, encouragement, and support.

THE NATURE OF THE WORKSHOPS

The nature of each workshop determined the type of student participation. For example, in the photography session offered by Ellen Carey, students created their own photographic images as ray-o-grams, by placing objects on photographic paper, and shot pictures with their self-made pinhole cameras. In the computer-generated art session presented by Katherine Delventhal, students were given a demonstration of how computer technology can be employed to create new images and had the opportunity to discover their own talents in this avant-garde art field. In addition to the activities directed by the workshop presenters, course instructors invited students in the follow-up sessions to share their ideas and creations with each other to enhance continuing integration, synthesis, and, of course, creativity. One example of integration followed a session in which students were asked to use the one-dimensional ray-o-grams of objects of their choice, such as a set of car keys and a wristwatch, to construct three-dimensional "sculptures" that presented a totally different "idea" from the photos alone.

An interesting phenomenon emerged as the course progressed and students began to buy into the premise that creativity evolves, in part, from risk taking as much as from dedicated hard work. Students did not want to be graded on their efforts, arguing that if they were willing to take risks then the instructors had no right to evaluate them on whether they were successful or not. A compromise was struck wherein students were led to recognize that the freedoms necessary to create well were not guarantees, in themselves, of success, nor were they license for the notion that "anything goes." By linking creative efforts with an intent to communicate an idea, students learned to appreciate that even at the height of creative freedom, standards did exist.

It should be noted that the creators and initial instructors of this course (the author and Anthony Maulucci) are from the same discipline, English. Overall, this proved useful in the follow-up classes that were divided between the two instructors. The workshops demonstrated the different disciplinary approaches to creativity. We knew that it was important to assist students in coming to a synthesis of so many variant art forms. Our similar backgrounds prevented the discussion sections from splintering unnecessarily. Because we were changing focus on a weekly basis in the workshops, it was essential that there be some stasis in the midst of all this change. The common background in English provided that.

In subsequent offerings of the course, the instructors have not always shared a common discipline, and it appears that what may have been lost in the discussion sections by having a more or less unified vision is made up for by the advantage of still more integrative insight. Using a team-teaching approach in some of the discussion classes might have provided interesting possibilities, but we ruled this out because of class size. The 40-plus students who gathered for each workshop strained the opportunities for hands-on interactive experience. By dividing this large group in half for discussion purposes, we created an atmosphere of unity and a sense of belonging, though sacrificing what a full team approach might have offered. We believe, on balance, this decision was correct.

ELEMENTS OF EVALUATION

Students' journals became an integral part of the course, serving as a springboard for discussion, a tool for cumulative integration of creative principles, a record of the evolution of observations and processes, and a critical response to each workshop. The instructors periodically collected these journals and evaluated them with written comments or in private conferences with students. Here again, given the nature of both creativity and student personalities, students did not want grades attached to their journal observations. Yet it became clear that some students engaged significantly in the expressive struggle between thought and performance while others simply reported what the workshop was about in as brief a manner as possible.

As instructors, we learned that there is always a bona fide relationship between a student's genuine effort and the ultimate grade for major projects. We offered examples of superlative journal entries compared with mediocre cursory ones in defense of our grades. In hindsight, our comments would have been sufficient without the accompanying grades, although some students' subsequent journal entries improved after the initial "shock" of a weak grade.

Two major assignments evaluated exclusively by the instructors were the formal critical paper and the final artistic project. It was expected that the critical paper would be a response to a theatrical production, a concert, or an exhibit and would incorporate the creative principles from at least three different workshop sessions or disciplines. The final creative artistic project was to represent the integration of at least two disciplines and embody a thematic idea approved by the instructor. Multiple examples were shared with students to help them appreciate this notion of integration. Each of the four types of course assignments (exploratory assignments in creativity, weekly journal, analytical paper, and final project) was worth about 25 percent of the final course grade.

In their final artistic projects, students were asked to synthesize the ideas expressed in their weekly journals and in the formal critical paper. Exploratory assignments in creativity, whether given by workshop leaders or by the course instructors, were critiqued and evaluated in the weekly follow-up sessions. Students' creative work was presented to the class as exhibits or through oral presentations, and comments were generated in a public forum where openness and a spirit of encouragement were expected.

In the presentation of the final projects students and instructors alike became aware of just how extensive was students' grasp of the interdisciplinary nature of creativity. Students were permitted to work in teams of up to three for these final projects. Some took full advantage of this collaborative opportunity, combining the particular skills of each participant to create effective presentations. One such group presented a video of the life of a dog exclusively from the dog's perspective relating to a dog's best friend, man. One student wrote the script, another directed the performance, and a third used his ability with a video camera to capture it all. All three were actors, along with the dog.

Another student who presented a solo performance provided a demonstration of the Samurai tradition, complete with cultural dress and Samurai sword-wielding flourishes, in an accompanying dance that sent the front row of the audience scurrying back for fear that their heads might be lopped off in the aggressive emotion expressed by the student dancer. In his presentation, this student combined information about the social meaning of the Samurai tradition with a visual enactment and performance that symbolically represented in dance movement information about the philosophy underpinning this cultural phenomenon. This synthesis helped reveal the multifaceted aspects of the culture. Many of the other projects were no less creative and no less integrative.

WHAT WE LEARNED

What did we learn from this experience? And, more important, what do we think our students learned about the interdisciplinary nature of the force we call creativity? In a word, they saw firsthand that creativity not only crosses disciplines, indeed it flourishes best when it draws upon that cross-pollination. When Robert Carl, for example, presented his workshop entitled "Making Your Life Into a Work of Art," students were unsure about what to expect when he asked them to arrive for the class with an object meaningful to them that made noise of some kind. The variety of objects almost defied imagination, ranging from perfume atomizers, to piggy banks that jingled, to more mundane musical instruments such as bongos and guitars. Carl asked each student why his or her particular sound creator was significant. The stories alone were informative about how objects of sound can play such critical roles at various junctures of an individual's life. But Carl, who is a nationally recognized composer, began to relegate kinds of sounds into categories, and he soon created an extemporaneous "orchestra" that had all the ingredients of a symphonic gathering. To the delight of the participants, some quite shy initially, what began as noise soon rose collectively as music. Students saw firsthand how the creative impulse can draw dissimilar individual noisemakers into a cohesive orchestration.

It was but a short jump to other workshops that were genuinely interdisciplinary, such as one combining the skills and knowledge needed to operate a personal computer with learning to create computer-generated art; or "Chasing the Poetic Muse," in which poets introduced the class to the connections between introspection and the expressive mode of using the metaphor to capture feeling and form in poetry; or Christopher Horton's workshop on painting in which an artistic eye for symmetry was married to the spatial plane of the design architect.

The concept of creativity evolved in the course as something that not only transcends the disciplines but also can shed new light on the disciplines. In addition to revealing the truly interdisciplinary nature of creativity, the course helped students understand their own roles in recognizing what is creative in themselves and in others. And their judgments gained an eclectic acceptance that did not seem to be present at the outset. Many in the class, for example, initially maintained that those individuals whom society deems to be creative appear also to be arrogant and self-serving to a fault.

In our investigation of the creative impulse, however, most students came away from the experience with an understanding closer to Csikszentmihalyi's observation that while society may often view creative people as aloof, cold, selfish, and arrogant because of their single-minded attention to pursuing their art, in fact, the very opposite is true. In such pursuits, says Csikszentmihalyi, "[creative artists] are making new connections between their art and adjacent areas of knowledge" (1996, 10). And while specialization is often favored as cultures evolve, it can lead to fragmentation. "Creativity generally involves crossing the boundaries of domains" (Csikszentmihalyi, 9) so that more substantive contributions can be made to the specialization of disciplines.

In the exposure students receive in Creativity: The Dynamics of Artistic Expression to how the imagination is used to create a variety of art forms that communicate an artist's ideas or feelings, they are led to see the integrative nature of creativity. In the process, they have the opportunity to become both creative audience and creative participant in the arts.

REFERENCES

Csikszentmihalyi, Mihaly. 1996. *Creativity: Flow and the Psychology of Discovery and Invention.* New York: HarperCollins.

Newell, William H., ed. 1998. *Interdisciplinarity: Essays from the Literature.* New York: College Entrance Examination Board.

ADDITIONAL RESOURCES

Maslow, A. 1974. *The Farther Reaches of Human Nature.* New York: Viking.

May, Rollo. 1975. *The Courage to Create.* New York: Norton.

Parnes, Sidney J. 1981. *The Magic of Your Mind.* Buffalo, N.Y.: Creative Education Foundation and Bearly Limited.

Stein, Morris. 1974. *Stimulating Creativity.* Vols. I and II. New York: Academic Press.

CREATIVITY: THE DYNAMICS OF ARTISTIC EXPRESSION: SAMPLE SYLLABUS

In this integrative course, students participate in a series of 10 to 12 workshops presented by different artists and instructors in a variety of media, ranging from the graphic arts to photography, writing, the performing arts, music, and other fine arts. The workshops and follow-up discussion sessions expose students to how the imagination is used to create art forms that communicate the artists' ideas or feelings. (Emphasis on oral and written communication, values identification, and critical thinking.)

Goals: Students will hone their skills as both creative audience and creative participant in a variety of art forms, learn how to write critically and analytically about the nature of those forms, and come to a fuller appreciation of the interconnectivity among them.

Texts: Germinal readings in their respective disciplines chosen by workshop presenters, augmented by selections from works such as Rollo May, *The Courage to Create* (1975); Mihaly Csikszentmihalyi, *Creativity* (1996); Abraham Maslow, *The Farther Reaches of Human Nature* (1974); and Betty Edwards, *Drawing on the Artist Within* (1986), *Drawing on the Right Side of the Brain* (1989).

Sample Workshops:

Be What Is: Dance Improvisation

Chasing the Poetic Muse

Computer Art

Creative Decisions in Exhibition

Creative Listening, Creative Notation, or "Do You Hear What I Hear?"

Creative Performance

Creativity and Learning Music

Creativity in Photography: The Magic Box

Drawing Without Looking

Electronic Musical Composition

Fiction Writing

Found-Object Symphony

Going on a Mystery Ride: Architecture and Creativity

Imagine a Scene From Childhood With Water

Martha Graham, Myth, and Movement

Music and Computers

Musical Choice: Planned and Spontaneous

Play Writing

Problem Solving and Play Acting

Scissors Are Swans' Wings: Making Metaphor and Poetry

Showing the Last Dance

Song Writing

Sound and Movement

Start Where You Are: Ceramics

Tour of the Artist's Work Place

Unity and Chaos in Geometric Drawing

Additional Student Activities: Workshop follow-up projects, ranging from drawing to poetry writing, mask making, or acting; weekly journal; critical essay exploring and synthesizing the elements and commonalities found in creative expression; final project (which students can create in teams of up to three) blending at least two art forms into a unique artistic statement of their own, with class presentation.

WHAT IS SCHOOL? THE ART OF INTERDISCIPLINARY ENGAGEMENT

Robert Fried and Holly DiBella-McCarthy

I: STUDENTS AS PLAYERS IN CONSTRUCTIVIST INQUIRY

GETTING INTO THE GAME

Fifty-five students—freshmen, sophomores, juniors, seniors, with majors ranging from business to history to the fine arts—wander into a large classroom designed for science lectures. They slowly fill the straight rows of chairs behind heavy, black-topped tables. Some converse (though few know each other); most just sit and wait for class to begin.

All are here for a course entitled What Is School? but few have even the slightest idea what they've signed up for. It's the course that fits their busy schedules, another of those pesky, required All-University Curriculum (AUC) courses that are supposed to "broaden" you. Most would rather do their own broadening, thank you very much. They have careers to prepare for, their parents pay a lot of money for them to attend a private university, and most are convinced they know best which courses to take. They don't like to be told.

As the students glance around the room, they see what looks like teacher-style graffiti—quotations of some sort printed in bold, inch-high letters that have been taped up on the wall. To the left, by the window, they read:

> *I'm only here because this course fits my schedule and they say I gotta take a number of these Mickey Mouse courses—not for any other reason. So take it easy, and don't push me too hard.*

> *See me? I'm right here, sitting up in front. That's to impress you that I'm a serious student. I've always been that way and teachers really like it. I'll do anything you ask of me—as long as I get my A.*

> *Hey Teacher! Leave those kids alone!*
> *All in all, you're just another brick in the wall. (Pink Floyd)*

To the right, by the doors to the corridor, is posted:

> *If you can't show me how this course is going to help me in my major, or help me get a job, I'm not going to waste my time. I'll do as little as I can possibly get away with and still pass.*

> *Most college profs don't realize how out of touch they are with people my age. It's hard for me to even pretend to be interested in what you have to say. You want to teach me? Find out who I really am!*

And behind them, across the back wall:

> *Just don't put us into little groups and tell us to teach each other. You're the one who gets the salary. You teach the course!*

> *I don't think anybody here understands how it feels to be me, to be different from the mainstream culture. Until you people take diversity seriously, I'm going to keep pretty much to myself.*

> *Let's face it, my parents want me out of the house for four years and are rich enough to send me to a place like this. And you want me to work?*

It is not quite what they expect to see, but those who've already had a few AUC courses have come to expect the unexpected. So they settle down and wait for what will probably come next: the arrival of professors armed with an interdisciplinary syllabus and introductory lecture.

Into their midst walk three instructors: Doug is a professor of biology with a passion for radical social reform; Holly, trained as a special educator, has directed a program linking the university with local public schools; Rob initially studied English literature but is now a professor of educational leadership. We are very much an interdisciplinary trio, having at least as much cross-disciplinary variety in our individual backgrounds as between us. Doug, who developed the course with Holly, taught it once before with mixed results. His idea is that our public school system is unfixable—blow it up and put something better in its place. Holly believes in a more evolutionary approach to educational reform and is convinced that as advocates for kids, we must invest in what is working in the public schools and build from these successes. Rob, who got hooked on the idea of this course through conversations with Doug, is first and foremost an advocate for student engagement. He envisions the course as a laboratory, where we try to undo the habits of docility that too many students bring with them from high school. It is Rob's design for an "opener" that we are about to embark upon.

Seeming to ignore the students, we position ourselves around the room—like three points of a triangle, about 20 feet apart. Rob has brought five grapefruit-sized, squishy, miniature soccer balls. We speak informally about the course: our hopes and concerns, why "school" is an issue worthy of attention, and whether our students will be able to "get into it" in the settings we have designed for them: a weekly classroom session, three breakout groups (also meeting weekly), and fieldwork explorations.

As we talk, the three of us begin tossing the puffy soccer balls back and forth, lobbing them over the students' heads. Soon we begin arching our throws beyond each other, so that they fall into the laps of startled students. At first, they toss the balls back to us (thinking we've missed our intended targets), but soon the balls are flying around the room with some abandon. After a few minutes of this, we collect them as they fly past us.

We then turn to the class and inquire: "What's going on here?" By this time, our students are probably thinking to themselves, "Hey! That's *my* question!" One of the bolder students offers the opinion that we are trying to get them involved. "You're trying to tell us that it's up to us, too, to figure out What is School?" Another connects what has just occurred to the phrases taped to the wall. "You're trying to get us to think about this stuff, to get it out in the open."

We acknowledge these responses and say that, yes, the balltossing emphasizes that we want the students to begin the course as players, not spectators. We say that we think learning means getting involved in issues, not simply hearing from the experts. And aren't we all experts of some sort when it comes to school? Haven't we all had at least 12 years of experience with that topic?

We let the questions hang in the air momentarily before moving to our next planned exercise—having students, by turn, briefly relate both the most positive and the most negative school experience they have had thus far in their lives. We take part in the exercise, explaining that everyone deserves an opportunity to address the class about things he or she knows more about than anyone else in the room.

It works. We hear from everyone, although some claim they have no best experience to relate, only a painful one. There are a lot of laughs, some awkwardness (less than one would normally expect on the first day, in a class this large). The exercise eats up an hour of our fast-evaporating time, and we instructors can't resist tossing in an occasional comment in response to a student's tale of glee or woe.

The students look pleased when we tell them that we, as faculty, expect to learn a lot from them, as well as have a good time contesting the issues among ourselves. We tell them we will also bring in guests who will offer different views on What Is School?

Our homework assignment is another challenge: by the next week, students are to choose one of the quotations posted on the walls that they identify with (or to invent one) and use it to write a one-page essay that describes, as truthfully as possible, why that quote reflects their experience of school. They are to make 55 copies of their one-page essay and bring it to be shared with their classmates. To protect their confidentiality, each student selects a pen name (e.g., Subzero, Bear, Pendragon). Only the instructors will know to whom each pen name belongs.

We apologize for the duplicating expense they will incur but explain that they will be creating one of the texts to be used in the class, and five dollars is pretty cheap as textbooks go. We use this moment to reiterate how earnest we are about students beginning the course as players, as people who have something to contribute to the learning of others, and as fellow explorers with us in the question posed by the course title. This first assignment, we explain, is a way of putting our values into action.

Class is over. Amid a friendly buzz as students get up and leave the room, we tell them we will explain more about the course next time, and that we will divide ourselves into three discussion groups that will meet each week. We are pleased, and a little relieved, that our unconventional kickoff has gone this well.

STUDENTS CONTRIBUTING AS PARTNERS

We don't want to suggest that this opening session resulted in a stream of intense student learning that lasted all semester. We were pleasantly surprised the following week to see most students return to class with copies of their one-page essays. But in some ways, our opening was a peak experience and not easily replicated. There were days when, at least in our general session, only a handful of students actively took part in the conversation. Participation was higher in the smaller discussion groups, but we hadn't eradicated student passivity. Two contrasting end-of-semester student reflections serve as an illustration. One confessed, *"I failed at improving relationships with the other students and the teacher. I have an empty feeling about my accomplishments in the course because I was a passive learner."* Another said, *"I definitely came out of my shell since day one. I have learned to speak up, disagree with class-mates, and ask a question if I don't understand what's going on."*

Beginning What Is School? the way we did sharpened our perspective on constructivist student engagement—an essential aspect of any interdisciplinary course (or course within a discipline, for that matter). To us it means promoting active student cognition and voice in making meaning from ideas and issues generated within the course that reflect upon the student's life. Such engagement is more than class participation—staged discussion groups or the occasional question and answer. We wanted our students to take their share of responsibility for the intellectual work of the class by doing some research about the attitudes of students in high schools, pondering questions that have no "right" answer, distilling personal experiences and communicating them to others, reflecting on their reading and, in some cases, taking action on their beliefs. Shor argues (and we heartily agree) that

> Until students experience lively participation, mutual authority, and meaningful work, they will display depressed skills and knowledge, as well as negative emotions. Teachers will be measuring and reacting to an artificially low picture of student abilities. (1992, 21)

Constructivist engagement requires of instructors that they not overwhelm students with their own erudition, but rather base a large portion of course content (perhaps 40 to 60 percent) on areas of inquiry and intellectual rigor in which students feel confident that they can make a substantive contribution to each other's learning. For example, we asked these college students to revisit their high schools and report on the quality of student engagement they observed. Other assignments included having them write about the kind of child they were before being exposed to formal schooling, or reflect on themselves as active versus passive learners. Our written assignments, weekly discussion sessions, and final demonstrations were all designed to help students see themselves as partners in our inquiry. One student said, *"I've come to think of school as more of a choice now that I am paying to be here. I am here now in order to expand my knowledge and make a contribution to this community and to the outside world."*

In designing our course, we attempted to create a reflective interdisciplinary laboratory in which students could use their current and prior school experiences to build a deeper understanding of What Is School? from multiple perspectives, including psychological, sociological, political, and aesthetic dimensions. In this we were assisted by guest speakers: a mathematics professor spoke on Teacher/Student Relationships at the University, a former school superintendent offered What Education Looks Like From the Top, a psychologist invited us to consider Two Separate Brains, and a parent discussed A Mother's Perspective on Disability.

Students took part in action research, which meant visiting a K-12 classroom on several occasions to observe teaching and learning styles and to gauge the quality of the learning climate. Students analyzed their experiences, shared them with each other during our weekly small-group sessions, and generated a list of issues for further exploration (e.g., *Are computers necessary for learning? Is student achievement affected by the classroom environment? Are students passive or active by nature or by indoctrination?*). As final projects, they created "happenings" in which a variety of expressive modes brought those issues to life. One group staged a brilliant role-play on the sex education controversy, in which the grown-ups (as advocates for abstinence or for value-free science) clash, while the teenagers are abandoned, forced to choose between moral guidance without information or information without moral guidance.

Working from an interdisciplinary and constructivist perspective, we challenged students to move beyond general statements such as "*When we did our group research, I was able to see the pros and cons of different classroom environments*" to dig deeper and think more critically about what they had seen. For the student who said this, a newspaper editorial he wrote as his final class assignment suggests that he had, indeed, achieved a deeper reflective insight. He said, in part, "*Teachers are so used to talking to their students and not with them. This is something teachers need to learn how to do, for the benefit of children*"—a sentiment not lost on his instructors.

As the course evolved in its dual focus on interdisciplinarity and constructivism, we encouraged students to discuss how prior schooling had shaped their views about our education system and what views they had carried with them to college. There was much talk about the "game of school" (Fried 1995), the tendency to passively accede to an instructor's agenda. "*You really have to test your knowledge in real-life situations, not just on a test some teacher made up,*" one student reflected. This kind of probing proved to be quite a challenge for most students, who were used to being given information by their teachers in a more-or-less lecture format: "*Every year I promised myself to become more active in class, but for some reason, I kept my passive pattern. . . . This year is different; my attitude is changing about school. I have taken more initiative to voice my opinion.*" A few resented our approach and tried to fade into the woodwork, while some spoke with their professors in other courses about making classes more participatory.

We deliberately posed questions and assigned tasks that placed a high value on student experiences and insights. It was not that we sought to devalue our own scholarship and life experiences, but we were convinced that we could be more passionately forthcoming in presenting our own interdisciplinary perspectives on school if we were in the company of students who saw themselves as intellectually active, not just as respectful spectators and note-takers. Shor puts it this way:

> A participatory classroom offers chances to hear the largely silent voices of students from which teachers learn how to integrate subject matter into their existing knowledge. Students routinely hold back their voices as a means of resisting traditional classrooms where authority is unilateral and where they lack an inspiring life of the mind which speaks to their dreams and needs. (1992, 42)

Such a pro-engagement stance does not require instructors to turn over the course to their students, or create a climate where anything goes so long as somebody thinks it's "meaningful." Our design was purposeful. We assigned readings, fieldwork, essays, collaborative presentations, and reflection papers. We required attendance—a departure, for one of us, from a previous stance in which it had been explicitly left up to the student to choose whether or not to attend class. Our thinking here was that, because being partners and contributing to each other's learning was an essential part of the course, students needed to be there to make and to benefit from such contributions.

We challenged them via class discussions and one-page essays to bring forth insights and experiences to heighten self-awareness and pave the way for them to use self-reflection as a learning strategy in all their courses: *"I learned that college did not have one sole purpose of landing you a job upon graduation. It also is useful in shaping my character, social skills, and in enhancing my attitude and values."*

As students became aware of their learning styles, we continued to challenge them to relate the issues raised by the three of us and our guest speakers to their own ideas. We relied heavily on the Socratic approach of learning-through-questioning, and we discussed this methodology in weekly meetings of the three of us. Responded a student, *"Though we may not have always been the most productive students, we learned how to change that based on our own frustrations, if the pace was too slow. Never before did I have the opportunity to change the way and manner in which I was being taught."*

FACULTY AS INTERDISCIPLINARY PARTICIPANT/FACILITATORS

By asking our students to explain *why* they felt as they did about their prior and current schooling, our class discussions went beyond the surface-level patter so common when adults try to engage adolescents in discussions. We assumed the role of participant/facilitators—knowledgeable people from different academic walks of life who care passionately about issues; who, because of academic diversity, bring varying frames of reference to bear on the issues; who have doubts; who disagree sometimes; and who might interrupt each other with a provocative comment or question (thus violating the unwritten law that while teachers can interrupt students at will, nobody ever interrupts when a teacher is talking).

The three of us attempted with our students, in Tredway's (1995) words, to engage in "structured discourse about ideas and moral dilemmas." Team teaching afforded us a chance to present our different disciplinary perspectives passionately—Doug in biology, Rob in English and education, Holly in special education—yet in a fashion that encouraged argument and dissent. If we did not often consciously highlight the integration of subject areas during class discussions, it was because such integration was part of the air we breathed, at the core of our search to find answers to the question posed by the course title. Perhaps, in teaching the course again, we would be more specific in acknowledging the contributions of our disciplines, to encourage students to see the value of approaching a complex issue through multiple disciplinary lenses and to underscore the need to search for thematic connections between the courses they are taking in the various departments of the university. This would allow us better to respond to students who recognize, as one of ours did: *"College is not just about earning a degree in a certain field. It should be more than getting facts from books. It's about feeding your brain with many different thoughts and views. It's about diversity."*

Being open to our own and our students' diverse ideas and experiences allowed a surprisingly large number of students to feel that they had become vital members of a learning community. In the environment we created, students were able to take leave of some old habits of passivity or deference. We would try to respond thoughtfully to their comments, to take their views seriously, even if they were awkwardly phrased or factually questionable: *"I had a different outlook on class because I realized the teachers had respect for us and our opinions. We were able to come to mutual agreements on how our grade would be determined, what the final demonstration should be composed of, and even on how to try to change the teaching styles of some of our other professors."*

By listening carefully to our students, we noticeably improved the quality of how students listened to each other and their ability to respect different points of view. Of course, some students remained skeptical and held back, frustrated that we were not telling them exactly what to do or waiting for us to reimpose teacher authority as soon as they failed to "give us what we wanted." But others basked in the freedom to range widely: *"For this class, we also had to do a group project. We were allowed to pick any issue and explore it. I was working with three classmates. Our project not only helped me learn more about the topic we chose, but also how to work with peers."*

This raises, for us, a central issue in our approach to interdisciplinary teaching through the AUC: Was our endeavor in What Is School? but one more example of faculty from multiple disciplines addressing a phenomenon like "schooling"? Or does our effort represent as much of a challenge to conventional interdisciplinary studies as to traditional discipline-based pedagogy?

II: INTERDISCIPLINARITY AND CONSTRUCTIVIST ENGAGEMENT

STUDENTS AS SPECTATORS IN A DANCE OF THE DISCIPLINES

Our focus on a discipline-crossing issue, What Is School?, combined with an emphasis on actively promoting student engagement (in sharp contrast to the teacher-centered, content-delivery pedagogy that most of us—instructors and students alike—faced in high school and college), made us realize that to adopt an interdisciplinary approach offers, in itself, no guarantee that students will be intellectually engaged and creatively challenged by the experience. The literature on interdisciplinary studies (IDS), strangely enough, often underplays the significance of student-as-active-learner in the interdisciplinary experience.

Some IDS advocates much prefer to speculate on the various ways disciplines can be combined, fused, linked, or intertwined than to reflect on the impact of such diverse comminglings on student behavior, imagination, intellect, or retention of skills and knowledge. In his editorial essay in the anthology *Interdisciplinarity: Essays from the Literature* (1998), Newell poses questions such as "What is interdisciplinary study?" "Why engage in interdisciplinary study?" "What assumptions underlie interdisciplinary study?" But he has rather little to say about the students who are the presumed beneficiaries of such interdisciplinarity. In fact his essay rarely mentions students at all.

The "Guide to Interdisciplinary Syllabus Preparation" developed by the Association for Integrative Studies and Institute in Integrative Studies (1996) does include several questions that relate to students' roles (e.g., "Is there collaboration between students and faculty in forging a synthesis/integration?" "Are students expected to undertake any integration without faculty assistance?"). But even here, for a document that is being prepared, we suppose, at least as much for students' benefit as for participating faculty, questions relating to faculty roles and the interplay among the disciplines outnumber those that mention students by eight to one. The tenor of the guide seems clear in questions such as "How dominant is one discipline? Do the less-dominant disciplines provide more than subject matter?" or "Is there a dominant-subordinate pattern to faculty interactions, where one faculty member tends to prevail?" or "Do faculty begin to understand each other's perspective, though their own remains unaltered?"

There is much to be considered about the implications for faculty members, departments, and the academy of breaking through traditional disciplinary boundaries, and Newell's collection of essays is clearly focused on the academic ramifications of IDS. But absent an explicit focus on student learning, the concept of IDS can seem a dance of disciplines at which students are but onlookers. The creative focus is on the choreography of the faculty as they pirouette around a theme or issue. When students are spotlighted, it is so that they might be "exposed to" or "encouraged to recognize" the achievements of their IDS instructors. The goal for students, it appears, is to enlarge their *receptive* capacities—to heighten their ability to appreciate what professors from various disciplines know and can illuminate for them. Student outcomes are generally phrased in fuzzy or passive language: "more sensitivity to . . . ," "enlarged perspectives . . . ," "more humility or listening skills" (Newell 1990).

Benson indulges in what he calls "a bit of enlightened devil's advocacy" as he lays out five arguments against IDS, the second of which "holds that it is pedagogically doubtful business to spend time in interdisciplinary learning projects when the student lacks a mature base in any of the contributing disciplines" (1982, 38, 41). He expands upon this theme, stating that undergraduate IDS programs

> appear fated to wander between two unattractive poles—either they assume disciplinary sophistication in the students, in which case most, if not all, of the students are left in the dark, unable to manipulate the central issues at stake or—and this is much more frequently the case—they assume little, and the program of study is diluted and homogenized to the point where it is almost totally devoid of a critical base. Under the guise of an invitation to wrestle with what are frequently fascinating and important issues, the student is cheated of a precious opportunity to develop the skills and background required for mounting a proper attack on the issues. (1982, 42)

Benson's argument points not so much to a conundrum for the student as to the long-standing pedagogical failure to frame issues in a manner that allows students to engage seriously in, and contribute significantly to, the conversation. We may find, in any field, topics of such rarefied scholarly discourse that mere amateurs (be they undergraduates or professors from another department) will quickly find themselves shunted to the sidelines.

But to claim that most college students are, by definition, incapable of taking part in intellectually valid conversations within an IDS framework is to insult the student and denigrate the teacher. To approach college students (or students in high school or elementary school or preschool, for that matter) from such a stance is to indulge in a self-fulfilling prophecy, namely, that if we talk down to our students we will inevitably succeed in silencing them. One student reflected, "*I hate the whole structure of a typical classroom. It seems so tense. The teacher stands in front peering at all the students, as the students sit in perfect horizontal and vertical rows, looking face-forward.*"

Trow pushes the "kids can't handle it" argument from a different vector, namely that IDS is only for the few, the proud, the self-motivated:

> it may be that interdisciplinary studies are not for everybody; that they are, so to speak, a curriculum for students (and teachers) who have an usual [*sic*] love of learning, who are self-motivated, and who are curious beyond the average about the world they live in. . . . We can, of course, try to engender and encourage that curiosity and motivation, but when those qualities are absent, and stubbornly absent, interdisciplinary studies may not be the best way to reach students who fear and resist the play of mind, the unfamiliar connection, the disturbing insight. (1984–85, 15)

Conceding he "would anticipate spirited disagreement within the [IDS] community" on this point, Trow seems to welcome being refuted. In fact, he himself offers the best possible brief for engagement when he acknowledges that "We can, of course, try to engender and encourage that curiosity and motivation" (1984–85, 15).

CONFRONTING OUR OWN PATRONIZING TENDENCIES

Engendering and encouraging that curiosity and motivation is precisely what we set out to do in What Is School? We will never know those among our students who actually "fear and resist the play of mind" unless we take the position that they all deserve an opportunity to lose or lessen such fear if, indeed, they have it. At least one student gave us credit for trying: "*I find it much easier to participate in class discussions*

based on the learning, rather than the teacher lecturing followed by ques-
tions. When the whole class is involved in a discussion, it makes it more
personal and more absorbing."

Shor contributes to this discussion the observation that

> In classrooms where this participation is meager, the low perfor-
> mance of students is routinely misjudged as low achievement. But
> the actual cognitive levels of students are hard to measure in
> teacher-centered classrooms where students participate mini-
> mally. An accurate picture of what students know and can do is
> possible only when students really want to perform at their best.
> (1992, 21)

In summary, the problem, as we see it, is not that students are too
narrow or unsophisticated or ill-prepared or unmotivated or incurious or
lacking background in the disciplines to become our learning partners
(though we have all seen such attributes aplenty in students whose enthusiasm and confidence as learners have been bleached out by previous
conditions of schooling or by the students' own intellectual torpor). It is
rather that we as teachers often don't know how to bring their potential for
thoughtfulness into the open—to put it to work and allow our students to
see its impact. It is our own narrowness that often precludes our capacity
for respectful conversation with young people about serious issues.

For example, one of the great taboos among some within IDS is for
students to have to witness their professors in debate about opposing
perspectives: "Students become more active in the process of exploring
the relative merits and weaknesses of competing disciplinary perspectives when they are not observing faculty arguing among themselves"
(Newell 1983, 12). We think constructivist interdisciplinary engagement should include the opportunity to witness and participate in
debate among faculty on issues of consequence.

Faculty arguments were a key feature of our course, insofar as
Doug and Rob held sharply different views on the possibilities of reform
versus revolution in the public school system. We scheduled a debate
in mid-semester, after most students had become comfortable with our
constructivist posture, and then announced that we would each give a
20-minute statement on our side of the issue. Our disagreement was

real, not staged, and we relied on our third colleague Holly and our students to referee. We do not know whether Newell or any of his IDS contributors would seek to keep such a debate between faculty out of their IDS classrooms, but we think it right to bring struggles—whether arising from personal or disciplinary differences—to student view as long as we feel our students are comfortable enough in our process not to be intimidated or overwhelmed by our disagreement.

We also regularly brought our concerns about the direction of the course out in the open for student reflection and comment. We sometimes held faculty planning sessions, fishbowl-style, in class, during which we discussed what was working and what was not and how we might improve the class to better meet our goals. We put extra chairs in our circle and students would occasionally join our planning session to make a suggestion or express an opinion.

THE CHALLENGE TO INTERDISCIPLINARY INSTRUCTION

The need to pay serious attention to student engagement is, if anything, greater in IDS, because it is here that many students experience an alternative to the traditional flow of content information from a single professor with a single viewpoint. Because students in interdisciplinary general education courses are less likely to face departmental pressures to acquire particular content information essential for their major, we believe the purpose of IDS is as much to develop students' intellectual habits as to present an issue or idea from several disciplines. Both goals reinforce each other but this by no means happens automatically.

This view is strongly supported by Kavaloski, who offers a significant challenge to his IDS colleagues:

> To the extent that interdisciplinary reform is thought to consist solely of manipulating course-content and curriculum toward some objectified "integration," the notion of the student as a creator or recreator of meaning, as a subjectivity capable of an ongoing *process* of inquiry seems entirely absent. Knowledge reduces to a content which must be "covered" and "possessed" by those persons (namely, students) who bear no intrinsic or ontological

relationship to it. The "bodies" of knowledge become inert, life-less—in a word, corpses—with professors authoritatively per-forming the appropriate mortuary rites. The feeling of deadness that pervades our classrooms is no accident. (1979, 229)

This is precisely where we saw our students as "coming from": 12 to 15 years of schooling had rendered most of them disinclined, if not unable, to see themselves as "creator or recreator of meaning," and we hoped our interdisciplinary approach might reverse the tide. But, as Kavaloski continues,

> The tragedy of the contemporary interdisciplinary movement is that despite its high humanistic aspirations, it has not yet fully extricated itself from the mortuary concept of education as the assimilation of bodies of knowledge—however interrelated—which are realities-in-themselves. . . . Interdisciplinary education is to that extent blocked from taking full account of the meaning of the human being engaged in the active process of intellectual growth. In form, if not in content, it begins to closely resemble dis-ciplinary education and thus leads to identical results. (1979, 229)

Kavaloski cites psychologist Carl Rogers for backup:

> When we put together in one scheme such elements as a *pre-scribed curriculum, similar assignments for all students, lecturing* as almost the only mode of instruction, *standard tests* by which all students are externally evaluated, and *instructor-chosen grades* as the measures of learning, then we can almost guarantee that meaningful learning will be at an absolute minimum. (Rogers 1969, 5)

These were the rallying cries of the much-maligned 1960s move-ments of liberation, radical reform, and social transformation, anchored by the writings of people such as Ivan Illich and Paulo Freire, whom Kavaloski leans on as spiritual guides. It is fashionable in the Reagan-Clinton era to dismiss such reformers, and we wonder how the IDS mainstream has responded to Kavaloski in the two decades since his essay was published in Kockelmans' *Interdisciplinarity and Higher*

Education (1979). From Newell's 1998 book it appears that the IDS field has chosen, in the main, to ignore Kavaloski's attack on "mortuary education" and concern itself instead with the ramifications, within the academy, of subject-matter boundary-crossings and other transdisciplinary comminglings.

Kavaloski, however, pulls no punches. Though we had not read him prior to our AUC course, his criticism of IDS presaged in some important ways our own design for What Is School? and he speaks to us in ways that mirror our experience. We fear that, if not alone within the IDS camp in sharing Kavaloski's view, we are distinctly in the minority:

> If, as seems the case, the subjects who legitimate a given body of theory and method as valid are simply the experts and professionals practicing in the area, then knowledge is still something considered to be external to students; *they* are not subjects of inter-subjectivity but rather still merely its objects. . . . They still experience it as an "other," as something outside the transcendental ground of *their* collective consciousness. After all, they do not play a part in planning the content and structure of the course or curriculum; it does not arise organically out of their process of inquiry but rather is grafted onto it as from the outside. No matter how integrated or interdisciplinary it may be, and no matter how "intersubjectively valid," if it is imposed on students as a prepackaged thing-in-itself, it will to that extent constitute a barrier to genuine inquiry that arises and is nourished in the individual's own subjectivity, the sense of wonderment, puzzlement or doubt. (1979, 233)

For us, creating a climate for Socratic dialogue gave shape and purpose to the interdisciplinary nature of the course. We began to see signs of a crossover effect as some students reported the impact of ideas and strategies generated in our class on other courses they were taking: *"Throughout my learning years, this is the first time I evaluated myself in depth. I found myself developing more in other classes as well. I actually participate in class and in outside learning, too."* Another reflected: *"I learned that being my own person can also mean challenging other people and their views. I should not just nod my head and agree, but ask people 'why' and 'how' they came to their conclusions. I think I have used this new knowledge to my benefit."*

It is high time we answer our own question: Does interdisciplinarity require constructivist engagement? We argue that it does, that little of value transpires in classrooms in which most students are busy pretending to pay homage to their teacher's agenda (all the while calculating just what it will take to get an A). Engagement is a vital attribute in any course and is at the heart of the learning experience for people of any age or circumstance. The IDS general education framework makes engagement especially desirable because instructors are not under pressure to "cover" a certain amount of material to prepare students for the next "deliverer of content" they will face.

Indeed, the great promise of interdisciplinary studies is that in allowing faculty to break free of the intellectual boundaries of a single discipline, IDS affords them the opportunity to empower their students as much through a constructivist pedagogy as through an interdisciplinary perspective. The two are wondrously complementary: IDS empowers faculty to collaborate with colleagues in addressing a vital issue or idea through the combined strengths of their diverse scholarship and experience. Constructivist partnership allows us to include our students as serious contributing players in the process of making meaning out of issues via dialogue, inquiry, shared personal experiences, and the clash of values. It may take us time and effort to overcome the awkwardness of venturing forth from our customary and comfortable teaching styles, but we can learn the steps if we are honest about our desire to do so. There is no room in interdisciplinary studies for a dance of disciplines that leaves students as wallflowers.

REFERENCES

Association for Integrative Studies and Institute in Integrative Studies. 1996. "Guide to Interdisciplinary Syllabus Preparation." *Journal of General Education* 45 (2): 170–73.

Benson, Thomas. 1982. "Five Arguments against Interdisciplinary Studies." *Issues in Integrative Studies* 1: 38–48.

Fried, Robert L. 1995. *The Passionate Teacher: A Practical Guide.* Boston: Beacon.

Kavaloski, Vincent C. 1979. "Interdisciplinary Education and Humanistic Aspiration: A Critical Reflection." In *Interdisciplinarity and Higher Education*, ed. Joseph J. Kockelmans. University Park: Pennsylvania State University Press.

Newell, William H. 1983. "The Case for Interdisciplinary Studies: Response to Professor Benson's Five Arguments." *Issues in Integrative Studies* 2: 1–19.

Newell, William H. 1990. "Interdisciplinary Curriculum Development." *Issues in Integrative Studies* 8: 69–86.

Newell, William H. 1998. "Professionalizing Interdisciplinarity: Literature Review and Research Agenda." In *Interdisciplinarity: Essays from the Literature*, ed. William H. Newell. New York: College Entrance Examination Board.

Rogers, Carl. 1969. *Freedom to Learn.* Columbus, Ohio: Charles Merrill.

Shor, Ira. 1992. *Empowering Education.* Chicago: University of Chicago Press.

Tredway, Lynda. 1995. "Socratic Seminars: Engaging Students in Intellectual Discourse." *Educational Leadership* 53 (1): 26–29.

Trow, Martin. 1984–85. "Interdisciplinary Studies as a Counterculture: Problems of Birth, Growth, and Survival." *Issues in Integrative Studies* 4: 1–15.

WHAT IS SCHOOL?: SAMPLE SYLLABUS

To realize American ideals, citizens need to understand the political, social, economic, and personal implications of their system of education. In this integrative course, students explore these issues in an effort to understand current problems in education and suggest possible solutions. They gain firsthand experience by engaging in community service in various school settings. These experiences serve as the basis for discussion and debate. (Emphasis on oral communication and critical thinking.)

Goals: Students will learn to reflect critically on their own school experiences with the aim of becoming more actively and constructively involved in issues of education confronting themselves, their families, their communities, and society at large; broaden their understanding of the complexities and choices within education; develop skills in defining issues and articulating and analyzing positions; and learn to collaborate as they work to synthesize diverse perspectives.

Texts: Anthology of articles on a variety of traditional and contemporary education topics, such as readings on "The Socrates Syndrome" illustrating the importance of questioning issues related to school and life; articles on school curriculum inviting discussions about student perspectives on school-to-life transitions (e.g., W. Glasser, "The Quality School Curriculum," *Phi Delta Kappan* 1992); book chapters on service learning; newspaper articles on the *Sheff v. O'Neill* school desegregation case in Connecticut.

Sample Topics (developed through shared experiences with students):

Learning Styles (including active and passive learning; forces and conditions in society and schools that encourage passivity in some people and assertiveness in others)

School Curricula and Educational Goals: Conflicting Views

Alternatives to Traditional Schools

Educational Role Models

Understanding the Brain From a Psychologist's Perspective

Parents' Perspectives on Their Role in Educating Their Children

Technology in Education

Issues in Special Education

Cultural Differences and Educational Approaches in the United States and in Other Countries

Current Reform Movements and Conflicts as Schools Adjust Their Historical Roles to Face Twenty-First Century Challenges

Selected Student Activities: Participating in "fishbowl" sessions in which students offer input on the direction of the course; responding to controversies aired by community members ranging from superintendents to psychologists to parents; sharing perspectives with one another through short focus papers distributed in class; conducting action research (school visits and observations); presenting group projects (e.g., role-plays, written editorials). Emphasis is on creative alternatives to traditional tests and papers.

ROMANTICISM IN THE ARTS: FACING UNCERTAINTY AND RESHAPING PERSPECTIVES

Jill Dix Ghnassia

OVERVIEW

The title of this chapter conveys not only the goals of the course Romanticism in the Arts but also my own struggles in teaching it. The challenges inherent in the course are twofold: those involved in teaching any interdisciplinary course and those involved in teaching about Romanticism. It is my belief, however, that no course on Romanticism can be taught other than interdisciplinarily. As a concept, Romanticism is a hydra: just when you think you have conquered the beast, it grows another head, and the animal is even more unruly than before. The complexity of the phenomenon of Romanticism is well known; I am not adding anything new here. To teach the course one must begin by accepting the virtual impossibility of finding any one universally acceptable definition. As with many classifications, the word "Romantic" seems to confuse as much as to explain. If there was a "spirit of the age," as Hazlitt wrote, it had many emanations and patterns. To pull together a sense of what it was to be alive during that time, to write, paint, or compose in those frequently contradictory currents, is no mean task—even within one discipline.

My own uncertainties eventually gave way to remolding my expectations for student success. In any attempt to give students a grasp of one of the last major European-wide intellectual and spiritual movements, one runs the risk of either oversimplifying or overspecializing. The old breadth versus depth dilemma reared its ugly head once more, and I had to slay it once and for all: the ancient dualities would not work. They had to be banished in favor of something else that allowed students to find their own way into the course. I did not have all the answers. But as I soon discovered, I did not need all the answers but only questions that my students could pursue and respond to according to their inclinations and abilities.

If I felt daunted by the task of teaching Romanticism in the Arts, I imagine that my students, when confronted by the material, must feel a little like Perseus attempting to slay Medusa. Some succeed in conquering the snaky-haired Gorgon; others are petrified before such a seemingly impossible ordeal. Making sense of three disciplines (art, music, and literature)—finding their commonalities while recognizing their differences—and relating them to the Romantic movement demands much of undergraduates. A colleague of mine once remarked that when he was a young boy, he used to go to London to visit his older brother during school holidays. While in London, he would take the underground all over the city, getting off at different stops and seeing the sights in the nearby area. It was only much later in life that he learned exactly where in the city these various metro stops were and how they were located in relation to each other. Like my colleague, some of our students finally make the connections despite the fact that first they pop up at a music stop, then a literature stop, and then an art stop. Some are able to identify the intersections of knowledge and culture. Others unfortunately fail to see how those points connect to form one vast, interlocking, and coherent network. Our work, the students' and mine, is to make as many of those connections as possible and to open up new questions and issues to be taken away and explored.

If, as Klein and Newell state, "interdisciplinary studies [is] a process of answering a question, solving a problem, or addressing a topic that is too broad or complex to be dealt with adequately by a single discipline or profession" (1997, 21), then Romanticism in the Arts fits this definition. The course strives to answer the question "What is Romanticism?" and others ancillary to it: Why and how did it originate? How have Romantic artists and their views affected the lives of their contemporaries? And conversely, how have people and events of that time influenced Romantic artists? How has Western culture evolved as a result of those individuals and their works? How has Romanticism influenced the way we live and think today?

What follows, then, is less an argument than a series of meditations about Romanticism in the Arts and about the importance of its interdisciplinary nature for engaging students not only in analyzing the art, music, and literature of the Romantic era but in developing an appreciation of the importance of these arts in actively changing as well as reflecting the world around them. Beyond the synchronic views of the arts of the late eighteenth and first half of the nineteenth centuries, the class benefits from a diachronic approach: opening up to question the assumptions of the period, examining the era for its universal perspectives and applications for today, and exploring the cultural side of the changes brought about in the decades surrounding the year 1800, the period known as the Age of Romanticism. For example, in studying Mary Shelley's *Frankenstein,* students confront an author, herself the only surviving strand of that enlightened Romantic band of Godwin/Wollstonecraft/Shelley/Byron, who not only writes one of the great Romantic masterpieces but manages to critique many of the beliefs of her group. Students at first find this subversion of Romantic ideals from someone firmly within that circle of writers puzzling.

This productive tension in Shelley's novel is a reflection of larger tensions, of the movement of Romanticism from a benevolent and democratic idealism (Wordsworth) to a more extreme form ("negative Romanticism" is Peckham's [1962] term for its emanation in later Romantic poets), where the high ground of political and moral idealism nearly leads to intolerance, uncompromising views, and a tyranny of ideals.[1] The logical outgrowth of Romanticism and its revolutionary views of art and life was a reversion to conservatism, greater conformity, even a degree of authoritarianism, and in England, Victorianism. This darker undercurrent present in the Romantic movement brings students face to face with precisely those tendencies within any ideological movement toward the very extremes from which it originally retreated, and as they begin to see the productive tensions of the movement both synchronically and diachronically, they see similarities to more recent times (political extremism, religious fanaticism) and start to venture their own ideas.

Getting students to the point where they voice their own views and questions can be a formidable task. Our students come to us underprepared, some of them never having had a course in art or music appreciation. Understandably, they are hesitant when faced with the prospect of learning not one but three new disciplines and their idiosyncratic discourses. Remedying these "black holes" in their education is compounded by student resistance to required arts courses. Yet increasingly students need to be exposed to the arts for their own well-being and for the sake of society. As we well know from our own century, there is no guarantee that those who study the humanities and the arts will be humanitarians. But exposing students to humanities and arts through interdisciplinary courses can remedy that gap between the "abstract" world of the arts and culture and its application to daily living. It is when students fail to see the connections between the courses they take and their own lives that culture fails to humanize.[2]

In an examination of interdisciplinary approaches to the humanities, Cluck observes that "literature and the other arts present the *experience* of humanity within the parameters of history, philosophy, and religion" (1980, 71). Indeed, the interdisciplinary study of the arts can play an important role in sensitizing students to the greater issues and questions of life and the problems of the human condition. Through examination of major issues of the Romantic era, most students gradually realize that these "stuffy old writers and artists" still speak to their generation. Gradually, they begin to reshape their perspectives on life and dare to cross those uncertain, foreign boundaries.

THE COURSE STRUCTURE

Over the 10 years that Romanticism in the Arts has been taught at the University of Hartford, the focus has shifted as faculty as well as faculty interests (reflective of disciplinary changes themselves) have altered; the focus has moved from an initial emphasis on the worship of nature to the current theme, "the progressive destruction of decorum" (Rosen and Zerner 1984, 38).[3] This focal point enables most students to enter into the midst of an ongoing and extremely contentious academic discussion about the nature of Romanticism and its relevance today. The current faculty changed the emphasis to reflect our interests and our view of the Romantic as well as our belief that previous unifying themes, such as the worship of nature, had been inadequate. They had resulted in some student confusion and were not comprehensive enough to allow a global perspective from which students could view the movement as a whole. Too many students indicated through their final examination answers that they had completed the course thinking that Wordsworth was a nature poet and Byron a poet of narcissism; they failed to see that the two had anything in common. Some believed that the Romantics' only contribution to culture was a love of nature.

The new integrative theme, compared with earlier ones, has elicited more discussion and made it easier to cross the boundaries of the formal properties of art as well as to examine shifting cultural points of view and "the contradictoriness, dissonance and inner conflict of the Romantic mind" (Schenk 1969, 1). Now discussions often lead to debates about the role of women in the Romantic movement. What kind of poet would Wordsworth have been without Dorothy and her journal? How does Mary Shelley portray men and women, biological predestination, love, and responsibility to others? One student asked, "Just how revolutionary and liberal was this movement anyway? Women seem to have had more freedom to act at the end of the eighteenth century." Despite possible criticisms of artificiality and oversimplification, the new theme has become the "'salient concept' . . . around which the course content and skill development processes are organized" (Hursh, Haas, and Moore 1983, 51) and has enabled faculty to approach the Romantic movement more fully.

During the initial week and a half of the course, the faculty lay the groundwork for the semester with discussions about the eighteenth century and the Enlightenment as an attempt to preserve decorum and to live and work within set social and artistic rules. The eighteenth-century artists presented in the first classes are then contrasted with artists from the Romantic movement, using a diachronic approach. To this end, students read an excerpt from the Rosen and Zerner book (1984) addressing the idea of the destruction of decorum; a fairly recent article, "New Romantics," by Colin McEnroe in the *Hartford Courant* (1991) about twentieth-century Romantics; and handouts with excerpts from Pope's *Essay on Man* and Byron's *Childe Harold's Pilgrimage*. While teaching team members spend about 20 minutes introducing their disciplines, they all refer back continually to the idea of decorum and the Romantics' progressive destruction of it, not only in this but in all subsequent classes.

The music professor usually begins because we want to engage students actively in the class as soon as possible. This engagement occurs when they are asked to sing "Yankee Doodle Dandy," a song most of them know. Once they have sung it, the professor asks them questions about the form of its composition: Is it easy to sing? Are the words simple to remember? Why? Gradually, students begin to come up with the ideas of a simple melody repeated in each stanza, of balance, of repetition, of moderate length, and so on. The musician must usually add a few details of background information; for instance, the song was originally sung by British troops during the American Revolutionary War to poke fun at (here the word "satire" is introduced) the ragtag American soldiers. Next, students are treated to the "Marseillaise," sung by their professor. Even if they do not understand the words, they feel them; they are also given a translation of the first stanza. By the time they are asked to compare this song with "Yankee Doodle Dandy," they begin to sense that something really different was occurring in Western Europe at the end of the eighteenth century. Concurrently, the instructor or one of the team writes the class-generated list of the characteristics of the periods on the board or overhead. This opening segment is the "hook" or "grabber" (Association for Integrative Studies 1996, 170) to engage students; we deliberately make the first large class meeting as nonthreatening as possible and work to build on what students already know or can easily observe.

By the time the discussion moves to literature, students are primed to continue. With reference to the handouts of Pope and Byron, students add to their list of the distinguishing traits of each period: greater emphasis on reason or emotion, objectivity or subjectivity and egocentricity, the social impulse or individual orientation, the artificial and man-made or the natural and organic, and the like. They also note differences in the formal structure of each poem in terms of stanza length, rhyme scheme, rhythm, imagery, and symbol. Inevitably, they also observe that while Byron's poetry contains certain marks and themes of Romanticism— heightened emotion, egotism, isolation, intensity, subjectivity, irregular stanza lengths, use of the specific and of nature—it also occasionally employs eighteenth-century diction and concepts. As a consequence, they realize that the lists they have been compiling reveal the directions of change and not clear-cut polarities. Finally, students are reminded of the differences between the two songs sung earlier and are asked to compare the literary passages with the musical ones, the Pope with "Yankee Doodle Dandy" and the Byron with the "Marseillaise." Admittedly, these first interart comparisons are frequently superficial, but the process of thinking comparatively, if not rigorously interdisciplinarily, has begun.

Last, the art historian shows slides of rococo paintings—Watteau's *Voyage to Cythera*, Vigée-Lebrun's *Marie Antoinette and Her Children*, Boucher's *Madame de Pompadour*, and Fragonard's *The Swing*—and juxtaposes them with David's *Madame Vérinac, The Oath of the Horatii, The Death of Marat*, and *Napoleon Crossing the Alps*, and Charpentier's *Mlle. Charlotte du Val d'Ognes*, among others. Students are first asked to contrast costumes and iconography or subject matter. Reactions to the costumes bring responses such as "They are frilly, rich-looking. Did men actually wear such things?" or "They are dressed like Roman matrons." Such comments lead to further discussion of the frivolity of the rococo, with its slightly naughty innuendos and hedonism, in contrast to the stark economy of the Neoclassical style, with its serious intent and call to civic duty and patriotism, often illustrated through representations of Republican Rome. Formal elements, such as color, linearity, and use of space, and different uses of those elements that generate various feelings in the viewer are addressed in the discussion. The concept of the progressive destruction of decorum develops as students gradually encounter the different texts and subtexts of the Enlightenment and Romantic eras.

The subsequent two class meetings are held in smaller sections and focus on a discussion and review of the material introduced during the first, larger meeting. During the first section meeting, the class learns a mnemonic aid and unifying hinge with which to work, the three Rs: Revolution, Radicalism, and Romanticism. When asked what revolutions occurred at the end of the eighteenth century, students usually answer "the American Revolution." From that point on, it is an easy step for students to remember the other two major revolutions, the French and the Industrial. In distinguishing the American from the French Revolution, we discuss the guiding forces behind both as well as the ideals and beliefs of the Enlightenment. Gradually, students see that when Enlightenment values met head-on with the French Revolution, society was in crisis—rationality was supplanted by irrationality, and philosophical, social, and political ideals gave way to passions, patriotism, and extremism. As Peckham notes, it was the beginning of the truly modern age (1962, 84).

Next, the class discusses what they understand by the word "radical": we first examine the word's etymology, working toward its various meanings of extreme and going to the root. Finally, they are asked to consider what they understand by the word "romantic." All this leads to a consideration of romanticism and Romanticism. For the following class they write a brief personal essay about whether they consider themselves more of a Romantic or an Enlightenment personality and why; they will be asked to repeat this exercise at the end of the course and to compare not only the labeling of their personality but their reasons for it. At the conclusion of class, students are assigned to read excerpts from Edmund Burke's *Reflections on the Revolution in France* and Mary Wollstonecraft's *A Vindication of the Rights of Men,* written in answer to Burke's pamphlet.

In the third class, students break into several groups and spend a few minutes sharing their personal essays. Those who find that they are Romantics frequently write: "I like to be able to do what I want," "I am an emotional person," "I like trying new things," "I hate being part of the crowd." By the end of the term, however, many realize they may not be so Romantic. One student wrote:

> I didn't realize how much guts it takes to be a true Romantic. Perhaps I'm not really a Romantic. As one of my friends puts it, it takes *cojones.* I really do have much more respect for these artists now that I have taken the class; many lived through difficult times. I wonder what they would think of society now. Perhaps they would cry—or laugh so as not to cry.

Then, still in groups, students discuss the passages from Burke and Wollstonecraft that they have prepared. These two passages refer to Burke's presentation of the violation of Marie Antoinette's bedroom by a mob of women on October 6, 1789, and include descriptions of both Marie Antoinette and the women. These passages encourage students to consider several issues: first, the issue of decorum emerges as students see the impropriety of breaking into anyone's bedchamber, let alone that of a woman and a queen. The second issue concerns political revolution and the ideals of a democratic society: Can there be limits in a revolution? What happens when traditional values and institutions are overthrown? How does a state revolution affect the individual? Gender issues are also discussed: What was the "proper role" for a woman at that time, for a "noble" woman? Was the queen behaving "decorously"? Questions arise about the furor of the women who were protesting for food and taking action, and about Burke's portrayal of the queen as a "Roman matron" and his disgust, verging on misogyny, as he describes the mob of women who marched to Versailles as a "swinish multitude." To conclude this class, the groups summarize the outcomes of their discussions and debate the issues that have emerged from their findings.

Such questions and issues integrate the basics of a liberal arts education, promote innovative thinking and synthesis, and encourage discovery and exploration (Hursh, Haas, and Moore 1983, 43). In the course of discussion, other questions arise: What exactly was the position of women in Europe during and after the French Revolution? In the wake of the women's movement of the twentieth century, have misogynistic views disappeared or just gone underground or taken another form? Is there a place for decorum? Just whose view—Burke's or Wollstonecraft's—of the French Revolution was more Romantic? With these issues and questions in mind, students begin to consider seriously the Romantic movement in the arts.

These first weeks set the stage for further interdisciplinary exploration. For instance, armed with the knowledge that Mary Wollstonecraft, the mother of Mary Shelley, worked for publisher Joseph Johnson, whose office was frequented by such liberal thinkers and Romantic artists as Blake, Godwin, and Cowper, students work with the ideas of influence and intertextuality early in the course. By centering on the aesthetic theme of the progressive destruction of decorum, they become detectives, hot on the trail of philosophical and historical ideas (Cluck 1980, 74–75) as they developed within artistic and intellectual circles. An interdisciplinary course such as Romanticism in the Arts that focuses on one period must explore both the context in which the various texts were created and the texts themselves. Critical theory has done an about-face since the heyday of the New Criticism. Most theorists now argue that there is no intrinsic meaning to texts, art objects, or musical compositions; indeed, that they cannot be read in isolation and that there is no possibility of a disinterested or objective reading of them. The study of influence and intertextuality and reading against the text create a rich fabric of meaning and a deeper understanding of the era, because Romanticism by its very essence demands a dissonant reading. Romanticism is by its very definition a reaction against and gradual destruction of earlier forms. Friedrich Schlegel's famous *Fragments*, in which he is the first to use the terms "Classical" and "Romantic" as an opposition, points the way to the breakdown of barriers not only between genres but between art and life (Rosen and Zerner 1984, 17–18).

THE EVOLUTION OF INTERDISCIPLINARITY IN THE COURSE

As the course evolved, it became more interdisciplinary as we realized through experience and reading the fuller implications of that term. Originally, we approached the course through discipline-specific lenses, merely juxtaposing disciplinary units and occasionally drawing comparisons among the disciplines. As the team worked together, we helped each other see connections that could be made from the wide array of themes and subjects. Team meetings have been vital to the growth of the course, as we exchanged ideas, argued over approach, and disagreed about or varied in our interpretations. These differences of opinion have carried over into the classroom, much to the consternation of the students who wonder, "If the experts disagree, who is right?" We not only teach the conflict, as Graff (1992) advises; at times we also become the conflict. Gradually, students begin to venture their own opinions right along with ours, tentatively at first, then rather pointedly. When a student finally challenged us last term about the appropriateness of our salient concept, we knew we had succeeded in getting students to engage with the issues and assumptions underlying the Romantic period. Little did he know that he was echoing parts of Schlegel's famous manifesto in Fragment No. 116 of the *Athenaeum*.[4]

Furthermore, the faculty have made deliberate efforts to bolster active learning. We encourage and offer opportunities for students to experience personally the works we study. When the course was first offered, the university had received a grant from the National Endowment for the Humanities to bring onto campus several distinguished speakers and exhibits as well as to take students into Manhattan to see a major exhibit, *William Wordsworth and the Age of English Romanticism.* In ensuing years students have viewed Romantic paintings in the Wadsworth Athenaeum in Hartford and attended concerts and operas at the Hartt School at the University of Hartford or at the Hartford Symphony. For many students, these field trips were their first visits to an art gallery or a live performance of a symphony or opera.

Students prepare for such experiences beforehand through class discussions and handouts that include a checklist of structural and thematic characteristics. Faculty also try to prepare students by taking them to the university's Joseloff Art Gallery or previewing the concert or opera before they go to a museum or attend a performance at Hartt or the Hartford Symphony. After the visit or performance, each student writes a critique that includes a consideration of the work's Romantic characteristics. Although students are provided with guides to writing about art, music, and literature and more recently, examples of good interdisciplinary critiques, these assignments have yielded student work of varying quality, many simply recounting either the iconography or libretto. Some students fail to venture out into the rough seas of interdisciplinarity, choosing to stay safely anchored in the shallows of description and summary or overgeneralization.

In addition to these field trips, especially designed units, assignments, and activities enhance interdisciplinary thinking and the use of synthesis as well as encourage creativity. One exercise, which I call "Metaphysical Portraits," originates in my own family, but its application to this course provides much fun as well as intellectual stimulation. Each student must create a metaphysical portrait of a figure or character from any of the disciplines we have been studying; classmates then take turns asking questions until someone guesses the figure the student has in mind. For instance, if a student has chosen William Blake, he or she must first tell the class that the figure is real as opposed to fictional. Then classmates begin the questioning: If this figure were a vegetable, what vegetable might he/she be? If he/she were an automobile, what kind would he/she be? A flower, a tree, a building, and so on. The answers can be as simple as "spinach," or as complex as "a gourmet radish, slightly bitter and difficult to peel." Once the class has guessed the figure, the student must justify his or her "metaphysical" answers and how they captured the essence of that individual or character. Thinking comparatively and figuratively breaks down the barriers of disciplines by forcing students to be imaginative and to synthesize what they have learned about a major figure or work.

Sometimes we emphasize the differences among the disciplines. In teaching Beethoven, for example, students must first learn to listen to music. And because we face a generation of boom-boxers and Walkman junkies with noise overload, in our class students start their exploration of Beethoven by sitting quietly, sometimes with eyes closed. After a few minutes of silence, I begin without warning to play the second movement of Beethoven's Third Symphony, "Funeral March on the Death of a Hero." Class continues as students struggle with questions such as "What is music?" "What does music do?" If no one questions the reason for the class first sitting in silence, I ask them, "What role does silence play in music?" Gradually, we work our way into the movement, and I point out to them Beethoven's innovations, among them the use of pauses, "silence expectant" to paraphrase Eliot.

Next, they listen to Haydn's Symphony No. 82, written conforming to the musical decorum of the eighteenth century. This short piece contrasts markedly with Beethoven's *Eroica* and its daring expansion of the symphonic form and breaking down and modification of the rules. Finally, students listen to an unidentified musical excerpt and must decide whether they consider it more Romantic or Classical. The answers come quickly: the dynamics vary greatly from loud to soft (extremes), the bagpipes sound sad and mournful (unusual or native instrument not usual in "classical" music), the vocalist sobs her solo (extreme emotional content), the accompaniment sounds like the pounding of a horse's hooves or the frantic beating of a heart (extreme emotion again). Few students recognize it as music from the recent film, *Rob Roy*, but most know it is Romantic.

At other times, we center on an aesthetic theme (Cluck 1980, 75) and encourage students to address an idea or set of related ideas, for example the theme of Prometheus with its clustered motifs of rebellion and revolution, defiance of authority and convention, suffering, the indomitability of the human spirit, opposition to tyranny, and the plight of humanity. As a transitional figure, Beethoven and his work embody both the eighteenth century's view of Prometheus as the enlightener and champion of freedom and the Romantics' view of him as a rebel. Undeniably, defiance of both social and artistic convention marked both Beethoven's life and his career. As the class considers his rebellious, almost pugnacious, personality, which punctuated his relations with patrons and servants alike, his almost vatic stance toward his profession, and his tenacious, uncompromising, and liberated approach toward the composition of music, they realize the extent to which he broke with tradition and decorum.

Later, students analyze the significance of the title of the Third Symphony, "The Heroic," and debate the characteristics of a hero, whether we have heroes as we enter the twenty-first century, and whether Beethoven may not have been thinking as much about himself as about Napoleon when he composed this symphony. In studying the fourth movement, "Theme and Variations," they discover that the musical idea that became the material of this great finale first appeared as a simple dance tune in Beethoven's ballet, *The Creatures of Prometheus.* Here, however, they find the Prometheus of Enlightenment thought and art and of the ideals of the French Revolution, liberty, equality, and fraternity. With these Promethean ideas in mind, student listeners experience this rousing set of orchestral variations as a musical celebration of the triumph of those values, preserved by the heroic determination of humanity.

As in his music, Beethoven the man reflects the Promethean spirit, because he championed the ideals of the French Revolution throughout his life. His only opera, *Fidelio,* extols the themes of justice and virtuous love and contains a great hymn to liberty, in which the liberated prisoners sing: "O happiness to see the light, to feel the air and be once more alive. Our prison was a tomb. O freedom, freedom come to us again." This view of Prometheus as arch-rebel, chained to the mountainside, defiant in his suffering, refusing to submit to the authority of Zeus, becomes a symbol of the Romantic generation, which embraced a different aspect of the myth than the thinkers of the Enlightenment while not ignoring its earlier significance. Students often interpret this aspect of the legend as emblematic of Beethoven's struggle with his deafness and representative of his defiance of traditional artistic rules, that is, his gradual destruction of eighteenth-century decorum.

Thus, the aesthetic theme (Prometheus) and the integrating concept intertwine and merge. Throughout the term, students revert back to the myth of Prometheus as they encounter Goya's *Third of May, 1808*, with its depiction of a French firing squad executing Spanish citizens in reprisal for their uprising the day before. It reappears as they read and discuss Byron's poem, "Prometheus," and Mary Shelley's *Frankenstein: Or, The Modern Prometheus*. They notice how the use of Promethean legend alters perceptively from the eighteenth century to the mid-nineteenth century. Its appeal—the appeal of the lone individual struggling against tyranny and superior force; of the rebel; of the individual attempting to alleviate human suffering, standing alone in suffering for his principles—reaches today's students. It also forces them to debate the role of the arts and the artist, still a heated issue.

Romantic art reflected its own time and attempted to influence the future, of that there is no doubt. Percy Shelley wrote and believed that "poets are the unacknowledged legislators of the world"; Byron wrote, "All contemplative existence is bad. One should do something"; in 1833 even Wordsworth stated that for every hour he had given to the writing of poetry, he had given 12 to the condition and prospects of society. "So long as the [arts] remained the weapon of men concerned by and involved in the real world, [they] remained a popular force" (Saul 1992, 545). All those artists were involved in some form of defiance.

But what is the position of artists today? Does the age of Romanticism continue to influence modern artists? Granted, it is sometimes difficult to make connections between them, especially stylistically; however, students frequently point out that many artists (for example, a Mapplethorpe) still take unpopular stands; others are perceived as cold, odd, arrogant, and out of touch with the "real world." As students who take our course discover, it takes courage to be an artist, even a Romantic artist in the age of Romanticism. These artists were not merely "ineffectual angel[s], beating in the void [their] luminous wings in vain"; they were, in fact, "[men] speaking to men."[5] They crossed the boundaries between art and life, because to them art was life. And the malaise of the Romantic artists, "far from being the itch of merely personal neurosis, discloses rather the human climate in which philosophers too, whether they knew it or not, drew their breath" (Barrett 1962, 146). After exposure to some major artists of the Romantic era, our students leave this course not only with a better appreciation of the arts but also having critiqued some of the major intellectual and political currents of that time and of all times.

Thus, I am a convert to interdisciplinary teaching. While I agree with Gunn that "interdisciplinarity is the pragmatist's response to the dilemma of disciplinary essentialism" (1992, 252), for me, it is more: it can and does work for me as a teacher. It is one answer for this teacher who wants students to learn not only content but also ways of thinking critically and creatively, eschewing easy dichotomies, and always trying to make those important connections with the world they face every day. The compartmentalization of intellectual pursuits did, and at times still can, benefit the advancement of knowledge, but as educators, researchers, and scientists are increasingly finding, we have often murdered to dissect. Innovative thinking and the ability to cross boundaries (a characteristic of Romanticism, according to Kierkegaard) and to synthesize ideas will be essential as the world enters the twenty-first century.

NOTES

1. I am indebted to Malcolm Kelsall for this idea. He writes:

As a man "uncompromising" in his views he [Shelley] was always "hostile" to those who opposed him. [Mary Shelley] concludes, therefore, that he is a writer whose ideas would cause "mischief". . . . Is Mary Shelley a Victorian quisling, or has she laid her finger on an essential paradox: that Shelley's absolute love is fuelled by absolute hate, and the least movement by the totalitarian Romanticism from the ideal to the real is fraught with danger? (1990)

2. As out of vogue as he currently is in many critical circles, Matthew Arnold has something to say to those of us who teach interdisciplinary studies today. About the gross misconception of the humanities by his contemporaries, he writes:

The culture which is supposed to plume itself on a smattering of Greek and Latin is a culture . . . valued either out of sheer vanity and ignorance or else as an engine of social and class distinction. . . . No serious man would call this *culture,* or attach any value to it.

Arnold is still correct in his assessment. Indeed, if culture were only for show and pol-ish or to set certain individuals apart from society, few serious people should attach any importance to it. Yet for Arnold there was another benefit to studying the humanities:

> But there is of culture another view . . . in which all the love of our neighbor, the impulses toward action, help, and beneficence, the desire for removing human error, clearing human confusion, and diminishing human misery, the noble aspiration to leave the world better and happier than we found it,—motives eminently such as are called social,—come in as part of the grounds of culture, and the main and pre-eminent part.

According to Arnold, the humanities (his word is culture) are vital because they enable us to be human, to empathize with others as well as to appreciate literature, art, and music. This, then, is his definition of a humanist, a far cry from the ivory-towered dreamer sometimes portrayed. For Arnold, there is—and should be—virtu-ally no distinction between humanist and humanitarian (1961, 407, 409).

3. The break with decorum was suggested by a passage in the book *Romanti-cism and Realism: The Mythology of Nineteenth Century Art* by Charles Rosen and Henri Zerner: "Perhaps an even better definition of Romanticism . . . would be a progressive destruction of decorum—not, we must emphasize, the absence of deco-rum but the *process* of its destruction" (1984, 38).

4. In Schlegel's words:

> [Romantic poetry] alone can become, like the epic, a mirror of the whole cir-cumambient world, an image of the age. And it can also—more than any other form—hover between the portrayed and the portrayer, free of all and ideal self-interest. . . . The romantic kind of poetry is still in the state of becoming: that, in fact, is its real essence: that it should forever be becoming and never be completed. (1971, 175–76)

Thus Romantic poetry, indeed Romantic art, is not merely a personal vision, stand-ing in opposition to Neoclassicism and breaking its rules; it stands on some middle ground and appropriates all forms of art and life.

5. Matthew Arnold, *Essays in Criticism*, 2d series, and William Wordsworth, Preface to *Lyrical Ballads*, respectively.

REFERENCES

Arnold, Matthew. 1961. *Poetry and Criticism of Matthew Arnold.* Edited by A. Dwight Culler. Boston: Houghton Mifflin. Riverside Edition.

Association for Integrative Studies and Institute in Integrative Studies. 1996. "Guide to Interdisciplinary Syllabus Preparation." *Journal of General Edu-cation* 45 (2): 170–73.

Barrett, William. 1962. *Irrational Man: A Study in Existential Philosophy.* Garden City, N.Y.: Doubleday Anchor.

Cluck, Nancy Anne. 1980. "Reflections on the Interdisciplinary Approaches to the Humanities." *Liberal Education* 66 (1): 57–77.

Graff, Gerald. 1992. *Beyond the Culture Wars: How Teaching the Conflicts Can Revitalize American Education.* New York: Norton.

Gunn, Giles. 1992. "Interdisciplinary Studies." In *Introduction to Scholarship in Modern Language and Literature,* ed. Joseph Gibaldi. New York: Modern Language Association.

Hursh, Barbara, Paul Haas, and Michael Moore. 1983. "An Interdisciplinary Model to Implement General Education." *Journal of Higher Education* 54 (1): 42–59.

Kelsall, Malcolm. 1990. "Sardanapalus: The Slave Woman in the Harem." Unpublished lecture presented at Yale University, March 1990.

Klein, Julie Thompson, and William H. Newell. 1997. "Advancing Interdisciplinary Studies." In *Handbook of the Undergraduate Curriculum,* eds. Jerry G. Gaff and James L. Ratliff. San Francisco: Jossey-Bass.

McEnroe, Colin. 1991. "New Romantics." *Hartford Courant* 6 March: C1, C6.

Peckham, Morse. 1962. *Beyond the Tragic Vision: The Quest for Identity in the Nineteenth Century.* New York: George Braziller.

Rosen, Charles, and Henri Zerner. 1984. *Romanticism and Realism: The Mythology of Nineteenth Century Art.* London and Boston: Faber and Faber.

Saul, John Ralson. 1992. *Voltaire's Bastards: The Dictatorship of Reason in the West.* New York: Vintage.

Schenk, H. G. 1969. *The Mind of the European Romantics.* Garden City, N.Y.: Anchor.

Schlegel, Friedrich. 1971. *Friedrich Schlegel's Lucinde and The Fragments.* Translated with an introduction by Peter Firchow. Minneapolis: University of Minnesota Press.

ADDITIONAL RESOURCES

Boime, Albert. 1987. *Art in an Age of Revolution, 1750–1800.* Chicago: University of Chicago Press.

Boime, Albert. 1990. *Art in an Age of Bonapartism, 1800–1815.* Chicago: University of Chicago Press.

Christiansen, Rupert. 1988. *Romantic Affinities: Portraits from an Age, 1780–1830.* New York: G. P. Putnam's Sons.

Eisenman, Stephen F. 1994. *Nineteenth Century Art: A Critical History.* London: Thames and Hudson.

Favret, Mary A., and Nicola J. Watson, eds. 1994. *At the Limits of Romanticism: Essays in Cultural, Feminist, and Materialist Criticism.* Bloomington: Indiana University Press.

Johnson, Paul. 1991. *The Birth of the Modern: World Society 1815–1830.* New York: HarperCollins.

Johnston, Kenneth R., Gilbert Chaitlin, Karen Hanson, and Herbert Marks, eds. 1990. *Romantic Revolutions: Criticism and Theory.* Bloomington: Indiana University Press.

Liu, Alan. 1989. *Wordsworth: The Sense of History.* Stanford, Calif.: Stanford University Press.

Mellor, Anne K., ed. 1988. *Romanticism and Feminism.* Bloomington: Indiana University Press.

Paulson, Ronald. 1983. *Representations of Revolution, 1789–1820.* New Haven, Conn.: Yale University Press.

Proctor, Candice E. 1990. *Women, Equality, and the French Revolution.* New York: Greenwood Press.

Rosen, Charles. 1995. *The Romantic Generation.* Cambridge, Mass.: Harvard University Press.

ROMANTICISM IN THE ARTS: SAMPLE SYLLABUS

This integrative course introduces students to several major works of Western art, literature, and music produced from 1775 to 1850 and investigates the Romantic impulse across the spectrum of the arts. Because of the many and profound changes during that period, historians have dubbed it "the age of revolution" and "the beginning of the modern world." This course explores the cultural aspects of these changes and asks students to read, discuss, and write about how Romantic views of issues such as creativity, sexuality, spirituality, and social change have persisted into the present. (Emphasis on written communication and values identification.)

Goals: Students will discover interart connections and conflicts, contextualize the creation of artworks, understand the role of the Romantic artist as a force for change and reform, articulate those changes and their effects, critique Romantic values and ideas in light of Romantic and contemporary notions about the nature and function of the arts, acquire the basic vocabulary of each discipline, improve their critical writing skills, and develop an appreciation of the arts.

Texts: *Romanticism in the Arts* (in-house course anthology, including study materials); William Vaughan, *Romanticism and Art* (1994); Mary Shelley, *Frankenstein* (1818); CDs or tapes of a Beethoven symphony, Schubert songs, Berlioz's *Symphony Fantastique*, and Verdi's *Rigoletto*.

Topics:

Introduction: Decorum; The Transition From the Enlightenment to the Romantic Movement; Burke and Wollstonecraft: Views of Revolution and Life

Revolutions in Art and Life: David, Blake, Beethoven, Goya

Nature in the Heart and Mind: Wordsworth, Schubert, Friedrich, Turner, Constable

Individualism and Its Costs: Coleridge, Berlioz, Gericault, Delacroix, M. Shelley, Verdi

Selected Student Activities: Position papers often making connections across the arts; reaction papers on musical performances and museum visits; a variety of five-minute essays at beginning or end of class. Other activities varying by the semester include guided reading journal, group project and class presentation on Romanticism in modern life, Oprah Winfrey-type interviews of Romantic figures, Frankenstein on trial (mock trial).

FINDING A VOICE
ACROSS THE DISCIPLINES

Marcia Bundy Seabury

"HOW CAN WE MANAGE ALL THIS?"

This essay draws on the Romanticism in the Arts course discussed in the previous chapter but applies to other interdisciplinary courses as well. As a member of the teaching team for the Romanticism course, I have found that before grappling with the complex question "What is Romanticism?" students often struggle with a more basic question: "In this course we're supposed to talk about a symphony, a painting, and a poem, with some history and philosophy thrown in too?"

Such concern recurs in a wide variety of interdisciplinary courses, as students feel they must master several unfamiliar modes of discourse for a single class. Assuring students that the multiple perspectives will focus on a single course theme and repeatedly drawing connections between works may not suffice to counter their discipline-based thinking: if a course involves three disciplines it must be triply difficult to understand. Instructors can assign a reasonable workload and explain that the course deals with only a fraction of the material from each discipline that is included in a traditionally structured course, but these efforts may pale in the light of students' sense that they will be overworked by having to learn several new languages at once. The history of our Romanticism course as well as others in the curriculum justifies this concern. Many teaching teams have found their assigned workload overly ambitious the first time they offered the course as they enthusiastically included the myriad fruits of their collaboration. Subsequent semesters have typically entailed progressive trimming, but student concerns persist.

The interdisciplinary site and these concerns may exacerbate familiar problems in student thinking and writing. When one has to produce in a new language, one may grope desperately for the appropriate vocabulary. Students who feel they are required to learn three new languages simultaneously may grope all the more desperately. They want to learn the languages fast, display fluency fast; thus they latch onto words they have heard bandied about in class or have underlined in their study materials and sprinkle them liberally throughout their essays, apparently the route toward sounding like their instructors and their texts. These are usually high-level abstractions: in the Romanticism course, such terms as nature, the individual, imagination, limits, the exotic. Students pick up the terms more readily than the structure of thinking that relates those terms to the works under discussion, the thinking that renders the terms meaningful. Asking for comparisons across disciplines may speed the rush toward high-level abstractions and generalizations, as students try to combine multiple new languages in a single essay; thus they look for any words the languages have in common—here nature, there nature, everywhere nature. Despite instructors' admonitions to "be specific," to "look closely at the individual works," students do what they think is expected of them, reaching up into the clouds for the "artist's meaning" and for vast, weighty generalizations about Romanticism, not coincidentally leaving the works far behind. Even professionals engaged in interdisciplinary projects typically spend time "wallowing in abstractions" as they seek "to find a common ground," notes Klein (1990, 71–72), citing a study by Sverre Sjölander. As Elbow puts it, "The interdisciplinary enterprise, in this sense, is in danger of beginning to rise from the earth and float impotently because of not being grounded in the concrete and unique. It seeks connections by moving as it were upward," in an extension of the disciplinary process of abstraction (1986, 32).

Another familiar problem of thinking and writing that may become all the more acute in an interdisciplinary setting occurs at the level of detail rather than generality. Many diligent students try to absorb as many details as possible from each new language and then recite them by mouthfuls without the contexts, the conclusions that could give the details meaning.[1] If an exam grade is low after they studied so hard and wrote so much that was accurate, anxiety about inscrutable modes of discourse and resistance to the interdisciplinary curriculum itself can build. Indeed that curriculum challenges many students' high school habit of dealing with disconnected facts and details from discrete classes.

Increasing our understanding of these student concerns and difficulties is of course an important first step. The next, obvious step of plunging in to deal with them may not be so obvious in practice. Some faculty, after years of reading essays written by nonmajors, have concluded that trying to deal with multiple disciplines plus develop the designated essential skill of writing is too much; perhaps the writing component should be dropped. Underlying this view are assumptions familiar to writing-across-the-curriculum advocates but intensified in an interdisciplinary course: not just that assigning writing means marking an endless stream of grammar and spelling errors or that reading frequently assigned essays or multiple drafts takes too much time, but more fundamentally that writing is an add-on, a separable "component" in an already over-busy course agenda.[2] Thus despite enthusiastic beginnings and continued lip service, active learning through writing in interdisciplinary curricula may face an acute version of the threats cited by White in "Shallow Roots or Taproots for Writing across the Curriculum" (1991) and by the many others concerned about the future of cross-college commitment to writing.

Especially in light of all the recent research on learning through writing, it is important not only to keep writing central in interdisciplinary courses but to develop ways to improve it. We would do well to base our approaches on the assumption, developed by Bizzell (e.g., 1982a) and illustrated in the classroom examples above, that students' anxieties and difficulties often stem not from cognitive deficiencies but from their situation as newcomers to academic discourse in general and to particular discourse communities.

Modeling this discourse does not suffice, as one notices vividly when team teaching—sitting in on colleagues' presentations, trying to understand the processes of thought in unfamiliar disciplines in order to plan discussion sections, watching students' reactions, and reviewing class notes with them. Even when a class session is well constructed, informative, and thought provoking, students may gain little conscious awareness of the processes of thought practiced so that they can use these processes on their own. Many students take copious notes, others take none because, as they tell us later, they "understand what's going on." But then comes an assignment asking them to discuss a new work using techniques learned in class, and students all along the spectrum often have no idea where to begin. Walvoord and McCarthy's classroom research supports these observations: in a wide variety of courses students are asked to apply learned "categories, concepts, or methods to *new data and new situations*," but "verbal descriptions of a process, whether presented in class or in a textbook, were difficult for students to translate into action." They conclude that "procedural knowledge often needs to be taught procedurally—by concrete experiences under the guidance of the teacher, who leads students physically and directly through the procedure" (1991, 7, 238).

LEARNING TO VISUALIZE LANGUAGE

One among many directions worth pursuing is to make more explicit and *visual* the processes of thought under study. Hayakawa (1939) offers the useful image of the abstraction ladder, based on the work of Alfred Korzybski. In brief, Hayakawa suggests that words can be seen as situated at varying positions along a ladder of abstraction, from the more concrete and specific lower down—for example Bessie the cow— on up through the more abstract and general: cow, livestock, farm assets, asset, wealth. Sentences likewise operate at varying levels of abstraction and generalization, from a lower-level sentence such as "Mrs. Levin makes good potato pancakes" on up through "Mrs. Levin is a good cook," "Chicago women are good cooks," and "The culinary art has reached a high state in America" (153, 159–60). To move up the ladder one abstracts, or selects, particular characteristics—what Bessie has in common with Daisy and Rosie or what potato pancakes have in common with roasts and pickles—and ignores differences. Abstracted characteristics make possible increasingly general terms and statements that refer to greater numbers of specific instances.

Hayakawa notes that good thinking involves movement on the ladder, the "constant interplay of higher-level and lower-level abstractions, and the constant interplay of the verbal levels with the nonverbal ('object') levels" (162). Perry (1970, 32), Shaughnessy (1977, 240–41, 246), and numerous other educators emphasize the centrality of connected movement among levels of abstraction in academic discourse. Moffett in fact comments that "a very large measure of what educators mean by 'teaching students to think' is in reality making them conscious of abstracting but is, unfortunately, seldom viewed this way" (1968, 27).

In a simple classroom application, one can jot faculty and student comments on the board at varying vertical levels to help students visualize and keep in mind the levels of abstraction in a discussion. Drawing on a discussion and handout by our art historian teammate, for example, the students and I have diagrammed some ways to talk about the subject, form, and content of the first paintings presented in the semester (e.g., form—line, color, composition, space, light, texture), with some rough notes underneath (color—many or few? bright or subdued? any striking objects or contrasts?) and below these notes, details from a painting on the screen. When students later attempted to analyze art on their own, they had an approach to try out. Such diagrams are helpful whether we are discussing the effects of iconography and formal devices or the social and political functions of art. Faculty can explicitly present such diagrams as "part of the picture," with other important parts undrawn for the moment. They suggest "*some* ways to talk about . . ." rather than "*the* ways." Students can be asked to generate examples of other kinds of categories and evidence.

Such board notes can likewise suggest ways of talking across disciplinary boundaries. If breaking with decorum is the topic of discussion, the instructor can jot students' comments on the board to illustrate varying levels of specificity: up high, the hypothesis; below, kinds of conventional "limits" such as appropriate subject matter, size, audience; below that, ways that Romantics pushed these limits; and, still lower, examples of each. Romantics brought the intensely personal into their art? Witness the portrayals of Berlioz's love for Harriet Smithson, Gericault's private obsessions, or the mind of the poet Wordsworth, with examples below that students can compare and contrast. The Romantics crossed the limits of the art form itself? Witness the program symphonies of Beethoven and Berlioz, Turner's attachment of long titles and explanations to his paintings, or Blake's merging of poem and image, again with examples below. We can talk about connections across disciplines, but such visualizing helps students think more clearly about them. The latter set of comparisons enables students to appreciate that an interdisciplinary approach to the arts, while useful in studying any period and culture, is particularly appropriate for Romanticism because so many Romantics crossed boundaries between artistic media in their works.

As a natural follow-up, students can practice discussing new works in section meetings, smaller groups, or pairs. Discussions need not be forced into rigid, linear structures, for as Mahala emphasizes, processes of inquiry are "inherently messy" (1992, 734). But the approach illustrated here, applied flexibly, serves as both a means of discovery and a means of supporting ideas. Paying close attention in a new field of study does not come naturally; ask any music instructor in general education what students try to do at the back of the room as the CD player runs. This approach helps students learn to observe, which "is central to all disciplines; learning to look and look again is learning to question" (Berthoff 1981, 116). And students who have differing viewpoints learn to argue using specifics.

Class discussion of photocopied student writing before a quiz or exam can be a next step. This general procedure has a long track record. In the late fifties, Harvard and Radcliffe asked students at orientation to grade sample essay exams (Perry 1963, 134). Bringing this type of exercise into the interdisciplinary classroom and focusing the discussion on how ideas are supported yields good results. A short handout might contain three excerpts from past exams: one filled with high-level generalizations, one with detail upon detail, and one with effective movement. In discussions with students, each of these writing examples may have its advocates, and a student's observation that one offers better analysis may not be enough to help other students see the difference and catch themselves when they are writing like the less effective examples. Together, we attempt informally to visualize the writings. Does the second sentence move up, down, or stay on about the same level as the first? What about the third? Students see that it is the movement that "answers the question" and "gets some depth"—we note the before-unexplored metaphor of height in this wording. They can see that the other examples contain "dead-level abstracting," a term Hayakawa borrows from Wendell Johnson's *People in Quandaries* to discuss such stasis at either higher or lower levels (1939, 161). Shaughnessy notes that "the problem in most BW [basic writers'] papers lies in the absence of *movement* between abstract and concrete statements" (1977, 240). These examples reveal that the problem resurfaces in more experienced writers' papers as they work in new contexts. We then try as a group to compose sample answers to a similar essay question.

Conferences with students can follow up on class discussions. One diligent but anxious student, responding to a question about how works from different fields of art use specific means to create an expressive, emotionally powerful transformation of historical events, began with *The Death of Marat* (1793). She noted that David uses several striking visual means to present the death, and then cited the blank background and the basically horizontal composition, with a downward slope of one arm. Her analysis of Wordsworth's "To Toussaint L'Ouverture" was similar in its rephrasing of the question, a learned exam-taking skill, followed by a basket of useful details. She was proud of herself for noticing so much in the works and thus unhappy with her grade. In conference our discussion helped her see for herself that she offered details but they did not connect to any mid-level comments about the specific effects of the artist's choices. Good high-level generalization plus good data equals wobbly thinking when the connecting links are absent. The student commented, "I've never seen it that way before"; note the literal and figurative "seeing." And she exhibited a sudden decrease in frustration. Our subsequent look at her writing in other courses revealed that such disconnected thinking had been a recurring problem but she had never understood what professors wanted with comments like "explain" ("I did!"), "vague" ("but I used lots of details!"), or "so?" ("so what?"). She wrote far better on later occasions by concentrating on the connecting rungs, which then allowed her to develop comparisons across the arts more effectively.

In another representative conference, a business student objected that in an arts discussion, "students just BS: I see a shadow there, I hear a drum there." Her mood was not bolstered by the feedback she had just received on an assignment—where, she reported, she didn't feel like writing "a lot of BS." What she did write was indeed that, unfocused and unsupported. One might hear such objections in any required course, but they took on added intensity because this was a second-semester senior who had avoided taking her arts course and now felt she had to learn many different kinds of BS at once to get through. Our sketches of the kinds of categories and evidence used in different disciplines helped her understand that some of those apparently BS'ing students were drawing on evidence to build an argument with as much rigor as she had come to expect in her own field. What she saw enabled her on the next exam to make and support her own points with greatly increased effectiveness. She could respect her own thinking in the arts as well as in accounting.

The approach suggested here shows students that they are already users of language at varying levels of abstraction and generalization, in their everyday lives as well as across the disciplines. At issue then are not processes and tools they lack and need to acquire to become "initiates" but rather varying and more conscious uses of tools they already possess and apply in a wide variety of situations. Disciplinary ladders enable us to see more even as they limit the kinds of things we see. Students can learn to understand the kinds of ladders frequently used in different disciplines but also realize that each is a socially constructed way of seeing, not *the* way and not the reality itself.[3] To "understand and remain conscious of the process of abstracting" helps us to "*realize fully that words never 'say all' about anything*" (Hayakawa 176, 175).

ONGOING CHALLENGES

The approach suggested in this essay is of course no panacea. A main ongoing challenge I and my Romanticism teammates face, implicit in the previous chapter, is maintaining a creative balance in class and in assignments between the artistic works and interdisciplinary thinking. Just as good thinking involves movement among levels of abstraction, so does a good course. Drawing connections across disciplines, while possible at varying levels of abstraction and generalization, necessarily entails "ascendant thinking," as van Leer discusses in an essay aptly entitled "Upwards and Across" (1987). Without sufficient attention to ascendant thinking, an interdisciplinary course remains multidisciplinary, juxtaposing works but not bringing them into meaningful relationship with each other. But without vigilance, ascendant thinking can lose the ongoing connection with the concrete that gives it vitality and validity.

Theorists of interdisciplinary studies typically express concern about the former limitation: that in many supposedly interdisciplinary courses faculty and students do not stretch upwards and across to interdisciplinary connections. To encourage this movement, the useful "Guide to Interdisciplinary Syllabus Preparation" poses questions that push toward quite abstract thinking: "Does the synthesis result in a larger, more holistic understanding of the issue?" "Have the perspective of each discipline and some of its key underlying assumptions been brought to light and made explicit?" and so on (Association for Integrative Studies and Institute in Integrative Studies 1996).

But faculty in interdisciplinary courses are likely to express more concern about too much of the upwards and across. Students in class discussions as well as essays may more readily hypothesize about the Romantics with a "holistic perspective" or compare the communicative potential of the various arts than discuss what they have heard in the *Pastoral Symphony,* which first of all entails actually sitting and listening to it. When critics of interdisciplinary courses worry that such courses may be "shallow"—the image of shallowness accords well with that of deadlevel abstracting—it is indeed this level of abstracting and generalizing they have in mind. And theorists not of interdisciplinary studies in general but specifically of interarts comparisons also share this concern.[4] Scher, for example, notes that literature-music parallels have been accused of holding "a fatal attraction for the dilettante, the faddist and the crackpot" (Calvin Brown's phrase) because we enter the "'interarts borderland' . . . on too high a level of generalization" (1982, 226).

Awareness of this tendency only reinforces my own teaching team's already-strong commitment, noted in the previous chapter, to immediate experiences with the arts. In addition to introducing students to new environments, we bring the new into class in forms students are not predisposed to disdain: for example, musicians they know as peers in their own dormitories, even if it is to demonstrate why they are not able to perform Romantic virtuoso works such as Paganini's *Caprices*.

We continue to experiment with the wording of assignments to encourage connected thinking. We may require a museum or concert visit and then an inductive essay structure so that instead of launching into a string of generalities, students begin by looking or listening closely and describing what they have seen or heard before moving on to guided analysis and comparison. Counteracting the here nature, there nature, everywhere nature tendency noted above—as if artistic medium is irrelevant, all the Romantics are similar, and they are all completely different from artists in the period before—we have altered our wordings by asking students to debunk syntheses as well as build them. An exam question may ask students to work with concepts but not blur the differences and tensions within them: "Your friend has not had this course. Explain to her some of what she is missing in her notion that the Romantics. . . . " As Hayakawa points out in a chapter entitled "The Little Man Who Wasn't There" (he discusses Jew and Arab, we might add Romantic), our constructed abstractions and generalizations are necessary for thought but also can blind us (1939).

We continue to work on progressions of assignments over the semester (as Haynes [1996] pursues further over an entire four-year span). Betanzos finds that "students needed to be trained first to listen, to look, and to hear/read carefully and skillfully; only then should one ask them to entertain probing questions into the meaning of what they had heard, seen, or read" (1989, 18). Clüver adds that the study of interrelations should be similarly postponed (1990, 17). These recommendations should encourage students to follow Weisstein's advice for interarts work: be wary of "vast syntheses and brilliant generalizations" but rather "proceed discreetly and with measured pace from the small to the large and from the particular to the general" (1982, 267). But progression from the more concrete to the more abstract, in class and from assignment to assignment, may not make sense pedagogically. Many students simply may not care enough at first to bother learning to listen, look, and read carefully: "I never listen to this kind of stuff." Our students are also comparing, contrasting, exploring connections with themselves and their world in class and in assignments from day one. They meet certain kinds of challenges again and again but with increasing ability to handle them.

The personal connections evolve, the analyses evolve, whether of the beginnings and structure of Romantic works, the possibilities of conveying through different media a sense of nature as a living organism, or "the artist's cultural role as image maker" (Lauter 1990).

To allow for these opportunities, we have found frequent short writings essential. Increasingly common across the disciplines under the influence of the writing-across-the-curriculum movement, they take on particular importance in an interdisciplinary course because they allow students to experiment with and bring together works and ideas in a variety of ways. It took us some time to escape captivity to the long papers that would supposedly allow students sufficient scope for creative integrative thinking but that often yielded less than optimal results.

MOVING TOWARD AND AWAY FROM SYNTHESIS

Our classroom struggles to encourage students' active movement among levels of abstraction and generalization, including ongoing "interplay of the verbal levels with the nonverbal" (Hayakawa 1939), may suggest a useful caution about interdisciplinary studies. Newell argues that "disciplines and not substantive facts are the raw materials of interdisciplinary courses" (1994, 44). But as Beethoven reportedly said, "There have been many princes [and, we might add, musicologists, music historians, interarts scholars] and there will be thousands more. But there is only one Beethoven." We need to stay in close touch with the "raw material" of his music as well—to value the creative motion.

Synthesis is often discussed as the high point of interdisciplinary studies (see surveys of the literature in Richards 1996 and Newell 1998). In terms of levels of abstraction and generalization, it may often be. But key for Hayakawa and many scholars since his time is the motion of the mind. Listen to the action words: Rorty discusses

> "the hermeneutic circle"—the fact that we cannot understand the parts of a strange culture, practice, theory, language, or whatever, unless we know something about how the whole thing works, whereas we cannot get a grasp on how the whole works until we have some understanding of its parts. . . . *we play back and forth* between guesses about how to characterize particular statements

or other events, and guesses about the point of the whole situation, until gradually we feel at ease with what was hitherto strange. (1979, 319, italics added)

And Geertz, noting the importance of the hermeneutic circle across the disciplines as well as in everyday experience, speaks of "characteristic intellectual movement, the inward conceptual rhythm . . . a continuous dialectical tacking"; "one oscillates restlessly . . . hopping back and forth . . . [in] a sort of intellectual perpetual motion" among specifics and generalizations (1983, 69).

In an interdisciplinary course, then, some of the important motion is toward integration, synthesis. It is also *away* from integration and synthesis toward specifics and toward the nonverbal level of event, object, and person, bringing to them a greater understanding gained from the more abstract thought. Interdisciplinary study entails bringing together data, tools, methods, concepts, and theories from multiple disciplines. It "draws on different disciplinary perspectives and integrates their insights through construction of a more comprehensive perspective" (Klein and Newell 1997, 393–94). Such study also entails moving in the opposite direction. It continually tests that comprehensive perspective, rejects syntheses and tries out others, sees of what value they might be for dealing with the more concrete. In the Romanticism course, interdisciplinary study yields both interarts comparisons and an enriched experience of particular works of Berlioz, Delacroix, and Mary Shelley.[5] Much of the power of interdisciplinary study, for professionals and students alike, lies not at a particular point within the intellectual action it entails—not just the integration—but in the enriched action among levels of abstraction and generalization. The action words cited above suggest a particular sense in which interdisciplinary study indeed calls for *active* student learning.

NOTES

1. See Perry's description of "cow" writing, the product of hard work but mired in raw data without evidence of the understanding that is the key to liberal learning: "The student who merely cows robs himself, without knowing it, of his

education and his soul" (1963, 129–33; Perry leaves unexplored the gender stereotypes in his cow-bull terminology, the "masculine context" and the "feminine particular"). Williams and Colomb comment on the "tyranny of the concrete" repeatedly experienced by writers entering unfamiliar disciplines (1990, 107).

2. Cf. Berthoff's warning about "the hazards of thinking of writing in the core courses as 'the composition component,'" and her emphasis that "one of the best ways to teach your subject is by teaching writing," "the chief means of making meanings and thus of laying hold on the speculative instruments of one discipline or another" (1981, 114, 113, 123).

3. McCarthy similarly recommends that faculty emphasize a discipline offers "one way of looking at reality and not reality itself" (1987, 262)—better amended to "*ways* of looking" to acknowledge the heterogeneity, the openness of the discourses. Also see Bizzell's caution that we not treat "conventions as if they simply mirrored reality" (1982a, 238; cf. 1982b, 203). For further analysis of the approach discussed in this essay in relation to recent writing-across-the-curriculum scholarship, including possible objections, see Seabury (1996, 45–50).

4. For comments on both the dangers and the possibilities of interarts comparisons and of periodization, see Wellek (1942), Steiner (1982, 1990), Green (1990), and other essays in Barricelli, Gibaldi, and Lauter (1990), especially the introduction. That collection offers various approaches to teaching interdisciplinary courses in the arts and a useful bibliography. While concerns continue among scholars, the editors note that recent theorizing about texts and contexts has increased interest in interarts comparisons, especially those that move beyond formal concerns (1990, 5). Steiner, for example, affirms that "interart *loci classici* may unlock doors to the very structure of cultural thought" (1990, 40).

5. Helen Vendler argued in her 1980 Modern Language Association presidential address that "a general interdisciplinary Poloniuslike religious-historical-philosophical-cultural overview will never reproduce that taste on the tongue . . . of an individual style," to which Graff rightly adds, "recent experience shows that bare, unmediated contact with the work does not necessarily inculcate that taste either" (1987, 254). Obviously, à la Hayakawa, stasis in either direction is less effective in generating active student learning.

REFERENCES

Association for Integrative Studies and Institute in Integrative Studies. 1996. "Guide to Interdisciplinary Syllabus Preparation." *Journal of General Education* 45 (2): 170–73.

Barricelli, Jean-Pierre, and Joseph Gibaldi. 1982. *Interrelations of Literature.* New York: Modern Language Association.

Barricelli, Jean-Pierre, Joseph Gibaldi, and Estella Lauter, eds. 1990. *Teaching Literature and Other Arts.* New York: Modern Language Association.

Berthoff, Ann. 1981. *The Making of Meaning: Metaphors, Models, and Maxims for Writing Teachers.* Upper Montclair, N.J.: Boynton.

Betanzos, Ramón. 1989. "Experiencing the Arts: Looking at Art, Listening to Music and Reading Poetry." *Humanities Education* (Winter): 17–21.

Bizzell, Patricia. 1982a. "Cognition, Convention, and Certainty: What We Need to Know about Writing." *PRE/TEXT* 3 (3) : 213–43.

Bizzell, Patricia. 1982b. "College Composition: Initiation into the Academic Discourse Community." *Curriculum Inquiry* 12 (2): 191–207.

Clüver, Claus. 1990. "The Comparative Study of the Arts." In *Teaching Literature and Other Arts,* eds. Jean-Pierre Barricelli, Joseph Gibaldi, and Estella Lauter. New York: Modern Language Association.

Elbow, Peter. 1986. "Nondisciplinary Courses and the Two Roots of Real Learning." In *Embracing Contraries: Explorations in Learning and Teaching.* New York: Oxford University Press.

Geertz, Clifford. 1983. *Local Knowledge.* New York: Basic.

Graff, Gerald. 1987. *Professing Literature: An Institutional History.* Chicago: University of Chicago Press.

Green, Jon D. 1990. "Determining Valid Interart Analogies." In *Teaching Literature and Other* Arts, eds. Jean-Pierre Barricelli, Joseph Gibaldi, and Estella Lauter. New York: Modern Language Association.

Hayakawa, S. I. [1939] 1972. *Language in Thought and Action.* 3d ed. New York: Harcourt.

Haynes, Carolyn. 1996. "Interdisciplinary Writing and the Undergraduate Experience: A Four-Year Writing Plan Proposal." *Issues in Integrative Studies* 14: 29–57.

Klein, Julie Thompson. 1990. *Interdisciplinarity: History, Theory, and Practice.* Detroit, Mich.: Wayne State University Press.

Klein, Julie Thompson, and William H. Newell. 1997. "Advancing Interdisciplinary Studies." In *Handbook of the Undergraduate Curriculum,* eds. Jerry G. Gaff and James L. Ratcliff. San Francisco: Jossey-Bass.

Lauter, Estella. 1990. "Images of Women in Contemporary Arts: Interart Discourse with a Social Dimension." In *Teaching Literature and Other* Arts, eds. Jean-Pierre Barricelli, Joseph Gibaldi, and Estella Lauter. New York: Modern Language Association.

Leer, Oscar van. 1987. "'Upwards and Across': An Essay on Cross-Disciplinary Thinking." In *Thinking: The Second International Conference,* eds. D. N. Perkins, Jack Lochhead, and John Bishop. Hillsdale, N.J.: Erlbaum.

Mahala, Daniel. 1992. "Daniel Mahala Responds." *College English* 54: 733–35.

McCarthy, Lucille Parkinson. 1987. "A Stranger in Strange Lands: A College Student Writing Across the Curriculum." *Research in the Teaching of English* 21 (3): 233–65.

Moffett, James. 1968. *Teaching the Universe of Discourse.* New York: Houghton.

Newell, William H. 1994. "Designing Interdisciplinary Courses." In *Interdisciplinary Studies Today,* eds. Julie Thompson Klein and William G. Doty. San Francisco: Jossey-Bass.

Newell, William H. 1998. "Professionalizing Interdisciplinarity: Literature Review and Research Agenda." In *Interdisciplinarity: Essays from the Literature,* ed. William H. Newell. New York: College Entrance Examination Board.

Perry, William, Jr. 1963. "Examsmanship and the Liberal Arts: A Study in Educational Epistemology." In *Examining in Harvard College: A Collection of Essays by Members of the Harvard Faculty,* ed. Harvard Faculty of Arts and Sciences. Cambridge, Mass.: Harvard University Press.

Perry, William, Jr. 1970. *Forms of Intellectual and Ethical Development in the College Years.* New York: Holt.

Richards, Donald G. 1996. "The Meaning and Relevance of 'Synthesis' in Interdisciplinary Studies." *Journal of General Education* 45 (2): 114–28.

Rorty, Richard. 1979. *Philosophy and the Mirror of Nature.* Princeton, N.J.: Princeton University Press.

Scher, Steven Paul. 1982. "Literature and Music." In *Interrelations of Literature,* eds. Jean-Pierre Barricelli and Joseph Gibaldi. New York: Modern Language Association.

Seabury, Marcia Bundy. 1996. "Writing and Interdisciplinary Learning." *Perspectives* 26 (2): 40–54.

Shaughnessy, Mina. 1977. *Errors and Expectations.* New York: Oxford University Press.

Steiner, Wendy. 1982. *The Colors of Rhetoric: Problems in the Relation Between Modern Literature and Painting.* Chicago: University of Chicago Press.

Steiner, Wendy. 1990. "Literature and Painting." In *Teaching Literature and Other Arts,* eds. Jean-Pierre Barricelli, Joseph Gibaldi, and Estella Lauter. New York: Modern Language Association.

Walvoord, Barbara E., and Lucille P. McCarthy. 1991. *Thinking and Writing in College: A Naturalistic Study of Students in Four Disciplines.* Urbana, Ill.: National Council of Teachers of English.

Weisstein, Ulrich. 1982. "Literature and the Visual Arts." In *Interrelations of Literature,* eds. Jean-Pierre Barricelli and Joseph Gibaldi. New York: Modern Language Association.

Wellek, René. 1942. "The Parallelism Between Literature and the Arts." In *English Institute Annual 1941.* New York: Columbia University Press.

White, Edward M. 1991. "Shallow Roots or Taproots for Writing across the Curriculum?" *Association of Departments of English Bulletin* 98 (Spring): 29–33.

Williams, Joseph M., and Gregory G. Colomb. 1990. "The University of Chicago." In *Programs That Work: Models and Methods for Writing Across the Curriculum,* eds. Toby Fulwiler and Art Young. Portsmouth, Mass.: Boynton/Cook.

(For sample syllabus, see previous chapter.)

WHAT IS SYMMETRY, THAT EDUCATORS AND STUDENTS SHOULD BE MINDFUL OF IT?

Laurence I. Gould

WHAT IS SYMMETRY?

Symmetry, at an elementary level, is something that we are all probably aware of in our everyday lives. In the faculty dining room, colleagues try to determine which of two apparently identical metal dispensers contains the hot water for tea (and, failing the determination, inadvertently release coffee onto a tea bag). And in the supermarket, shoppers attempt to find another tomato in the pile that looks just like the nice one already selected.

We can open many doorways to a more detailed understanding of the term because the subject of symmetry has been written about extensively. There are numerous works on symmetry in science, art, mathematics, philosophy, music, poetry, and information processing. On the World Wide Web and in two journals alone (Darvas and Nagy 1990–1996; Hargittai 1986a, 1986b) we can find many examples covering all of those subjects and more.[1]

In Seeing Through Symmetry, a course I created in 1991, students work up to a definition of symmetry, starting in a qualitative way by observing pleasing patterns in the arts and in the sciences. We then go on to characterize symmetry using elementary mathematical notions. These give us the raw material from which to abstract and conceptualize and ultimately to formulate a general definition of symmetry as the course's key concept.

The term "symmetry" as used in the course has no meaning apart from some *operation*. With this in mind, we can put forth the following (fairly standard) definition: An object is symmetric under a particular operation if it appears unchanged after that operation has been performed. For example, a square has rotational symmetry because after rotating it about its center through 90 degrees, in its plane, the square appears as it did prior to the rotation.

If, in addition, we define an object's "image" as the result of having performed a particular operation on the object, then a more concise definition of symmetry is: An object is symmetric under a particular operation if it is identical to its image. Even more briefly: Symmetry means invariance under change (cf. Mackay 1986, 19).

WHY BE MINDFUL OF IT?

The concept of symmetry comes fundamentally from the field of philosophy, the most basic of all the disciplines. It is therefore not so surprising that the concept applies to such a diverse set of disciplines (see, e.g., Van Fraassen 1989). I would even argue that it applies to *all* disciplines. (Indeed, thinking is itself an activity that appears to require the identity of ideas under change of mental state.)

So a small but important part of the course is devoted to understanding the philosophical aspects of symmetry. One such aspect could be called the epistemology of symmetry: How valid is our concept of symmetry? What are its limitations? For example: Do we mean that an object is symmetric if it *appears* so? (Is the right side of your face the true mirror image of the left side?) Are there symmetries that lie below appearances? (Are all the laws of physics symmetric? If you drop an object at one place will its motion be the same as when you drop the same object after having moved two feet to the right or after having waited for one minute?)

Educators at other universities have also thought about the value of teaching symmetry.[2] A particularly good description of the value of symmetry for education in general and for science education in particular is given by Klein:

It aims at [an] *interdisciplinary* approach since it deals first with formal conditions of understanding applicable to all possible objects of experience;

It relates objects of learning to each other, thus rendering possible *shaped, understanding* learning;

All formal laws raise from and remain closely related to *sensual experience;*

A deep feeling of comfort is raised by having symmetrical orders open to our senses; this affects our sense of *beauty;*

Learning with symmetries may be based on *action,* and action will continue to give a basis of understanding for complicated problems: the promoting unity of action, of sensual and intellectual activity in understanding will be experienced;

These activities may be abstracted and *formalized* towards mathematics, simple enough, yet basic, thus *evolving* the mathematical interpretation of the world. (1990, 86)

Symmetry, as presented in the Seeing Through Symmetry course, is what I would call a "hub concept." It is as if it stood for the axis of a cylinder consisting of a multidisciplinary world with ties to disciplines constituting the surface, and with the disciplines, as a consequence, tied to each other. Through this hub many aspects of the scientific and artistic worlds can better be understood and appreciated. For example, a concept of symmetry common to mathematics, physics, and music enables students to interrelate those disciplines—not only by acquiring some new understanding of each through the concept but also by seeing a commonality of each through it. By using that commonality, it is possible for advances in one discipline to lead to advances in another. To explain further, the concept of "translational symmetry," when given its precise mathematical formulation, can be used to explain the physics of sine waves, which in turn can be applied to understanding why a musical tone sounds the way it does. The physics of sound and the sound of music can then feed into each other, each contributing to the other. The interrelationship of such disciplines perhaps seems strange to many academic specialists, but in the Middle Ages it was a matter of course. For example, music was part of the mathematical sciences called the "quadrivium," a division of the seven liberal arts. It was personified by Pythagoras because he was able to relate sounds made by a taut string that was plucked, after holding down one part of it to divide the string's length into the ratio of lengths corresponding to positive integers.

According to some critics, such integrations are not always possible. For example, Richards, taking into account the work of several prominent writers, explains what he sees as a problem of interdisciplinarity for the humanities and the sciences. He mentions that subjects from those two areas may only complement each other so that

> What results from interdisciplinary cooperation is an accumulation of different *types* of knowledge about a particular issue. . . . the two can yield a "synthesis" only in a *loose* [my emphasis], "enriched-view-of[-]the-world" sense. There would seem to be unbreachable epistemological barriers preventing genuine integration in such cases. (1996, 122)

But the aim of Seeing Through Symmetry is to facilitate a *strong* synthesis.

The aim is to use what students know about symmetry in their everyday life not only as a launching ground for the formulation of a precise definition but also to give them new insights into their own disciplines and to reveal the interconnection of different disciplines. In this way they can better understand both science and math, thus, as Carlisle says, "creating the cross lines [between disciplines] and helping students understand that the phenomenon they are studying is simultaneously a number of things" (1995, 11).

> Can you hear symmetry? Can you see it in space? In solids? Can you see it in movement? How is it that the left and right hands playing scales that start simultaneously at the top and bottom of the keyboard have symmetry? How is ABA form like a farmhouse with a porch in the middle and two pairs of windows on each side? . . . Can there be symmetry in male and female relationships? Can there be symmetry in historical development? (Carlisle 1995, 12)

SEEING THROUGH SYMMETRY: THE COURSE

Seeing Through Symmetry integrates nonscientific areas with science, using nonscientific disciplines as a *feedback gateway* to scientific ones. The course enables students explicitly to develop their quantitative abilities and analogical thinking by using symmetry both as a method within a discipline and as a bridge between disciplines. (A brief statement of the need for something like such a bridge is provided by Fisher [1995].) Starting with the topics of symmetry in art, in poetry, and in music, we then go on to display and interrelate those topics to symmetry in areas such as mathematics, physics, chemistry, biology, and cosmology. Thus students "see through" (i.e., understand) the concept of symmetry as well as "see the world through" (i.e., by means of employing) the concept of symmetry. They develop interrelational and scientific abilities, in part through the medium of a highly graphical laboratory experience that uses computers to explore the many facets of symmetry, including generating their own patterns with the use of software packages and elementary programming.

This course develops integrative skills in a variety of ways. A primary one is the use of communication skills, speaking, writing, and class presentation, in a term project. The term project incorporates the concepts of science and math presented in the course and requires students to display their creative and analytical abilities. Throughout this project, as one of the course's integrative benefits, students not only identify interrelations between subjects within the realm of science but also between that realm, the humanities in general, and their own discipline in particular.

Lectures

Class sessions are multimedia interactions. Students view two films. One, presented during the first class meeting, is an easily understood general introduction to a variety of symmetries. The other, shown about halfway through the course, stresses the glories of learning as seen through the mind of the prototype Renaissance man, Leonardo da Vinci. An audiotape demonstrates the use of the Golden Ratio in Bartok's

"Divertimento for Strings." A laser exhibits both the wave interference phenomenon called diffraction and the manner in which light waves can interfere to produce a hologram. A special feature of the course is a computer animation and sound show composed by me and a colleague from the Biology department (D. P. Buckley, an expert in multimedia presentation). The show illustrates symmetry in art, geometry, geophysics, and both cellular and molecular biology. It also dynamically demonstrates broken symmetry by presenting a portion of a motion picture showing the sickling (change of shape from circular to crescent moon) of a red blood cell to microscopically manifest the disease called sickle cell anemia.

The course is currently taught by a single instructor because the other team members have left the university (although I hope to rebuild a team). While I have had occasional guest lectures (from the art school, the college of music, and outside the university), course evaluations indicate that students appear to be satisfied with the format.

On the first day of class students list their majors. Thus we can immediately start to connect aspects of symmetry, as they understand the term, to their current career choice. (One example is a painting major who considers symmetry to be the use of balance in art.) The list of majors engenders a lively class discussion.

In fact, the course has moved more and more toward encouraging students to refer to their own experiences throughout the development of any topic. They are also able to try things out on the computer that illustrate ideas discussed in class. The point here is that science begins from an individual's observations of the world. It is a highly imaginative probing into the workings of nature, not just a rigid compilation of facts and formulas.

Over the years, the subject matter of the course has been broadened. Some of the more recent topics are the structure and function of DNA, the nature of the chemical bond through explanations of electric forces, scientific bases for common uses of electricity, an introduction to the mathematical theory of groups with applications to computer algorithms, the application of waves to some aspects of the strange world of quantum physics, and the very important issue of scientific methodology (presented in part through the use of Venn diagrams to illustrate class inclusions and methods of concept formation). As a result of learning that students want greater challenge, I have introduced a variety of more intriguing and complex topics (including group theory) into the course.

A colleague and I were able to outfit a multimedia classroom, in part as a result of a 1993 National Science Foundation Instrument and Laboratory Improvement grant (No. DUE-9352670) for the course. The room contains 12 nodes (each with a Mac computer, plus desk lamp, in a space that easily accommodates two students), an instructor node with another Mac tied to a projection system at the front center of the classroom, and a laser printer, all connected via an Ethernet network. Because each node's computer screen faces the front of the room, the instructor can monitor all activity. There is also a VCR player connected to a large monitor and an overhead projector. The instructor node permits access to each of the student nodes (e.g., for loading software or transferring files). The equipment is completed by a variety of hardware and software packages used both in teaching and in the laboratory portion of the course.[3]

Labs

Once-a-week labs give students a deeper understanding of the course. Discussion is continually encouraged. Although students work in pairs, an individual typed report is required for each lab exercise. Earlier labs feed into later ones as lower-level abstractions feed into higher-level ones. The labs are briefly described below in relation to the question: What is the activity and how does it relate to other areas of the course to convey the interdisciplinary experience? (The subjects referred to are covered earlier in lectures.)

1. *Computer Drawing: Reflections, Rotations, and Designs.* This lab (a) introduces students to the computer and (b) enables participants to create and understand designs that have reflectional or rotational symmetry. Students test for those symmetries by using the software package to compare an image of the design with the design itself. They can also do a comparison by getting a printout of their design on which can be laid a transparency for tracing it. They can then fold or rotate the tracing. In

addition, they can create their own colored designs using a variety of reflectional and rotational symmetries. In this way students explore the relation between symmetry and art.

2. *Learning Algorithms Through the Language of Logo.* Students learn about a computer algorithm: how a repetitive command, or algorithm, can be used to create certain simple figures. Hence they experience "time-translational" symmetry that they can, for example, interrelate to rhyme schemes in poetry.

3. *Drawing and Hearing Patterns: Polygonal Symmetry and Fibonnaci Tones.* In this continuation of Lab 2, students (a) employ algorithms (via Logo) to simplify the creation of regular polygons that have both reflectional and rotational symmetry and (b) use the Fibonnaci sequence, an example of an algorithm discussed in lectures, to hear tones and thus learn more about the musical scale. In this lab students discover the connections between music, design, and computers; for example, by using the concept of an algorithm they may create certain musical patterns.

4. *Intricacies of Coloration: Coordinates, Translations, Groups, and Tessellations.* Continuing from Lab 3, students observe (a) how coordinates of points can be represented by the computer, a prelude to learning (b) how different colors are determining factors in the nature of translationally symmetric designs, (c) how the mathematical theory of groups can be introduced, and (d) how algorithms can be created to tessellate the screen. Here students learn (or relearn) the analytical geometry basics of locating objects in space; see how this is related to design, to poetry, and to music through the creation of symmetries and broken symmetries; understand how art can be a manifestation of group theory in mathematics and how the latter can be used to create art; and glimpse infinity in terms of symmetries that can go on and on through time and space.

5. *Patterns in Music: Sound and Sight.* At our school of music (each pair of students is in a small room containing a piano), students gain a literal hands-on introduction to elementary ideas in music and music symmetry through exploration of the visual and aural aspects of the

keyboard. Students (a) learn about symmetrical patterns that can be associated with the keyboard, both visual and what I would call *aural temporal;* (b) relate the psychophysical concepts of pitch and frequency to each other and to the Fibonnaci sequence; and (c) perform the broken symmetry of musical rounds. In this lab, students interrelate music, mathematics, art, and physics, with even a little psychoacoustics.

6. *Experiencing Motion in Space and Time.* In this lab and the ones that follow, students learn to appreciate the value of technology for investigating aspects of certain natural phenomena, including those that exist beyond the range of human vision and hearing. The computer with auxiliary devices attached to it "extends" our visual and auditory senses. This in turn makes it possible for us to understand the manner in which symmetric aspects of nature contribute to our sense of the world of motion, sound, and light.

Students build on their experience of graphical representations (introduced in Lab 4) through the visualization of scientific data obtained via the simultaneous monitoring and display of different phenomena by computer equipment. This enables them to (a) appreciate the value of technology's omnipresent concept of voltage through the display of battery outputs as a function of time; (b) understand aspects of motion by experiencing the movement of their hand using an ultrasonic motion detector; and (c) conceptualize some details of a periodic phenomenon that has time-translational invariance, called "simple harmonic motion," using a mass on a spring connected to a force probe. Students begin to recognize the obvious tie to mathematics, as well as to epistemology (i.e., how we acquire knowledge about the world; in this case, scientific knowledge). They also make connections to art, music, and poetry. For example, the stressed and unstressed pattern in the sonorous iambic pentameter may be represented through the use of visual voltage steps exhibiting a similar periodicity in time.

7. *Symmetry of Oscillations: Sine Waves and Sound.* This lab, drawing from concepts learned in the previous one, serves as an introduction to some elementary properties of sound by using the computer to measure periods that are thousands of times shorter than one second. Students learn (a) how to

measure the frequency and amplitude of periodic sinusoidal signals produced by tuning forks and then apply that knowledge to the observation of periodic *non*sinusoidal signals and (b) what gives rise to the remarkable symmetrical patterns, called "Lissajous figures," that result from combining two sinusoidal signals whose frequencies stand in a simple numerical relation to each other. Ties to epistemology are demonstrated by experiments on consistency: students compare the measured value of a frequency with the standard value stamped on the tuning fork. (Is the standard value the "correct" one? What do we mean by "correct"? Do we use similar methods to acquire knowledge in the arts?) The exercise in (b) reveals obvious ties to mathematics as well as to the visual arts, and with a little more imagination, students begin to understand how both music and poetry benefit from such insights. An example is the tuning of a piano string by means of a visual comparison of a given input frequency with that from the string.

8. *Building Symmetry From Symmetry: The Fourier Spectrum.* In this introduction to symmetrical wave patterns, students learn about (a) Fourier synthesis, as manifested in complex periodic sounds, with their corresponding shapes, occurring when two or more simple periodic sounds with their corresponding shapes, resembling sine-wave shapes, are combined, or synthesized (although true sine-wave shapes are referred to as Fourier components, our simple approximate shapes are also so referred to); (b) Fourier decomposition, a method showing how complex periodic shapes can be broken down (or decomposed) into their Fourier components, enabling students to look at the shape of their voice and their heartbeat; and (c) how to synthesize their voice and heartbeat from the Fourier components.

A variety of interconnections emerge from this lab. Ties to mathematics are obvious, but in addition, connections can be made to the technology of electronic music and voice production, the visual arts, biology (e.g., how does the structure and function of the vocal chords and heart relate to the nature of the waves they produce?), and, most remarkably, to the limitations of a certain type of knowledge through the Heisenberg Uncertainty Relation in quantum physics (e.g., why is it that to be able to precisely locate a particle's position is to be unable to precisely locate its velocity?).

9. *Waviness: In Water and Light.* The addition of wave patterns in the lab introduces a far-ranging investigation because the patterns apply to almost all waves in the universe. Here the focus is on the visual as students learn about (a) brightness and light waves through the experience and measurement of the intensity of light as well as through the observation of a spatial and temporal invariance (each a symmetry property) of that intensity under certain conditions. By modeling light as a transverse wave and using polarizers, they also demonstrate and explain how such polarizers work in altering the intensity of light; and (b) waviness in water by computer simulation of waves, through which students can observe the wavelength of waves, measure their speed, see how waves interfere with each other, and observe the effects of their interference. The connections are of course to mathematics (and once more emphasize an important epistemological point about methodology in the physical sciences), but also to the visual arts, to music (the phenomenon of the "intensity of light" is analogous to the "loudness of sound"), and to cosmology (e.g., how do we know the distance to stars and what they are made of?).

Other labs in the planning stage are "Slipping" Symmetry: Crystals, Fractals, and Chaos; Bounced, Flipped, Rotated, and Decomposed Light: From Mirrors to Spectra; and On Balls and Bombs: The Geometry of Projectile Motion.

Problems Related to the Labs

The labs are explicit enough that there is almost no need for instructor supervision, important for a single instructor overseeing 24 students in a lab that must normally be completed within two hours. Nevertheless, it sometimes takes more than a two-hour period to complete some of the labs, so I am considering trimming those labs and replacing others with more intriguing explorations—chaos and fractals in particular.

Could it be that students are having difficulties because they are not adequately prepared in the various disciplines presented in the course? I do not think so. They are shown during the first class that no algebra is needed beyond solving one equation in one unknown. As to geometry, I also explain that none is needed beyond a small subset of concepts from high school (such as points, lines, and angles). Furthermore, I always offer a brief review of the mathematical ideas when they are needed. Concepts from science, no matter how elementary, are also carefully presented to relate them to students' everyday experiences. As a consequence, even some of the most profound concepts in mathematics (such as group and limit) are understandable. It appears, from class discussions, exams, and term projects, that students are adequately prepared for the course. Indeed, a past complaint from student evaluations was not that the topics were too difficult but that the course moved too slowly because of too much time spent reviewing elementary ideas.

Museum Report

As a result of visiting several science museums in the United States and Canada, I have experienced the joys of seeing creative exhibits that frequently employ a hands-on approach to science. (The Reuben H. Fleet Space Theater and Science Center in San Diego, California, even has an entire exhibit on symmetry: Symmetry: A Universe by Design.) Consequently, I ask my students to visit a science museum and submit a rather open-ended report of their experience. They are asked only to describe their observations, explain what they saw, and critique exhibits they found notable.

The reports (to my surprise and joy, given the lack of structured requirements) have been one of the most successful parts of the course. They are not focused on symmetry per se but on the scientific method, discussed in class, of making observations and drawing conclusions. Students, often going with their friends so they can compare their experiences, are genuinely delighted to see the exhibits and critically examine them.

Although the Connecticut Science Museum is closest to the university, students are permitted to visit museums in places that are convenient for them (which they usually do during spring break). The reports often show glimmers of a scientific understanding of the world—such as the "winding symmetrical patterns" in a mollusk's shell—and intricate descriptions of "a chaos pendulum . . . a curious device kept in motion by a system of gears." The reports illustrate that students are not only observing and assessing what they observe but also enjoying doing it.

Term Project

This is the capstone experience of the course. Students are advised to start researching possible topics early and are invited to consult with the instructor throughout the course. To maximize the value of this experience, it is divided into several stages spread out over half a semester. These consist, in order, of a report on their preliminary idea, a progress report, a class presentation, and the final report.

Over the years students have completed some outstanding projects. One was by a philosophy major on the application of symmetry principles to metaphysics. Another, by a business major, identified concepts of symmetry in the stock market. One student did in-depth research for her video-supported report on "Symmetries in Synchronized Swimming," a sport in which she also participated. Another student grew crystals and researched "Crystal Structure and Symmetry." A music student wrote an original composition to explain symmetry in tonal elements using set theory and vectors; he titled his project "The 4 Arms of Chenrezi" because of the manner in which the "moods" of this Tibetan Tantric deity relate to the moods of his composition. Going beyond the course's mostly two-dimensional symmetries in geometry, one student did a project titled "Polyhedra and Tessellations of Space." Another very creative and highly interdisciplinary project was titled "Symmetry in Human Relationships." Supported by the use of graphs and space-time diagrams, it integrated (fairly successfully) concepts from geometry, wave theory, and simple harmonic motion with the student's own observations of the manner in which humans interact.

Those were among the best. Some of the projects, however, lack sufficient integration of quantitative scientific ideas, thus missing the significance of the course's interdisciplinary message. Part of the reason appears to be students' failure to realize how rich are the connections that can be made (in spite of the manifold connections shown through lecture and lab). Further, some students do little or no library research (even though I require it as part of the project and give them a two-page list of suggested references). To correct this problem I have been emphasizing the value of research and giving students more information on where they can go to learn more about their topic. I will not simply put more materials on reserve in the library because that would defeat the goal of making *students* responsible for their research. In future classes the research aspect will count more heavily in the grade given for the term project.

CONCLUSION

Seeing Through Symmetry is designed to help students find pleasurable values in the areas of science and technology by focusing on the interactions among a variety of disciplines. As a result students have ample opportunity to relate concepts of symmetry to their own disciplines. The course thus enables and motivates them to gain understanding of technical areas outside their majors. Such understanding can then feed back (as it has for some) to give them a better grasp and appreciation of their own fields of study.

More broadly, Seeing Through Symmetry is intended to give students an understanding and appreciation of the many important areas of study spawned by human creativity. It shows them that the world is of a piece. And it conveys the sense that where the human mind journeys there are no barriers.

NOTES

1. The integration of my own interdisciplinary teaching and scholarship on symmetry has resulted in three articles (e.g., in *Symmetry: Culture and Science*, the quarterly of the International Society for the Interdisciplinary Study of Symmetry); nine talks, mostly invited (e.g., at Harvard University; the Third Interdisciplinary Symmetry Congress and Exhibition of the International Society for the Interdisciplinary Study of Symmetry in Washington, D.C.; and the East/West Invitational Seminar on New Technologies in Education at Charles University, Prague); and two grants. As a result of a variety of interactions at such meetings, I obtained a wealth of new information for my course. I have also met with colleagues who teach about symmetry in Warsaw and in Budapest. The further internationalization of Seeing Through Symmetry has resulted from discussions of our respective teaching methods and experiences.

2. Only a small number of institutions have offered courses explicitly on symmetry. Some examples are those taught by G. Darvas at the Institute for Advanced Symmetry Studies in Budapest, I. Halpern at the University of Washington, R. Hazen at George Mason University, J. Kapraff (1986) at the New Jersey Institute of Technology, E. Merzbacher at Williams College, D. Nagy at Arizona State University, A. Rosenberg at Swarthmore College, M. Senechal at Smith College, and S. Wait at Rensselaer Polytechnic Institute. But those courses do not appear to have taken quite the same approach as the one discussed here with regard to the method used, the kinds of disciplines discussed, and the laboratory-enriching laboratory-based hands-on experiences.

3. The software equipment used in the labs and lectures includes Super Paint™ (Version 3.5; ©1993 by Aldus Corporation; Micro Worlds Logo (© by Logo Computer Systems Inc.); Data Logger 4.5 (© 1989–95 by the Center for Science and Mathematics Teaching, CSMT, Tufts University); MacMotion 4.5 (© 1989–95 by CSMT, Tufts University); Sound 4.5 (© 1989–94 by CSMT, Tufts University); MultiMap (©1991–92 by Bolt Beranek and Newman, Inc.); SoundWaves (© 1993, 1994 by Bill Moran); Mathematica 2.2 (© 1993 by Wolfram Research, Inc.); Physics Explorer 2.0: Ripple Tank (© 1993 by LOGAL Educational Software and Systems, Israel); Songworks 1.7 (©1992–1994 by Jeffrey Evans).

The hardware used in the labs and lectures includes, for each pair of students, a Mac Performa 636; Universal Laboratory Interface (ULI) box plus test leads, ultrasonic motion detector, student force sensor, microphone/amplifier, heart rate monitor, and light sensor (all obtained from Vernier Software, Oregon); headphones, tuning forks, masses, clamps, aluminum rods, 1.5 V batteries; high-low intensity lamp; and polarizers. In addition there are diffraction gratings through which students can view the spectrum from different sources of light (the sun, incandescent bulbs, fluorescent bulbs, and hydrogen and mercury discharge tubes).

Other materials required for the course are meager but necessary for students to understand that the scientific enterprise is heavily dependent on quantitative measurements and computations. In addition to the two texts mentioned in the syllabus, only the following are needed: blank 3.5" diskettes; a calculator (whose display should show at least five places to the right of the decimal point but need only perform the operations of addition, subtraction, multiplication, and division); pencils and erasers; a ruler that can be used as a straightedge for drawing lines and measuring lengths; a compass to draw arcs of circles; and a protractor for measuring angles.

REFERENCES

Carlisle, Barbara. 1995. "Music and Life." *American Music Teacher* 44 (June/July): 10–13.

Darvas, György, and Dénes Nagy, eds. 1990–1996. *Symmetry: Culture and Science.*

Fisher, Melvyn L. 1995. "Symmetry: The Needed Bridge between the Arts, the Sciences and their Mathematics, and the Humanities." *Symmetry: Culture and Science* 6 (2): 214–17.

Hargittai, István. 1986a. *Computers & Mathematics with Applications.* Special Issue on Symmetry (Part 1) (January-April), 12B (1/2).

Hargittai, István. 1986b. *Computers & Mathematics with Applications.* Special Issue on Symmetry (Part 2) (May-August), 12B (3/4).

Kapraff, Jay. 1986. "A Course in the Mathematics of Design." *Computers & Mathematics with Applications.* Special Issue on Symmetry (Part 2) (May–August), 12B (3/4): 913–48. See also Kapraff, Jay. 1990. *Connection: The Geometric Bridge between Art and Science.* New York: McGraw-Hill.

Klein, Peter. 1990. "On Symmetry in Science Education." *Symmetry: Culture and Science* 1 (1): 77–91.

Mackay, Alan L. 1986. "But What Is Symmetry?" *Computers & Mathematics with Applications.* Special Issue on Symmetry (Part 1) (January–April), 12B (1/2): 19–20.

Richards, Donald G. 1996. "The Meaning and Relevance of 'Synthesis' in Interdisciplinary Studies." *Journal of General Education* 45 (2): 114–28.

Van Fraassen, Bas C. 1989. *Laws and Symmetry.* Oxford: Clarendon.

ADDITIONAL RESOURCES

Besides the References and the wealth of information that can be found on the World Wide Web, the following are some additional resources on the topic of symmetry:

Aihara, Jun-ichi. 1992. "Why Aromatic Compounds Are Stable." *Scientific American* 266 (3): 62–68.

Bevlin, Marjorie Elliott. 1980. *Design Through Discovery.* Brief Edition. New York: Holt, Rinehart and Winston.

Budden, F. J. 1972. *The Fascination of Groups.* New York: Cambridge University Press.

Cook, Theodore Andrea. 1979. *The Curves of Life.* New York: Dover.

Curl, Robert F., and Richard E. Smalley. 1991. "Fullerenes." *Scientific American* 265 (4): 54–63.

Escher, M. C. 1960. *The Graphic Work of M. C. Escher.* Translated by John E. Brigham. New York: Ballantine.

Field, Michael, and Martin Golubitsky. 1992. *Symmetry in Chaos: A Search for Pattern in Mathematics, Art and Nature.* New York: Oxford University Press.

Forman, Paul. 1982. "The Fall of Parity." *The Physics Teacher* 20 (5): 281–88.

Hofstadter, Douglas R. 1980. *Godel, Escher, Bach: An Eternal Golden Braid.* New York: Vintage.

Huntley, H. E. 1970. *The Divine Proportion: A Study in Mathematical Beauty.* New York: Dover.

Judson, Horace Freeland. 1980. *The Search for Solutions.* New York: Holt, Rinehart and Winston.

Kornberg, Warren, ed. 1985. "Symmetries and Asymmetries." *Mosaic* 16 (January/February). [The entire issue is devoted to symmetry.]

Montgomery, Robert L., Jr. 1969. *Symmetry and Sense: The Poetry of Sir Philip Sidney.* New York: Greenwood.

Nelson, David R. 1986. "Quasicrystals." *Scientific American* 255 (2): 42–51.

Oster, Gerald. 1969. *The Science of Moire Patterns.* Barrington, N.J.: Edmund Scientific Co.

Schattschneider, Doris, and Wallace Walker. 1977. *M. C. Escher Kaleidocycles.* New York: Ballantine.

Shubnikov, A. V., and V. A. Koptsik. 1974. *Symmetry in Science and Art.* Translated by G. D. Archard. New York: Plenum.

Thompson, D'Arcy Wentworth. 1966. *On Growth and Form.* New York: Cambridge University Press.

Weyl, Hermann. 1952. *Symmetry.* Princeton, N.J.: Princeton University Press.

Wigner, Eugene P. 1967. *Symmetries and Reflections.* Bloomington: Indiana University Press.

In addition, a variety of films on symmetry are available (both 16 mm. and VHS); I am grateful to A. Rosenberg, emeritus professor from Swarthmore College, for bringing some of these to my attention.

SEEING THROUGH SYMMETRY: SAMPLE SYLLABUS

In this integrative course, symmetry is used as a basic concept through which many aspects of the scientific and artistic worlds can be better understood and appreciated. The course begins by illustrating pleasing patterns in the sciences and arts. This leads to a general definition of symmetry, which is then characterized using elementary mathematical notions and explored through examples of symmetry in art and architecture as well as in poetry and music. Finally, the existence of symmetry is demonstrated in chemistry, biology, physics, and cosmology. A brief excursion into asymmetry concludes the course. (Lab course.) (Emphasis on written and oral communication and critical thinking.)

Goals: Students will discover that the world is an integrated structure; use concepts such as reflectional, rotational, translational, and exchange symmetry to understand aspects of art, poetry, and music; and, coupling those concepts with rudiments of scientific methodology, explore aspects of science and technology such as DNA, group theory, and computer algorithms (which, in turn, feeds back further insights to the former subjects).

Texts: Laurence I. Gould, *Notes and Labs for Seeing Through Symmetry* (©1991–1999, under development as a book); Phares G. O'Daffer and Stanley R. Clemens, *Geometry: An Investigative Approach* (1992).

Topics:

Symmetry in Nature and in Art: An Overview

Building Blocks for Symmetry: Points, Polygons, and Philosophy

Tessellating Space: Constructions in the Plane, Diversions in Space

Symmetry Patterns in Flatland: Translations, Rotations, Reflections, . . . Escher!

Patterns of Motions in the Physical World: Sliding, Turning, Flipping, and the Theory of Groups

Rhyme and Reason: Patterns in Poetry and Music

Regularities in Waves: From Water Through Sound . . . to Light and Chance!

Symmetry Through Space and Time: Projectiles and Planets

Symmetry in Spacetime: Black Holes and the Cosmos

Coordination in Chemical Structures, Crystals, and Life

Labs: Computer Drawing: Reflections, Rotations, and Designs; Learning Algorithms Through the Language of Logo; Drawing and Hearing Patterns: Polygonal Symmetry and Fibonnaci Tones; Intricacies of Coloration: Coordinates, Translations, Groups, and Tessellations; Patterns in Music: Sound and Sight; Experiencing Motion in Space and Time; Symmetry of Oscillations: Sine Waves and Sound; Building Symmetry From Symmetry: The Fourier Spectrum; Waviness: In Water and Light; On Balls and Bombs: The Geometry of Projectile Motion; Bounced, Flipped, Rotated, and Decomposed Light: From Mirrors to Spectra; "Slipping" Symmetry: Crystals, Fractals, and Chaos; The Ambidextrous World of Light; Symmetry Broken: Chaos and Fractals . . . and the World of Elementary Particles.

Additional Student Activities: Museum report; term project with class presentation (often linking course concepts to student's major).

WHAT IS SCIENCE?

Doug Dix, Regina Miller, Mike Horn, and Dale Brown

Although much is written about science and the need for reform in science education, there is little in the way of definition. It is as if that definition were common knowledge. We profess that it isn't, and suggest that much of what is commonly portrayed as science isn't. In our course on Reasoning in Science, we explore the disciplines to discover what they have in common and how they are distinct. How does science compare and contrast with religion, music, art, and the humanities? What defines science?

QUESTIONS

Experts representing "the informed thinking of the scientific community as nearly as such a thing can be ascertained" define the purpose of science education as helping "students to develop the understandings and habits of mind they need to become compassionate human beings able to think for themselves" (Rutherford and Ahlgren 1990, xv, v). This is a fine-sounding definition, but it isn't accurate. Compassion isn't taught in science courses, and thinking for oneself is more characteristic of courses in the arts and humanities. Even science majors find science courses dull (National Science Teachers Association 1997a, 15) and even the National Research Council (1990, 2) realizes that "something is profoundly wrong" with science education.

On the one hand experts espouse compassion and independent thinking, but on the other they measure science achievement by content knowledge (Rutherford and Ahlgren 1990, vii; National Science Teachers Association 1997b, 45; Stedman 1997a, 4; Baker 1997, 16; Bracey 1997, 19; Stedman 1997b, 27). On the one hand they argue that "Scientific habits of mind can help people in every walk of life" (Rutherford and Ahlgren 1990, vi), but on the other they focus science courses on topics—for example, the solar system, periodic chart, genetic code, photosynthesis—that many find irrelevant to their walks of life. The most important question—"Why should I study science?"—is typically unacknowledged, unanswered, or answered incorrectly. As a result, students reject science before they even come to know what it is.

We suggest that science is

- motivated by a passion for truth
- an antidote to dogma, deceit, and delusion
- born out of curiosity, pervaded by doubt, governed by data, and stifled by agreement
- ethical
- rebellious
- rooted in instinctive behavior

Unfortunately, science courses tend to inhibit the scientific instinct. Passionate inquiry is routinely submerged beneath a tide of content knowledge (National Research Council 1990; Yager 1993; American Association for the Advancement of Science 1993; Colburn and Clough 1997). "Science is about things—objects and their relations—that must be known before process can be applied to problems of real interest. . . . In the absence of content, process is just another intellectual toy" (Arch 1998). We disagree. Science *is* process, the process of exploration and discovery. We can find all or part of the scientific process operating in disciplines other than science and, conversely, we can often fail to find all or part of the scientific process operating in so-called scientific disciplines. Writing poetry, for instance, is about hypothesis and experiment and rehypothesis. Learning biology, on the other hand, is too often about rote memorization.

Natural science is natural. Just as geese and caribou know how to migrate, humans know how to explore. You can see this in preschoolers. Investigation is coded in their genes. No one teaches or pushes them, yet they work tirelessly and call it play (Montessori 1964; Elkind 1993). But by third grade many begin to lose interest, and by high school too many are apathetic. In the course of "education," children's authentic instinct for inquiry is too often replaced by ulterior motives. The dominant concern of nonscience majors in a required science course is the grade. Under such circumstances they are incapable of playing. We try to change the circumstances by challenging each student to be free and authentic as they were as preschoolers.

We ask our students to study children, to appreciate their instinct for inquiry, and to remember being curious themselves. Can they get that authentic curiosity back? Where would it take them? What would they like to become? What quality would they most want to find within themselves and within their own children? For Coles (1997), the answer is kindness, which seems strangely similar to the experts' definition of science education. Can we achieve kindness or compassion by cultivating our natural instinct for inquiry?

REASONING IN SCIENCE

"It just may be that counterrevolutionary, old-time lecture hall education is still with us after all these centuries because . . . it's still the best thing anyone has yet invented" (Arch 1998). We disagree. Preschool is the best, and our course operates something like an old-time Montessori preschool. We begin each class by asking who wants to begin. Typically, at least in the beginning, no student answers. So one of us will begin with a story that leads to a question or moral. Storytelling is among the most ancient and enjoyable human activities (Coles 1989) and the essence of research (Smith 1997). We ask, "What do you think?" and focus on the process of thinking. How do we use definitions, assumptions, logic, and data? How do we know when conclusions are and are not warranted? Gradually the undergraduates begin their own stories and class becomes a show-and-tell session. Because we draw students from all disciplines except the sciences, these stories consist of art, music, poetry, sport, travel, politics, philosophy, biography, etc. In all cases, we probe the reasoning process, asking, in particular, what is and isn't science? Our purpose is to promote the passion and the skills and attitudes—confidence, questioning, experimentation, perseverance, collaboration—that facilitate discovery.

We begin with music in part for its shock value. No one expects to study music in a course on science. But research is about discovering the unexpected (Kuhn 1970), so we do the unexpected. And we begin with music in part for its power to capture our minds independently of reason and in part because it is pleasant and ever present (Bloom 1987). Beethoven's Sixth Symphony (1806) and Stravinsky's *Rite of Spring* (1913) are antagonistic expressions of a similar theme. We discuss the themes and the history and philosophy of music and mention Stravinsky's criticism of Beethoven (Stravinsky 1936). Which philosophy, Beethoven's or Stravinsky's, is more valid? Which music is better? The students are quick to conclude that there is no absolute scale by which to measure music. They see nothing perverted in one orchestra performing both pieces even on the same program.

From music we move to religion, not only for its shock value but for the point that opinions can matter. Which religion is correct? It is not a trivial question. We recall the history of religious war and persecution. But religious answers are a matter of faith. Typically children inherit this faith from their parents. It isn't based on reason or data, but on authority—parents and clergy. The faithful call it virtue. Scientists call it bias. By either definition, integrity matters. The same parents and clergy cannot espouse different religions without loss of integrity. But, when all is said and done, we are left with the question: Which religion is correct?

After music and religion, we turn to science. What is it? How is it similar to and different from music and religion? We shock the class with the idea that science is a religion. Believing correctly is essential. But which belief is correct is a matter of faith. Learning science is like learning catechism. Science teachers are like clergy. They teach children what to believe not by reason or data but by authority. Perhaps students resent science because it is not their religion and yet it is forced upon them in violation of religious freedom.

We ask whether the sun moves around the earth or vice versa. They say it is the earth that moves. The sun is still. They know this for a fact. They learned it in third grade and every grade since. We ask how they know. Do they not see the sun rise in the east and ride like a golden chariot across the sky? Do they not feel the earth to be still? What reasons justify their betrayal of sensory experience? Not one undergraduate has ever offered a cogent argument to support his or her beliefs in the operation of the solar system. Such faith is based on the authority of science teachers who act like clergy.

We assault with reason: If the earth were moving as they believe, would there not be a constant wind in a constant direction? How fast do they believe the earth to be moving? One rotation per day. If the earth is, as reported, 24,000 miles in circumference at the equator, that would be 24,000 miles per 24 hours or 1,000 miles per hour. Imagine a wind of 1,000 miles per hour. How can the earth be rotating so fast if there is no wind at all? And if the earth were rotating, why would people fly to distant locations? Why not simply hover (helicopter) and let the world slide underneath until landing on the desired spot? Of course, there are scientific answers for these questions, but the students don't know them. They enjoy the challenge and laugh but offer no defense for their beliefs. Their beliefs are not based on reason, but on faith.

We suggest that our students ask preschoolers about the sun and earth. Which do the children say is moving? Should we teach children to believe what doesn't make sense? Should we call such teaching science? How is it different from brainwashing? Is it any wonder that children learn to resent science? Is it any wonder they stop exploring when they lose confidence in their senses?

We demonstrate a different scenario: Imagine a preschool class. Bring a coconut for the children to explore. Ask them to look at it carefully, noticing its shape and color and texture; to feel it, noticing its texture and weight; and to smell it, noticing that when unopened it has no odor. Ask them to notice that it is a quiet thing and that it doesn't move by itself. Shake the coconut. What is that noise? Some child will answer that there is water or milk in the coconut. Deny this. State emphatically that there is no liquid in the coconut. Ask the children to agree with this statement. Search for dissenters, point them out to the class, and ask them pointedly to conform. Tower over these children and tell them of your own importance. Insist that they conform. Here is a true David-Goliath controversy. How can it be resolved? Let the children *think*. One of them will suggest opening the coconut. Notice that no one has to teach children how to think. Use the word "experiment" to describe the opening of the coconut. Be astonished at the discovery and admit defeat. Congratulate the nonconformists. Let them bask in peer admiration. They are champions at science. Let all the children see the power of reason to overthrow authority, even Goliath authority.

This is the great science lesson. Remember it, repeat it, reinforce it. Give the children unshelled peanuts and ask them to explore the peanuts in the manner of the coconut. What is that sound? Be careful. Do not open the shell. There is water in there. What? Yes, there is water in the peanut and it will get you soaking wet. Do not open the shell. Let the kids rebel and prove you wrong again. Repeat the process with almonds.

Is this good teaching? What do the children learn? What should we call this sort of teaching? Clearly it isn't art or religion. Diverging opinions are not valid, and faith in these circumstances is no virtue. If we call this critical thinking, this testing of answers by means of experiment, science, then we must recognize the antagonistic relationship it bears to that other catechism-like learning called science. The same teachers cannot espouse both forms of science without loss of integrity. Which should they espouse? Which will yield compassionate, independent thinkers?

We discuss Plato's cave allegory (*The Republic*, Book VII), and ask students to look at their classroom. Are they chained to face front? What prevents them from turning their chairs to see the light streaming through the back windows? Winslow Homer thought the important lessons were in nature, not school (Flexner 1966, 26). See his painting *The Country School*. Is he right? Should we look more to nature for our education, at least for our science education?

Scientific discoveries are paradigm changes (Kuhn 1970). Science education should be about preparing to change, preparing to refuse convention, to rebel against history, to create, invent, or discover something new and better. But change is as important to the arts and humanities as it is to science. What is uniquely scientific? Measurement, the means by which we reject hypotheses. Conformity to a rejected or untested hypothesis is bias. Science, therefore, is a means to separate bias from truth.

Consider the Gettysburg Address. Appreciate the hypothesis: "The world will little note, nor long remember, what we say here, but it can never forget what they did here." Is that so? Do the experiment. Ask students what they remember of the battle and of the address. Which do they remember? Many will know, or guess correctly, the outcome, but few will know when the battle occurred or the names of combatants, the manner of fighting, or the cost, or consequence. The truth is that what was done at Gettysburg is largely forgotten. Yet the words are immortal. Everyone takes note of them, and many memorize them without even realizing that the prophecy has been proved false. Science is about separating true from false. The Gettysburg Address is an opportunity to see not only how science differs from politics and rhetoric but to appreciate the role of science in the most important matters of daily life. Should we die or kill for political prophecy, or should we demand first to see truth beyond some reasonable doubt? Which option will more likely yield "compassionate human beings able to think for themselves"?

THE EXPERIMENTAL METHOD

Poetry

We ask students to create poems and, in the process, to notice how they experiment with words, rhyme, rhythm, and meaning. Most resist, but those who try are often surprised by the interesting, even beautiful, results. We discuss these eureka moments that testify to the reality of inspiration and luck and convey a sense of science process.

But there is another, more important, lesson: Poems without passion, even if mechanically correct, are shallow and defeat the very purpose of poetry, which is to express passion. Science is like that, "raw passions . . . are the essential ingredient" (150th Essay Committee 1998). Without passion, students may go through the motions of science, they may weigh, mix, pour, shake, incubate, and read the various meters, but they cannot experience the process of science. To do that, they must genuinely want a true answer to a question that matters.

Measurement

The best rock and the peanut butter experiments (see the Appendix) are designed to force confrontation between measurable and unmeasurable criteria. Here is a student response to the best rock and peanut butter experiments:

> *The best rock experiment seemed like an exercise in futility. But I think now it is a lot like my discovery project. It is completely subjective and not at all grounded in the truth. The scientific truth is measurable, and in the best rock experiment, we had no agreed-upon measure of best. Everyone had their own criteria. The result was anarchy. When an agreed-upon measure is used, it is possible to come to the truth. For example, if we had decided that the best rock was the heaviest, we could have easily agreed whose was the best. There is no room for dispute on scientific measure. Two pounds is two pounds. The only thing you can argue is the method of measurement, whether the scale was calibrated correctly, etc. But since we have all agreed that a pound is this much, we can measure by that standard. A standard is needed to scientifically judge the best. But in the peanut butter experiment, we weren't looking for the best, scientific or otherwise. We were told to pick our favorite. And that's a word that has certain connotations. We're all very used to the fact that our personal favorite is not necessarily someone else's too . . . I did learn that subjectivity has no place in science. Science is about the objective truth. What we accept as truth is a whole other issue. Science can only measure in terms of what we as a society agree on as standards. . . . I think I get it.*

Discovery

In discovery projects, students design and conduct their own experiments. Here is a response from the same student:

I had a brainstorm for a possible topic. I'm thinking of investigating in what situations people accept a statement and in what ones they question it. I've noticed that sometimes people believe what they hear without questioning the validity of it and other times they refuse to listen to that information because they believe differently. Other times they listen carefully and then question the information and go off to do some research to find out if it's true or not. I am curious about what makes the difference. Is it only in how the information is presented? Is it true that you can get some people to believe anything if you only tell them in the right tone of voice? I can imagine designing an experiment around this question.

CONCLUSION

When students are coerced, their performance is determined largely by their vulnerability. Students who cannot afford less than an A will jump through hoops to get the grade. Does the A then mean they are excellent students? Or does it mean simply that they jumped as directed? In content courses, jumping as directed can have merit, but science is about process, and the process is manifested by refusing to jump as directed. We cannot cultivate refusal skills by coercing obedience.

Coercion breeds resistance and creates an adversarial student-teacher relationship (Glasser 1992). Students conceal their weaknesses in an effort to fool their teachers. Integrity is irrelevant. How many students worry that their grades may be too high? Coercion has convinced them that education is a game, that teachers are their opponents. As long as they don't violate the rules—or as long as they aren't caught—everything is fair. This attitude is appropriate to boxing or football but it is artificial and incompatible with natural science. Students can learn this by struggling with freedom, by struggling to be honest. Nothing is more important to scientific reasoning (Gunsalus 1997; Vandervoort 1997).

Integrity determines what questions we choose to pursue and in what order (Bloom 1998). The authentic answer requires an honest appraisal of natural curiosity, a weighing of costs and benefits, and an examination of consciences. This is where compassion and independent thinking play their roles. Should sequencing the genome or exploring Mars take precedence over providing adequate food and shelter to all children? The answer determines whether children suffer or not. This struggle to *see* is akin to art and should dominate science education, but it doesn't, because ulterior motives get in the way. People find employment sequencing the genome and exploring Mars, with the result that our natural sense of priority becomes irrelevant. People do science as a profession and the questions they pursue are determined more by profit than curiosity. These questions and answers then become the content of textbooks. Under coercion, students learn to recognize these questions and answers as important. Professional science is portrayed as the model for children (D. Kuhn 1997; Metz 1997). But it would be better if "professional science" were more authentic, more like preschool. Accepting bribes—money or grades—to do what isn't authentically interesting is scientific misconduct. To prevent misconduct and enhance compassionate independent thinking, students need to become nonconformists (Emerson 1926). And that is why they should study science.

Benson (1982) has summarized some criticisms of interdisciplinary courses. First, what does it mean to connect the disciplines? What is the value of making those connections? Is there some substantial bond that is established between the different disciplines?

We suggest that science is the instinctive process of inquiry and that it is similar in all disciplines that involve inquiry. The poet and painter use the same process of trial and error as the physicist. We can study reasoning in science by considering hypotheses and experiments about rhythm and rhyme, or color and perspective, or matter and energy. The difference is that science culminates in objective measurement, and as long as the measurement doesn't change, it can be considered true. In this sense, science is a search for truth, objective truth that is independent of time and personality. The laws of buoyancy and gravity and thermodynamics are evidence that such truth exists.

Second, Benson argues that it is premature to pursue interdisciplinary study before the student acquires competence in one or more disciplines. However exhilarating the discussion, interdisciplinary study has little of substance to offer the undisciplined student. As a result, interdisciplinary studies are superficial and devoid of lasting benefit. "Under the guise of an invitation to wrestle with what are frequently fascinating and important issues, the student is cheated of a precious opportunity to develop the skills and background required for mounting a proper attack on the issues" (1982, 42).

We suggest that science is a refusal skill that can protect students from becoming too disciplined. It is important that they hone this skill *before* being brainwashed in the name of discipline.

Third, in Benson's view, interdisciplinary studies "are characteristically shallow, trading intellectual rigor for topical excitement" (1982, 45).

We suggest that science, when taught using methods of independent study or thesis research, helps students become nonconformists and "develop the understandings and habits of mind they need to become compassionate human beings able to think for themselves" (Rutherford and Ahlgren 1990, v).

Acknowledgment: This work was supported in part by U.S. Department of Health and Human Services award 90CD1113/02. The authors are grateful to University of Hartford faculty members Sue Buckley, Pat Cohen, Larry Gould, Jane Horvath, Marcia Seabury, and Jay Stewart, to the Hartford Head Start staff, and to our students and their parents.

APPENDIX

Readings

The following are our major sources of discovery stories. Faculty from any discipline can enjoy these stories and tell them to students. In this way, students can be inspired to discover and to tell their own discovery stories to each other and to children.

The Making of the Atomic Bomb by Richard Rhodes (Simon and Schuster 1986) won several book awards including the Pulitzer Prize. It is filled with history and philosophy as well as physics and forces the question of who should control the uses of science. It fits perfectly with books on Hiroshima.

The Dancing Wu Li Masters, An Overview of the New Physics by Gary Zukav (Bantam Books 1979) is an interesting description of quantum physics and relativity with philosophical and theological implications.

Mathematics, The Loss of Certainty by Morris Kline (Oxford University Press 1980) is an extremely interesting history with references to Pythagoras, Plato, Aristotle, Archimedes, Euclid, Ptolemy, Aristarchus, Eratosthenes, Copernicus, Kepler, Descartes, Pascal, Galileo, Newton, and the Non-Euclideans and excellent examples of paradigms.

Microbe Hunters by Paul de Kruif (Harcourt Brace 1954) is a collection of inspiring essays on some of the most dramatic discoveries in medicine, with excellent examples of hypothesis-experiment relationships.

The Mismeasure of Man by Stephen Jay Gould (Norton 1996) is, perhaps, the best description of the role of bias in scientific research.

The Statue Within, An Autobiography by Francois Jacob (Basic Books 1988) is, perhaps, the best description of the role of luck in scientific research.

The penicillin story as told, for example, in *Alexander Fleming: The Man and the Myth* by Gwyn Macfarlane (Hogarth Press 1984), is an excellent example of failing to see the obvious.

Experiments

The following experiments are suitable for students of every age:

1. To demonstrate the difference between subjective and objective reasoning, ask students to bring their favorite stick (or rock or flower or leaf) to class and prove to the class that it is the best. The result will be unresolvable controversy. Next, ask students to determine which stick is longest (or shortest or heaviest or lightest). There will be unanimity. Ask why. What is the difference between asking which is longest and which is best? When we ask which is best, there is no agreement on how to measure best and no agreement in the conclusion. When we ask which is longest, everyone agrees on how to measure length and there is unanimity in the conclusion. This is a good opportunity to point out that science is our means to unanimity and that unanimity is

our stated goal: *E Pluribus Unum*. We achieve unanimity by finding measurements that do not change.

2. To demonstrate the power of bias, show students unopened jars of brand-name, creamy-style peanut butter. Ask them to identify in writing their favorite brand. Then conceal the labels with paper and ask the students to identify in writing which of the number-coded, paper-covered jars is their favorite. Provide plain crackers and water to facilitate taste testing. Be sure all jars are of identical size. In our experience, the vast majority of students have strong opinions on their favorite but are unable to distinguish their so-called favorite in the blind taste test. And they tend to enjoy this experiment and to be quite impressed with the results. This is an excellent opportunity to discuss the role of bias in everyday life and the power of science, e.g., in blind taste testing, to overcome bias. But beware of food allergies and always elicit appropriate informed consent.

3. To demonstrate the tendency to overgeneralize, bring a rabbit to class and ask the students to determine its favorite food. No doubt they will place dishes with different foods in the cage, and, after some period of time, declare the dish with the least food to be the favorite. Does the result demonstrate the rabbit's favorite food? Perhaps the results would be different tomorrow or the day after. How often would the experiment need to be performed to demonstrate the favorite? Does the result apply to rabbits in general? How many rabbits would need to be sampled to generalize the conclusion? Perhaps the rabbit's favorite food was not among the choices. This is an animal experiment and an opportunity to discuss animal rights. Did the rabbit enjoy this experiment? Should we do experiments that animals do not enjoy? If so, under what circumstances?

4. To demonstrate a paradigm and the power of science to overthrow authority, ask students to classify groceries into fruits and vegetables. The edible roots, stems, leaves, flowers, and seeds are clearly vegetables. Some seed packages, e.g., apples, pears, peaches, plums, and nectarines, are clearly fruits. But what of the tomatoes, cucumbers, squash, melons, nuts with shells, and peas and beans in pods? Are they vegetables as the grocer says? How do they differ from the fruits? How are they similar to the other vegetables? What are vegetables? What are fruits? What definitions make sense? Why are groceries classified as they are?

5. To demonstrate imprecision in definition, display a loaf of Italian bread. It is common to find the words "authentic" and "freshly baked" on the package. Ask what it means to be Italian. What is Italian opera? What are Italian shoes, cars, violins, etc.? The students will agree that Italian things are made in Italy. Is the bread made in Italy? Is it authentic? The so-called Italian bread is really American bread baked, perhaps, in an Italian tradition. It isn't difficult to find other foods that are labeled similarly, such as English muffins, commonly made in America.

6. To demonstrate unsupported claims, show a bottle of Frank's Original Red Hot Cayenne Pepper Sauce. The label claims this product has been "America's favorite for over 75 years." Is that true? No evidence is offered to support this claim, and it is difficult to imagine how such evidence could be collected.

REFERENCES

150th Essay Committee. 1998. "Passionate Science." *Science* 282: 1821.

American Association for the Advancement of Science. 1993. *Benchmarks for Science Literacy.* New York: Oxford University Press.

Arch, Stephen. 1998. "How to Teach Science." *Science* 279: 1869.

Baker, David P. 1997. "Good News, Bad News, and International Comparisons: Comment on Bracey." *Educational Researcher* 26: 16–17.

Benson, Thomas. 1982. "Five Arguments against Interdisciplinary Studies." *Issues in Integrative Studies* 1: 38–48.

Bloom, Allan. 1987. *The Closing of the American Mind: How Higher Education Has Failed Democracy and Impoverished the Souls of Today's Students.* New York: Simon and Schuster.

Bloom, Floyd. 1998. "Priority Setting: Quixotic or Essential." *Science* 282: 1641.

Bracey, Gerald W. 1997. "On Comparing the Incomparable: A Response to Baker and Stedman." *Educational Researcher* 26: 19–25.

Colburn, Alan, and Michael P. Clough. 1997. "Implementing the Learning Cycle, A Gradual Transition to a New Teaching Approach." *Science Teacher* 64: 30–33.

Coles, Robert. 1989. *The Call of Stories, Teaching and the Moral Imagination.* Boston: Houghton Mifflin.

Coles, Robert. 1997. *The Moral Intelligence of Children.* New York: Random House.

Elkind, David. 1993. *Miseducation: Preschoolers at Risk.* New York: Knopf.

Emerson, Ralph Waldo. 1926. "Self-Reliance." In *Essays by Ralph Waldo Emerson.* New York: Thomas Crowell.

Flexner, John Thomas. 1966. *The World of Winslow Homer 1836–1910.* New York: New York Times.

Glasser, William. 1992. *The Quality School: Managing Students Without Coercion.* New York: HarperCollins.

Gunsalus, C. K. 1997. "Ethics: Sending Out the Message." *Science* 276: 335.

Kuhn, Deanna. 1997. "Constraints or Guideposts? Developmental Psychology and Science Education." *Review of Educational Research* 67: 141–50.

Kuhn, Thomas S. 1970. *The Structure of Scientific Revolutions.* Chicago: University of Chicago Press.

Metz, Kathleen E. 1997. "On the Complex Relation Between Cognitive Developmental Research and Children's Science Curricula." *Review of Educational Research* 67: 151–63.

Montessori, Maria. 1964. *The Montessori Method.* New York: Schocken.

National Research Council. 1990. *Fulfilling the Promise: Biology Education in the Nation's Schools.* Washington, D.C.: National Academy Press.

National Science Teachers Association. April 1997a. "Poor College Teaching Turns Students Off to Sciences." *NSTA Reports.*

National Science Teachers Association. April 1997b. "NSF Survey Finds Americans Don't Know Science Basics." *NSTA Reports.*

Rutherford, James F., and Andrew Ahlgren. 1990. *Science for All Americans.* New York: Oxford University Press.

Smith, John K. 1997. "The Stories Educational Researchers Tell About Themselves." *Educational Researcher* 26: 4–11.

Stedman, Lawrence C. 1997a. "International Achievement Differences: An Assessment of a New Perspective." *Educational Researcher* 26: 4–15.

Stedman, Lawrence C. 1997b. "Deep Achievement Problems: The Case for Reform Still Stands." *Educational Researcher* 26: 27–28.

Stravinsky, Igor. 1936. *Chronicle of My Life.* London: Gollancz.

Vandervoort, Frances S. 1997. "Scientific Integrity." *American Biology Teacher* 56: 72.

Yager, Robert E., ed. 1993. *The Science, Technology, Society Movement.* Washington, D.C.: National Science Teachers Association.

REASONING IN SCIENCE: SAMPLE SYLLABUS

This integrative course relates fundamental concepts from the history, philosophy, and sociology of science to concepts in science and mathematics. Comparison and contrast of the process of discovery in different disciplines is combined with the actual practice of experimental observation. Topics in class and in laboratory encourage the exercise of higher-level thinking skills. (Lab course.) (Emphasis on written communication and critical thinking.)

Goals: This course focuses more on the question "How do scientists know?" than on "What do scientists know?" Students will develop an understanding of scientific method and apply it to a variety of content. They will improve their abilities to observe, think abstractly, solve problems, and think about their own thinking; learn that science is a human enterprise firmly embedded in the culture; and learn to detect pseudoscience and to distinguish between argument and assertion. They will suspect ulterior motives, question what they are taught, appreciate the value of uncertainty, and awaken to the importance of scientific reasoning in enhancing our public and private lives.

Texts: Packet of articles from journals, newspapers, magazines; discovery stories drawn from sources such as those listed in the Appendix to this chapter; varied materials to enrich student projects.

Topics (developed in collaboration with students):

Science as Catechism or as Process

Instinctive Inquiry; Children as Scientists; How Are Professional Scientists Similar or Different?

Seeing What We Take for Granted (asking good questions)

Subjective and Objective Reasoning

Bias

Science as Rebellion Against Authority

Theory Versus Experiment; Guessing Answers and Testing Guesses

Data: Kinds; Quality; Reproducibility; Reasoning in the Face of Incomplete Data

Laws of Nature; Truth; Changes in Knowledge

Discovery Stories Across the Centuries and Across the Disciplines: Similarities and Differences

Selected Student Activities: Volunteering in Hartford Head Start classrooms (federal preschool program for low-income families); labs, developing skills of observation, hypothesis building, experimentation (see examples in the Appendix to this chapter); individual "discovery projects" in consultation with instructor, often linking student's major to course concepts; ongoing e-mail with instructors about research projects.

PART II
FRAMING ISSUES AND DEALING WITH PROBLEMS

DEALING WITH MULTIPLE PERSPECTIVES

Parts I and II of this volume discuss closely related challenges. As Neil Browne emphasized during a workshop at the University of Hartford, in critical thinking both attitudes and skills are essential: students need to develop the desire to ask tough questions as well as to acquire and use evaluative criteria to address them. As with active engagement, issues of interdisciplinarity and critical thinking often intersect, accompanied in classroom practice by multiple ironies and challenges.

Critical thinking has been defined in a wide variety of ways and in any case covers a huge array of mental activities. In a committee report 10 years ago, faculty at the University of Hartford outlined various aspects of inductive and deductive reasoning to be developed through interdisciplinary courses. But the problems explored in the courses that emerged typically do not lend themselves to clear-cut solutions via such logic; a key goal of many of these courses is to teach students to think well about complex issues. One way in which the languages of interdisciplinary study and critical thinking most clearly intersect is in their mutual emphasis on developing the ability to look at such issues through multiple perspectives.[1]

Even as habits of passivity and obeisance to disciplinary experts impede students' question-asking, as discussed in Part I, the further habits of holding tightly to preconceptions and distancing oneself ("Yes, it is a problem, but it's not my problem") impede students' wrestling with difficult issues. The authors in Part II explore approaches that help students bring to light, examine, and critique assumptions and try out and evaluate other ways of seeing. Through such approaches students relate social problems to their own lives: for example, seeing power not just as something "they" wield but as something "we" wield as well, encountering hunger not just in the third world but in our own cities, and putting a human face on the statistics of AIDS.

But a metaphor invoked here deserves note: wrestling. In a traditional model of critical thinking an individual wrestles face-to-face with a problem, learning to define it, select pertinent information, recognize assumptions, formulate hypotheses, and draw valid conclusions (Dressel and Mayhew 1954, 179–80). Recent scholars, however, increasingly emphasize the context within which a problem is set, and thus the importance of teaching critical thinking skills within disciplinary contexts (see the summary in Kurfiss 1988, 19–20; cf. Meyers 1986). As scholars increasingly view discovery and argument as social processes, references to conversation, both literal and figurative, abound—"Argumentation is a *dialogue*" (Kurfiss 1988, 22). Graff (1992) urges that we introduce students to a more social model of knowledge based on ideas and disciplinary approaches in conversation with each other rather than only to the traditional teacher-thinker-in-monologue model. Applebee, in *Curriculum as Conversation*, argues similarly that teachers should help students to gain "knowledge-in-action" through "participation in ongoing conversations about things that matter, conversations that are themselves embedded within larger traditions of discourse," thereby approaching knowledge as "socially negotiated through the process of conversation itself" both spoken and written (1996, 3, 40).

In the light of this more social model of critical thinking, team-taught interdisciplinary courses such as those described in Part II are particularly appropriate. They can create something of the effect of a symposium or think tank as faculty from different disciplines negotiate their way through a problem together and invite students to participate in the process. People have always wrestled and will always wrestle with problems as individuals, as will the student coming out of a class on AIDS and deciding whether to buy a condom. But people wrestle as teams as well, through tough conversations on AIDS policy. When faculty colleagues challenge each other in class they are forced to think out loud with their students, a too-rare phenomenon in academia that encourages students to relate to them as humans rather than as would-be gods (Belenky et al. 1986, 216), get a sense of ideas in action, and learn to construct the various schemas of expert thought (Kurfiss 1988, 42). And of course working on problems in small groups, as described for example in the essay by Smith and her coauthors, gives students important practice with knowledge-in-action.

Readers interested in further discussions of interdisciplinarity and critical thinking might consult Hursh, Haas, and Moore, who trace the emphasis on dealing with multiple perspectives back through Dewey (1933, 1938), Piaget (Inhelder and Piaget 1958), and Perry (1968). They summarize Piaget's "cognitive decentering" as

> the intellectual capacity to move beyond a single center or focus (especially the innate tendencies toward egocentrism and ethno- centrism) and consider a variety of other perspectives in a coor- dinated way to perceive reality more accurately, process information more systematically, and solve problems more effec- tively. (1983, 44–45)

With complex problems this move entails a shift among "perspectives, frames of reference, or even disciplines" (1983, 45). More recently, Paul argues that "multilogical thinking," the ability to think "within opposing points of view and contradictory frames of reference," is cen- tral to the concept of the critical person, and that schools need to do more to develop students' ability to recognize and address "multi-sys- tem" issues, such as those discussed in Part II (1990, 109, 561–62). Probing in a similar direction, King and Kitchener focus on "messy" or "ill-structured problems" that "can be neither described with a high degree of completeness nor solved with a high degree of certainty" (King 1992, 4). They approach thinking about such problems as the "outgrowth of a developmental process" and join the Association of American Colleges in emphasizing the responsibility of institutions of higher education to further that process:

> In the final analysis, the challenge of college, for students and fac- ulty members alike, is empowering individuals to know that the world is far more complex than it first appears, and that they must make interpretive arguments and decisions—judgments that entail real consequences for which they must take responsibility

and from which they may not flee by disclaiming expertise. (Association of American Colleges 1991, 16–17, cited in King and Kitchener 1994, 3)

Thus we need to give students ongoing practice in dealing with multiple perspectives.

Theorists of both critical thinking and interdisciplinarity emphasize that this practice entails the central activities of "identifying and challenging assumptions and . . . exploring and imagining alternatives" (Brookfield 1987, 15). Worded even more strongly, "all assumptions are open to question" and "divergent views are aggressively sought" (Kurfiss 1988, 2). Theorists in these areas focus on different optimal results: in the critical thinking literature, a "decision on what to believe or do" or a more complex understanding of the issue, among other possibilities (e.g., Ennis 1985, Meyers 1986, Johnson 1992, respectively); in the interdisciplinary literature, a new synthesis or again a recognition of complexity, with synthesis questioned in terms of both feasibility and desirability as an overarching goal of interdisciplinary general education (e.g., Newell 1990, Richards 1996, respectively; see also Newell 1998). The essays in Part II describe instructional approaches that, like the various situations students will encounter outside the classroom, call for responses all along this spectrum. Some case study approaches yield specific conclusions; courses on hunger or AIDS may yield specific individual or group actions but also emphasize noninstrumental analysis of the multiple dimensions of a problem.

CHALLENGES

Interdisciplinary learning, then, involves processes that critical thinking theorists have been emphasizing for years. A paradox to be faced in the classroom is that critical thinking and interdisciplinary thinking are arts as well as sciences. The authors in Part II have designed a wide variety of activities to encourage particular kinds of thinking. It is possible, and theorists and teachers in both areas have done so, to draw diagrams and flowcharts to describe the learning processes involved. But as Brookfield notes, some of the best insights may arise when faculty and students depart from the plan. *"There is no standard model of facilitating critical thinking,"* "no one way to instructional enlightenment":

> When one considers the bewilderingly complex configuration of capacities represented in a group of individuals, it becomes evident that any closely prescribed pursuit of predetermined, standardized objectives is meaningless for anything other than closely specified instrumental skill learning. . . . It is certainly possible to devise exercises and simulations that are intended to help people become aware of internalized assumptions, scrutinize these critically, and think of alternatives. It is likely, however, that dramatic insights, revelations, and understanding of how knowledge, behaviors, and values are culturally constructed will frequently come unexpectedly to individuals. (1987, 232, 233, 244)

Accepting this paradox requires devising the best case studies, role plays, and so forth that we can to encourage integrative thinking while acknowledging that we cannot and should not expect to control the processes of insight and integration.

A catch here, as with active engagement, is that faculty tend to report a greater commitment to critical thinking than we practice (Paul 1990, Browne and Keeley 1989), as we may likewise do with respect to interdisciplinary thinking. After all, if we model effective integrative thinking, we feel we encourage it in our students. And if we give assignments asking students to compare and synthesize, we feel we help them learn to do so. But familiar routines exert power. We need continually to resist the gravitational pulls on both ourselves and our students back to traditional lecture/reception modes and discipline-bound thinking. Doherty et al. point to the limited awareness many faculty have of the burgeoning literatures on intellectual skill building and ask pragmatically how much of that awareness would be necessary to make a difference for students (1997, 182–83). Similarly, most faculty will not read volumes of interdisciplinary theory, but without some conscious awareness of interdisciplinary approaches, the pull into serial disciplinary approaches can hold sway, with synthesis expected but not sufficiently coached.

Another practical irony in developing critical thinking through interdisciplinary conversations—"teaching the conflicts" in Graff's terms—is that it can be hard to get faculty members with conflicting views into the classroom together or to keep them there (even as it is with faculty with potentially provocative differences of personality or pedagogy). In meetings one may hear wonderful arguments between a sociologist and a biologist with differing viewpoints about the dynamics of the history of science; in the hallway one may hear why instructor X will not, or will no longer, teach with instructor Y because their approaches to the subject are too different. Students should have the opportunity to hear just those sorts of disagreements and add their voices to the discussion. It could be exciting for them. But amidst the demands of teaching, scholarship, and service, confronting friendly adversaries three times a week is more than many faculty want to take on.

OVERVIEW

All the essays in Part II discuss issue- or problem-based courses. The courses begin with what the instructors themselves consider to be problems and help students to see what is at stake, thus taking into interdisciplinary sites procedures Meyers recommends to develop motivation and critical thinking within a discipline (1986, 47). In the lead essay, Ralph Aloisi, Karen Barrett, Margaret Ciarcia, and Jill Dix Ghnassia discuss their course on Epidemics and AIDS, which was developed with the assistance of a grant from the Alfred P. Sloan Foundation to meet a specific social need. This laboratory course approaches the subject from a wide variety of disciplinary perspectives with the goal of increasing students' knowledge and changing attitudes and behaviors. Students not only become more critically aware of the epidemic and come to feel differently toward those with AIDS but also engage in various kinds of service-oriented action in the university or wider community.

A pair of follow-up essays discuss case study approaches. Marilyn Smith, Ernest Gardow, and Laura Reale-Foley are part of a team of philosophers and professional school faculty teaching Ethics in the Professions. They ask students not simply to receive and absorb knowledge but to produce knowledge, based not on biases and hunches but on work with a variety of materials from different disciplines. Their students learn to collaborate as seekers and synthesizers. The course becomes fully interdisciplinary as students explore and compare moral dilemmas in various professions. The underlying questions of "what is a professional?" and "what is professionalism?" plus comparisons of codes of ethics of various professional groups further encourage interdisciplinary thinking.

Next, Charles Canedy argues the benefits of bringing business school faculty and their methodology of the choreographed case study into the liberal arts and general education. Discussing the one course in Part II focused on an historical period, the United States since 1945, he encourages students not only to juxtapose competing perspectives but to think in action-oriented terms: given these perspectives, what actions are warranted and why? (See the essay by Thomas Grant in Part III for some background on and a different view of the Discovering America course series.)

A second pair of follow-up essays offer brief overviews of courses that aim less explicitly at decision making than at developing a more complex understanding. In Jane Horvath's Sources of Power, students analyze examples of power within their personal lives, their college environment, and beyond, as well as within written narratives, in the light of various theoretical approaches from across the social sciences. They thus learn to build the "bridges between concrete, everyday ideas and more abstract, academic concepts" that are central to critical thinking (Meyers 1986, 77–78). Students become conscious of their preconceptions, learn to critique them, and explore, evaluate, and compare other viewpoints. Because Horvath has experience in both team and nonteam formats, she can offer a perspective on which works better to develop these processes.

The course on Hunger described in the final essay by Horvath, Doug Dix, and Bernard den Ouden crosses not only the social sciences but the humanities and natural sciences as well, even as effective policy on issues of hunger must be grounded in disciplines crossing those areas. This course on an uncomfortable topic is designed in part to make students uncomfortable, to break them out of their academic routines and intellectual assumptions about poverty and hunger. In contrast to the more structured approaches of the case study and the application of different theoretical models emphasized in the previous essays, this discussion highlights the benefits of freewheeling, unpredictable interdisciplinary conversations. Armstrong cites an example of faculty team members who "chose to ensconce themselves in three of the four corners of the room," their physical separation symbolic of the lack of integration of ideas (1980, 57). In contrast, the Hunger course team members can often be found in their four corners creating a large action space with students at the center.

As in Part I, then, the essays in Part II focus on particular courses but explore approaches with wide-ranging applicability, from case studies to labs and community service. They illustrate how students can learn to bring together materials, methods, and ideas from diverse disciplines to address the complex issues and problems of their world.

NOTE

1. For a recent discussion of the importance of this ability for student achievement, see Browne 1997, a guide for students on active learning and critical thinking. For a research report on critical thinking and interdisciplinary courses based on the All-University Curriculum (AUC) and utilizing Perry's theory of intellectual and ethical development, see Wright (1992). Wright, one of the authors in this volume, used the Learning Context Questionnaire (Griffith and Chapman 1982) to measure intellectual development in a 19 percent random sample of a freshman class at the University of Hartford with reference to Perry's stages. The results showed a statistically significant shift along Perry's continuum from late dualism to early multiplicity, as students began to realize the uncertainty and complexity of the search for understanding. The data also revealed a statistically significant relationship between intellectual growth and the number of AUC courses taken during the year.

REFERENCES

Applebee, Arthur N. 1996. *Curriculum as Conversation: Transforming Traditions of Teaching and Learning.* Chicago: University of Chicago Press.

Armstrong, Forrest. 1980. "Faculty Development through Interdisciplinarity." *Journal of General Education* 32 (1): 52–63.

Association of American Colleges. 1991. *Liberal Learning and the Arts and Sciences Major.* Vol. 1: *The Challenge of Connecting Learning.* Washington, D.C.: Association of American Colleges.

Belenky, Mary Field, Blythe McVicker Clinchy, Nancy Rule Goldberger, and Jill Mattuck Tarule. 1986. *Women's Ways of Knowing: The Development of Self, Voice, and Mind.* New York: Basic Books.

Brookfield, Stephen D. 1987. *Developing Critical Thinkers: Challenging Adults to Explore Alternative Ways of Thinking and Acting.* San Francisco: Jossey-Bass.

Browne, M. Neil. 1997. *Striving for Excellence in College: Tips for Active Learning.* Upper Saddle River, N.J.: Prentice Hall.

Browne, M. Neil, and Stuart M. Keeley. 1989. "The Need for Critical Thinking Courses." *Intellectual Skills Development Association* 3 (2): 1–2.

Dewey, John. 1933. *How We Think.* Lexington, Mass.: Heath.

Dewey, John. 1938. *The Theory of Inquiry.* Troy, Mo.: Holt, Rinehart and Winston.

Doherty, Austin, James Chenevert, Rhoda R. Miller, James L. Roth, and Leona C. Truchan. 1997. "Developing Intellectual Skills." In *Handbook of the Undergraduate Curriculum,* eds. Jerry G. Gaff and James L. Ratcliff. San Francisco: Jossey-Bass.

Dressel, Paul L., and Lewis B. Mayhew. 1954. *General Education: Explorations in Evaluation.* Washington, D.C.: American Council on Education.

Ennis, Robert H. 1985. "A Logical Basis for Measuring Critical Thinking Skills." *Educational Leadership* (October): 44–48.

Graff, Gerald. 1992. *Beyond the Culture Wars: How Teaching the Conflicts Can Revitalize American Education.* New York: Norton.

Griffith, J. V., and D. W. Chapman. 1982. *Learning Context Questionnaire.* Davidson, N.C.: Davidson College.

Hursh, Barbara, Paul Haas, and Michael Moore. 1983. "An Interdisciplinary Model to Implement General Education." *Journal of Higher Education* 54 (1): 42–59.

Inhelder, Bärbel, and Jean Piaget. 1958. *The Growth of Logical Thinking from Childhood to Adolescence.* Translated by Anne Parsons and Stanley Milgram. New York: Basic Books.

Johnson, Ralph H. 1992. "The Problem of Defining Critical Thinking." In *The Generalizability of Critical Thinking: Multiple Perspectives on an Educational Ideal,* ed. Stephen P. Norris. New York: Teachers College Press.

King, Patricia. 1992. "How Do We Know? Why Do We Believe? Learning to Make Reflective Judgments." *Liberal Education* 78 (1): 2–9.

King, Patricia M., and Karen Strohm Kitchener. 1994. *Developing Reflective Judgment: Understanding and Promoting Intellectual Growth and Critical Thinking in Adolescents and Adults.* San Francisco: Jossey-Bass.

Kurfiss, Joanne G. 1988. *Critical Thinking: Theory, Research, Practice, and Possibilities.* ASHE-ERIC Higher Education Report No. 2. Washington, D.C.: Association for the Study of Higher Education.

Meyers, Chet. 1986. *Teaching Students to Think Critically.* San Francisco: Jossey-Bass.

Newell, William H. 1990. "Interdisciplinary Curriculum Development." *Issues in Integrative Studies* 8: 69–86.

Newell, William H. 1998. "Professionalizing Interdisciplinarity: Literature Review and Research Agenda." In *Interdisciplinarity: Essays from the Literature,* ed. William H. Newell. New York: College Entrance Examination Board.

Paul, Richard W. 1990. *Critical Thinking: What Every Person Needs to Survive in a Rapidly Changing World.* Ed. A. J. A. Binker. Rohnert Park, Calif: Center for Critical Thinking and Moral Critique, Sonoma State University.

Perry, William G. 1968. *Forms of Intellectual and Ethical Development in the College Years.* Troy, Mo.: Holt, Rinehart and Winston.

Richards, Donald G. 1996. "The Meaning and Relevance of 'Synthesis' in Interdisciplinary Studies." *Journal of General Education* 45 (2): 114–28.

Wright, Sheila. 1992. "Promoting Intellectual Development in the Freshman Year." *Journal of the Freshman Year Experience* 4 (2): 23–39.

EPIDEMICS AND AIDS: CONFRONTING FEAR, DISCRIMINATION, AND MORTALITY

Ralph Aloisi, Karen Barrett, Margaret Ciarcia, and Jill Dix Ghnassia

IN THE BEGINNING

In the fall of 1996, a class of college students from the University of Hartford viewed the AIDS Quilt in Washington, D.C. Students mingled with the two million visitors who included families, friends, and lovers of the more than 70,000 individuals represented by coffin-sized panels. The students knew that these 70,000 pieces of cloth represented only about one-third of the total deaths in the United States caused by AIDS, but to have 70,000 "deaths" laid out in front of them was almost over-whelming. Not long after embarking on this emotional weekend trip, our students met the complexity of the issues surrounding AIDS face-to-face. While two million visitors observed the quilt, speaker after speaker rose to the microphone to read out the names of 10 people who had succumbed to AIDS. Two protests in the distance, however, stunned our students more than the sorrowful tocsin of names: members of the gay activist group ACT UP screaming for justice, support, and help, and a group of conservative extremists yelling, "Kill all the queers; they deserve AIDS."

The devastating nature of AIDS makes it mandatory for students of all ages to learn how to protect themselves and those they love from the HIV virus and AIDS. But AIDS is more than the biology of a virus or an epidemiological problem; it is, as Keeling says, "an unwelcome messenger of unwanted news about the integrity of our social fabric, the quality of our sense of community, and our tolerance for suffering" (1996, 1). This epidemic demands an interdisciplinary approach if students are to understand the complex issues that have no boundaries in disciplines. It involves a broad spectrum of interrelated issues that simultaneously allow students to gain perspectives on AIDS and humanity, on personal freedoms and government control, on the rights of the individual and the rights of the community, on the role of health care, and on death and dying. Because of its far-reaching effects, AIDS may go down in history as the most significant event of the latter half of the twentieth century.

Clearly, the study of epidemic diseases and AIDS is well-suited to college-level interdisciplinary courses and provides scholars with insights far beyond the epidemic itself. If, as Klein and Newell suggest, interdisciplinary study often begins with a question (1997, 393), then the main question our course seeks to answer is: What are epidemic diseases and how do societies respond to them? The course Epidemics and AIDS strives to answer this question by studying epidemics in general and the AIDS epidemic specifically and by examining the historical, social, economic, political, medical, and biological aspects of the current epidemic of AIDS in the United States and around the globe.[1] When students enter the classroom, they immerse themselves in an active learning environment that for many will change their lives forever. Students learn principles of science and scientific reasoning, develop critical thinking skills, and challenge established social and personal values related to death, dying, discrimination, and AIDS. To these ends, science as a way of knowing (Moore 1984, 42), within the context of epidemic diseases and AIDS, becomes the unifying theme that ties the course together and provides the basis for developing an understanding of complex scientific paradigms such as evolution, herd immunity, and change and survival in an ecosystem.

Funded by a grant from the Alfred P. Sloan Foundation in 1988, course development involved faculty members from very different disciplinary orientations. Each team member was responsible for developing and writing one or more units to be included in a text that could be used by educational institutions and other groups to educate their constituencies, including nonscience majors, about AIDS, and each would, at some point, teach a section of the course. The original team included two faculty from medical technology, two from biology, one from English who had an interest in literature and medicine, one from communication, and the last from public health. In developing the course, the team encountered many obstacles. First and foremost was the obvious difficulty faced by faculty working outside their fields of expertise. Those with expertise in the humanities felt much like the faculty member in English who expressed these sentiments:

> I wondered whether I was undertaking too much; could I teach this course if I was only one step ahead of my students, and could I, in good conscience, adequately teach the science portion of the class and not disadvantage those students in my section? How could I possibly explicate scientific theory, let alone DNA and genetics, or answer those inevitable questions that only students can come up with to stump the professor?

Conversely, those of us with a scientific background were not apprehensive about the science portion of the course but felt ill-prepared and uncomfortable about competently discussing themes related to death and dying from the perspective of the social sciences and the humanities, never mind dealing with those issues from our own personal perspective.

These problems, however, turned out to be a blessing in disguise, because our colleagues are excellent students and teachers themselves. Each of us, then, not only developed units for the students but also an instructional packet for faculty, replete with teaching guides, additional readings, references, suggested topics for discussion, and possible questions to be probed. We taught each other and integrated this new knowledge into our disciplinary view of the world. And because our colleagues in the sciences were faced with the daunting task of teaching the science portion of the course to those of us in the humanities and social sciences, they were exposed to some of the conceptual difficulties nonscience majors might actually face in the classroom. Furthermore, the mere fact that we were teaching material outside the normal realm of our instruction made the approach become interdisciplinary.

Consider the science faculty member teaching the social value of diversity in a community and hoping students will understand the necessity of diverse people within a population. Of course, from a biological viewpoint, that issue alone is a fundamental underpinning of evolutionary theory. If it were not for diversity, there would be no evolution, no change, and the species would quickly become extinct. Moreover, the greater the diversity within a population the more likely the species will survive changes in the environment.

Because the course was, and still is, team-taught, team members decided to attend every lecture, reinforcing what we had studied and, at times, learning along with our students. Thus, we mastered the material in an interdisciplinary context rather than as isolated units. Now, as new faculty prepare to join the team, they first spend a semester auditing the class before actually teaching it. This approach has enabled the originators of the course to allay the fears of newcomers about teaching outside their field and to ensure a continuing supply of instructors.

EVOLUTION OF THE COURSE

At the time we were developing the course in 1988–89, misinformation about AIDS, its cause, and its prevention was widespread. During the planning process, we agreed that we wanted to correct misconceptions, stir public awareness, and involve students in working toward controlling the epidemic and preventing its spread. If we were to attain our goals, we had to design a course that spoke to those issues. To put our thoughts into context, the AIDS epidemic was first recognized in the United States in 1981. Not until 1985 did the first test to detect HIV infection become available. This was the same year Rock Hudson died of AIDS, and at that time the press and conservatives alike were calling AIDS "the gay plague." From 1981 to 1985, the significance of the epidemic was downplayed by some members of the medical/scientific community, the federal government, the press, and society at large. Very few people seemed to understand or care that AIDS was an equal opportunity virus that struck without regard for sexual preference, age, nationality, or race (Shilts 1987). On October 22, 1986, the then-Surgeon General of the United States, C. Everett Koop, released his report on

AIDS to the American people and began his educational campaign to control the epidemic. Because education was (and still is) the best means to control the spread of the disease, he urged that AIDS education begin in childhood. Following closely after this report, in 1987 the Centers for Disease Control (CDC) recognized that AIDS would become a major killer of young people. In the 1988–89 school year, it sponsored a national study with the American College Health Association to determine the influx of HIV into this population by performing serological studies on college students. The resulting data indicated that three of every 1,000 students on college campuses were already infected with HIV. By 1988, AIDS had become a major killer of men between the ages of 24 and 43.

Furthermore, the fact that at that time AIDS in the United States, unlike its manifestation in Africa, was to a great extent a disease of gay men added a degree of complexity both to the epidemic equation and to our curriculum design; the spread of AIDS occurred concurrently with the increased activism and openness of gay groups:

> When they come to write the history of AIDS, socio-ethnologists will have to decide whether the "practitioners" of homosexuality or its heterosexual "onlookers" have been the more spectacular in their extravagance. The homosexual "life style" is so blatantly on display to the general public, so closely scrutinized, that it is likely we never will have been informed with such technicophantasmal complacency as to how "other people" live their lives. (Leibowitch 1985, 3)

A growing intolerance toward homosexuals, reflected in numerous reports of "gay bashing" in campus communities throughout the nation, was manifested in the early 1980s. Homophobia has always been present, but open and very public expressions of homophobic thought (such as the words of Congressman William Dannemeyer in October 1985 during a debate on a homosexual rights bill: "God's plan for man was for Adam and Eve and not Adam and Steve") and physical beatings and intimidation began to rise as AIDS came to be viewed as the "gay plague" or the "wrath of God" syndrome. In our early classes, some students expressed another response to this epidemic: "If I'm not gay or an

IV drug user, the AIDS epidemic doesn't concern me." This attitude was prevalent throughout society in general in the early 1990s.

Clearly, this type of reaction, coupled with lack of knowledge about high-risk behaviors, prompted the faculty team to develop this laboratory science course for nonscience majors in the hope that once students knew the facts about AIDS they would alter their behavior as well as increase their understanding about the disease, and practice tolerance toward others. The course had to reach beyond personal and narrowly academic goals to address broader issues. We also hoped that the course would provide a powerful tool for outreach to the campus and local community. We all agreed that everyone needed to understand that AIDS is everyone's problem.

At the time we were developing the course, there were no appropriate introductory biology texts on AIDS nor were there texts that incorporated the diverse issues and facets of epidemic disease and AIDS that we believed essential to the integrity of the course. The struggle between the needs of our disciplines and the goals of interdisciplinary education was often difficult to manage. While everyone agreed on the relevance and integration of the science components, the English faculty member rather testily observed that literature, philosophy, and the arts seemed "tacked on" and useful only to meet the All-University Curriculum (AUC) requirement that such courses include disparate disciplines. She noted that the humanities had been relegated to one week near the end of the course and worried that students would fail to see the significance of the literature component of the course and view it as merely busywork. Initial student evaluations indicated that while we had successfully developed a multidisciplinary course, we might have failed to meld the disciplines sufficiently to create a new field of exploration (Klein 1990, 56). Students often had difficulty seeing the relationship between the literature they had to read and the science they had to master.

Over the years, the course has become more truly interdisciplinary, especially now that we realize more fully, both through experience and professional development, what that term actually means. We originally analyzed course material from our own discipline-specific perspective but in time, as we came to recognize the interconnectedness of the content, we began to integrate the subject matter more successfully. Topics were initially presented as discipline-specific modules, for instance, Virology and HIV, the Cell, Society and AIDS, Communication and AIDS, Literature and AIDS. While at least 50 percent of the course focused—and still focuses—on science, with each successive semester it has changed so that topics are now integrated throughout the entire course. For example, instead of encountering all the literature in one of the final units, students now read and discuss *The Plague* by Camus and *And The Band Played On* by Shilts during the first third of the course. These readings complement their understanding of the history of epidemics and the epidemiology of plagues, virology, and immunology; develop their empathy for people with AIDS; and move them toward the later discussions about death, their own mortality, and the ability of art to engender vicariously emotions they have not personally felt. In the Camus novel, each of the main characters comes to a realization concerning his role during the epidemic of plague, which is what we are attempting to guide our students toward with regard to the AIDS epidemic.

THE CURRENT COURSE

Many of the issues, problems, and behaviors described in *And The Band Played On* and *The Plague* are identical and demonstrate further the typical human response to epidemic disease, still seen in our society today. Early in the course, students are challenged to reflect on their assumptions about the concepts of xenophobia, victim blaming, mortality, the value of human life, and cultural and sexual diversity. They later learn that history is replete with records of blaming the victims for epidemic disease. This behavior is particularly well-documented during the great plagues of the fourteenth and fifteenth centuries when Jews in Christian Europe were tortured, burned, and killed for contaminating the drinking water despite the fact that they drank from the same wells and died from the same plague as the Christians. Students realize that even today we get some comfort in blaming others for epidemic disease, as seen annually with the Asian or the Hong Kong flu, for example. Thus, the course has incorporated a rich synthesis of disciplines and modalities of thought.

Throughout the course, whenever possible, we attempt to humanize the objectivity of scientific investigation for our students and help them attach a human face to the terrible disease called AIDS. This deliberate tempering of the facts through the introduction of social science and humanities perspectives forces students to address issues such as their own mortality, rising health care costs, past and present reactions to epidemics, economic and social repercussions of epidemics, and future problems in coping with a pandemic such as AIDS. Beginning with the initial class, students are challenged in their thinking and assumptions: they are presented with facts and they are presented with people. First, they learn a few basic facts about AIDS. The class is told, "Do you know that approximately one in 250 people in the United States is infected with HIV, the virus that causes AIDS? If accurate, that would mean that at the University of Hartford there may be at least 15 members of the student body who are HIV-infected." If this statistic were not enough to catch their interest, they then view a video that is a compilation of the broadcast tapes of Dr. Peter Jepson-Young, a Canadian physician who contracted HIV through homosexual behaviors. Dr. Peter, as he was known to his admiring viewers, convinced a local television station to allow him to document the last years of his life with a brief weekly report after the evening news. This video is the "hook" or "grabber" (Association for Integrative Studies 1996, 170) to draw students into the human aspect of the epidemic.

Students are forced immediately to confront an individual with a different sexual orientation and lifestyle from most of them and to begin thinking about the costs of AIDS in very real human terms. The video of Dr. Peter dramatically illustrates the effects of HIV infection and AIDS on the remaining years of his life. The initial segments introduce Dr. Peter as a young, vibrant individual with a wonderful sense of humor. In each short segment the tape archives the decline of his health through Kaposi's sarcoma, blindness, pneumonia, wasting, and finally his death, funeral, and burial. The Dr. Peter episodes link the study of the natural history of HIV disease to a likable individual dying a most tragic death. It is this video that initiates the integration of the scientific, psychosocial, and cultural aspects of infectious disease and, we hope, moves our students toward the development of a new, personal perspective that ideally results in a larger, more holistic understanding (Newell 1990, 76) of epidemics and AIDS as well as the effects of discrimination and persecution.

In later discussions of death and dying, students read and analyze further examples of literature that deals with this theme, for instance, *The Death of Ivan Illych* by Dostoevsky and poems by Keats, Dylan Thomas, and Larkin. They discover how the arts help us to understand and explain the unexplainable through visual representation, music, or language when science proves helpless against illness, disease, and death. Through the arts, for example, students study issues crucial to epidemic disease that are impossible to deal with within the limitations of science. The arts invite them to share in life's struggles, to confront elemental realities, unpleasant as these are, and to feel what they have not experienced or do not desire to know empirically: what it is like to die young, what happens after death, and what emotions assail the terminally ill. Students can begin to relate to persons with HIV who perhaps face discrimination at work, at school, or in the community. Addressing these topics eventually leads to further discussions about the limitations of science and helps students understand that science encompasses an exploration of the physical world only.

In addition to focusing on literature and art to explore issues of death and dying imaginatively and vicariously, we have found that popular movies also provide an excellent medium to enable students to explore difficult questions. For instance, in the film *Glory*, a black Union troop in the Civil War attacks a Confederate fort in a suicidal march that is presented as a "glorious" death. In the attack, Union soldier after soldier raises the American flag only to be killed and to drop it. The death of these young men, while tragic, is glorious—a proud way to die. Another popular film presented in the course is *Ghost*, in which banshees come and take away the evil characters and the dead hero speaks one last time to his lover and tells her that death is wonderful if you have lived a good life. Discussions addressing our views of death and dying accompany the viewing of these films. Do they merely reflect our cultural view of death or do they create it? Finally, in the film *Philadelphia* we see the devastation AIDS causes in the life of a young, productive lawyer. We ask students what they think it is like to die from

AIDS: Is it a kind of suicide? Is it a crime against nature and God? Or, as Father Paneloux in *The Plague* states in a sermon to the people of Oran, "Calamity has come to you, my brethren, and my brethren you deserve it." Is it a deserved calamity?

Death and dying are issues that young people often avoid in their consideration of science. Of the many questions addressed in Epidemics and AIDS, several cause much consternation and even distress: "Does it matter when and how you die?" "Where and how do we develop our images of death since no one has survived to tell us what death is like?" The course questions the creation of priority lists, for example, the often unconscious prioritizing of the "acceptable" order of the deaths of loved ones. Students jump into discussions, often talking about young friends and relatives who died before their parents. Building on their knowledge of the past and their increasing understanding of the history of disease and epidemics, students arrive at the conclusion that until relatively recently, dying old was the exception. Many have visited historic churches, and hence, old graveyards, and have observed that they are filled with the bodies of the young—infants, children, adolescents, and young mothers. With the advent of antibiotics and vaccination, however, that pattern changed; now dying old is the norm and dying young the exception. Parents expect to die before their children. But no matter what era they consider, students seem to understand almost intuitively that dying old is natural and expected and that dying young seems to be a disruption of the natural order of life.

Finally, in studying death, dying, and AIDS, students in the course meet young people living with AIDS. Local support groups have regularly provided contacts with remarkable individuals who bravely come to small-group sessions to discuss what is happening to them and how they are preparing for a life that is far different from the one of their dreams. Last year, Jennifer, a 21-year-old student, told of years of drug abuse that ended with pregnancy, withdrawal from school, and AIDS. She described the signs and symptoms of AIDS she was experiencing and reflected on how things would be different if she could only relive her life. Jeff, a 19-year-old gay man with AIDS, sat next to her. Jeff's concerns were dramatically different. While Jennifer wondered how her daughter was and where she would get money for AIDS treatment, Jeff knew that he had only 20 T-lymphocytes, the blood cells essential for proper immune function, and clearly was near the "end." He worried whether his parents would forgive him, if they would understand, and who would come to his funeral. Would anybody know that he had ever been alive? Students saw first-hand that Jennifer and Jeff really were not very different from themselves. They were not homeless outcasts. They were young, attractive, educated people dying from AIDS. These were young people who had thought that they were invincible and would live forever, young people who had thought AIDS was not their problem.

It is worth noting at this point that what started as a lecture on the pathophysiology of HIV disease and AIDS evolved to include discussion related to the psychological effects the disease has on those infected and eventually led to the visit by these young people with AIDS. This encounter brought the true holistic nature of the disease, as it affects those afflicted with it, to the reality of the class. After these visits by infected peers who still look like any other young adult, students view for the first time slides of the shocking, disfiguring effects of opportunistic diseases that assail a human body weakened by AIDS. Discussion now centers on questions that explore, investigate, and analyze issues fundamental to having a sense of living with HIV: for example, "In a society where we are so concerned with physical appearances, how does one deal with the disfiguring 'Scarlet Letter' markings of Kaposi's sarcoma?" or, "Imagine looking in the mirror and seeing a once-healthy image now reflecting back the effects of physical wasting. Describe your reaction." Such questions integrate the basics of the liberal education we are striving to convey in this course (Hursh, Haas, and Moore 1983, 43).

Throughout the semester, as we address ethical issues, specially designed learning activities promote interdisciplinary thinking, synthesis, and creativity. Teaching students to ask perceptive questions, first about scientific fact and social science practice and then about the assumptions underlying them, is a main pedagogical goal. In one exercise, students examine, for signs of bias, scientific articles written at the time the medical/scientific community was first becoming aware of the AIDS epidemic, along with articles from the popular press. Handouts include copies of the actual *Morbidity and Mortality Weekly Report* from the CDC that first announced the death of five young gay men from an unknown disease (June 5, 1982) and later reports that document growing awareness of the scope of the new epidemic. These reports and the news they generated are compared with other public health dramas that unfolded in that same period, such as Legionnaires' disease in Philadelphia or the Tylenol poisoning. Students are asked to compare these events. Why is it that until Rock Hudson's death few were aware of this new and deadly disease, yet front-page news around the globe extensively covered the relatively few calamities associated with Legionnaires' disease and the Tylenol poisoning. Clearly, the media did not think that AIDS was worthy of video or print coverage. Gay men walking hand-in-hand just weren't newsworthy, while coffins carrying World War II veterans and draped in the U.S. flag provided poignant images for magazines and television.

Eventually, class discussions lead to an examination of the role that homophobia played in preventing widespread news coverage of the events surrounding the early years of the AIDS epidemic, an issue that will likely be discussed for decades. If this epidemic had begun in the United States in the young heterosexual population, would the media have treated it differently? Would the government have provided more extensive funding for research and care? Would the public health community have taken a more active role in mandatory testing and tracking of those who were HIV positive? Would the epidemic have been under control in 1999? Such questions encourage students to probe the underlying social and cultural attitudes that had a profound influence in the early days of the AIDS epidemic in the United States and to make connections between the various disciplines.

As students address these questions, they also examine the role homophobia may have played in scientific research. They ask whether scientific and medical discourses, which traditionally seek to draw the line "between the facticity of scientific and nonscientific (mis)conceptions," are indeed free from bias, from the same "ambiguity, homophobia, stereotyping, confusion, doublethink, them-versus-us, blame-the-victim, wishful thinking, popular forms of semantic legerdemain about AIDS" (Treichler 1988, 37). Students are often surprised to learn that the underlying assumptions of many researchers early in the AIDS epidemic prevented them from recognizing the truth about AIDS: that it was not a "gay disease." Such assumptions also prevented many scientists and researchers from recognizing the syndrome in women, thus denying those women early treatment and palliative medication as well as the benefits of medical coverage through Medicaid. Ideally, scientific discourse attempts to eliminate bias, but in reality this does not always occur. As long as there exists a human element, all discourse, all communication, is fallible.

To impress this idea upon students even more strongly, they view a video about epidemics that illustrates the concept of scientific bias by portraying the conflict between Dr. John Snow, who discovered the causative organism of cholera, and an associate, Dr. Pettenkopher, who manipulated the results of his experiment to prove *Vibrio cholera* did not cause cholera, thus showing that scientists sometimes can be biased in their interpretation of scientific data if they have a strongly held, preconceived notion of how the experiment will turn out. Students learn that the scientific process is a process of global communication that often clashes with economic reality and social, cultural, or political biases. Gradually, they come to understand the importance of asking the right questions and never assuming too much. This type of learning and critical thinking would not easily be accomplished within the parameters of a single-discipline approach to AIDS.

ACTIVE LEARNING

Mindful that we charged ourselves with the mission not only to create a laboratory science course for nonscience majors that integrates the sociological, psychological, and historical perspectives on epidemics but also to effect a modification of behavior through education, we needed activities that would reinforce student learning. It had become evident that more than factual information was required to bring about fundamental behavioral change, thereby decreasing the practice of high-risk behaviors related to disease transmission. Study after study has shown that a strange paradox occurs in health education—despite knowing the facts, we often choose the riskier behavior (Fan, Conner, and Villareal 1996, 67). We needed to apply teaching strategies that would demand critical thinking, cultural exploration, and social analysis. As a team, we decided that if students took an active role and had first-hand experience in AIDS education, they would feel more connected to AIDS prevention and make it a more significant part of their lives. By emphasizing student involvement, we felt we could encourage responsible behavioral change. We selected the field of communication as the discipline through which to encourage increased involvement. Thus, we required students to develop AIDS education campaigns designed to teach others, either on campus or in the community, about the virus, AIDS, high-risk behaviors, and/or discrimination.

Requiring students to develop health education campaigns results in a number of positive outcomes. This component of the course is, in fact, a problem-based learning activity (Doig 1994, 2). Students must work together in groups to design a persuasive campaign, then implement the campaign and evaluate its effectiveness. As an example, many of our education majors choose to develop AIDS education classes for local schoolchildren. In the process they not only must know the science thoroughly but understand the ramifications of presenting unpalatable, possibly offensive, material and ideas to a fearful public. They indeed come head-to-head with, and must deal with, parental concerns and obstacles posed by school policy. In terms of enhancing public awareness and encouraging civic action, to our suprise students run immensely effective campaigns. While their target audiences learn about AIDS, students become effective AIDS advocates. Over the years, student groups have developed many wonderfully creative AIDS education campaigns: they've published articles in both local and student newspapers; participated in concerts, plays, and other events to increase AIDS awareness; written and performed a musical based on a young person with AIDS; written and produced a book about AIDS for elementary schoolchildren; and even developed a game for adolescents to teach them about the disease. Students have also raised funds for AIDS causes. As they absorb information related to HIV and AIDS, they learn to teach others effectively about the disease and to analyze their health communication efforts. Because students often choose projects related to their major field of study, such as analyzing portrayals of AIDS in gay literature or producing artworks about AIDS for campus display, the campaigns help them link their study in general education to their major.

Additional AIDS learning activities related to the field of communication focus on the posters, radio spots, videos, and print materials produced as part of the federal government's "America Responds to AIDS Campaign." Students analyze and evaluate communications on AIDS both to learn from the messages conveyed and to learn how to be critical consumers of information. They also analyze various public service announcements and determine the goals or objectives of the campaigns. They ask questions about the effective dissemination of information, such as: Is the intent of the public service announcement to change behavior? Change attitudes or values? Create interest? Motivate? Encourage awareness? Disperse knowledge? Who is the target audience (sex, age, cultural background, etc.)? What is the source of the message (peers, celebrities, experts)? What type of appeal is used (rational, emotional, one-sided)? What is the style of the message (entertaining, long, short)? Finally, students evaluate the media strategies used. Integrating communication, education, social and political issues, economic factors, psychological principles, and the science of HIV and AIDS provides a framework for student involvement and reflection.

In another hands-on portion of the course, the science laboratory component, students complete experiments in hematology, microbiology, and immunology. They are provided with individual kits for each experiment and summarize their results in standard lab reports. For example, in the clinical immunology experiment, students learn how to perform three assays: total protein using refractive index (T/S meter), protein electrophoresis in agarose gel to evaluate the gamma globulin fraction of serum proteins, and radial immunodiffusion to quantify specific classes of immunoglobulin. Each student is then given three serum samples and told that one is a normal control, one is from a normal patient, and the other is from a person with an immunodeficiency. The objective is to determine, using the first two assays, which sample was taken from a person with an immunodeficiency and to confirm the theory by performing the immunoglobulin assay on only one sample.

Background information for the labs is presented in class lectures and discussions and the significance of the laboratory experiments is explained. Because these lab assignments are fairly sophisticated for non-science majors and at a level far beyond typical introductory biology labs, laboratory instructors demonstrate complex or intricate techniques step-by-step before students attempt them. Thus lab work gives meaning and relevance to the study of basic science and biology. The experiments they conduct do not deal with abstract scientific paradigms but rather are tools of diagnosis and means of understanding AIDS as a disease.

In one of the early labs, students create a mock epidemic and learn first-hand how quickly epidemic disease can spread throughout a community. In the case of AIDS, they see clearly that the frequency of high-risk behaviors is directly associated with the likelihood of contracting HIV infection. Complementing these activities, students learn how epidemiologists analyze a disease in a population through the study of the host, the environment, and the agent. In the labs, they explore the relationship of dose, time, and frequency in determining causation, and they find out how a controlled study is developed and paid for. Students also learn about different variations of the AIDS epidemic. They learn that on some continents, AIDS is primarily a disease of gay men and IV drug users, as it is in North America, while on other continents like Africa, AIDS is primarily transmitted through heterosexual activity. In Botswana, for example, the epidemic is widespread among heterosexuals; 15 percent (1 out of every 6 people) is HIV-infected. The economy is dramatically affected and a growing population of orphan children flood communities. The epidemic among young people in the United States is much like that in Botswana but differs in scope and time. While still in its early stages, this epidemic is characterized as primarily a sexually transmitted disease. But, we ask, what will happen in our society 10 years from now? Will young people change their ways? Will we speak out clearly and definitively to our children about AIDS and promiscuity? Will the sexually transmitted epidemic progress as it has in Africa? Will the government respond? Will the media cover this story more responsibly than they did when AIDS first surfaced in the gay community?

The final message in the course is that we are now living in the time of AIDS. After two decades, we have made substantial progress in understanding the disease and the epidemic. We know more about AIDS than many diseases like arthritis or the common cold that we have struggled with for centuries. While this knowledge has led to new therapies that for the first time give hope to those infected with HIV, even if a cure existed, the devastation and global disruption this epidemic has caused and continues to inflict are tremendous. According to the World Health Organization, close to 15 million people are currently infected with HIV in Africa, the Americas, and Europe alone, and by 2005, AIDS will produce untold misery and depress the global economy by 4 percent. In studying epidemics and AIDS in this interdisciplinary course, faculty and students have an opportunity to delve into social, political, economic, and scientific issues, using this tear in the social fabric as a medium to explore the human condition.

NOTE

1. This chapter builds on an earlier published analysis of this course, within the context of innovative college science teaching; see Aloisi et al. 1990/1991.

REFERENCES

Association for Integrative Studies and Institute in Integrative Studies. 1996. "Guide to Interdisciplinary Syllabus Preparation." *Journal of General Education* 45 (2): 170–73.

Aloisi, R. M., K. Barrett, H. Birden, R. Carveth, M. Ciarcia, W. Coleman, and J. Ghnassia. 1990/1991. "Epidemics and AIDS: An Interdisciplinary Course." *Journal of College Science Teaching* (December/January): 162–67.

Doig, Kathy. 1994. "Problem-based Learning: Developing Practitioners for Today and Tomorrow." *Clinical Laboratory Science* 7 (3): 172–77.

Fan, Hung, Ross Conner, and Luis Villarreal. 1996. "Models of Health Behavior Change." *AIDS Science and Society*. Boston: Jones and Bartlett.

Hursh, Barbara, Paul Haas, and Michael Moore. 1983. "An Interdisciplinary Model to Implement General Education." *Journal of Higher Education* 54 (1): 42–59.

Keeling, Richard. 1996. "HIV and Higher Education: From Isolation to Engagement." *Liberal Education* 82 (4): 1–8.

Klein, Julie Thompson. 1990. *Interdisciplinarity: History, Theory, and Practice*. Detroit, Mich.: Wayne State University Press.

Klein, Julie Thompson, and William H. Newell. 1997. "Advancing Interdisciplinary Studies." In *Handbook of the Undergraduate Curriculum*, eds. Jerry G. Gaff and James L. Ratcliff. San Francisco: Jossey-Bass.

Leibowitch, J. 1985. *A Strange Virus of Unknown Origin.* Translated by Richard Howard. Introduction by Robert Gallo. New York: Ballantine.

Moore, John. 1984. "Science As a Way of Knowing—Evolutionary Biology": Opening Remarks. *American Zoologist* 24 (2): 421–22.

Newell, William H. 1990. "Interdisciplinary Curriculum Development." *Issues in Integrative Studies* 8: 69–86.

Shilts, Randy. 1987. *And the Band Played On.* New York: Penguin.

Treichler, Paula A. 1988. "AIDS, Homophobia, and Biomedical Discourse: An Epidemic of Significance." In *AIDS: Cultural Analysis, Cultural Activism,* ed. Douglas Crimp. Cambridge, Mass., and London: MIT Press.

EPIDEMICS AND AIDS: SAMPLE SYLLABUS

This integrative course in the sciences is an interdisciplinary exploration of plagues, epidemics, and AIDS. It reviews historical, social, political, and scientific perspectives on the current AIDS epidemic. Knowledge of basic scientific concepts enables students to develop an understanding of the disease based on fact and a personal perspective on AIDS and their role in the epidemic. (Lab course.) (Emphasis on written and oral communication and critical thinking.)

Goals: Students will learn the facts about HIV/AIDS; take an active role in combating the epidemic; develop an understanding of epidemics and their effect on societies, politics, and human behavior; learn to appreciate the complexity of the scientific method and how advances are made in science; understand risk behaviors and the pathophysiology of AIDS; and understand the importance of education in preventing the further spread of the epidemic.

Texts: Albert Camus, *The Plague* (1947); Hung Fan, Ross F. Conner, and Luis P. Villarreal, *AIDS, Science, and Society* (1996); Randy Shilts, *And the Band Played On* (1987).

Topics:

Introduction: AIDS Timeline 1981 to the Present

History's Lessons: Past Epidemics and Plagues

Epidemiology and the AIDS Epidemic

The Cell: Structure and Function

Microbes and Infection

Natural Resistance and Anatomy of the Immune System

The Immune Response and Immunity

Retroviruses and the Pathophysiology of HIV Disease

Medical Management of HIV Disease

Life, Death, and Culture

AIDS Communication and Education

Social, Ethical, and Political Issues Related to AIDS

Selected Student Activities:

Class: Group discussions and presentations—distinguishing between bias and reason, fact and opinion; writing assignment on death and dying; debates on current political and social policies and views on HIV/AIDS; analysis of printed media focusing on HIV/AIDS.

Lab: Introduction to microbiology and a simulated epidemic; white blood cell identification and differentiation; serum protein electrophoresis; simulated HIV antibody detection; HIV/AIDS health education campaign or service learning.

REFLECTIVE JUDGMENT AND MORAL DILEMMAS: ETHICS IN THE PROFESSIONS

Marilyn S. Smith, Ernest Gardow, and Laura Reale-Foley

The University of Hartford is a federation of nine colleges, much the way the cantons of Switzerland constitute the Swiss confederation. The intellectual and professional differences among these colleges are great. Recognition of this fact was the main motivating force behind the creation of the All-University Curriculum (AUC) and of the course Ethics in the Professions. How to represent the ethical dimensions of each of the professions represented by these colleges was the procedural question. The natural answer was to make this course as interdisciplinary as possible.

Kockelmans writes, "The alternative to narrative education is dialogical education, which commits itself to relentless self-reflection by both teachers and students as co-inquirers engaged in the unfinished task of the humanization of man and his environment" (1979, xi). Ethics in the Professions began with a full commitment to dialogical education and to interdisciplinarity. We also decided early on that we would employ some kind of problem-solving methodology to emphasize a Socratic approach to the course and encourage reflective judgment on the part of students (King and Kitchener 1994).

We also were committed to the goals and characteristics of an AUC course. This meant developing students' written and, especially, oral skills. By combining oral skills with values analysis and social interaction, we arrived at the idea of case study presentations by students of carefully structured moral dilemmas. The obvious approach was to examine serious moral dilemmas that confronted each of the professions; in order to achieve that goal, we needed to further our understanding of both reflective judgment and interdisciplinarity.

Because a single semester was insufficient to cover every profession, the four original faculty examined our areas of expertise and decided to focus on those we could most easily handle. The professions covered, therefore, include medicine with its many thorny ethical dilemmas such as genetic engineering (now cloning as well), patient confidentiality, euthanasia, physician-assisted dying and suicide, abortion, and modes of fertilization; business and the role of professionals in business; engineering in a variety of modes; public service (forms of law enforcement); and environmental issues. In addition to the professions themselves, we examine their practices and ask whether they contribute to completing the "unfinished task of the humanization of man and his environment" (Kockelmans 1979, xi).

We believe that resolving and justifying a moral dilemma is inherently interdisciplinary. Both critical thinking and reflective judgment are central foci in Ethics in the Professions. Throughout this chapter we argue for the necessary inclusion of these two modes of thinking as goals of interdisciplinary education.

Dewey in his often misunderstood book *How We Think* discusses the place of judgment in reflective activity. He writes of the features of judgment:

> There are three such features: (1) a controversy, consisting of opposite claims regarding the same objective situation; (2) a process of defining and elaborating these claims and of sifting facts adduced to support them; (3) a final decision, . . . closing the particular matter in dispute while also serving as a rule or principle for deciding future cases. (1933,120)

His aim, of course, was for our institutions of learning to "turn out their pupils in that attitude of mind which is conducive to good judgment." In the same manner, it was our aim to show that the professions under discussion all contained "controversies" with opposite claims and that we, students and faculty alike, needed some framework that would enable us to arrive at a tentative conclusion by first defining and elaborating all possible alternatives and their consequences. "The principle for deciding future cases" would be one of the known ethical theories that assigns moral conduct for rational and autonomous human beings.

THE NATURE OF MORAL DILEMMAS

To understand reflective judgment at work on moral dilemmas, let us look at a concrete illustration. Although the dilemma (in Beck and Orr 1970) dates back to 1915, it is not old-fashioned and nicely illustrates ethical questions and concerns in the discipline of medicine. In November 1915, a Chicago surgeon named J. H. Haiselden refused to operate on a baby boy four days old. Though contrary to the accepted medical ethics of the time, he did this, he said, "in the interest of the human race." The baby was born with a severe defect and would probably have this defect throughout his life. Dr. Haiselden believed the infant to be dying, although his life could have been prolonged if an operation had been performed. The doctor's position was that, given the consent of the parents (which consent was given), "nature should be allowed to take her course." When no other doctor or nurse intervened, the result was that the child was allowed to die. Here we have a genuine moral dilemma, albeit one for which we do not quite have sufficient information. Nonetheless, it serves our purposes well. First, a decision has to be made (we make it very clear to students that, when presenting their case studies, in no way can they avoid making a decision). In Dewey's terms, the question, for Dr. Haiselden, is full of doubts and uncertainties; there are indeed opposite claims regarding the objective situation. The doctor has to clarify these claims in his mind and sift the facts that he is sure of (e.g., the nature of the baby's defect, previous instances of infants with that defect, and so on) as a prelude to making a final decision that may serve as a principle for deciding future cases.

With this illustration in mind, we analyze the constituent parts of a moral dilemma, remembering that this analysis holds true for all dilemmas, no matter what the discipline. First, moral dilemmas must have a human agent—rocks and chairs do not make moral decisions—who is faced with alternatives that are laden with doubtful and, occasionally, contradictory consequences. The moral agent must employ imagination in projecting for herself or himself what the consequences of each alternative are. For example, Dr. Haiselden knows that, should he operate, the life of the infant will be prolonged but will certainly lack quality; on the other hand, if he does not operate, the infant will just as certainly die. Once as many consequences as possible are foreseen, a decision must be made based on some value. It is at this point in the presentation of the nature of a moral dilemma that we come to the heart of a course concerned with ethical decision making, namely, values. We provide students with "Guidelines for Case Study Presentation" (a four-page handout summarized in Figure 1), which includes a section on Clarifying the Conflicting Values and Ethical Principles. These guidelines are relevant for case study presentation and for moral decision making in all the disciplines we discuss in the course.

We maintain that it is only through an interdisciplinary approach that we can attempt to solve the ever-increasing ethical problems challenging our society. Wolfram W. Swoboda writes:

> Amongst proponents of interdisciplinarity, there is little dispute over the need for an alternative to the present organization and transmission of knowledge. . . . Since disciplinary, specialized knowledge has come to be applied to a growing number of social problems, attempts at short-term solutions often engender further problems graver than the ones they have "solved." (in Kockelmans 1979, 49)

The "social problems" to which Swoboda refers are clearly ethical in content. Students are particularly attracted to those social problems that involve overt conflict, including questions of police enforcement that leads to brutality, problems involved in alternative means of conception such as in vitro fertilization, and issues surrounding patient-assisted dying.

Carl Hausman writes, "Philosophy has the longest tradition of any formal discipline that might be considered essentially interdisciplinary" (in Kockelmans 1979, 9). In ancient and medieval times, all disciplines were taught as forms of philosophy; for example, science was taught as natural philosophy. In the modern period, under the aegis of philosophy falls not only the philosophy of science but the philosophy of art or aesthetics, the philosophies of religion, of law, of mind and more. The interdisciplinary nature of Ethics in the Professions is expressed not only in our discussions of morality and ethics as illustrated above but also in the attempt to answer the questions: What does it mean to be a professional? What are the characteristics of professionalism? We sometimes encounter almost insurmountable disagreement among students and faculty when attempting to answer these questions.

FIGURE 1

Summary of Guidelines for Case Study Presentation

1. Identify the Relevant Facts
   By first identifying a list of facts that are relevant in the case, the student group confines the dilemma to a limited number of options. This gives the problem some identifiable boundaries.

2. Enumerate the Apparent Options
   By enumerating the apparent options available in the case, the ability to come to closure is enhanced.

3. Clarify the Conflicting Values and Ethical Principles
   The difficult task of articulating the relevant ethical values is undertaken at this step in the process. The student is assisted by referring to a list presented in a handout.

4. Reflect on Your Options
   Reflective judgment is the key activity in this interdisciplinary effort. The group dynamic created by members with varying backgrounds becomes apparent at this point in the process. Sufficient ethical theory has been presented to students so that reflection on the options is an important learning experience.

5. Determine Which Theory Should Prevail
   Students assess the values presented earlier and determine whether a teleological or deontological viewpoint should prevail in the conclusion. The application of the values to the facts results primarily from the reflective thinking of the individuals in the group.

6. Anticipate Criticism and Clarify the Costs
   If the group has been properly primed, there should be conflict and criticism prior to reaching a consensus. Conflict resolution techniques are necessary abilities that are nurtured and honed in this process.

7. State Your Decision Clearly
   When the group reports its findings, describing the steps listed in the guidelines, a clear resolution of the moral dilemma should have been reached. Grades are based on arriving at a conclusion with appropriate reference to ethical theory.

If we define interdisciplinarity as "an attempt to view different disciplines as related through some principle of interaction more fundamental than any one of them" (Hausman in Kockelmans 1979, 10), we can identify two principles of interaction in Ethics in the Professions. One, discussed above, is the use of reflective judgment when analyzing moral dilemmas; the second is the nature of professionalism. We learned on the first day of the course that defining a "profession" was going to be a huge sticking point for faculty and students alike. Were we, the faculty, to be dialogic and Socratic in attempting to arrive at this extremely important definition? Or were we to be didactic and Draconian? As we began team-teaching this course—two engineers and two philosophers at the outset—we knew that we could not remain discipline-based in our attempts to get at meanings of profession and professional that would be acceptable to all. Thus it was that we examined more than 20 scholarly treatises on the nature of professions (e.g., Millerson 1964) and arrived at 13 different characteristics. The faculty subsequently condensed these to six. Here is a further condensation of those six: professions are organized and represented by associations of distinctive character (e.g., the American Medical Association), have a stated code of conduct, involve a skill based on theoretical knowledge, require extensive training and education, serve the public good, and entail assuming responsibility for the affairs of others.

As an initial exercise, faculty and students examined each of the disciplines represented by the students in the class; by their friends and relatives; by the faculty's acquaintances, colleagues, and friends; and by people in general. The major bone of contention was that while the literature and the faculty stressed the importance of an intellectual component in a definition of a professional, students, on the whole, disagreed. The garage mechanic was, to them, as much of a professional as the mechanical engineer. Through Socratic exchanges, it was determined that a professional could answer the question "why" as well as "how." In this manner the entire group arrived at a consensus across disciplines of a working definition of a professional. By so doing, we uncovered principles more fundamental than those of any one discipline (Hausman in Kockelmans 1979, 8). (It should be added that, no matter what the mix of faculty—for example, one philosopher and one economist—there was little agreement as to a hard and fast definition of a professional.)

REASONING ABOUT MORAL DILEMMAS

Practicing resolving moral dilemmas and analyzing the results are key teaching methods in the Ethics in the Professions course. Both methods combine some important branches of the discipline of philosophy with content from other disciplines. Reasoning about moral decisions combines moral judgments with empirical facts. The reasoning processes needed to solve any problem, whether moral or not, are based on the science of right reasoning or logic, the major tool of philosophy. When the problem is a moral one (such as the case of Dr. Haiselden), the concepts of ethics always frame the analysis. Thus ethics and logic interact in the formation of moral judgments. The empirical facts or the content of the dilemmas can come from any discipline, however. We draw from the professions of engineering, medicine, education, and others. For example, we must learn the procedures of decision making in engineering before searching for the answers to moral dilemmas in that field. Moreover, the entire faculty team needs to understand the nature of "safety" as perceived by the engineering profession. This combination of a philosophical framework and nonphilosophical content results in an interdisciplinary construct. (Of course, it is theoretically possible to formulate a moral dilemma entirely within philosophy itself: Is it immoral to be illogical? Such an arcane question, however, seems outside the commonsense boundaries of undergraduate general education.)

Oddly, a sophisticated level of disciplinary knowledge is not necessary; in fact, complex knowledge of a discipline can be a hindrance to perceiving an ethical conflict. This is particularly true with our business and education students. The former often see only utilitarian solutions and the latter often seek unrealistic solutions that overlook the legal as well as ethical dimensions of the problem. For example, in a case about a Jehovah's Witness who refused a blood transfusion for her child, some education students suggest removing the child from the family altogether.

EXPLICIT CRITICAL THINKING

The branch of philosophy that is crucial to any reasoning process is logic, which is closely related to critical thinking and reflective judgment as formulated by Dewey (1933). Improvement of critical thinking skills has frequently been identified as an overall goal of general education (Newell 1998). This goal is not unique to our course. What is unique is that the specific steps in critical thinking are self-consciously discussed and followed (see Figure 1). This focus seems appropriate in that the source of theories of critical thinking, the discipline of philosophy, is one of the fundamental bases of the course. In fact, the course perhaps should pursue more deeply than it currently does the open consideration of the principles and concepts of the art of critical thinking.

The crucial steps in the process of critical thinking include, first, clear formulation of the problem and the goal (Paul 1990). In the resolution of all moral dilemmas, the goal is to determine which possible action is morally optimal. Because answers may differ depending on the perspective, it is always important in attacking a moral problem to identify who the moral agent is and the alternatives available to that agent. We discussed above the difficulty of formulating moral dilemmas; they are imperfect (ill-structured) problems. The second step is the selection of the relevant data to be used in solving the problem. This step is of itself interdisciplinary because it combines empirical facts from the content discipline (e.g., engineering) with specific ethical theories. A duty or utility ethic considers the rightness or wrongness of a specific action within the context of a particular discipline. Dr. Haiselden had to be aware of the medical ethics of his time as well as of his ultimate concern with the quality of life. The third step in the process of critical thinking is assessing the appropriate ethical principles. From relevant moral principles, one is chosen as particularly applicable to the resolution of a moral dilemma. Students use the Guidelines and the diagram of moral principles in Figure 2 as they attempt to solve the case studies presented to them by the faculty team.

FIGURE 2
Moral Principles

THE PRINCIPLE OF RESPECT
In every action and every intention, in every goal and every means, treat every human being, yourself and others, with the respect befitting the dignity and worth of a person.

THE PRINCIPLE OF NON-MALEVOLENCE

In all of your actions, avoid harming people.

THE PRINCIPLE OF BENEVOLENCE

Promote the well being of others.

THE PRINCIPLE OF INTEGRITY

Maintain personal standards of conduct befitting a professional; respect yourself in all of your decisions so as to be worthy of living a fulfilling professional life.

THE PRINCIPLE OF JUSTICE

Treat others in a manner that is appropriate to them as human beings; be fair, treating people equally, i.e., in similar ways in similar circumstances.

THE PRINCIPLE OF UTILITY

Given that the intention and the goal of your action treat people with respect, choose the course of action that produces the greatest benefit for the greatest number of people.

THE PRINCIPLE OF DOUBLE EFFECT

Given that the intention and goal of your action treat people with respect, make sure that there are no foreseeable bad side effects that are disproportionate with the good of the main effect.

Source: Beabout and Wennemann (1994, 61).

Let us take the factual example of a policeman in New Jersey faced with the choice of whether to dive into a wildly raging river to save three children who are swirling around in a small rubber raft. He chose to try to save their lives and as a result he drowned, as did the children. Was this a foolhardy or a courageous act? The major ethical principles (teleological and deontological) answer this question differently. *After* their immediate reaction, that is, upon reflection, students engage in discussion about the variations in the principles themselves. In other words, the case studies lead to reflection about ethical theory.

The faculty team also presents other "principle-like concepts" such as living a virtuous life, caring about relationships, and following traditional religious principles (e.g., the Golden Rule). Because these are not theories in the ordinary sense, students find their inclusion in the course difficult to understand. Often these concepts represent rival or less-accepted frameworks and merit full discussion of their pros and cons. Discussing the inconsistencies among ethical theories contributes to a broadening of student *and* faculty perspectives.

The final step in the process of critical thinking is the development of logical connections to produce supportable conclusions. The apparent absence of universally accepted right answers to ethical questions helps to maintain the course's focus on the processes of thinking and problem solving rather than on hidebound solutions. The imperfect match between ideal moral principles and professional interests, as found in business, for example, makes the dilemmas interesting and challenging for students while, at the same time, highlighting the importance and difficulty of remaining impartial when addressing a moral dilemma as exemplified in the case studies (see Appendix A).

KOHLBERG'S THEORY

Ethics in the Professions introduces Lawrence Kohlberg's well-known theory of moral development. Kohlberg (1927–1987), a developmental psychologist, borrowed from Jean Piaget's model of intellectual and conceptual development to propose a six-stage, three-level model of moral development. His long-range empirical study of moral decision making by young men and boys at different stages of youth and young adulthood identified a fairly common and orderly progression of moral views. The subjects' moral attitudes generally began with selfish concerns that grew into group concerns and, finally, ideally into impartial universal concern for all representatives of humanity (see chart, e.g., Kohlberg 1984, 174–76, summarized in Beabout and Wennemann 1994, 24). Kohlberg applies his empirical data to the two mainstream theories that have received the most theoretical support and attention from philosophers since the Enlightenment: John Stuart Mill's (1806–1873) principle of utility and Immanuel Kant's (1724–1804) principle of duty. These theories are at once similar and different; occasionally they offer contradictory resolutions to moral problems. To justify his model of the stages of moral development, Kohlberg stresses the similarities: the autonomy of the moral agent, the use of universal principles, and a scientific decision-making process. Kohlberg disregards the serious differences between the two theories and therefore leads us to believe that there is a consistency between them that does not, in fact, exist.

(It should be noted that we also examine Gilligan's (1982) critique of Kohlberg and present her "ethic of caring" as an alternative moral principle. In fact, the ethic of respect is often chosen by faculty and students alike as the more feasible theory or principle.)

It should also be noted that Kohlberg's model is particularly useful for studying professionalism (see Beabout and Wennemann 1994). Professionals—defined as those having complex skills and knowledge—are potentially able to use their knowledge-based power with the intent of manipulating people. Thus, a professional at Kohlberg's Level 1 (preconventional, defined by self-interest) or Level 2 (conventional, defined by social conformity, roles) might make choices that are unprofessional by definition. Being a professional also means having a responsibility to society as a whole, in fact, serving society, as well as being concerned with universal ethics.

TEACHERS AS CO-INQUIRERS

The team-teaching arrangement in Ethics in the Professions turns teachers into learners, although all too frequently it has been impossible to organize teams successfully because of scheduling constraints. When we have used teams, however, the philosophers learn professional ethics from the engineering professors, while the latter in turn learn to place their own ethical code in a theoretical context. Faculty collaboration on curriculum, tests, grading, and discussion of the ethical dilemmas (case studies) helps to engage students as they witness teachers engaged in active learning themselves (see the comments of Colarulli and McDaniel in the Appendix to this volume). Contrary to Richards's (1996) view that team teaching is a poor vehicle for interdisciplinary undergraduate education, we find that team teaching is the preferred vehicle. Richards does argue persuasively that synthesis should not be the only goal of interdisciplinary education (1996, 125–26); there are, in addition, three commonsense results of combining disciplines: an enriched understanding of the issues, a new understanding of the limitations of the disciplinary perspective, and the contextualization of competing ideologies. The Ethics in the Professions faculty believe that the course accomplishes all three.

REFLECTIVE JUDGMENT AND ETHICAL CODES

All but one of the professions investigated in our course (the exception, oddly enough, is education) over time have developed professionwide codes of ethics. These codes are usually set down by the premier professional organization, e.g., the American Medical Association, to be followed by members of the profession. The codes of course differ but, on the whole, they define the fundamental canons relevant to moral behavior. See Appendix B for a sample code from the American Society of Mechanical Engineers. The mechanical engineering profession has developed this code to address the following behaviors: (1) maintaining continued competence; (2) maintaining personal integrity; (3) being accountable to society; (4) having concern for the welfare of others; (5) respecting the rights of others; (6) demonstrating social responsibility; (7) maintaining autonomy; (8) maintaining privacy; (9) avoiding conflicts of interest; and (10) maintaining confidentiality. These 10 concerns of the Society of Mechanical Engineers are in general also the concerns of all other professions. To illustrate this in detail, we developed a matrix of codes from various professional groups (Figure 3). The matrix shows that there is a large degree of commonality among the professions, which points to the conclusion that there are indeed basic moral values that have universal application. The professions listed in the matrix are accounting, education, engineering, finance, law, nursing, medicine (physicians), psychology, and social work. Even a quick glance at the matrix reveals that these professions are universally concerned with competence and integrity.

By examining the preambles to the codes of the above professions, it is evident that the reflective nature of morality is embodied in their statements. For example, the physicians' code states that doctors are responsible not only to the patient but also to other health professionals, society as a whole, and themselves. To ensure such responsibility, the physician must constantly weigh the alternative values, and such evaluation necessarily involves reflective judgment. Another indication of the need for reflective evaluation is found in the code established for attorneys. That code states that lawyers' responsibilities include maintaining competence, improving the ever-changing law, and administering justice. (A tall order, indeed.) As members of the legal profession, attorneys should cultivate their knowledge beyond its use for clients and work to reform the law at all times and to strengthen legal education. Surely, these activities are close, if not identical, to those stated by Dewey (1933). Space does not allow for discussion of the codes of other professions, but they all, in one form or another, emphasize the importance not only of being aware of the moral dimension of their profession but of weighing opposing claims or obligations in an objective manner and coming to some closure regarding a particular matter in dispute that contains a principle for deciding future cases (Dewey 1933, 120).

CASE STUDY PRESENTATIONS

The major component of the course Ethics in the Professions is student case study presentations. As noted above, faculty from various disciplines (business, engineering, medicine, and others) teach the course on a regular basis in conjunction with a philosopher. The students also come from diverse colleges in the university, including engineering, technology, business, arts and sciences, education, art, and music. Teams of four or five students are randomly assigned to groups to orally present case studies to the rest of the class. Presentations begin, typically, in the fifth or sixth week of the semester after adequate time has been devoted to explicating ethical theories and identifying conflicting values. Normally two oral presentations are required of each student. The whole range of ethical topics is covered: euthanasia, physician-assisted dying and suicide, abortion, animal rights, homelessness, police ethics, AIDS, business and journalism ethics, environmental and engineering (safety) ethics, confidentiality and truth telling. The emphasis in evaluating these presentations is on preparation, exposition, and creativity; the goal is to move from prejudicial and stereotypical thinking to thinking of a more reflective nature. (See Appendix A for an example of a more-or-less typical case study.) The case studies usually consist of detailed narratives of 1,000 words or more.

CONCLUSION

Newell and Green, in their article "Defining and Teaching Interdisciplinary Studies" (1982), quote Gresham Riley's comment that "never more than at the present time has there been a need for citizens to be able to focus the insights of various disciplines on the problems and issues which beset our collective existence." Those of us engaged in teaching Ethics in the Professions strive with both enthusiasm and conviction to combine the insights of the various disciplines considering the question of values. We, together with the students, identify situations in which values are involved, examine the many ethical principles that have been advanced by the great philosophers from Aristotle to John Rawls, and attempt to develop the skills of integration and synthesis so frequently demanded by the ethical problems of our ever-changing culture. We strive for these goals, often in an atmosphere of skepticism, yea even cynicism and hostility, because we are absolutely convinced of the importance of both reflective judgment and interdisciplinary education.

FIGURE 3
Comparison of Ethics Codes

	A	B	C	D	E	F	G	H	I Social Work	Total
	Accounting	Education	Engineering	Finance	Law	Nursing	Physicians	Psychology	Social Work	Total
1. Continued Competence	X	X	X	X	X	X	X	X	X	9
2. Integrity	X	X	X	X	X	X	X	X	X	9
3. Accountability	X	X		X		X	X	X	X	7
4. Others' Rights	X	X	X		X		X	X	X	7
5. Others' Welfare			X			X	X	X	X	5
6. Social Responsibility			X	X	X	X	X	X	X	7
7. Autonomy					X		X	X	X	4
8. Privacy		X			X	X			X	4
9. Conflict of Interest	X		X		X					3
10. Confidentiality	X	X		X	X			X		5

X denotes specific reference in code.

Data as of July 1997.

References: Callahan (1988, 439–64), Beabout and Wennemann (1994, 99–125), British Columbia Teachers' Federation (1998).

APPENDIX A

Summary of a Case Study

Police officers Bill Simmons and Chuck Fisher, both tested veterans of the inner-city Washington, D.C., police force, now patrol a downtown and northwest Annapolis, Maryland, beat spanning a wide range of socioeconomic classes. One night their radio directs them to be on alert for a 1987 gray Volvo sedan (no license plate number available) seen leaving the scene of a fatal accident about six blocks away. When they spot such a car they give chase, and the Volvo pulls over. The driver, a muscular black male about 25 years old dressed in soiled, working-class clothes, rolls down the car window. When asked for his identification, he appears annoyed and makes no effort to produce it, instead asking whether the officers are having a slow night and thus are "out to bust D.C. niggers." Bill now determines that the other passenger is a white female who appears to be unconscious. Bill orders the driver out of the car as Chuck crouches beside the patrol car, weapon drawn. The suspect protests as he emerges that the woman needs a doctor, having "had too much white stuff." Bill strong-arms suspect A by shoving his face against the sideview mirror just as the passenger door begins to open. Alarmed, he clubs suspect A on the head with the back of his revolver. Chuck sees all this but cannot respond to his partner because of the movement on the passenger side. Chuck shouts "drop it," but when the shining object in suspect B's hand is not dropped within the next second, he discharges his weapon.

The police report notes that suspect B is critically wounded but will recover after several months of physical therapy. Suspect A is treated for a concussion and released. Charges of possessing an unlawful substance will be filed against suspect B, Maureen Smithers. Police investigators accept the reasonableness of Chuck's discharging his weapon on the grounds that he saw a flash of metal that he presumed was a weapon that would be used against the officers. It is later discovered to be the metallic glitter on the purse clutched by Maureen and containing the cocaine that had been used in her drug OD. Another gray Volvo sedan with Maryland plates is found abandoned several hours later, with a damaged right fender with paint that matches the color of the vehicle involved in the fatal accident. The hit-and-run crime remains unsolved.

At home a week later recuperating from the blow to his head, Frank Johnson (aka suspect A) explains to his retired parents, whom he helps support,

> It isn't right to be treated like this when all I was doing was bringing Maureen home from a party. Yes, she was high, but I didn't supply her and I wasn't using the drug. Now she's in the hospital and is probably going to lose her job, and yet she wasn't even conscious of what was happening. And now the word has gotten out that I had a run-in with the police and Holiday Inn notified me that I'll be getting my last paycheck from them—something about not having their reputation blemished. Professionals? They're just hired guns in uniforms, those SOBs.

Directions: Using the Guidelines for Case Study Presentation supplemented by Lawrence Sherman's "Learning Police Ethics" (1982), consider whether officers Simmons and Fisher exercised unreasonable or professionally appropriate force. Why?

APPENDIX B

THE AMERICAN SOCIETY OF MECHANICAL ENGINEERS
FOUNDED 1880

CODE OF ETHICS OF ENGINEERS
THE FUNDAMENTAL PRINCIPLES

Engineers uphold and advance the integrity, honor, and dignity of the Engineering profession by:

    I. using their knowledge and skill for the enhancement of human welfare;

    II. being honest and impartial, and serving with fidelity the public, their employers and clients, and

    III. striving to increase the competence and prestige of the engineering profession.

THE FUNDAMENTAL CANONS

1. Engineers shall hold paramount the safety, health and welfare of the public in the performance of their professional duties.

2. Engineers shall perform services only in the areas of their competence.

3. Engineers shall continue their professional development throughout their careers and shall provide opportunities for the professional and ethical development of those engineers under their supervision.

4. Engineers shall act in professional matters for each employer or client as faithful agents or trustees, and shall avoid conflicts of interest or the appearance of conflicts of interest.

5. Engineers shall build their professional reputation on the merit of their services and shall not compete unfairly with others.

6. Engineers shall associate only with reputable persons or organizations.

7. Engineers shall issue public statements only in an objective and truthful manner.

8. Engineers shall consider environmental impact in the performance of their professional duties.

BOARD ON PROFESSIONAL PRACTICE AND ETHICS

REFERENCES

American Society of Mechanical Engineers [ASME]. 1998. "Code of Ethics of Engineers." ASME Society Policy P-15.7. 8 January 1999. <http:www.asme.org/asme/policies/p15–7.html>.

Beabout, Gregory R., and Daryl Wennemann. 1994. *Applied Professional Ethics: A Developmental Approach for Use with Ethical Case Studies.* Lanham, Md.: University Press of America.

Beck, Robert M., and John B. Orr, eds. 1970. *Ethical Choice.* New York: Free Press.

British Columbia Teachers' Federation. 1998. "Code of Ethics." 8 January 1999. <http://www.bctf.bc.ca./about/membersguide/code.html>.

Callahan, Joan C., ed. 1988. *Ethical Issues in Professional Life.* New York: Oxford University Press.

Dewey, John. 1933. *How We Think.* Boston: D. C. Heath.

Gilligan, Carol. 1982. *In a Different Voice.* Cambridge, Mass.: Harvard University Press.

King, Patricia M., and Karen Strohm Kitchener. 1994. *Developing Reflective Judgment: Understanding and Promoting Intellectual Growth and Critical Thinking in Adolescents and Adults.* San Francisco: Jossey-Bass.

Kockelmans, Joseph, ed. 1979. *Interdisciplinarity and Higher Education.* University Park: The Pennsylvania State University Press.

Kohlberg, Lawrence. 1984. *Essays in Moral Development.* Vol. II: *The Psychology of Moral Development.* San Francisco: Harper and Row.

Millerson, Geoffrey. 1964. *The Qualifying Associations: A Study in Professionalization.* New York: Humanities Press.

Newell, William H. 1998. "Professionalizing Interdisciplinarity." In *Interdisciplinarity: Essays from the Literature,* ed. William H. Newell. New York: College Entrance Examination Board.

Newell, William H., and William J. Green. 1982. "Defining and Teaching Interdisciplinary Studies." *Improving College and University Teaching* 30 (1): 23–30.

Paul, Richard E. 1990. *Critical Thinking: What Every Person Needs to Survive in a Rapidly Changing World.* Rohnert Park, Calif.: Center for Critical Thinking and Moral Critique, Sonoma State University.

Richards, Donald G. 1996. "The Meaning and Relevance of 'Synthesis' in Interdisciplinary Studies." *Journal of General Education* 45 (2): 114–28.

Sherman, Lawrence. 1982. "Learning Police Ethics." *Journal of Criminal Justice Ethics* (Winter/Spring): 10–19.

ETHICS IN THE PROFESSIONS: SAMPLE SYLLABUS

This integrative course provides students with the theoretical tools for resolving dilemmas that arise in professional life. Practical experience is stressed through group efforts to resolve challenging case studies in the health professions, business, the media and the arts, and engineering. (Emphasis on oral and written communication and critical thinking.)

Goals: Students will gain enhanced skills in assessing values, both their own and those of different value systems; enhanced communications skills, both oral and written; more sophisticated critical thinking skills about issues that cannot be resolved simply by appealing to the facts; and heightened awareness of the similarities and dissimilarities in the ethical dilemmas encountered in diverse occupations, both professional and nonprofessional.

Texts: Beabout and Wennemann, *Applied Professional Ethics* (1994); Harris, Pritchard, and Rabins, *Engineering Ethics* (1995); G. E. Pence, *Classic Cases in Medical Ethics* (1995).

Topics:

The Moral Climate and the Concept of "Professional"

Moral Development, Ethical Theory, and Professional-Client Relationships

Public Service and Accountability

Medical Ethics: Classic Questions About Truth and Death; Questions About Abortion and AIDS

Business Morality: On Privacy and Social Responsibility; Deception in the Name of Profit

Engineering Ethics: Conflict of Interest; Public Safety; Corporate Responsibility; Whistle-Blowing

Ethics and the Environment: The Law and Nature

Ethics in Education

Sample Case Studies: Blood Transfusions and Religious Beliefs; The Space Shuttle "Challenger" Disaster; Bribery in Business Ethics; Pregnancy and Cancer; Public Disclosure of School Disciplinary Actions; Advertisement and Marketing of a Product Potentially Damaging to the Environment; Conflicts of Interest and Competing Demands on Engineers.

Selected Student Activities: Two group oral presentations of case studies (including a range of modes, such as dramatic role-plays and videotapings); composing of an original case study; final paper analyzing a moral dilemma.

A BUSINESS SCHOOL CASE METHOD, CLIO, AND INTERDISCIPLINARITY

Charles R. Canedy, 3rd

THE INSTITUTIONAL BACKDROP

Fin de siècle jeremiads on the reputed decline of higher learning in trans-century America abound in scholarly writings and in the popular press. Since the mid-1980s, it seems, U.S. colleges and universities have lurched from one point of crisis to the next. To many observers, most at risk in crisis-laden academia is the state of undergraduate learning. Deprived of a coherent sense of the world and adrift in a disjunctive curriculum caused by faculty discord and inaction, undergraduates have become steeped in cynical relativism, if not nihilism. Aimless and devoid of deep-seated conviction, they have relapsed into primal collegian behavior, obsessed with grades and the acquisition of narrow vocational skills.

Professors of business administration, who have always claimed to excel in classroom instruction with their choreographed delivery formats, now have an opportunity to make a contribution to the turnaround and revitalization of undergraduate education, the academic sphere most in need of dramatic change in the troubled multiversity. As fortune would have it, a vehicle is available for the diffusion of business school teaching techniques—particularly the case method of instruction—to the university at large: interdisciplinary studies.

INTERDISCIPLINARITY AND THE
PROFESSIONAL SCHOOL

Heretofore languishing on many college campuses in a state of intellectual marginality, interdisciplinary studies have been thrust into the mainstream reform of undergraduate education. Devotees hold aloft the banner of the general education movement and are propelled by a millennial zeal to rescue U.S. higher education from a mindless curricular jumble of vocational training and liberal learning without any overarching synthesis or grand vision of the whole.

The general education movement seems to be committed to three major changes in American academia. The first item on the agenda is the virtual interchangeability of interdisciplinarity and integration. Student intellectual abilities should include higher-order reasoning skills such as conceptualization, synthesis, and integration. So equipped, the undergraduate would then have the ability to scope out alternative solutions to complex problems, critique their relative merit by means of "rational actor theory," which in the Anglo-American business world is only another version of common sense, and derive a rigorously reasoned synoptic integration and subsequent plan of action. In the decisional process, the college student would be expected to deal with ambiguity, paradox, and contradiction in a simulated problem environment perplexed by imperfect information.

A second desideratum in the world of interdisciplinarity, a derivative of the objective of synoptic integration, is a skills orientation to teaching. Interdisciplinarians recognize that the acquisition of knowledge is an essential component of cognitive development, but in the Information Society with its abundance of myopic specialized experts, the well-rounded citizen must be endowed with a probing capacity, almost as a survival skill, to identify fundamental processes and question the basic assumptions in various domains of expertise. Interdisciplinary courses therefore should be delivered with the aim of developing and refining critical thinking faculties, the posing and solving of problems, the framing of issues, and the artistry of decision making. Most of these basic knowledge skills are patently not closely linked to specific occupationally relevant competencies.

Last, interdisciplinarians are keen on the delivery of instruction that is activist and participatory, immersing all students in the "dialogic" currents swirling through the classroom. To elevate classroom discourse into a genuine dialogue, the didactic lecture mode, the single most common delivery approach in higher education and a caricature of teaching as a simple, linear information transfer process, is relegated to the dustbin of failed instructional formats, fatally afflicted with what Freire diagnosed over two decades ago as "narration sickness."

The interdisciplinary classroom is characterized by a creative engagement of open, searching inquiry; alert minds in the quest of wide-ranging competencies and synoptic integration; and the cohabitation of instructor and protégés in a co-learning knowledge community. At least this is the theory, but what is the paradigmatic profile of an interdisciplinary instructor?

According to some educators, the model presenter of an interdisciplinary course is an "analogic" thinker rather than a "digital" thinker, the latter regarded as too narrow to integrate domain-crossing issues. He or she is an assertive individual with a tolerance for ambiguity, a broadly educated person chafing under the conventional constraints of a monodisciplinary academic regime. Behavioristically, interdisciplinarians are "divergent" thinkers as opposed to "convergent" thinkers; they savor the messiness and muddle of the world beyond the guarded, gated campus governed as it is by the exotica of chaos theory and its offshoot, self-organized criticality. A new breed of academic is emerging who has had life experiences with problems and challenges outside the Halls of Ivy. Perhaps the French noun, *bricoleur*, translated by Howard Rheingold as one who constructs things "by random messing around without following an explicit plan," most aptly depicts the would-be interdisciplinarian. Be that as it may, it is certainly remarkable that most general education programs have not tapped to any great degree that reservoir of college instructors approximating this ideal profile: the schools of professional studies in the multiversity, particularly colleges of business and management.

Business faculty by training and disposition have an applied problem focus. Both in the classroom and in outside practice, most have had experience in solving problems that are open-ended, multidimensional, ambiguous, unstable, and interstitial, thus more than satisfying the pragmatically based "instrumental" justification of interdisciplinarity.

These "academic intellectuals" also have delivered courses in disciplines with high permeability: that is, in subject areas that are more holistic, less codified, less theoretically specific, and characterized by a more open-ended epistemological structure. One of the offsets of teaching in an immature discipline, one that lacks the canonical texts and defining methodologies of more rigorous fields of study, is that such teaching is often described, if not defined, as "inherently interdisciplinary." To effectively teach these permeable courses, professors of management studies have cultivated in their role as classroom discussion leaders a dual instructional competency, a mastery not only of content but also of the techniques of process.

Tools and methods in the intellectual baggage of nomadic business school faculty that may be of some utility in interdisciplinary studies include familiarity with problem-centered curriculum design, experience with competency-based education, and long involvement as both graduate student and classroom teacher with case-driven instruction. A business school faculty member in tandem with a like-minded colleague from the college of arts and letters can remodel most courses in a general education curriculum with high humanistic content not only to fit the interdisciplinary standard but also to introduce the case method of instruction as the preferred vehicle of delivery.

THE CASE METHOD IN GENERAL

The case method can be used as a research tool or as a teaching method. As the former, a mode of research and a strategy of inquiry for theory development, it acknowledges its derivation from clinical studies in medicine and psychology. The rigorous sense in which the term is used in these fields notwithstanding, case study as a research tool in some domains of knowledge is a metaphor for all nontraditional research methods.

As an active learning approach, the case method has persevered in academia for virtually a century and has spread from its origin in

schools of law into practice-oriented fields such as management studies, public policy, international affairs, and education. Business school
faculty point with pride to the fact that the case method of instruction dates back to the foundation of the Harvard Business School in
1908. The first dean, Edwin F. Gay, a former professor of economic history, encouraged his faculty colleagues to use cases as teaching instruments to enliven the classroom dynamic and engage students in the
learning process instead of relying on rote lectures and discussions of
anthologies.

As case methodology has matured in academia and attempted to
offset the traditional decontextualized learning of the classroom with the
simulation of a professional setting, its advocates have made various
claims as to its effectiveness as a pedagogical format. While it certainly
galvanizes the until-now diffident student to participate and fosters the
development of critical thinking skills in most undergraduates, the case
method of instruction does not automatically generate the integrative
learning enhancements sought by interdisciplinarians. Also, still in dispute among case study theoreticians is the role of the classroom instructor in this "messy" process. Listener? Facilitator? Debriefer?

A 1996 revised teaching note from the Harvard Business School
prepared by faculty member V. Kasturi Rangan addresses these concerns and outlines four approaches to presentation of cases in the
classroom. Each of them has an appropriate role to play in the delivery of a robust, case-oriented curricular offering but each differs quite
markedly in terms of student learning. First, case teachers with an
engaging classroom persona, charismatic stage presence, and superb
platform skills can lecture in and out of a case discussion, particularly
when content new to students is critical for analysis and resolution.
Second, at key junctures in a case course, the instructor might use a
given case as a vehicle to convey conceptual and theoretical knowledge. This stratagem is especially effective at the end of a multi-case
series, when students have constructed inductive frameworks in previous case discussions, understand the themes under consideration, and
are now primed for convergence.

A third tack is case illustration. During the verbal thrust and
parry of the discussion, the instructor intervenes at pregnant points

with "war stories" gleaned from real-world practice, some perhaps based on personal experience, to illuminate the application of certain management techniques. This method of illustration is most advantageously used during the discussion of issues of implementation following the resolution of the case decision.

These three approaches can be used here and there at suitable opportunities during a case course or even integrated into the discussion of a single case. However, their contribution to student learning ranges from suspect to dubious. Of course, learning in a case environment can be measured only by the success of students in appropriating their inductive frameworks, which are relatively grounded in context and time, to related critical issues in future cases and beyond.

Thus only the fourth approach in the Rangan typology—the choreographing of a case—satisfies the learning philosophy of the case method and speaks to all items on the interdisciplinary teaching agenda. Under the tutelage of the case instructor as choreographer, inductive frameworks are erected, alternative solution paths staked out and analyzed, and a decision point followed by an action plan of implementation arrived at. The use of this case approach is tempered with risk (both to the learning process and to the teaching plan of the instructor) and forces the case instructor to play a more intercessionary leadership role than normal in case dynamics.

The choreographer guides students through a discussion of the four or five premapped significant themes of the case, manages points of transition from intellectually exhausted to unexplored materials, reframes deflected issues, refocuses wayward discussions, and reasserts a high rational standard of argumentation when oral commentary degenerates into analytic trivia or ad hominem exchange. Finally, the case instructor encourages students to probe possible contingencies to the solution and secures closure with a final decision and plan of implementation. The exact amount of intercessionary vigor and class redirection exercised by the case instructor in the problem-solving flow is still an unresolved issue at this hour in case management. After all, learning in the Piagetian sense is a discovery process, and students, according to case philosophy, have to "learn how to learn."

THE CASE METHOD: AN ANALYTICAL FRAMEWORK

Although most case teachers have a preferred or even proprietary analytical framework, the variance among business school faculty delivering case-oriented courses is quite small. Invariably, the approach in decision-forcing cases consists of a five- or six-step process commencing with a situational analysis and ending with the implementation of the solution of the case. A representative choreographed case presentation usually includes the following sections:

- Section One: situational audit
- Section Two: problem or decisional statement
- Section Three: identification of heuristic frames
- Section Four: critical issue analysis
- Section Five: recommendation and implementation

Section One is a situational audit—partially diagnostic, partially descriptive, partially synoptic—that profiles the backdrop of the case. This first section focuses on the key factors, major trends, historical forces, and strategic capabilities that must be analyzed and summarized by the case reader to understand in detail the case environment. One way to organize a situational audit is by means of designated rubrics. These are topics or categories—substantive in scale and scope—around which case content may be reorganized to reveal a more penetrating insight into the situation. Rubrics are case-specific (although a few hardy perennials recur in many business cases) and are selected for their ability to assist the student-analyst in making a rational choice among the possible solutions to the problem posed by the case. In a written or oral presentation of a case, the four or five rubrics are discussed sequentially from the most general to the most specific. Some case presenters enfranchise student learners with the right of unrestricted inquiry or the privilege to search for pertinent information beyond the given facts and data of the case text and exhibits.

Section Two is the decisional statement. Problem setting involves defining the problem space in which the solution can be found and is the linchpin of any case presentation, because in the definition of the problem space, the student contours the scope, aggregation level, and domain of the problem. Failure to correctly identify the central problem of a case unleashes a spillover effect that will probably skew the selection of the heuristic frames, distort the designation of the rubrics, and so on. A central problem statement is best communicated in a one-sentence question.

Section Three is the identification of heuristic frames. These are the strategic options that appear to be viable solutions to the problem. Case analysis recognizes that in real-life environments, the management principle of equifinality prevails in that more than one alternative may solve the problem. This is a stretch for novice undergraduates because they generally lack the experience from which to retrieve alternatives for decision making and for the most part must rely on book knowledge. It is not common practice among case-oriented professional school faculty to label alternative solution paths as heuristic frames, but I tend to favor that term.

Individual heuristic frames should be mutually exclusive and collectively exhaustive whenever feasible. These objectives are generally easier to achieve in the logical flow of a business school case than in some of the interdisciplinary cases written for a general education curriculum. The collectively exhaustive rule can be satisfied with four or at most five alternatives.

The mutual exclusion consideration is more challenging. Heuristic frame overlap may have to be conceded in the real world, and there is at times a combination of two or more frames in the admitted set of solutions. The bottom line for inclusion always takes into account logic and operational practicality. Needless to argue, there must be a logical fit between the problem statement and the heuristic frames of the solution set.

Section Four is critical issue analysis. In this section the case analyst spells out a number of decisional criteria to be used in the assessment of the relative attractiveness and utility of the heuristic frames for the resolution of the problem. In a business case these criteria are normally divided into monetary and nonmonetary considerations with profitability, variously expressed and quantified, conventionally the dominant factor. Nonbusiness cases are not so constrained, but the selection process should follow the rule that the criteria reflect the objectives of the decision maker, the organization, or the nation in the case environment.

One quick method of assessment is to assign relative weights to each of the decisional criteria and then value the heuristic frames on each criterion by some scaled rating. The products of the relative weights times the scaled ratings are then summed to derive a global score for each frame. The final scores of all frames are then scanned to determine the decision. However, this analytical aid should not be regarded as a substitute for thorough, rigorous analysis, clear thinking, and enlightened decision making.

Section Five contains two parts: a rather brief recommendation and a more lengthy implementation. In the recommendation subsection, the main reasons for the selection of a given heuristic frame are succinctly stated. The second part of this section addresses the implementation and undertakes—if written, in parsimonious prose, and if class recitation, pointed verbal delivery—a plan of action for the implementation of the case decision.

OUTLINE OF A CASE ANALYSIS

A skeletal framing of a case delivered in the All-University Curriculum (AUC) at the University of Hartford follows to illustrate the application of this particular method of case analysis. I wrote the text of the case after burrowing through a maze of secondary sources. The *lingua franca* of case analysis is the clinical, unemotional language of the corporate executive or the government policymaker. The case exhibits consist of primary materials (diplomatic correspondence, presidential and cabinet member memoirs, committee reports, decrypted radio transmissions, participant recall, and so on), cartographic aids, and other resources (demographic, military, cultural, anthropological, sociological, scientific, and economic charts, diagrams, and tabular data calculations and summaries, which are appended to the case).

The AUC course Discovering America III was designed to examine various issues in American civilization since the Second World War. Each semester students are offered a variety of choices because each section has a different theme. These range from social change in postwar America to the response of artists and literati to lifestyle trends to explorations of American society through biographical narratives. The section discussed here focuses on the cumulative social, cultural, political, and strategic transformations in the United States during its Golden Age. It features a pedagogical repertoire of lectures as well as classroom discussion of anthology articles such as sociological treatises, political commentaries, and excerpts from literary works. Also, a number of cases interspersed throughout the course deal with *Pax* Americana. The case inventory begins with the Asian-Pacific War triptych.

The A Case in this section, the Mukden Incident of 1931, details the course of events in the wake of the attempted derailment of the Dairen Express on the night of September 18 by a group of ultranationalist officers in the Kwantung Army stationed in Manchuria. It focuses on the range of choices available to the Nanking regime as the Japanese military proceeds to overrun the northernmost provinces of the Republic of China and eventually transforms that area into a client state, Manchukuo.

The B Case traces the historical evolution of the prewar *nanshin ron* or "southward advance concept" in Japanese business, government, and naval circles. This penultimate phase of Japanese expansionism, with its vision of hegemony in Southeast Asia, was seen as a solution to the twin dilemmas confronting Japan after 1938. These questions included the war of attrition with China and the increasing difficulty in procuring strategic raw materials from the overseas possessions of the Western powers. The case explores the backdrop of the "fateful" decision to strike south and, predicated as it was on an aerial-naval assault on Hawaii, to initiate an open *casus belli* with the United States.

These two cases are discussed in class to introduce students to the case method. The means of delivery is a methodical progression through the cases to the solutions to teach students the framework, dynamics, and style of this pedagogical approach.

The C Case covers the war in Oceania between the Empire of Japan and the Allied coalition and reviews the strategic options considered by the eventual victors in the Pacific conflict endgame. As originally presented, the case proved too lengthy and has been abbreviated to conform to the general rule of thumb of approximately 15 pages for regular class discussion or write-up. As a consequence, the pendular flow of battle during this struggle has been consigned to a teaching note or briefing paper accompanying the case. Sections one through five of the case presentation follow in sparse outline:

1. Situational Audit
    a. The Japanese strategy in the Asian-Pacific War
    b. The U.S. strategy in the Asian-Pacific War
    c. Tide-of-battle analysis and summary
2. Decisional Statement
   How can the U.S.-led coalition bring the Asian-Pacific endgame of World War II to a successful conclusion—the surrender of the Empire of Japan?
3. Heuristic Frames
    a. Continue with the modified Plan Orange siege strategy of strangulation, economic disarray, and starvation through sustained sea-lane interdiction, hermetic coastal blockade, and heavy conventional bombing to compel Japan into submission.
    b. Pursue the scheduled two-step Operation Downfall: the amphibious and airborne storm of Japan.
    c. Initiate a shock-into-surrender strategy of progressive force: the contingent encouragement of the Soviet Union to honor its Yalta Conference pledge of entry into the Asian-Pacific war, the use of "new-type" bombs, and, only as a last resort, the assault of Kyushu Island and the Kanto Plain.
    d. Negotiate the conditional surrender of Japan by means of back-channel contact or formal diplomatic exchange.
4. Critical Issue Analysis
   Possible decisional criteria:
    a. Unconditional surrender formula
    b. Atomic diplomacy or proxy intimidation of the Soviet Union
    c. One-year-after-defeat-of-Germany deadline enunciated at the Quebec Conference in August 1943
    d. Certitude of victory
    e. Postwar political and territorial implications for the Far East
    f. Cost of strategy in terms of blood and resources
    g. Impact on the morale of the homefront and war-weary troops redeployed from the European theater

h. Domestic political situation
i. Bureaucratic momentum of the Manhattan Project
j. Wartime Roosevelt legacy
k. Desire for retribution and revenge (for Japanese atrocities committed in the field and the "sneak" attack on Pearl Harbor)
l. Infamy of being the first nation to deploy atomic weapons

The arithmetic exercise described in the section on the analytical framework of the case method is not hazarded here because of limitations of space.

5. Recommendation and Implementation

Students who resolve the C Case in terms of the first heuristic frame scope out an implementation scenario closely contoured to the architecture of War Plan Orange, the contingent master plan designed over three decades of U.S. military planning. During the final stage of the Pacific War, the amphibious island-hopping U.S. campaign across the central Pacific would be followed by a siege of bombing and blockade of Japan. There would be no invasion, no engagement with the fearsome Japanese army on a wide front, no casualties of the magnitude of Tarawa Atoll, Guadalcanal, Peleliu, and Okinawa. Urban incendiary attacks by B-29s would reduce a proud nation to ashes and embolden Japanese peace proponents anguished by the mounting horror and devastation of the great fire raids to prevail upon the Emperor to overrule the military bitter-enders and sue for peace terms.

The second heuristic frame is not selected by many undergraduates, but those so inclined script a game plan based on Operation Downfall, the coded project for the invasion of southern Kyushu in November 1945 and Honshu in March 1946. These students believe that the last-ditch psychology of the Japanese Army, despite the toll of air bombardment and offshore naval shelling, would require the use of ground troops to strike and occupy Japan. While it was the prevailing viewpoint among U.S. Army planners skeptical of air corps and naval claims for a siege strategy, Operation Downfall, portending thousands of U.S. casualties, is difficult to justify after the successful atomic detonation at Trinity Site. The mix of official projections of ghastly casualty counts on the beaches and inland, the expenditure of $1 billion tax dollars on the Manhattan Project, and the momentum generated by government agencies and the scientific community render this frame the least attractive to students.

A strategy of progressive force, the third heuristic frame, appeals to those who are skeptical that Japan could be smashed into capitulation by unrelenting air and naval attacks. To these students, the Japanese military may have been virtually defeated everywhere in Oceania and on the Asian continent, but it is not yet willing to surrender. In Japan alone more than 50 infantry divisions reinforced by a *levée en masse* (mass mobilization) were being urged to pit flesh against iron, spirit against material to defend the sacred land from the expected Allied ground invasion. If numerous casualties were inflicted on the invader by a resolute beachhead defense, then the war-weary Western democracies might be willing to end the war on terms far better than unconditional surrender. To dispel these illusions, held in high Japanese circles, some students argue that only a strategy of escalation—Russian entry into the war coupled with the serial obliteration of targeted cities by the "superbomb"—will shock the Japanese into a realization of the total hopelessness and futility of their cause. If for some inconceivable reason the irradiated land still did not sue for peace, tactical atomic weaponry would be used in the invasion of southern Kyushu.

Students who recommend the fourth heuristic frame, conditional surrender, contend that Japan has already been defeated. Its metropolitan areas have been gutted, its economy devastated, its transportation infrastructure bottlenecked, and millions of its people malnourished and homeless. If it were not for the unconditional surrender doctrine, Japan probably would have surrendered in the spring or early summer of 1945. These students therefore suggest offering terms of conditional surrender to the Japanese government, including the retention of the imperial system, the thorny issue dividing the belligerents. By this back-channel or formal diplomatic move, the United States would be spared the human agony of invasion and the moral stigma of atomic terror. This frame might include a noncombat demonstration to Japanese observers of the atomic bomb on a neutral site. Some students believe, however, that a negotiated peace is tantamount to losing the war and argue that it would accepted by a war-fatigued U.S. public only if the Pacific endgame became a protracted struggle of attrition.

Other cases presented in Discovering America III include the Truman Doctrine, the outbreak of civil war in the Korean peninsula, the Dien Bien Phu debacle, and the Cuban missile crisis. Cases in various stages of development from late conceptualization to testing in the classroom explore U.S. strategy with regard to events in China, South Vietnam, Afghanistan, the Persian Gulf, and Bosnia-Herzegovina. All these cases profess to discover America by selectively analyzing how Washington has conducted international relations during the last half-century. The "informal empire" of *Pax* Americana projects volumes about the exceptionalism of the American experiment in world history.

Case studies integrate analytical and thematic materials from various disciplines into a chronological and narrative representation of an essentially historical decision-making situation. The materials may include the economics of land reform and the formation of an entrepreneurial class in a Confucian society, the clash of confessional and cultural norms, the feminist as combatant and insurgent, and theories of nuclear deterrence. Public policy issues at the national and state levels also could be similarly reframed in a case method format. For instance, the Kennedy School of Government at Harvard University displays in its online catalog a collection of nearly 1,500 case abstracts in public policy probing contemporary national and local issues such as youth violence, federal drug control, zoning restrictions on social services for the underclass, and civil rights reform. I plan to extend the case dimension of this course to areas of American experience other than foreign policy in the near future. Instructors who seek to deliver in their courses both content enhancement and the development of critical thinking and problem solving skills have in the case methodology a tested vehicle of instruction to achieve these learning objectives.

Has genuine interdisciplinarity really been achieved by this teaching praxis? It certainly exhibits two characteristics of interdisciplinary interaction: method interdisciplinarity, or the use of tools and techniques of one discipline in other fields of study; and composite interdisciplinarity, or the instrumental solution of problems without a conceptual unification of knowledge. It is a superb vehicle for integration of existing content from multiple disciplines. On the other hand, it does little to contribute to the emergence of a new branch of knowledge—an interdiscipline.

The case method detailed in this essay incorporates the synthesis of selective content abstracted from a number of disciplines housed in the college of arts and letters and a reengineered process of decisional analysis common in professional school instruction. The liberal arts content has been reconfigured, cross-fertilized, and lodged in a problem-laden text to make it amenable to analysis and discussion in a case-method format. The case method represents a new metalevel mode of discourse that bridges institutional divides and normatively projects, from its rational actor approach, what best decisional practice should be. After all, theorizing in any field of knowledge oblivious to empirical application is conjectural fantasy at best, and vice versa, case studies not grounded in theory may not aggregate beyond interesting "combat" anecdotes.

All in all, this particular intellectual bond of content and process perhaps constitutes a building block, a Mertonian middle-range theory, on the steep path to a master paradigm of what an interdisciplinary field indeed ought to look like and how its granular texture can be smoothly communicated to undergraduates.

REFERENCES

Harvard University, John F. Kennedy School of Government. 1998. *Case Studies in Public Policy and Management*. 8 January 1999. <http:www/ksgcase.harvard. edu>.

Rangan, V. Kasturi. 1996. *Choreographing a Case Class*. Boston: Harvard Business School Publishing.

ADDITIONAL RESOURCES

Christensen, C. Roland, David Garvin, and Ann Sweet. 1991. *Education for Judgment: The Artistry of Discussion Leadership.* Boston: Harvard Business School Press.

Christensen, C. Roland, and Abby Hanson. 1987. *Teaching and the Case Method: Text Cases and Readings.* Boston: Harvard Business School Press.

Cohen, Myron, ed. 1992. *Case Studies in the Social Sciences: A Guide for Teaching.* Columbia Project on Asia in the Core Curriculum. Armonk, N.Y.: M. E. Sharpe.

Corey, E. Raymond. 1980. *Case Method Teaching.* Boston: HBS Case Series, Harvard Business School Press.

Dyer, Robert, and Ernest Forman. 1991. *An Analytic Approach to Marketing Decisions.* Englewood Cliffs, N.J.: Prentice-Hall.

Easton, Geoff. 1982. *Learning from Case Studies.* Englewood Cliffs, N.J.: Prentice-Hall International.

Eckstein, Harry. 1975. "Case Study and Theory in Political Science." In *Handbook of Political Science,* Vol. 7, eds. Fred I. Greenstein and Nelson Polsby. Reading, Pa.: Addison Wesley.

Erskine, James, Michiel Leenders, and Louise Mauffette-Leenders. 1981. *Teaching with Cases.* London, Ontario: School of Business Administration, University of Western Ontario, Canada.

Gijselaers, Wim, Dirk T. Tempelaar, Piet K. Keizer, Jos M. Blommaert, Eugene M. Bernard, and Hans Kasper, eds. 1995. *Educational Innovation in Economics and Business Administration: The Case of Problem-Based Learning.* Dordrecht, Netherlands: Kluwer Academic Publishers.

Klein, Hans, ed. 1989. "Case Method Research and Case Method Application." *Selected Papers of the Sixth International Conference on Case Method Research and Case Method Application.* Needham, Mass.: World Association for Case Method Research and Application.

Klein, Julie Thompson. 1990. *Interdisciplinarity: History, Theory, and Practice.* Detroit, Mich.: Wayne State University Press.

Klein, Julie Thompson. 1996. *Crossing Boundaries: Knowledge, Disciplinarities, and Interdisciplinarities.* Charlottesville: University Press of Virginia.

Leenders, Michiel, and James Erskine. 1989. *Case Research: The Case Writing Process.* 3d ed. London, Ontario: School of Business Administration, University of Western Ontario, Canada.

Locke, Rovert. 1996. *The Collapse of the American Management Mystique.* New York: Oxford University Press.

Lucas, Christopher. 1996. *Crisis in the Academy: Rethinking Higher Education in America.* New York: St. Martin's.

O'Dell, William, Andrew Ruppell, Robert Trent, and William Kehoe. 1988. *Marketing Decision Making: Analytic Framework and Cases.* 4th ed. Cincinnati, Ohio: South-Western Publishing Company.

SVHE Task Force. 1990. "SVHE Task Force Report on Interdisciplinary Studies." *Issues in Integrative Studies* 8: 9–33.

Yin, Robert. 1984. *Case Study Research: Design and Methods.* Applied Social Research Series, Vol. 5. Beverly Hills, Calif.: Sage.

DISCOVERING AMERICA III: 1945 TO PRESENT: SAMPLE SYLLABUS

This integrative course is an inquiry into American society, culture, and thought in the post-World War II era. The topics chosen for investigation represent significant themes and issues that have been and continue to be influential in shaping the contours of recent American cultural experience. Readings for this course emphasize the diverse perspectives of major American writers, historians, and social scientists. (Emphasis on written communication and critical thinking.)

Goals: Through an active inquiry classroom approach that has both ancient pedagogical roots and latter-day professional-school refinements, students will gain an understanding of complex issues of international and domestic policy in the second half of the twentieth century. They will become proficient in the use of the case method as a tool of interdisciplinary discourse and develop critical thinking faculties and presentation skills in reasoning to decision-point about landmark issues.

Texts: Paul Boyer, *Promises to Keep: The United States Since World War II* (1999); Thomas Frazier, ed., *The Many Sides of America: 1945 to the Present* (1996); Charles R. Canedy 3rd, *Discovering America Coursebook* (typescript).

Topics With Case Content:

Endgame in the Pacific, the Collapse of the Grand Alliance, and the Shattered Peace
  Cases: The East Asian-Pacific War Trilogy; The Truman Doctrine

The Asian Cockpit: Reinventing Japan, Lost Chance in Mainland China, Divided Korea, *Agonie de l'Indochine* and the "Forgotten War"
  Cases: Civil War in Korea; The Indochina Crucible

The Vicissitudes of the [Aronite] Imperial Republic: Thirteen Days on the Thermonuclear Brink and Thirteen Years of Quagmire War
  Case: The Cuban Missile Crisis

Other Topics:

The American Business System and Postwar Global Dominance Race, Gender, and Generation on the Home Front During World War II

The Years of Conformity and Protest

The McDonaldization Hypothesis

Contemporary Generational Cohorts

A Half-Century of American Political Cycles

Major Intellectual Issues at the Fin de Siècle

Selected Student Activities: Oral and written case exercises.

SOURCES OF POWER: INTEGRATION IN THE SOCIAL SCIENCES

Jane Horvath

Victor F. D'Lugin was a member of the original development team for the course and was the political theorist with whom I team-taught it. He died of AIDS-related complications in August 1996. He is missed as a teacher, scholar, colleague, and friend. This chapter is dedicated to him.

The University of Hartford's Sources of Power course was designed by faculty from communication, economics, political science, and sociology. It is one of the courses in the All-University Curriculum's (AUC) "Living in a Social Context" category, in which inquiry is focused on aspects of social exchange. Although individual courses in many of the traditional social science departments are devoted almost exclusively to the study of this issue, the faculty who developed the course on Power hold the view that if students are to gain a full understanding of power, in all its dimensions, an interdisciplinary approach is essential. As Kockelmans observes:

> any single one of the social sciences, psychology, sociology, and the rest, cannot validly develop in scope and depth without cross-borrowing from the others. This interdisciplinary borrowing is not a matter of choice, but is a necessity to achieve the needed scope and depth within each discipline. (1979, x)

The faculty team built an integrative social science course around a single concept, power, to enable students to examine that concept thoroughly using the perspectives of multiple social science disciplines.

Early in the development process, the team adopted an approach integrating readings from the various disciplines. Theories and terminology from those disciplines would, of course, be identified for students, but that would not be the primary focus of the course. Thus the team rejected a model that presents each discipline's contribution to the study of power in a rigid, sequential manner; we wanted to avoid what Richards has since termed "serial multidisciplinarity" (1996, 127). Class sessions minimize disciplinary boundaries and serve as a model for an integrated study of power. The interdisciplinary approach provides what Richards describes as "a more adequate accounting of the subject than strictly disciplinary approaches can" (1996, 125). Students gain what has been termed in the literature an "enriched understanding" of the concept while examining the limitations of a single-discipline approach.

The course has two goals. The intellectual goal, as stated in the syllabus, is to teach students to "recognize and understand the nature of power and how it is used in society, and to apply this understanding in their own lives." The second and related goal is to develop students' skills in oral and written communication and critical thinking. Oral assignments include group and individual presentations as well as ongoing class participation. Students are evaluated on the basis of their ability to ask questions, participate in debate, and orally defend positions. They must also exhibit an understanding of and competence to analyze different perspectives. Written assignments may or may not involve library research. Students write several essays based on assigned short narratives, in which they must explain the arguments made by the authors and evaluate them in light of the concepts and theories presented in class. Students also compare and contrast differing viewpoints expressed in the assigned readings.

The course thus is geared to the development of critical thinking skills. In both oral and written assignments, students identify and evaluate perspectives and arguments presented in class and in assigned readings and critique them in light of data, evidence, alternative perspectives, and their own observations. Through this process students not only come to know *what* they think but gain some insight into why they hold particular views and how they arrived at those views.

COURSE FORMAT: OPTIONS AND ADVANTAGES

The course has been taught by an economics/political science/sociology team and by an economics/political science team, as well as by a single faculty member. We have used two different team-teaching models. The first is a variation of the dispersed-team model described by Colarulli and McDaniel in the Appendix to this volume: after meeting as a large group once a week, we devote the second weekly meeting either to small-group discussion, with each of the three instructors leading his or her section, or, if the material warrants, to another combined group meeting. This model provides maximum flexibility in instruction. It also ensures that the instructors meet regularly to discuss and plan class activities, because we must not only do the groundwork necessary for effective team teaching but also make decisions each week about the configuration of the sections with respect to various topics and classroom activities. This requires planning so that students have adequate lead-time to arrange schedules.

This format has two disadvantages. In weeks when we choose to hold a combined class for our second meeting, we underutilize scarce university classroom space. Meeting in combined sections leaves two classrooms unoccupied for the 75-minute period, which obviously works against the usual efficiencies associated with the team-teaching model (see the Appendix to this volume). Also, students express some confusion about changing formats. We might argue that because they receive timely notification of the format for the next week, their complaints are without merit. Nevertheless, these complaints reflect students' discomfort with a variable format for class meetings that deviates from the set class format they have come to expect from traditional course scheduling models.

When two instructors teach the course, we meet as combined sections twice weekly and both faculty actively participate in each class session. Both are in front of the classroom at all times and interact with students and each other on a continuous basis. We do not divide up class meetings so that one instructor is "responsible" for the lecture on a given day and the other plays a passive or more limited role. Sharing the classroom throughout the semester results in a great deal of spontaneity. This approach, however, requires considerable trust as well as a willingness to engage in risk-taking behavior. Students do have "their instructor" because they register for a section with one of the instructors and receive grades from that faculty member. However, because presentations, lectures, and discussions are truly team-taught, students do not identify with their instructor as much as in the AUC's usual team-teaching setting.

I have also taught the course alone on several occasions. Each time I rely heavily on guest speakers and use the university as a laboratory to explore issues of power on the interpersonal, institutional, and system levels. Guest speakers, primarily from within the university, include representatives of various constituencies on campus, such as the editor of the campus newspaper, the head of the student government, the director of the Multicultural Center, the associate provost/dean of undergraduate studies, and select members of the faculty. This cross section allows us to study the power dynamics among students, staff, faculty, administrators, and regents. We are able to apply the concepts developed in class to an environment with relevance to the students, and the class gains valuable insight into the world around them. As Newell observes, it is difficult to "enforce interdisciplinarity" when a team-developed interdisciplinary course is taught, for budget or other reasons, by a single faculty member (1990, 77). The guest speakers reinforce the interdisciplinary emphasis of the course. Use of the team's syllabus, as well as my experience teaching the course as a member of a team, further counters the tendency for Sources of Power to evolve into a disciplinary course. Students reinforce interdisciplinarity by integrating relevant concepts from their discipline-based courses into our discussions and analysis.

Nationwide, the debate continues on the advantages and disadvantages of team-teaching interdisciplinary courses, based on cost (Benson 1982, 46; Newell 1983, 10; Colarulli and McDaniel, in this volume) or pedagogical value (Kockelmans 1979, 140; Stember 1991; Richards 1996, 127). Accompanying research has identified those conditions necessary for successful team teaching. Stember notes that team members must have a "commitment to a common interest" and that "successful interdisciplinary teams require a common focus for their work" (1991, 6). The teams working on Sources of Power certainly meet these conditions. Whether coming from an economic, political theory, or sociological perspective, we are all committed to the study of power in a social context and prefer a macro approach to the subject. That is, we tend to place more emphasis on the structural, institutional, and systemic issues than on the interpersonal and psychological aspects of power. It is perhaps because of this shared preference for a macro level of analysis that we communicate easily and across discipline borders. We reflect Klein's comment that "individuals interested in cross-disciplinary problems and questions often find it easier to communicate with individuals in other disciplines or disciplinary subgroupings, even though they retain disciplinary labels reflecting their original graduate training" (1993, 190).

Richards argues that team teaching is not the best approach to undergraduate interdisciplinary courses. He maintains that team members do not succeed in achieving interdisciplinary synthesis because of the time and effort involved. The result is the serial multidisciplinarity, apparent to students (Richards 1996, 127), that we are determined to avoid. We do not have these problems, perhaps because we share what Stember describes as "the right combination of commitment to the common interest, disciplinary competence, broad interests, and personal attributes" (1991, 6). Further, team members are secure enough in their own individual disciplines and competence that interdisciplinary work is in no way a threat to our egos or sense of self. Finally, we all share a trust in each other that facilitates risk-taking behavior, exemplified either as forays into new and less familiar teaching formats or the use of innovative texts.

Based on my experiences, team-teaching an interdisciplinary course is of greater value to students than the one-instructor format, which in my mind is a second-best solution. When instructors are actively involved in team teaching, students benefit enormously from the interplay across disciplines. When a single instructor teaches an interdisciplinary course, students benefit from that instructor's prior experience in a team-teaching setting. My understanding of power in a social context has been enriched through team teaching and I bring that experience with me when I teach the course alone.

Why have I taught the course in a single-instructor format? Identifying and forming faculty teams is a difficult and lengthy process. Ensuring the continued vitality of teams also requires attention, and even if that attention is forthcoming, people's interests and commitments change. Therefore new teams continually have to be recruited, developed, and nurtured. In the case of Sources of Power, that process can take several semesters. Just recently, after being confined to the single-instructor format for three years because of faculty unavailability, the course has a new communication/economics team.

FRAMEWORKS FOR ANALYSIS

The course begins with a discussion of student expectations. Responses range from "I heard it was a good course" and "It was a required course that fit into my schedule" to "I want to learn how to be powerful; to get what I want." Through preliminary questioning in the first few days of class, it becomes apparent that students bring with them preconceived ideas—for example, a tendency to acknowledge power being exercised over them while resisting the acknowledgment of their own power. They also tend to see authority figures as all-powerful and prefer to identify power with persons rather than with role or institutions. Further, they lack a framework in which to analyze the concept of power.

Early in the semester we provide such a framework through the work of sociologist Dennis Wrong (1979), whose discussion of "forms of power" helps students understand the difference between influence and power and identifies different forms of power: force, persuasion, manipulation, and authority. To teach students how to distinguish between various forms of power, we ask them to identify and classify power where and when they experience it. In one early assignment, they explore instances in which they have been both the power holder and the power subject, discussing their roles in terms of Wrong's four forms of power.

Throughout the semester two additional concepts provide a more complete understanding of the dimensions of power. Bachrach and Baratz's (1963) concept of "nondecision-making" introduces students to the idea that individuals and institutions most effectively exercise power when they set agendas for people who are unaware that they face constrained choice, at best, or no choice, in the extreme. One example illustrating nondecision-making is Reynolds's article "Rape as Social Control" (1974). The "decision" to view rape as an individual act of violence rather than as a social act that serves to control all women and limit their deviation from traditional roles reinforces the orthodoxy of appropriate sex roles. After gaining an appreciation for Reynolds's argument, students often get caught up in the gender issues it raises. The class often splits along gender lines, with female students feeling angry and victimized by the accepted view of rape as an individual act and male students feeling the need to distance themselves from this view.

At this point we read the bell hooks essay "Seduced by Violence No More" (1994), in which the author urges both heterosexual males and females to engage in a critical self-examination of their own views of the erotic. The essay challenges students to recognize how their own uncritical acceptance of the dominant culture's definition of the erotic contributes to what hooks terms "a rape culture." The introduction of the hooks essay immediately following the Reynolds article reinforces the concept of nondecision-making. Another work used to illustrate this concept is "On the Merits" by essayist Katha Pollitt (1975). It forces students to reconsider the accepted definition of affirmative action. Pollitt identifies special privileges often given to high-income white males that we do not tend to see as affirmative action. These include civil service points for veterans and preference in college admission for children of alumni. Pollitt asks why the debate on affirmative action focuses on perceived advantages given to nonwhites and nonmales and those not from the upper class. If the terms of the debate are defined in this way, those seeking to limit affirmative action will much more likely be successful in exercising power and achieving their desired results.

Next we introduce the concept of privilege, drawing primarily on the work of McIntosh (1988). While McIntosh focuses chiefly on white male privilege, we broaden the concept to include heterosexual and social class privilege. Students struggle with this concept. Again, exercises are useful, as are the instructors' acknowledgments that we too grew up in a sexist, racist, heterosexist, and classist society. Thus the discussion becomes less value-laden and students can acknowledge their own privilege(s).

Course materials have changed over the years, but several important readings have remained constant, including our main text, Parenti's *Power and the Powerless* (1978). Parenti, a political scientist, elaborates the concepts of nondecision making and privilege while maintaining students' focus on role and institutions rather than individuals and personal character. Readings to supplement the Reynolds article and the Pollitt essay vary from semester to semester to keep the course current. They have included the works of James Baldwin, Audre Lorde, Toni Morrison, and Sarah Schulman. Issues of racism, sexism, homophobia, and social class conflict play an important role in Sources of Power. As a result, the supplementary readings deal heavily with these subjects and reflect "hot" topics that get media attention. For example, in a recent semester we read articles from gay and lesbian as well as mainstream business publications to explore the power issues associated with the coming-out of the lead character on the *Ellen* television show, the first sitcom with an "out" lesbian in the starring role.

In one particularly effective assignment, students research and write about the confrontation between George Wallace and the Kennedy White House over the integration of the University of Alabama. The integration of the university serves as a case study on the uses of and limits to power in a political context. The assignment has two parts. Students first do library research and write an historically correct description of the clash between Wallace and Kennedy. They then analyze the effectiveness of the strategies used by various parties in the dispute. They must use Wrong's framework of the forms of power to critique the actions taken by the various players. This assignment gives students the opportunity to apply the different analytical approaches to power introduced early in the semester to an event in which the dynamics of power are key.

After students submit their papers, we view the 1963 Robert Drew video *Wallace v. Kennedy: A Crisis Up Close*, in which students see the Kennedy and Wallace camps strategizing to resolve the conflict. The video is especially effective in conveying the limits of power facing even the president of the United States. This limitation often surprises students because many have a notion that those in authority are all-powerful and always able to achieve their intended results.

The exercise concludes with a reading of the activities of the president and his advisers on June 11, 1963, the day of the confrontation with Governor Wallace, in *President Kennedy: Profile of Power,* by Reeves (1993). After students research and write about this confrontation for several weeks, it comes as a great surprise to them that the crisis in Alabama was but one of several pressing issues the White House dealt with that day. Through the Reeves book students gain a more realistic view of how power is wielded at the national level.

We often end the semester with a reading of the play *Galileo* by Brecht (1940), which allows us to examine why people listen and acquiesce to authority. The play also emphasizes, in a dramatic and compelling way, the importance of role in understanding the concept of power. By ending the semester with this work, students gain fuller understanding of the interplay of social, political, and economic issues in situations in which authority is questioned and threatened.

CONCLUSION

Faculty who have taught Sources of Power describe it as their favorite course to teach. Working in an interdisciplinary setting with trusted colleagues allows for lots of intellectual play. In the course, we push the limits. We ask students to question—to question what they know and what they believe. Our goal is for students to gain an understanding of power, to see how it is used and how it affects their lives. Several years ago, a popular bumper sticker read "Question Authority." At the time, I pointed out to students that the bumper sticker was quite often spotted on Volvos, and, referring to the people who typically drive Volvos, I asked, "But I thought they *were* authority?" We want our students to ask that question and see the possible irony in the statement being made by the Volvo driver.

REFERENCES

Bachrach, Peter, and Morton S. Baratz. 1963. "Decisions and Nondecisions: An Analytical Framework." *American Political Science Review* 57 (September): 632–42.

Benson, Thomas. 1982. "Five Arguments against Interdisciplinary Studies." *Issues in Integrative Studies* 1: 38–48.

Brecht, Bertolt. [1940] 1966. *Galileo,* translated by Charles Laughton, ed. Eric Bentley. New York: Grove Weidenfeld.

hooks, bell. 1994. "Seduced by Violence No More." In *Outlaw Culture: Resisting Representations.* New York: Routledge.

Klein, Julie Thompson. 1993. "Blurring, Cracking, and Crossing: Permeation and the Fracturing of Disciplines." In *Knowledges: Historical and Critical Studies in Disciplinarity,* eds. Ellen Messer-Davidow, David R. Shumway, and David J. Sylvan. Charlottesville: University of Virginia Press.

Kockelmans, Joseph J. 1979. Preface. *Interdisciplinarity and Higher Education,* ed. Joseph J. Kockelmans. University Park: Pennsylvania State University Press.

McIntosh, Peggy. 1988. "White Privilege: Unpacking the Invisible Knapsack." In *Experiencing Race, Class, and Gender in the United States,* ed. Virginia Cyrus. Mountain View, Calif.: Mayfield.

Newell, William. 1983. "The Case for Interdisciplinary Studies: Response to Professor Benson's Five Arguments." *Issues in Integrative Studies* 2: 1–19.

Newell, William. 1990. "Interdisciplinary Curriculum Development." *Issues in Integrative Studies* 8: 69–86.

Parenti, Michael. 1978. *Power and the Powerless.* New York: St. Martin's.

Pollitt, Katha. 1995. "On the Merits." In *Reasonable Creatures: Essays on Women and Feminism.* New York: Vintage.

Reeves, Richard. 1993. *President Kennedy: Profile of Power.* New York: Simon and Schuster.

Reynolds, Janice M. 1974. "Rape as Social Control." *Catalyst* 8 (Winter): 62–67.

Richards, Donald G. 1996. "The Meaning and Relevance of 'Synthesis' in Interdisciplinary Studies." *Journal of General Education* 45 (2): 114–28.

Stember, Marilyn. 1991. "Advancing the Social Sciences Through the Interdisciplinary Enterprise." Presidential Address. *Social Science Journal* 28: 1–14.

Wrong, Dennis H. 1979. *Power: Its Forms, Bases and Uses.* New York: Harper and Row.

SOURCES OF POWER: SAMPLE SYLLABUS

This integrative course employs perspectives from the various social science disciplines to help students recognize and understand the nature of power and how it is used in society. Students examine power on the interpersonal, group, institutional, and societal levels. They gain insight into contemporary issues and controversies and apply this understanding in their own lives. (Emphasis on written and oral communication and critical thinking.)

Goals: Students will understand the application of scientific methods to the study of human behavior and understand the variety of analysis and explanation in the social sciences; distinguish individual, group, and mass levels of analysis and explanation; critically evaluate the need for, implications of, and biases of each perspective; directly apply and integrate understanding of the various social sciences through study of a particular shared issue; analyze the power dynamics in particular situations; and develop the skill to evaluate the effectiveness of strategies employed to achieve a desired effect.

Texts: Michael Parenti, *Power and the Powerless* (1978); Bertolt Brecht, *Galileo* (1940); selected articles.

Topics:

Introduction to the Social Sciences

Definitions of Power

Forms of Power: Dennis Wrong

Orthodoxy and the Nondecision-Making Model

Applications: Nondecision-Making and Privilege; Rape as Social Control; Affirmative Action; University Life

Case Study: The Integration of the University of Alabama

Authority: *Galileo*

Selected Student Activities: Group discussions encouraging critical evaluation of situations at the interpersonal (such as parent-child interactions or dating), group (students versus the university administration), and societal levels (e.g., the public debate surrounding affirmative action); short papers analyzing and evaluating assigned readings; research paper on the integration of the University of Alabama.

THE RIGHT TO FOOD: HUNGER AND THE PROBLEMS OF SCARCITY AND CHOICE

Jane Horvath, Doug Dix, and Bernard den Ouden

PURPOSE

The course Hunger: Problems of Scarcity and Choice is designed to give students a clear understanding of the problem of hunger, its causes, and, we hope, some possible solutions. In addition, students are introduced to the concept of global interdependence. Students gain an appreciation of the reality that hunger, poverty, disease, and pollution in any corner of the world have an effect on everyone.

One effective way of heightening students' awareness of the many problems associated with global interdependence is to present the scenario of "life-boat ethics" (an uncommon moral dilemma) through which the paradoxes of survival and interdependency are vividly portrayed (Hardin 1974, 38). Through case studies, students learn that ignorance of the problems of hunger and poverty leads to choices that bring with them profound and serious consequences. This holds true, as well, for choices concerning aid to needy countries, development assistance, or other models of intervention (Hardin 1968, 1243).

As illustrated in the sample syllabus following this chapter, we always begin our discussion with a geographic lesson on where most of the world's hungry live: the developing countries. We focus on the major problems associated with hunger in those countries and emphasize the interconnectedness of the developing world with our own. From there, we move to the hungry in the United States, Connecticut, and ultimately, Hartford. Concluding the course with a look at the city nearest to the university reinforces the understanding that hunger is not a foreign phenomenon.

INTERDISCIPLINARITY

In his article "Why Interdisciplinarity?" Kockelmans (1979) makes a compelling case for interdisciplinary study. He asserts that certain questions cannot adequately be investigated within a single discipline but rather must be examined from the standpoint of many disciplines. As Fuller puts it, some problems "require that practitioners of several such disciplines organize themselves in novel settings and adopt new ways of regarding their work" (1993, 33). We, the teaching faculty in the course Hunger: Problems of Scarcity and Choice, identify the problem of hunger as one such topic. We would go one step further: a sound policy solution to the problem must be firmly grounded in several disciplines. In fact, a single-discipline approach can lead to destructive planning, policy, and consequences. We are not alone in holding this view. For example, van Dusseldorp and Wigboldus (1994), in discussing rural development projects, assert that policymakers and planners need a knowledge of several disciplines to effectively develop and implement sound policies. They observe that as the problems facing planners and policymakers become more complicated, the need for interdisciplinary research increases.

How do faculty interest undergraduate students in interdisciplinary work? The students are usually exclusively familiar with learning inside the bounds of a single discipline. Oddly enough, we often then criticize them for not making the connections between disciplines and courses that we think should come to them quite naturally. In recent years much of the research on learning and teaching has centered on the need for educators to address and accommodate divergent learning styles (Gardner 1993). As part of that critical self-analysis, we must also address the role of interdisciplinary study. If it is the case that students do not naturally acquire knowledge within disciplinary boundaries and that this is a learned behavior, taught by successful faculty participants in an institution known for turf wars and battles over the ownership of key ideas, then learning new ways to think about and order problems will not come easily or without a certain level of discomfort and perhaps outright resistance.

TEAM TEACHING AND SPONTANEITY

In the All-University Curriculum students learn in a setting that is not only interdisciplinary but team taught. The faculty believe that the study of hunger is an interdisciplinary effort in which "the work can most often be done effectively only by teams" (Kockelmans 1979, 140). The team typically includes an anthropologist, a biologist, an economist, and a philosopher. In joint sessions once a week, one instructor, on an alternating basis, begins with a traditional lecture on the relevant facts or concepts within her or his field of expertise. While one instructor has primary responsibility for each weekly large-group session, that does not mean that the others are passive observers. Rather, each discipline-based instructor has something to contribute to the discussion of each theme or topic. As a result, there is a lot of interaction among the instructors during the sessions. The instructors interrupt, question, discuss, debate, criticize, and expound on the theme presented. Because no one can predict how any given session will evolve, faculty cannot prepare for class in the traditional manner. Spontaneity and risk-taking become paramount.

These processes do not develop automatically and can be quite difficult. Most of us were trained in discipline-bound settings and students likewise are unaccustomed to interdisciplinary study. We are acutely aware that we are asking students to engage in a form of inquiry with which they are not familiar. To make students feel more comfortable in this situation, we have a frank discussion at the first meeting about how the large-group setting works. We explain to students that the instructors will be interacting with each other. We outline a strategy that emphasizes disagreement and debate as means of exploring the interdisciplinary nature of the subject and indeed, of conducting any complex inquiry. We let them know that we are comfortable interacting with each other in this manner, although it is new to many of us. We use respect, humor, and friendship to counter any attempts by students to "keep score." This introduction to the course is especially important when the teaching teams include faculty of different genders and races, because critical interruptions can be perceived as sexist or racist by students (Nieto 1996; Simpson and Erickson 1983).

Many students are reticent and refuse to speak in the full group sessions, but we encourage them to be active participants in their own learning. Like Hursh, Haas, and Moore, we find that interdisciplinary learning works best when students are not merely passive observers in the classroom (1983, 57). Therefore we discourage students from sitting back and watching the interaction among the instructors. They are asked, encouraged, angered, and cajoled into speaking in these sessions. Moreover, they are encouraged to debate issues with each other and with the faculty.

Much of our effort is directed at overcoming student inertia, because it is essential that students, as well as faculty, question commonly held assumptions about hunger by means of spontaneity. In this regard we follow the lead of Kavaloski, who points to the need in interdisciplinary study to think beyond the assimilation "of subject matter, and begin to think of how it can become an integrative process of becoming more human" (1979, 234). We encourage as much participation as possible to ensure that students actively engage the facts surrounding hunger while confronting how their own behavior and values affect the world's hungry. Beyond our own example and strong encouragement to students to participate, we have had some success providing students with a microphone to engage with and debate each other.

Many students of course feel much more comfortable speaking in smaller groups, and the weekly small-group sessions conducted by individual instructors provide this opportunity. Usually, these more intimate sessions emphasize in-depth discussions about readings and issues raised when we are all together. Quizzes, exams, and the presentation of group and individual projects also occur in the smaller sessions, which in addition give students practice for presentations to be made to the full group. Faculty act as coaches and students learn to support each other.

INTERDISCIPLINARITY IN THE STUDY OF HUNGER

Course faculty encourage students to analyze and integrate the layers of meaning that shape the dilemmas of hunger. As social scientists, humanists, and natural scientists, we use a pluralistic approach to the issues surrounding hunger, poverty, and scarcity and choice, that is, from a number of sound and viable perspectives. The interdisciplinary approach and methodology of the course are supportive when we discuss differing values. One main concern is to demonstrate that just because values differ, they are not necessarily mutually exclusive. Different perspectives often have significant spheres of overlap or shared domains of relevance and applicability. For example, when opposing ethical theories are discussed, students are encouraged to dig deeply into the historical and cultural circumstances that influenced the development of the theories and to scrutinize their own religious and cultural backgrounds. As co-inquirers we make it clear that the world's religions, such as Islam, Christianity, Judaism, Buddhism, and Hinduism, all have specific mandates and principles emphasizing responsibility for the poor. In addition, students are urged to take their own heritages seriously and use them as a starting point for the development of their perspectives on poverty.

After an in-depth examination of both the Kantian and utilitarian ethical theories, students are asked to relate them to questions of hunger and the hungry. By so doing, they move from the discipline of philosophy to sociology and ultimately to questioning the uncritical acceptance of competitive models of income, wealth, and food distribution. Thus the inherent interdisciplinary nature of the topic becomes clear. Furthermore, we explore another element that adds to the complexity of this issue, namely the environmental. We may begin a discussion with a general assertion, for example: There is only one earth and we all have the same survival needs that we fill from the same atmosphere and oceans. In spite of the fact that we claim ownership of different land and different sources of fresh water, ultimately all property is integrated into the same global ecosystem. Indeed, as the human population increases, the resources to support survival shrink. Here, once again, ethical issues combine with economic and biological concerns.

Through class discussion we learn that many students and faculty alike have been taught to regard economic disparity, particularly growing and vicious disparity, as wrong. Yet poverty continues to exist in the midst of affluence. Currently, 22 percent of the world's population control approximately 85 percent of the world's wealth (Miller 1996, 10).

Moreover, the vast majority of the fortunate 22 percent are only vaguely aware of this disparity, have no idea of its magnitude or vicious implications, and never intentionally act to perpetuate it. This disparity—economic and cultural—continues to grow. Multiple disciplines must address this problem and in a multifaceted, interdisciplinary manner, especially given that the fortunate are often unaware of the interrelationship between the hungry and the nonhungry (Singer 1972).

As the course proceeds, students begin collectively to address a variety of topics that are of both global and personal significance. Students and faculty together examine, from multiple perspectives, the realities and contingencies surrounding basic nutrition and food production. We assiduously try to avoid compartmentalizing problems of nutrition, food production, or the "right" to food in terms of particular disciplines. As a team, we also examine the circumstances in which food is sought or eaten because of either compelling necessity or a desire for frivolous consumption. The question "Should a minimum daily diet be regarded as a fundamental human right and not as a privilege?" is paramount in our discussions, for students and faculty alike.

These are value-laden problems and realities that are biological, economic, ethical, and cultural. For example, faculty ask why food is often regarded as an earned privilege when, indeed, it is a biological necessity. The methods used in answering these thorny questions are mainly classroom discussion, presentations, and often videos that examine the implications of historical instances in which food was used as a weapon of social control. In past semesters we have studied the Irish famine, the famine in the Ukraine, and the multidisciplinary implications of the dust bowl phenomenon in the United States through both video and student-led presentations.

HUNGER AND GLOBAL INTERDEPENDENCE

By focusing on the integration of all the world's people, students learn that they have a direct stake in all these issues. For example, as the poor concentrate in the major cities of the developing nations, they become a threat to everyone. They may revolt, if not in overt civil war then by turning to crime. Civil contempt threatens everyone, but there are even greater threats. With the rise in population and worldwide migration to ever more crowded urban slums, hunger can precipitate epidemics. With regard to infection, students learn that there is no person or place from which we are isolated. Jets travel daily between cities throughout the world. A plague in one part of the world is a potential plague in all (Garrett 1994). By studying the history of medicine, students learn that although we have depended on antibiotics to protect us, the germs grow ever more resistant (Service 1995). A plague of antibiotic-resistant germs would threaten everyone. There would be no safe haven, not even for the most affluent in the developed world.

When we integrate economic analysis into the discussion, students discover that we have the means to prevent such a catastrophe: worldwide public health. But we hardly consider it among our priorities. The U.S. health care system fosters the illusion that the health of the poor, and particularly of foreigners, is not our problem. In fact, it is one of our most urgent problems. Primary health care for all is, the students learn in the course, in our own self-interest not just from an ethical point of view but because it makes economic and biological sense as well.

Enlightened self-interest suggests the need to eradicate squalor everywhere, to ensure that everyone has a minimally decent standard of living, adequate food and shelter, safe water, sanitary sewers, and vaccinations. These interventions are simple and extremely cost-effective. To demonstrate that such actions go beyond ethical concerns, we use a case study to compare the costs and outcomes of these interventions with examples of the high tech, costly, and sometimes exotic medical treatments increasingly available in the developed world.

From an historical perspective students learn that the rich and poor are coming to live side by side in growing disparity. In every major third-world city, there are neighborhoods of affluence. In every major U.S. city, there are ghettos of poverty. The United States leads the developed world, and Connecticut leads the United States, in economic disparity.

In the last segment of the course, we look at Connecticut as a case study of economic disparity. The state is extremely wealthy but, at the same time, it has cities parts of which approach conditions in the third world. Connecticut is America's most affluent state, yet its major cities consistently rank among the poorest and most segregated. In a study of the 200 U.S. cities with populations greater than 100,000, the Children's Defense Fund (CDF), using 1990 census data, found Hartford's poverty rate to be the fifth highest (48 percent) among U.S. cities for children of all races, the fifth highest (62 percent) for Hispanic children, and the seventh highest (33 percent) for white children. In the same study, the CDF found New Haven's poverty rate to be twelfth (49 percent) for Hispanic children and Bridgeport's to be twentieth (25 percent) for white children (Children's Defense Fund 1992). In a nationwide survey of U.S. cities by the Food Research and Action Center, Hartford had the highest percentage (41 percent) of hungry children (Waldman 1991).

Hartford residents brought suit against the state (*Sheff v. O'Neill*) charging unconstitutional inequality of educational opportunity. In the summer of 1996 the court found in the plaintiffs' favor and ordered the state to rectify the situation. In the course on Hunger, we use data on income and the inequality of educational opportunity in Connecticut as a case study to bring home to students their close interconnections with the poor around them. The *Sheff v. O'Neill* case reinforces what students see in case studies from the work of Jonathan Kozol (1991): the court, while finding for the plaintiffs, offered no method to equalize educational opportunity and no time frame in which to accomplish it.

Students are encouraged to engage in service learning activities such as feeding the hungry (volunteering in soup kitchens and homeless shelters) or participating in tutoring and after-school programs in the Hartford school system. This active learning is an integral part of the course and forces students to go beyond statistics and confront, in an overt way, their own preconceived notions of poverty. It also broadens their concepts of community and diversity and better prepares them for future employment (Hendershott and Wright 1997, 315).

CONCLUSIONS

Breaking with convention is always difficult. Interrupting is a new and uncomfortable skill to learn. Faculty are constantly tempted to fall back on familiar routines, lecturing when it is our turn, acting interested and respectful when it isn't. Most of the faculty teaching the course on Hunger began their careers in settings in which disciplinary boundaries were rigid and stable and the faculty member had total control over the classroom. Over the years these same faculty have grown to appreciate, if not become fully comfortable with, the "improv" qualities inherent in teaching a class that demands much less structure and control than most of us were socialized to expect.

It takes effort to change, and usually it doesn't seem worthwhile, particularly when students seem so comfortable with the standard routine and so uncomfortable exposing their real selves. But hunger isn't comfortable and we need to become less comfortable with comfort. When we, the instructors, push ourselves to struggle, we teach our students to do the same.

Much of the course is presented in a manner intended to provoke debate. One of the most effective means is to challenge clichés and untested beliefs concerning our culture and our relationship to the world's poor. We frequently remind our students that the purpose of the course is to dispel life's illusions so that we can experience reality.

Team teaching, if done well, is about taking risks. As Newell notes, "Faculty need to experiment, to take risks; they need to be able to fail with impunity" (Newell 1990, 78). When we come together to teach the course on Hunger, we move out of the comfortable model of the single-discipline expert holding forth in a classroom filled with students accustomed to being fed compartmentalized offerings. Increasingly the teaching faculty in the course are coming to believe that, although comfortable, that model does not work well. Certainly, discipline-based instruction and knowledge are important and they need to be supported and nurtured. However, we cannot expect students to address and solve complex problems unless we give them the training to do so prior to entering the work environment. The model of instruction used in the course is one way to prepare students for a future that will require the use of such skills.

REFERENCES

Children's Defense Fund. August 11, 1992. News Release.

Fuller, Steve. 1993. "The Position: Interdisciplinarity as Interpenetration." In *Philosophy, Rhetoric, and the End of Knowledge*. Madison: University of Wisconsin Press.

Gardner, Howard. 1993. *Multiple Intelligences: The Theory in Practice*. New York: Basic Books.

Garrett, Laurie. 1994. *The Coming Plague: Newly Emerging Diseases in a World Out of Balance*. New York: Farrar, Straus, and Giroux.

Hardin, Garrett. 1968. "The Tragedy of the Commons." *Science* 162 (December): 1243–48.

Hardin, Garrett. 1974. "Life Boat Ethics: The Case Against the Poor." *Psychology Today* (September): 38–41, 126.

Hendershott, Anne Barnhardt, and Sheila Phelan Wright. 1997. "The Social Sciences." In *Handbook of the Undergraduate Curriculum*, eds. Jerry G. Gaff and James L. Ratcliff. San Francisco: Jossey-Bass.

Hursh, Barbara, Paul Haas, and Michael Moore. 1983. "An Interdisciplinary Model to Implement General Education." *Journal of Higher Education* 54(1): 42–59.

Kavaloski, Vincent C. 1979. "Interdisciplinary Education and Humanistic Aspiration: A Critical Reflection." In *Interdisciplinarity and Higher Education*, ed. Joseph J. Kockelmans. University Park: Pennsylvania State University Press.

Kockelmans, Joseph J. 1979. "Why Interdisciplinarity?" In *Interdisciplinarity and Higher Education*, ed. Joseph J. Kockelmans. University Park: Pennsylvania State University Press.

Kozol, Jonathan. 1991. *Savage Inequalities: Children in America's Schools*. New York: HarperCollins.

Miller, G. Tyler, Jr. 1996. *Living in the Environment*. Boston: Wadsworth.

Newell, William H. 1990. "Interdisciplinary Curriculum Development." *Issues in Integrative Studies* 8: 69–86.

Nieto, Sonia. 1996. *Affirming Diversity: The Sociopolitical Context of Multicultural Education*. New York: Longman.

Service, Robert. 1995. "Antibiotics That Resist Resistance." *Science* 270: 724–27.

Simpson, A., and M. Erickson. 1983. "Teacher Verbal and Nonverbal Communication Patterns as a Function of Teacher Race, Student Gender and Student Race." *American Educational Research Journal* 20: 83–98.

Singer, Peter. 1972. "Famine, Affluence and Morality." *Philosophy and Public Affairs* 1(3): 229–43.

van Dusseldorp, Dirk, and Seerp Wigboldus. 1994. "Interdisciplinary Research for Integrated Rural Development in Developing Countries: The Role of Social Sciences." *Issues in Integrative Studies* 12: 93–138.

Waldman, Hilary. 1991. "Report Says 80,000 Children in State Go Hungry." *Hartford Courant* (March 27).

HUNGER: PROBLEMS OF SCARCITY AND CHOICE: SAMPLE SYLLABUS

This integrative course, combining perspectives from the social sciences, health, and philosophy, introduces students to the multiple dimensions of hunger. Various models are used to examine the causes and consequences of, and treatment for, hunger in the developing world and the United States. (Emphasis on written communication and values identification.)

Goals: Students will be able to distinguish various sociological, political, economic, and biological explanations for the hunger problem; describe the worldwide demography of hunger in its various manifestations; evaluate the strengths and limitations of proposed solutions to the problem of hunger; defend positions regarding the causes and consequences of, and solutions to, hunger; analyze the roles of various agencies in providing hunger relief; clarify personal values and principles; and appreciate our individual and collective power to alleviate poverty and hunger.

Texts: E. M. Young, *World Hunger* (1997); Jonathan Kozol, *Savage Inequalities* (1992); Frances Moore Lappé and Joseph Collins, *World Hunger: Twelve Myths* (1986); John Steinbeck, *The Grapes of Wrath* (1939); Frank McCourt, *Angela's Ashes* (1996); UNICEF, *The State of the World's Children* (1998); United Nations Development Program, *Human Development Report* (1998).

Topics:

What Is Hunger? Definitions: Famine Versus Chronic Persistent Hunger

Food Production Versus Food Distribution

Population: Not Enough Food or Too Many People? Population Policy

Is Free Trade the Answer?

Trade, Colonialism, and Foreign Aid

Health in the Developing World

Environmental Issues: One Small Planet

Food As a Weapon—Famine in History: Ireland/The Ukraine

Hunger in the United States: Historical Examples/The Present

Economic and Educational Disparity in the United States, Connecticut, and Hartford

Selected Student Activities: Group discussions and presentations structured to differentiate between chronic persistent hunger and famine, examine historical examples of famine, and evaluate the effectiveness of policies and programs designed to alleviate hunger; a journal to encourage reflection on the issues raised in readings and discussions; and various community service projects, such as volunteering at homeless shelters, soup kitchens, and public schools in Hartford and in Head Start classrooms, to gain greater understanding of the complex issues and challenges experienced by those facing poverty and hunger.

PART III

EXPLORING CULTURES AND
UNDERSTANDING OURSELVES

CROSSING DISCIPLINES, CROSSING CULTURES

Intersections between interdisciplinarity and cultural pluralism are implicit in the introduction to this volume in the many geographical metaphors used to describe interdisciplinary work. Disciplines—as described by King and Brownell (1966) and summarized in Davis (1995, 25–26)—in many ways have their own cultures: traditions, languages, communication patterns, values, and perspectives shared by a community of persons. To learn about ourselves and our world we need to cross borders, build bridges, both disciplinary and cultural. As the Association of American Colleges (AAC) *Strong Foundations* report puts it, "it is the task of general education to prepare students to understand and deal constructively with the diversity of the contemporary world, a diversity manifested not only in ideas and ways of knowing but also in populations and cultures" (1994, 4). What students learn in interdisciplinary study about the cultures of disciplines reinforces what they learn about world cultures and vice versa. No particular country has a monopoly on the "correct" values, even though students may have taken up residence and feel at home in that country; no single discipline has a monopoly on the "correct" lenses through which to view the world, even though students are taking up residence and learning to feel at home in that discipline.

Some of the authors in Part III note that students often enter their courses with strong convictions about the universality of their own beliefs. The essays propose challenges to such existing mental constructs that can lead students to create new ones. But the authors typically express concern about allowing students to move into an easy relativism. They work to build the critical skills discussed in Part II of this volume: looking at an issue through multiple perspectives, examining assumptions, supporting viewpoints with evidence. Thus they apply to the study of cultures the AAC's recommendation that students be expected not just to "*understand, appreciate, enlarge, refine*" perspectives but more specifically to "describe and summarize, . . . analyze, compare, critique, theorize, and extend theory," which implies not just looking in from the outside but engaging issues within domains (1988, 11). This engagement is a social process, not a withdrawal into relativistic isolation. As faculty teams model the process, students enter conversations (a concept also introduced earlier in this volume) that are both interdisciplinary and intercultural. Hill's model is particularly applicable here: he discusses the limitations of cultural relativism and urges democratic pluralism embodied in "conversations of respect," a paradigm he bases on his experience in interdisciplinary communities. Participants need each other, expect to learn from each other, admit they cannot answer a question on their own (Hill 1994, 23–24; cf. AAC 1995, 38).

As demonstrated throughout Part III, the interdisciplinary study of cultures, our own and those of others, helps students to see both the familiar and the strange with new eyes.[1] This combination could call to mind William Wordsworth's and Samuel Taylor Coleridge's approaches in *Lyrical Ballads* (an analogy arising from my own interdisciplinary work that I would not press too far). Wordsworth shows the strangeness of the familiar: he makes us look and look again at the everyday that we have taken for granted and see it with new eyes, thus "awakening the mind's attention from the lethargy of custom." Coleridge moves in something of the opposite direction: he brings us into a realm that is quite different from our own, that remains so even as we venture through it, but that also connects with our own, showing us more about ourselves and our world ([1817] 1961, 98–99). They saw these different approaches as working toward a similar end of enlivening our imaginations, opening our eyes. And they saw this end as integrally connected with effecting political and social change.

The AAC report *Integrity in the College Curriculum* suggests that "any subject, if presented liberally, will take students into a world beyond themselves, make them again and again outsiders, so that they may return and know themselves better" (and their communities as well, adds a 1995 AAC report). But thus the particular importance of broadening students' horizons through "access to the diversity of cultures and experiences that define American society and the contemporary world" (1985, 22). Similarly, any course within a liberal education curriculum may push students into new ways of seeing, but thus the particular effectiveness of helping students to "reexamine the world that we take for granted" and gain "enlarged perspectives or horizons" (Newell 1994, 43; Field, Lee, and Field 1994, 70) through study focused on diverse disciplinary perspectives.

One useful resource on the link between interdisciplinary and intercultural studies is Cornwell and Stoddard's "Things Fall Together: A Critique of Multicultural Curricular Reform" (1994), cited as a keynote in some of the essays to follow. These authors argue that cultures demand interdisciplinary understanding, and indeed their analysis fits quite closely Klein and Newell's definition of interdisciplinary studies as "addressing a topic that is too broad or complex to be dealt with adequately by a single discipline or profession" (1997, 393). In terms of student learning, it is especially worth emphasizing that this process entails a restlessness. No disciplinary perspective offers stability; no methodology, set of concepts, or body of data offers a "home" even for a semester. Rather, we shift perspectives, we look at an issue or a culture through various lenses while remaining aware of additional lenses through which we might also look. This process mitigates against premature, unreflective closure. And well we might resist such closure in understanding our own culture or those of others. Familiar blind spots and stereotypes lie in wait.

CHALLENGES

Parts I and II of this volume note that although most faculty say they encourage active learning and critical thinking, actual practice may be less than claimed. With reference to cultural pluralism, the problem may be a shortage of faculty who even claim to deal with it. And when courses cross both cultures and disciplines, the shortage of faculty trained and willing to teach them may be doubly acute. The University of Hartford continues to work to resolve this problem through retraining as well as new hiring, though much remains to be done. Our International Center now gives modest grants to faculty to encourage more cross-cultural study in courses across the curriculum; the Epidemics and AIDS course discussed in Part II recently received one of these grants. Thus while most of the courses described in Part III explicitly center on cross-cultural study, a wider array of courses would be candidates for inclusion in the future.

An irony of interdisciplinary and intercultural courses is that they aim to move students beyond simplistic views. They should enable students to understand particular cultural features and artifacts in context rather than in isolation. But given the complexity of both interdisciplinary and intercultural study and the limited time frame of a 14-week semester, the combination can heighten the ongoing tension between understanding and stereotyping. After seeing Puerto Rican films and reading Puerto Rican poetry, students naturally move to generalizations about Puerto Rican culture. How accurate are such generalizations? How much time is there to deal with differences within a culture, for example in terms of region, class, gender, much less within a discipline?

And of course a further challenge is trying to deal with moving targets. Both world cultures and disciplines are dynamic rather than static. We do our students an injustice by attributing a sense of static reality to either: This is what Japanese culture is like, this is how a literary critic would discuss the haiku. But again, given the time limitations, how full a sense of cultures and disciplines in process can a course convey? Obviously team teaching such courses, with faculty from different cultures as well as different disciplines, is particularly helpful in avoiding some of the too-easy generalizations; so is an explicit in-class challenge, as illustrated in some of the following chapters, to "the belief that blackness, femaleness, or Africanness are essential, unchanging qualities" (Graff and Robbins 1992, 435).

Finally, the territory is disputed. Any interdisciplinary team, as Davis (1995) notes, faces the challenge of "inventing the subject" in the absence of the more established structure of many disciplinary courses. This challenge of invention is particularly acute in a course exploring cultures, in which both intellectual frameworks and instructional approaches may be highly contested (as discussed in the chapter by Thomas Grant); agreeing to "teach the conflicts" still leaves the questions of which and how.

OVERVIEW

The first essay to follow, by Jane Edwards, serves as a bridge between Parts II and III. Edwards, cofounder of the Sex, Society, and Selfhood course and now a Director of International Studies, describes the origin of this course in "framing issues and solving problems." The designers wanted to help students explore assumptions underlying their behavior, to encourage interaction and respect, and to improve campus culture through rigorous academic study. Edwards shows how cross-cultural study can contribute to these ends. Her course serves as a model of the integration of cross-cultural study into interdisciplinary courses across the curriculum. Because faculty can individualize any All-University Curriculum course in accord with their interests and expertise, the gender course has varied over the years but has retained several strong commonalities, including cross-cultural study and direct connections to students' experiences. Whereas faculty in the Hunger course described in Part II encourage students' productive discomfort, the gender team has explored ways to release students from a sometimes overwhelming sense of personal responsibility so that they can freely engage the issues. Students can then respond to efforts to shake loose some of their assumptions about what is "natural" and about the logic of their own thinking on gender.

A paired lead essay describes a course actually centered on cultural diversity. In Ethnic Roots and Urban Arts, Cheryl Curtis, Anthony Rauche, and Edward Weinswig's students experience some of the richness of cultural life in U.S. cities. Students look at their own ethnic identities through the lenses of expressive culture and the arts and then use those lenses to explore the African American and Puerto Rican communities, two of the many large ethnic populations in the city of Hartford. Students examine the arts within their political, social, and historical contexts and within the contexts of ethnicity and multicultural theory. Their insights about themselves and others are manifested visually in individual and collaborative squares of an "ethnic arts quilt." This essay thus contributes several important elements to the discussion, including integration of course work with a campus's surrounding community, encounters with a multiplicity of arts and folkways as ethnic expressions, movement from self to other, and nonverbal ways to express learning.

A pair of follow-up essays turn to interdisciplinary courses focused on international cultures and highlight the difficulties and rewards of such study. Narratives, which figure to some extent in all the courses discussed in Part III, are in the forefront of Virginia Hale's course on Literature and Film of Other Cultures. Students study and compare specific techniques across literature, film, and anthropology as they explore cultures and values distant from their own. For example, what can an integrated study of haiku and film reveal about Japanese culture? And how do Japanese values relate to their own? Hale's portrayal of the cumulative effect of the course illustrates the importance of "reconstrual" in critical thinking: as new elements enter the conversation we continually resee all that has gone before (Applebee 1996, 77). But the process is not easy. She describes encounters with values that conflict and the numerous barriers and pitfalls along the way.

Harald Sandström and Errol Duncan suggest that in interdisciplinary and intercultural general education courses students gain skills they can transport to their work in other courses, and faculty gain transportable skills as well. The authors draw on their experience team teaching both Cultures and Transnational Corporations and The Caribbean Mosaic to discuss how students learn to make meaning across cultural and disciplinary boundaries. They use the image of the epic quest, composition theory, and contemporary political economy to shed light on the process. Students learn to relate individual attitudes to political and social struggles, thus avoiding emphasis only on tolerance for differences, a shortcoming of human relations multiculturalism (see Bensimon 1994, 13). The risk-taking involved in crossing cultures and disciplines cannot occur without trust among faculty and students. Sandström and Duncan explore how that trust can develop, for example through an exercise comparable to the "Ethnic Me" described by Curtis and her coauthors but exploring memories of ethnocentrism rather than artifacts of ethnic identity.

To conclude Part III, Thomas Grant offers a "cautionary tale" dealing more with faculty planning for interdisciplinary learning than

do other essays in this volume. Courses crossing both cultures and disciplines may face compounded difficulties of conceptualization and
team building. Faculty such as Grant who work in American Studies,
"once called the oldest interdiscipline" (Klein 1990, 113), may have
more colleagues with whom to create an interdisciplinary general education course than those studying particular other countries or cultures.
But because approaches to American history and culture are so varied
and contested, the result may not be fuller integration but rather a certain amount of ongoing fragmentation as faculty fail to agree on how the
course or courses are to be structured and focused. Grant expresses
concern about the consequences for student learning, although other
faculty teaching the Discovering America courses hold more positive
views (see the Charles Canedy essay in Part II).

Each of the essays to follow, then, explores the processes of interdisciplinary and intercultural study—processes of teaching and learning during a semester as well as changing practices over the years in
the light of evolving understandings.

NOTE

1. Given the emphasis in this volume on student learning, we have not
dwelled at length on curriculum structure. Suffice it to say here that we are aware of
the artificial distinction between "Western" and "other" cultures as curriculum categories and the problems of the terms themselves—issues pointed out by Schmitz
(1992) and participants in the AAC's Engaging Cultural Legacies project, among
many others. Faculty have considered various alternatives in terminology or structure, but so far those have met with objections as well. In practice, we work with
students who come from many cultures within the United States and abroad and
thus may be studying "other" cultures in reading founding documents of the United
States. And cultural interactions are central in our courses on both Western and
global cultures.

REFERENCES

Applebee, Arthur N. 1996. *Curriculum as Conversation: Transforming Traditions of
Teaching and Learning.* Chicago: University of Chicago Press.

Association of American Colleges. 1985. *Integrity in the College Curriculum.* Washington, D.C.: Association of American Colleges.

Association of American Colleges. 1988. *A New Vitality in General Education.* Washington, D.C.: Association of American Colleges.

Association of American Colleges. 1994. *Strong Foundations: Twelve Principles for Effective General Education Programs.* Washington, D.C.: Association of American Colleges.

Association of American Colleges. 1995. *American Pluralism and the College Curriculum: Higher Education in a Diverse Democracy.* Washington, D.C.: Association of American Colleges.

Bensimon, Estela Mara, ed. 1994. *Multicultural Teaching and Learning: Strategies for Change in Higher Education.* University Park: National Center on Postsecondary Teaching, Learning, and Assessment, Pennsylvania State University.

Coleridge, Samuel Taylor. [1817] 1961. *Biographia Literaria.* In *Prose of the Romantic Period,* ed. Carl R. Woodring. Boston: Houghton Mifflin.

Cornwell, Grant H., and Eve W. Stoddard. 1994. "Things Fall Together: A Critique of Multicultural Curricular Reform." *Liberal Education* (Fall): 40–51.

Davis, James R. 1995. *Interdisciplinary Courses and Team Teaching: New Arrangements for Learning.* Phoenix, Ariz.: American Council on Education and Oryx.

Field, Michael, Russell Lee, and Mary Lee Field. 1994. "Assessing Interdisciplinary Learning." In *Interdisciplinary Studies Today,* eds. Julie Thompson Klein and William G. Doty. San Francisco: Jossey-Bass.

Graff, Gerald, and Bruce Robbins. 1992. "Cultural Criticism." In *Redrawing the Boundaries: The Transformation of English and American Literary Studies,* eds. Stephen Greenblatt and Giles Gunn. New York: Modern Language Association.

Hill, Patrick J. 1994. "Multiculturalism: The Crucial Philosophical and Organizational Issues." In *Multicultural Teaching and Learning,* ed. Estella Mara Bensimon. University Park: National Center on Postsecondary Teaching, Learning, and Assessment, Pennsylvania State University.

King, Arthur R., Jr., and John A. Brownell. 1966. *The Curriculum and the Disciplines of Knowledge: A Theory of Curriculum Practice.* New York: Wiley.

Klein, Julie Thompson. 1990. *Interdisciplinarity: History, Theory, and Practice.* Detroit, Mich.: Wayne State University Press.

Klein, Julie Thompson, and William H. Newell. 1997. "Advancing Interdisciplinary Studies." In *Handbook of the Undergraduate Curriculum,* eds. Jerry G. Gaff and James L. Ratcliff. San Francisco: Jossey-Bass.

Newell, William H. 1994. "Designing Interdisciplinary Courses." In *Interdisciplinary Studies Today,* eds. Julie Thompson Klein and William G. Doty. San Francisco: Jossey-Bass.

Schmitz, Betty. 1992. *Core Curriculum and Cultural Pluralism: A Guide for Campus Planners.* Washington, D.C.: Association of American Colleges.

CONSTRUCTING A GENDER COURSE: MESSAGES IN THE MARGINS

Jane Edwards

A PURPOSE-BUILT COURSE

The structures of the All-University Curriculum (AUC) at the University of Hartford provide exceptional opportunities for faculty members interested in creating what might be called "purpose-built" courses. What follows is a discussion of such a course, Sex, Society, and Selfhood, constructed to help students develop their understanding of the complex issues surrounding gender.

In the early 1990s, the Women's Studies program already in place at the university was serving students well, but the students selecting those courses were overwhelmingly female. Our working group[1] agreed that we needed to design a general education course that would serve the needs of male as well as female students; in fact, our imagined audience from the very beginning included just those groups of male students (stereotypically imagined as fraternity members and athletes) least likely to sign up for a course that they might perceive as either "feminist" or focusing on women. We sought to create a course that was inclusive and not exclusive; that would provide students with analytical tools they could use in dealing with their experience outside the classroom; and that would be exemplary in building, within the classroom, patterns of thoughtful interaction and mutual respect that could serve as models in other arenas of students' lives.

Thus "the gender course," as we called it during the planning process, was grounded first in concern with outcomes and with the day-to-day dynamics of social life on campus. This seems at first glance a weak academic base for any course, but the subject matter of this course—gender—is widely recognized as a powerful nexus for analysis in a wide range of disciplines. The explosion of research in this area, generated in so many fields, from the life sciences through the social sciences to the humanities, provides rich sources of theory and content. It was clear to us that gender is a defining focus for issues under examination within our own disciplines and on the margins between them. Recent work on gender issues has been so influential, and so widely disseminated, that the appropriateness of an interdisciplinary course examining such issues did not need to be questioned. For those of us already teaching Women's Studies courses, the shift in perspective necessary as we began to focus not on women (one gender) but on gender itself was an easy one: the premises and methods of feminism served us well in this enterprise.

We had pragmatic as well as conceptual goals. At the University of Hartford, as on many other campuses, issues of sexual harassment, and particularly issues surrounding relations between male and female students, have for some time been under constant examination. As public discourse becomes more heated, universities develop programming designed to make students aware of patterns of behavior between male and female students that could lead to such events as date rape and to behaviors categorized as sexual harassment. Unfortunately, interventions designed to improve the climate may make male students feel threatened and resentful, while female students become increasingly anxious and defensive. We felt that the creation of a course in which gender was treated as an appropriate subject for sustained investigation could help address this problem, and could even prepare a core of well-informed students who would become agents for changing campus culture.

Sanday's work on fraternity culture and rape (1990), Roiphe's controversial *The Morning After: Sex, Fear, and Feminism on Campus* (1993), and Tannen's work on gendered conversational strategies (1990), as well as the growing body of research on the impact of gender in the classroom (for example Holland and Eisenhart 1990; Kleinfeld and Yerian 1995), support the need for such grounded academic intervention. It was clear to us that on-campus relations between the sexes were characterized by levels of confusion and anxiety that had reached crisis point. We therefore wanted to develop a course the goal of which was to make transparent to our students the assumptions about gender governing their behaviors, offering them new knowledge, based on intellectually rigorous methodologies, which they could take out of our classroom into the rest of their lives.

This is not to suggest a self-improvement program, 12 steps to better gender relations. On the contrary, the premise of the course was to encourage students to develop a capacity to ask serious questions: first about phenomena, whether contemporary events, culturally specific behaviors, or physical realities; and then about the usefulness of the methods and assumptions used by scholars in analyzing such phenomena. The real intellectual tasks for students are to develop their own capacity to analyze, to assess the analyses of others, and to develop new perspectives on the significance of gender in their own lives and in contemporary society.

The course designers and teaching teams (working with shared guidelines but great flexibility in choice of texts, disciplinary foci, and pedagogical methodologies) have included faculty from a variety of disciplines including English, theater, philosophy, sociology, and educational psychology. We agreed on certain premises: that teaching teams would include both male and female faculty; that we would work to ensure that issues of concern to both male and female students remain central to the course, so that this would be an addition to and not a substitution for courses in Women's Studies; and that two elements—cross-cultural components and continual direct reference to personal experience—should be present in all incarnations of the course.

We were all concerned from the very beginning with the potentially problematic classroom dynamics of such a course: how could we avoid the female/male, blame/resentment, hostility/defensiveness dichotomies that often plague discussion of these issues? We found a solution in two strategies. First, we introduce the theoretical model of patriarchy early in the course as a way of releasing our students from the overwhelming burden of personal responsibility for the entire history of male dominance and female outrage. Examining, in small groups, ideas about how the structure of patriarchy dominates and places great pressures and limitations on the lives of men as well as women gives male students a place to stand, and offers female students constructive ways of approaching the experience of their fathers, brothers, and partners. Second, we determined that the rules for classroom interaction must be very clear, and we lay them out in terms of encouraging students to make a conscious personal negotiation with the existing social structure and to respect the personal nature of that negotiation for their peers. Radical and conservative students are then able to discuss explosive issues without expecting that adversarial lines will be drawn. Some students leave the class ready to engage in activism, others to return to traditional value patterns. We believe that at the very least all are more aware of the choices they are making.

WHAT IS "NATURAL"?

Other essentials of the course no doubt reflect more clearly the disciplines in which we were prepared. One of these essentials took us, however, into territory outside the disciplinary expertise of anyone working on the project. Both the popular and the academic literature emphasize essentialist definitions of gender, manifested primarily in the search for biological, and specifically genetic, explanations for gendered behaviors. We wanted students to learn not only to approach gender issues with an informed perspective but to approach the ways in which such issues are presented with the same degree of critical skepticism. Gender, galvanizing much groundbreaking (and mold-breaking) work in many disciplines, also acts as a magnet for political and emotional agendas outside higher education.

When questioned about behavioral differences between the sexes, students often voice the view that such differences are "natural" or "the way people are born" or "biological." This signaled that one of the assumptions we had to address most conscientiously was an unquestioning essentialist perspective: if differences—and conflicts—are due to "natural" causes, then they are not susceptible to change, cannot be helped, and cannot legitimately require effort on the part of those doing the behaviors. We needed to shake that comfortable assumption. This is not to say that we wished to espouse a behaviorist analysis. What we wanted to do was to beg the question, in a coherent and rigorous manner.

Had a biologist been a member of the working group at that time we might have used a different strategy for managing our concerns. Because that proved impossible, we were faced with the most serious dilemma those who wish to teach in an interdisciplinary mode can encounter: we could hardly masquerade as scientists, and what we could hope to learn would inevitably be insufficient to provide more than a sham of any kind of biological analysis. This was not a matter of needing "to loosen the shackles of the disciplines" (Hursh, Haas, and Moore 1983, 43). Faculty teaching in the AUC are open to interdisciplinarity by definition, and our teams were already working in the interdisciplinary, multidisciplinary, or emergent field of Women's Studies. We were not afraid of inability to explicate the assumptions, methods, and theories of the social sciences and humanities. This was, rather, the waking mirror image of the most common faculty nightmare—that of standing before a class to teach about a totally unfamiliar field. We concluded that the best way to handle this leap was to be honest with students about our limitations, extremely conscientious in preparing classes, and energetic learners as well as teachers in the classroom. One of the great virtues of the AUC is surely that it gives faculty space to take these risks, and support in expanding their knowledge with the help of their colleagues. Briefly laying aside the notion of expertise in favor of a collaborative exploratory process involving teachers as well as students can be very exhilarating.

It may, in fact, be clearer to the reader than it then was to me that what was called for was not, in fact, a doctorate in the life sciences. In a recent analysis of issues of "synthesis" in interdisciplinary studies, Richards examines the goals of interdisciplinary, or multidisciplinary, approaches to general education. Cutting through the mass of conflicting views on the virtues and drawbacks of various rigidities, Richards suggests that "authentic interdisciplinary efforts possess as a defining characteristic the ability to identify and illuminate the connections between disciplinary insights and materials" (1996, 124). Our course on gender is not a course in the biology of gender, obviously the province of the Biology department: what we offer our students is an understanding of the ways in which biologists think about, analyze, and write about gender. The pedagogical goal is for students to learn to identify the kinds of answers biology gives, and then consider the competing claims of other disciplinary perspectives and the relationships between these different sets of questions and answers. Ultimately they have at their disposal a variety of perspectives, which together yield a complex analysis that may genuinely gloss reality. Through tracing the connection between disciplinary orientations students can construct a meaningful whole.

The text we use as a basis for a biological perspective is Fausto-Sterling's *Myths of Gender: Biological Theories About Men and Women.* Fausto-Sterling's goals match those we had established, and encouraged us to believe that, even with our slender knowledge of the sciences, we could nonetheless achieve our learning objectives:

> In the pages that follow we will look closely at many scientific claims about men and women. We will start with the assertion that male and female brains differ physically, with the result that the members of each sex end up with different abilities for verbalizing and doing mathematical work. Since at the heart of this and other arguments is the idea that genes cause behavioral differences between the sexes, we will ask just what is meant by the idea of genetically caused behavior. At the same time we will also see what is known about the embryological development of gender differences. Women's hormonal ups and downs, some would say, make them emotionally unstable, while men's hormones make them the more aggressive sex. But is there scientific evidence to support such ideas? Finally we will look at a body of thought that, within the framework of knowledge about human evolution, tries to find explanations for present-day male/female interrelationships. For each of these topics we will not only discuss the views of some scientists and physicians, we will ask just how well the scientific literature backs up a particular viewpoint. (1992, 12)

GENDER ISSUE OF THE DAY

Issues of the above kind are extremely prominent in the media. For my section meetings, it became my habit to reach for the *New York Times* every morning with great expectations that the genetic basis of homosexuality, of mother love, of rape would once again be the subject of debate. It was this media coverage that inspired the element of my section that students valued most: Gender Issue of the Day. The class examined at the start of each session a newspaper clipping, an anecdote, a report of an incident, a piece of music, brought in by me or, increasingly, by one of the students, which raised an issue of relevance. We discussed articles about gays in the military, the role of the president's wife, genital mutilation, Saudi Arabian women's protest of the ban on their driving cars, the aggressiveness of female hyenas, date rape on campus, sex education in schools, contrasting cultural norms for women's weight, fraternity culture. The goal was always to see how what we were reading and learning related to the issue.

This segment of the class had rules: both sides (or all sides) of any issue must be presented; opinion must have an evidentiary basis (that guideline is extremely important in all aspects of this course, in which everyone has opinions about everything); there were no assumptions that everyone would agree and every assumption that differences of opinion would be courteously expressed and appropriate to the classroom. With a diverse student body such guidelines are essential, because feelings often run high. Control of such a class can never, in fact, be surrendered by the teacher, although the illusion that that surrender has taken place is carefully sustained by both teacher and students.

Gender Issue of the Day turned out to be extremely important during our reading of Fausto-Sterling, particularly in the light of new research on the biological basis of homosexuality. Through a combination of the text, newspaper articles (e.g., "Quayle Contends Homosexuality Is a Matter of Choice, Not Biology" [De Witt 1992], and a range of articles on the "Rainbow Curriculum"), and readings from other sources (Burr 1993; Pronger 1990), we were able, as a class, to make significant progress in understanding the issue, the discourse, and the premises of the debate. In this context of immediacy we also succeeded in bringing class participants with very different attitudes into genuine dialogue. More than one evaluation of the course commented on the new level of understanding achieved concerning this issue, an important one on any campus, as gay and lesbian rights are more fully recognized and opposition crystallizes.

INTEGRATING CROSS-CULTURAL STUDY
INTO AN ISSUE-BASED COURSE

If students assume that many gender-related behaviors are "natural" they also believe their own attitudes are "universal." If biological issues are central to consideration of the natural, anthropological theory is indispensable to addressing assumptions of universalism. Working with a combination of literary and anthropological materials, students gradually develop a critically relativistic view. This became an essential goal of the course for me and for my colleagues in later incarnations of the course.

Students, consistently and without proselytizing, respond strongly to coherently presented ethnographic case materials, and equally strongly to carefully selected fiction. The groundbreaking studies of feminist anthropologists (for example Rosaldo and Lamphere 1974; Errington and Gewertz 1987; Moore 1988) offer theoretical direction and substantive ethnographic materials that lay the foundation for a creatively relativistic perspective. A course taught on the margins of the disciplines, rather than as part of a major in anthropology, offers additional opportunities for different combinations of materials. Geertz, in his seminal essay on the blurring of boundaries in the social sciences, describes the panorama:

> we more and more see ourselves surrounded by a vast, almost continuous field of variously intended and diversely constructed works we can order only practically, relationally, and as our purposes prompt us. It is not that we no longer have conventions of interpretation; we have more than ever, built—often enough jerry-built—to accommodate a situation at once fluid, plural, uncentered, and ineradicably untidy. (1980, 166)

While within the context of attempting to train students within a major this situation can be dauntingly complex, for an interdisciplinary, issue-focused course it suggests an exhilarating freedom to engage in bricolage. Our course confronts the cultural specificity of what are often considered by students to be universal assumptions about equal rights, romantic love, generational relations, and the nature of families.

Because the Arab world, and Islam in general, are so poorly understood and often presented in such pejorative ways in the United States, particularly in respect to the lives of women, a study of women in Saudi Arabia provides a productive source of ethnographic description (Altorki 1986). This reading can be supplemented by careful presentation of the basic premises of Islam. Our campus, like many others, has numbers of Malaysian and Middle Eastern undergraduates. We therefore stress the variations in the practice of Islam among sects and cultural groups so that students understand that range of variation and will not expect all Muslims to subscribe to the same ideology as the Saudis about whom they are reading.

This section provides an opportunity to elaborate on a topic very specific to the discipline of anthropology—the study of kinship—and at the same time to clarify the significance of this subject in the context of gender studies. The structure of extended families and parallel cousin marriage, common in the Arab world, is fascinating to students who have read enough of the ethnographic material to develop some curiosity. They learn through this approach about a completely different system of defining relationships and constructing economic units based on kinship. This material, which dramatically illustrates the concept of cultural norms as a skeleton clothed by the flesh of individual human choices, leads to an understanding of the importance of technological development and the basis of the means of production as predictors of the social structures that so fundamentally determine the nature of gender differentiation in any society.

We wished to go further, however, and add to this new understanding of the importance of these issues the possibility of empathy with the emotions and choices of people living in completely different circumstances. A growing body of work stands between fiction and ethnography, a wonderful example of which is Friedl's *Women of Deh Koh: Lives in an Iranian Village* (1989). These fictionalized biographical narratives bring to life individuals whose problems and choices are deeply foreign to students. Because the writer is herself an ethnographer, questions about the reality she depicts and her positioning in respect to it, while always compelling in a post-modern era, can legitimately be shelved temporarily in favor of the immediacy of the sense of walking through the page into another world. As students learn about this radically different construction of reality, assumptions about the universality of their own views (even about the absolute rightness of those views) begin to melt.

The third layer of material is fiction itself. Most students have some experience in literary analysis, and are intrigued and challenged by the opportunity to use these methodologies to evaluate stories as foreign to them as those written by women from the Arab world and Iran. One of the great pleasures of reading fiction today is the variety of novels and short stories from many parts of the world now available in translation (e.g., Abouzeid 1989; El Saadawi 1987; Sullivan 1991). If by good fortune students from this part of the world are enrolled in the class (in the first semester of the course an Egyptian woman brought considerable insight to our work) then so much the better. Visiting speakers can authenticate interpretation and clarify the apparently inexplicable. The outcome of working with such stories is that students carry with them concrete examples of situations and behaviors that illuminate the cultural construction of gender.

To test the effectiveness of this section of the course, we created a class exercise I thought of, flippantly, as "Oprah goes to Riyadh." Using class readings, we developed situation descriptions, such as this one:

> Khadija, a 15-year-old girl whose parents are traditionalists, was caught by her brother Faisal going out at night to meet his friend Fahd, an engineering student in the United States home on vacation. She says she loves him, but her father Mohamed has promised that Khadija will marry his old friend Ahmed. Plans for the wedding have been speeded up, and it will take place next week.

Students are assigned roles and asked to think about culturally appropriate responses to this situation. They advise, criticize, and correct each other cheerfully, and rapidly grasp that the goal of the assignment is to see the hypothetical situation through new eyes.

Explicit focus on the condition of women in this section of the course is legitimate and useful, but requires balance. As watchdog for male gender equity in this course (a new role for me), I was delighted to come upon Gilmore's (1990) study of cultural variation in the concept of masculinity. This book serves us well by introducing the importance of initiation rituals into adult gendered statuses, a theme that, because of student response, has become increasingly important in the course. It also provides a means of focus specifically on the problems that men face. There are, of course, two schools of thought about the appropriateness of this concern, but attention to this theme was mandated given the goals we had established for the course. As discussed above, we eventually made our own negotiation by introducing the concept of "patriarchy" (using the model presented in simple and accessible terms in *Patriarchy as a Conceptual Trap* [Gray 1982]). Women students in the course, while sometimes militant, are willing to subscribe to the understanding that our classroom is a place for calm discussion of the way in which social structure impinges on everyone's lives. Male students, as they feel more fully included in the dialogue, become less threatened, and less burdened, by the history of male dominance. Reassured that they are not, at least in this context, going to be held personally responsible for the entire system, they become more open to knowledge about and take interest in the situation of their female classmates in what may be completely new ways.

Continuing to challenge the assumption of universalism, we read Gilmore's chapter (1990, 123–45) on male initiation rituals among the Samburu, a society that segregates young men from the rest of the village for a lengthy period as they mature. This interstitial status, which gives them years of all-male adventure before they return to assume new and responsible status in the community, is marked, as might be expected, by a series of rituals. We present this "exotic" example to leverage discussion of the problems associated with entering gendered adult status in U.S. society. We examine Freudian theory, studies such as Pronger's (1990) work on men and sport, the work of Gilligan (1986), and the importance of differential socialization in the construction of gender identity. Discussion about the vagueness of American definitions of appropriate gendered adulthood, different patterns of gender identity formation for males and females, and the significance of the absence of transitional rituals into adulthood produces a new awareness of the concepts and processes attached to becoming male and female in contemporary America.

CONCRETIZING THE THEORETICAL

Concretizing the theoretical, we discuss bar mitzvahs, sweet-sixteen parties, and initial experiences with sex and alcohol. A group exercise in designing rituals for marking the transition from childhood to adulthood raises awareness about the desirable qualities American society assigns to adulthood for both men and women. Diversity among class participants often leads to insightful discussions of cultural differences among the diverse ethnic populations of the United States. Such discussions loosen the hold of stereotypical thinking on students, who suddenly discover that individual members of different ethnic groups articulate different values and norms that, although unfamiliar, have a validity they can recognize. A young woman whose family came from the Dominican Republic, for example, introduced the class, articulately and in detail, to gender relationships and the complex roles of adult women in her community. These ideas were unfamiliar to almost everyone in the class. To my relief, rather than automatically rejecting them, students enthusiastically discussed their significance and (with some assistance) pursued the topic to a broader discussion of the ways in which economic and cultural factors interact in creating social roles.

To examine the influence of socioeconomic factors and the agendas of social analysts, particularly sociologists, in the United States, we use a variety of materials, many of them fairly obvious and conventional. Stack's (1974) work on low-income African American households provides interesting and controversial substance in this section of the course: students struggle as their assumptions about "welfare fraud" and about the irresponsibility of males in this community are challenged by descriptions of the daily struggle of this disadvantaged population. Recent debates on welfare reform offer new material that will be more topical and serve the same purpose. This section is important because students get the opportunity to ask questions about the lives of so many young minority men not in college but desperately trying to survive in a society that can seem implacably hostile. We use this time to examine the differences between the lives of African American men and women and to draw on the experience, and also the knowledge of history, that some students bring to the classroom. The calm description by a student of his daily experience of being feared by others instructed us all: a gentle and courteous man, he was well over six feet tall and very dark skinned, and every day he was reminded, as people crossed streets to avoid him, that in this society he represented a threat to other people simply because of his physical presence. We read, tell, and listen to such stories, anecdotal and fictional, and then we analyze their implications. Discussions of such materials use ideas and analytical tools from a range of disciplines to broach issues of pragmatic importance in students' lives beyond the classroom.

Other segments of the course, on Freudian and feminist studies of socialization practices (using, on occasion, fiction, child-rearing manuals, and children's books to assist in our analysis) and on television representations of gender, follow a similar pattern of eclectic use of sources, attention to individual student experience, and critical examination of theoretical studies and methodology. Because students have learned these practices with us in the most challenging section of the course, that dealing with biological issues, they are adept by these later stages and respond energetically as they find themselves dealing with more familiar materials on which they can with confidence exercise their new-found critical facility.

ONGOING CHALLENGES

The gender course as we invented it is challenging to teach. Team teaching in this course often means bringing highly cohesive individual sections together for visiting speakers, panels, or student presentations. In this larger group it can be difficult to develop coherence. Some semesters this has worked well, but by no means always—depending, as always with team teaching, on the nature of the relationship among the members of the faculty team and on the chemistry of the particular class of students. My colleague from theater engineered a marvelous acting out of *Cloud 9* (Churchill 1986), a play that challenges almost every imaginable assumption about age, race, and gender. We also had some spectacular student projects, including a particularly charming fashion show designed to reveal the absurdity of gendered dress.

Another problem is that the course materials are heavily loaded and things can come close to getting out of hand: in a section discussion of Gilligan's (1986) theories, a fraternity president who had a deep belief in the importance of male bonding and a student from one of the tougher parts of New York City whose father had explicitly taught him that a real man needs no emotional support almost came to blows. I did not handle it well. I can only say that the students were wonderfully willing to help solve that and other difficulties as they arose, showing great goodwill and engagement. The immediacy of the issues seems to produce a certain sense of urgency, and the tensions that come with strong opinions can be productive. No one ever falls asleep, that much can be said with certainty.

But the success of any segment of the course varies, semester by semester, in an almost random way. I realize that this observation begs the question because writing about pedagogy is always an effort to reduce this kind of randomness, but in all the team-taught courses in which I have participated the same phenomenon is observable. Very careful collaborative preparation is the best antidote to uncertainty, and I agree with a colleague's observation that any course taught for the first time needs a Surgeon General's warning label. But courses focusing on current issues must by definition cultivate flexibility and always seek to innovate, and reducing their elements to formulas can stifle innovation and smother just the kind of discovery process that we most often advocate for students grappling with materials of this kind.

Above all, teaching in this way means taking risks (guiding students as they study materials that may be relatively unfamiliar to the faculty) and more than anything else, remaining alert. Depth of knowledge is for once less important than lightness of touch. But at no time has it seemed that what we are doing in the gender course—cruising on the margins of the disciplines—is less than a legitimate academic activity, and our nightmares of being revealed as bankrupt in scientific knowledge have never been realized. Disciplines are inventions of convenience, after all, as we often remind ourselves in this era of reevaluation. The questions we are interested in asking are untidy, broad, and pragmatically framed: appropriate, then, for us to take seriously the mandate we have established for ourselves. We therefore created a course untidily located in the margins, but one that fosters analytical energy, clarity, and a spirit of intellectual openness that students can bring out of the classroom into the tumult of their lives.

NOTE

1. Jane Edwards served as convener of the working group that designed the Sex, Society, and Selfhood course and taught it several times before she left the University of Hartford. She speaks here on behalf of the ongoing course teams.

REFERENCES

Abouzeid, Leila. 1989. *Year of the Elephant.* Austin: University of Texas Press.

Altorki, Soraya. 1986. *Women in Saudi Arabia: Ideology and Behavior among the Elite.* New York: Columbia University Press.

Burr, Chandler. 1993. "Homosexuality and Biology." *Atlantic Monthly* (March): 47–65.

Churchill, Caryl. 1986. *Cloud 9.* In *Plays/Caryl Churchill.* London; New York: Methuen.

De Witt, Karen. 1992. "Quayle Contends Homosexuality Is a Matter of Choice, not Biology." *New York Times* (September 14).

El Saadawi, Nawal. 1987. *She Has No Place in Paradise.* London: Minerva.

Errington, Frederick, and Deborah Gewertz. 1987. *Cultural Alternatives and a Feminist Anthropology.* Cambridge: Cambridge University Press.

Fausto-Sterling, Anne. 1992. *Myths of Gender: Biological Theories About Men and Women.* 2d. ed. New York: Basic.

Friedl, Erika. 1989. *Women of Deh Koh: Lives in an Iranian Village.* New York: Penguin.

Geertz, Clifford. 1980. "Blurred Genres: The Refiguration of Social Thought." *American Scholar* 49 (2): 165–79.

Gilligan, Carol. 1986. "In a Different Voice: Women's Conceptions of Self and Morality." In *Women and Values,* ed. Marilyn Pearsall. Belmont, Mass: Wadsworth.

Gilmore, David D. 1990. *Manhood in the Making: Cultural Concepts of Masculinity.* New Haven, Conn.: Yale University Press.

Gray, Elizabeth Dodson. 1982. *Patriarchy as a Conceptual Trap.* Wellesley, Mass.: Roundtable.

Holland, Dorothy C., and Margaret A. Eisenhart. 1990. *Educated in Romance: Women, Achievement, and College Culture.* Chicago: University of Chicago Press.

Hursh, Barbara, Paul Haas, and Michael Moore. 1983. "An Interdisciplinary Model to Implement General Education." *Journal of Higher Education* 54 (1): 42–59.

Kleinfeld, Judith S., and Suzanne Yerian. 1995. *Gender Tales: Tension in the Schools.* New York: St. Martin's.

Moore, Henrietta L. 1988. *Feminism and Anthropology.* Minneapolis: University of Minnesota Press.

Pronger, Brian. 1990. *The Arena of Masculinity.* New York: St. Martin's.

Richards, Donald G. 1996. "The Meaning and Relevance of 'Synthesis' in General Education." *Journal of Education* 45 (2): 114–28.

Roiphe, Katie. 1993. *The Morning After: Sex, Fear, and Feminism on Campus.* Boston: Little Brown.

Rosaldo, Michelle Z., and Louise Lamphere, eds. 1974. *Woman, Culture, and Society.* Stanford, Calif.: Stanford University Press.

Sanday, Peggy Reeves. 1990. *Fraternity Gang Rape: Sex, Brotherhood and Privilege on Campus.* New York: New York University Press.

Stack, Carol. 1974. *All Our Kin: Strategies for Survival in a Black Community.* New York: Harper.

Sullivan, Soraya. 1991. *Stories by Iranian Women.* Austin: University of Texas Press.

Tannen, Deborah. 1990. *You Just Don't Understand.* New York: William Morrow.

SEX, SOCIETY, AND SELFHOOD: SAMPLE SYLLABUS

This integrative course examines some of the questions asked about gender within the context of biological and social scientific paradigms. Challenging the assumption that gendered behaviors are "natural," students consider the agendas of analysts as well as the evidence they present. Developing an understanding of the social construction of gender from a broad, cross-cultural perspective, the course uses ethnographic and literary sources to shake loose assumptions about universalism. Contemporary themes in U.S. society are addressed through examination of media representations, investigation of current issues, and study of seminal and current theory, as students reexamine their own attitudes and assumptions about gender in the light of discussion and critical reading. (Emphasis on values identification, critical thinking, and written communication.)

Goals: Students will develop an understanding of the questions asked, theories proposed, and issues studied in relation to gender; gain experience in critically examining those issues and the various disciplinary perspectives commonly brought to bear on them; and develop tolerance and empathy for perspectives and behaviors related to gender that differ from their own, while clarifying and reexamining their own values.

Texts: Soraya Altorki, *Women in Saudi Arabia: Ideology and Behavior among the Elite* (1986); Nancy Chodorow, *Feminism and Psychoanalytic Theory* (1989); Anne Fausto-Sterling, *Myths of Gender: Biological Theories about Men and Women* (1992); John Fiske, *Television Culture* (1990, 179–223); Sigmund Freud, "Femininity," in *New Introductory Lectures on Psychoanalysis* ([1933] 1965); Carol Gilligan, "In a Different Voice: Women's Conceptions of Self and Morality," in *Women and Values*, ed. Marilyn Pearsall (1986); David Gilmore, *Manhood in the Making: Cultural Concepts of Masculinity* (1990); Elizabeth Dodson Gray, *Patriarchy as a Conceptual Trap* (1982).

Topics:

Approaches to Biological Issues in the Study of Gender

Cross-Cultural Perspectives on Gender

The Formation of Gender Identity

Gender in American Society: Social, Economic, and Cultural Issues

Media Representations of Gender

Selected Student Activities: Gender Issue of the Day, a collaborative exploration of current issues ongoing throughout the course; a guided reading journal for *Myths of Gender*; creative writing and role-play assignments in connection with cross-cultural study; group projects on gendered socialization including critical analysis of readings; analytical reports on the representation of gender in television shows.

UNDERSTANDING ETHNIC IDENTITY THROUGH EXPRESSIVE CULTURE: AN INTERDISCIPLINARY APPROACH

A. Cheryl Curtis, Anthony T. Rauche, and S. Edward Weinswig

Ethnic diversity is one of the hallmarks of U.S. cities that enriches the fabric of our shared American heritage. Artistic forms provide each ethnic group with unique venues for presenting and reaffirming its own identity. For many groups, the best way of presenting "who they are" is through the arts—music, painting, poetry, dance, literature, theater, and storytelling. These expressive cultural activities also foster communication with other ethnic groups and the general community. The result is that contact with one another builds understanding and acceptance.

Culture and identity permeate all facets of life, and the reflection of that impact through multiple artistic disciplines was a logical starting point for the course Ethnic Roots and Urban Arts. Cornwell and Stoddard (1994) discuss the role of general education in "foregrounding" issues of culture and identity. They think this task is best approached through interdisciplinary and intercultural curricula. Three faculty with distinctly different backgrounds (music, education, and reading and academic development) but mutual interests collaborated at the University of Hartford to create a course focusing on the expressive arts of ethnic groups. With an urban center as the backdrop, the team chose two groups, African Americans and Puertoriqueños, as the initial focus. These groups are prominently represented in the greater Hartford area.

Since the inception of the course, students have explored a wide range of selected ethnic arts and their critical, historical, and sociological contexts. Community resources are tapped for classroom presentations. In addition, students visit sites that celebrate or preserve the contributions of African American or Puertoriqueño arts. Students have experienced, first-hand, griots (storytellers), poets, musicians, artists, ethnomusicologists, curators, and writers, and have attended exhibits. Incorporated in the course are core curriculum values that strengthen and enhance written and oral communication, values identification and analysis, research, and synthesis of theoretical and practical issues.

Originally, the faculty team chose the metaphor of an "ethnic arts umbrella" for the course to illustrate the various elements that are the components of any expressive culture. These include music, visual arts, theater, dance, literature, religion, fashion, advertising, food, language, oral traditions, television, and film. The umbrella metaphor provided a visual icon that helped students interpret each discipline as part of a "common enterprise" under which the traditional boundaries of disciplines may be interconnected and transformed. The metaphor drew students into the processes of making analogies, recognizing similarities and differences, and respecting diversity.

We have since explored additional metaphors, because the notion of crossing cultural and disciplinary borders in the sense of a brief tourist visit does not convey the synthesis we advocate or the complexity of materials we study. While we may not be at the radical stage proposed by Fuller (1993) of dismantling the traditional disciplines, we find the transformative orientation he suggests appealing. His exhortation to critique disciplinary structures, methods, and assumptions is appropriate for the arts, which continually "push the envelope," testing "what is art?" For example, is rap music "music"? Or is graffiti art "real" art? Can the concept of "soul food" be expanded to include ethnicities other than African American? Can foodways events (seders, birthday parties, family reunions) be seen as artistic ethnic expressions? How is art expressed in the rituals of religion?

To prepare students to explore the complexities and interrelationships of ethnic arts, the course begins with who they are—an exploration of their own cultural sense of self. They are asked to design a narrative of themselves, becoming their own storytellers. They eventually come to see this as an empowering experience. They do not always enter into the assignment willingly, frequently voicing panic and protests. It does, subsequently, become for them a self-discovering, self-revelatory touchstone.

This initial section of the course focuses on an exercise called "The Ethnic Me." Each student is asked to present who he or she is in terms of personal ethnic background, however that might be interpreted. Students bring in an "icon" that is personal and meaningful to them for an oral class presentation followed up by a short written summary. As a model for these student presentations, each faculty member presents his or her own Ethnic Me artifact and background. Examples include a 1905 Italian passport symbolic of the peasant dream of a new life in America; the discovery of black female poets as a doorway to African American identity; Sabbath and memorial candles representing Jewish rituals and traditions. Family photo albums and documents, flags, music, food and food memories, clothing, inherited objects or gifts handed down from one generation to the next—all have found their way into these presentations. Inevitably, even when students suggest that they are simply "American" without any particular ethnic group identity, their search in this assignment triggers associations and embedded levels of personal meaning that have contributed to their unique "ethnicity." For many students this is the first time they have confronted their ethnic identity and the learning process is quite fruitful.

Students discover particular beliefs or activities that are part of their personal history and become evocative storytellers as they begin to make connections. Not only do they have the opportunity to look into their own past, they also reconnect with family members, especially grandparents. They listen to the experiences of others in the class and begin to understand how ethnicities differ yet are fundamentally alike. Students have found ethnic connections in dance traditions (Irish step dancing, the Jewish hora, the Italian tarantella, and the dance rhythms of Puerto Rico) as well as in etiological and historical storytelling. Ultimately, the Ethnic Me exercise frames the introduction to an interdisciplinary approach that considers not only the traditional arts but also their sociological, philosophical, historical, and personal roots.

Based on the personal storytelling exercise, the thread of the power of narrative and especially the naming of one's self is interwoven throughout the course. Exploring multiple forms of narrative, for example the words of a griot, a song, or the text of a painting, invites comparative analysis. These forms may be represented by the oral tradition of African American etiological tales, the power of the metaphors of salvation and redemption in spirituals and gospel music, or the symbolic use of light and dark color compositions in artistic works that convey similar spiritual concepts. As these examples show, questions of identity are a richly varied and intrinsic part of the subtext of the images represented in artistic expression. Newell poses the question, "must interdisciplinary integration lead to a solution, or merely an appreciation of the complexity of the problem?" (1998, 548). For our students, the answer is that they must both recognize the complexity and seek solutions. They must first develop an appreciation of these artistic expressions and acknowledge their inherent complexity. If there is a "solution," ours is recognizing and respecting the differences encountered in the multiple cultural voices present in various artistic forms. Interdisciplinarity encourages students to think more openly and to understand and embrace the spectrum of ethnic and artistic possibilities.

WHAT WE HAVE LEARNED: MOVING FROM "SELF" TO "OTHER"

How we identify ourselves is a complex process, and as teachers, we have learned to expect an enormous variety of responses to the Ethnic Me exercise. We emphasize process because this is a rich, multilayered, and multidimensional exploration for each student and for the group as a whole, soon to build relationships and bonds as a temporary classroom community. Each begins this process with a unique background as well as shared experiences. We must be constantly attentive to the ideas, feelings, shared beliefs, and differences expressed, in their actual substance and in their effect on a particular individual. By doing so we can then bring them to the attention of the entire class for analysis and discussion.

　　Understanding differences and similarities, beginning to develop an appreciation of tolerant thinking and reflection, and breaking down the walls of ignorance about others are central at this point in the course. We seek to open our students' minds to the concept of identity through direct contact. What is unknown is often feared or misunderstood. Establishing an understanding of self at the outset is a stabilizing and equalizing experience. All voices are heard equally and all experiences are valuable. Each student gets to know the others without asking the question, "Who are you?" which is often too direct for everyday social interaction, despite a natural curiosity about the backgrounds and lives of others.

The concept of self-identity is the link to understanding what characterizes an ethnic group. Our discussion begins with reference to a standard definition by Royce:

> The ethnic group is a reference group invoked by people who identify themselves and are identified by others as sharing a common historical style. Our discussion . . . emphasizes the changing image of ethnicity and the strategies devised to use it. (1982, 184).

This definition enables us to reinforce three central focal points in the course. First, we focus on "sharing a common historical style" and what that means. Thus the discussion is immediately rooted in an historical perspective, which is essential to understanding any ethnic group, and in particular, African Americans and Puerto Ricans for obvious reasons; both are situated somewhat outside the mainstream historical dialogue. We endeavor to restructure students' historical thinking to include both these groups as vibrant participants in history in the broadest sense, as the creative and resourceful people they are, and as important components of the "ethnic quilt" of American society.

Second, "the changing image of ethnicity" highlights the organic qualities inherent in an ethnic group. The historical perspective emphasizes that the images of an ethnic group do indeed change over time, and that established or accepted "tradition" is always changing. Ethnic groups present themselves and are perceived differently through changing social and political eras. Students learn to interpret the ideas of the past in historical context and to examine changing images and attitudes in relation to these historical anchors. If the ethnic group shares a common historical style, it is our job to establish the links between the present and the past to understand both stylistic continuity and change. We look for old images reinterpreted or refreshed, or negative images turned into positive expressions of ethnic pride and culture.

Third, "the strategies devised to use it" leads us directly to those strategies we wish to emphasize with respect to the arts and expressive culture. Expressive culture is behavior. The activities and products of expressive culture identify what an individual has experienced and has come to value in his or her ethnicity, communicated through subjective and iconic metaphors and the images they evoke. The individual also establishes a link to the larger ethnic group, identifying with it and its other members (the "shared" aspect Royce suggests).

The application and implementation of Royce's definition continues with a three-part focus: identity, understanding, and expressive culture. This approach provides a "personal-to-community" structure for our discussions, leading students from self-discovery to discovery of others through learning to appreciate similarities and differences and then observing the variety of expressive activities that constitute a group's culture.

Identity

We have already described how, through the reflexive Ethnic Me activity, students begin to learn about themselves (individual identity). Later they apply that information to another ethnic group (community identity). Through this exercise students begin to consciously consider themselves as racial and ethnic beings juxtaposed to people in other groups who are also racial and ethnic beings. For many students it is the first time they have viewed themselves in these contexts. As Tatum (1992) discovered with her classes, our students, too, are at different stages in the development of their racial (and for us, ethnic) identities. Some initially are scarcely aware of the roles that race and ethnicity play in the development of identity. Many are clearly at the stage labeled *preencounter* (for blacks, characterized by a belief that race does not affect individual achievement) or *contact* (for whites, a lack of awareness of white privilege). Other students are frequently in a back-and-forth "spiral" between different stages. Our course provides the catalyst for examination and exploration. Students leave the classroom and face a campus, or home community, or organization where knowledge about the racialized nature of our society expands understanding and meaning.

Understanding

> Before you come to understand a person, to deserve a people's love, you must know them. You must learn to appreciate their history, their culture, their values, their aspirations for human advancement and freedom. (Colon 1995, 21–22)

To bring students to a common or shared understanding, a knowledge base must be established about an ethnic group. Students need a foundation through which to interpret their acquired learnings. It is important to introduce different perspectives and not just that of the instructor. The course materials covered, therefore, range from ethnocentric philosophies to adaptations that emerge from cross-cultural contacts and ethnic assimilation.

As students are exposed to diverse ideologies, they begin to question and challenge and to develop their own interpretations. Through several readings that provide a basis for defining culture and exploring the many issues related to reaching a personalized focus, students begin to construct a foundational base and integrate new learning. We choose readings that provide a comprehensive assessment of cultural associations, the ideas, myths, and symbols that are meaningful within a specific cultural group. Because we examine two ethnic groups in the span of one semester, we assign short, focused, powerful essays that establish a basis for comparison of these two groups and in addition are applicable to the experiences of other groups that migrated to America. It is important that the readings be sensitive and emotional, yet educational. The Irish American student, the Jewish American student, the Polish American student, among others, can readily make associations between their own ethnic group experiences and those of African Americans and Puertoriqueños. We all marvel that though some materials were written decades ago, they maintain a timeliness for groups new to the complexities of American society.

Not all assigned readings and films, especially *Ethnic Notions* (1992) by the late filmmaker Marlon Riggs, are comfortable for students. They sometimes respond with shock and rage at images of denigration and pernicious, systematic stereotyping, their sensibilities affronted. But out of this unexpected and unsettling intellectual stimulation grows understanding, reflection, and reassessment of previously held ideas. Through exposure and the acquisition of knowledge, students begin to realize that the eradication of ignorance, bigotry, and hatred comes only through their commitment to understanding as a catalytic force of change. It is essential that students explore an ethnic group's identity from historical, sociological, philosophical, and political perspectives.

As we focus on the images that have been used to portray African Americans, no matter how evil or demeaning, we also show the popular and deceptively entertaining *West Side Story* (1983) to depict the stereotypical images of Puertoriqueños. *West Side Story* created stereotypes of Puerto Ricans that are hard to eradicate. In fact, Prinze (1995) writes that the play set Puerto Ricans back 200 years. The Puerto Rican male is seen as a blade-carrying chauvinist whose life is devoted to gangs, and the Puerto Rican female as someone who cares only for her children and family, especially her macho mate. Through selected scenes, with particular emphasis on the song "America," students engage in an educated analysis based on a new awareness. They see the film as a powerful instrument in creating a cultural perspective.

The artworks of Jacob Lawrence, John Biggers, William Johnson, Elizabeth Catlett, Benny Andrews, Faith Ringgold, Marina Gutierrez, Imna Arroyo, Miguel Trelles, Angel Rodriguez Diaz, and others are indeed stories about the gifts, talent, and beauty of those who convey their messages through visual images. As an extension of the storytelling tradition, music such as blues, gospel and spirituals, la plena, la bomba, and salsa enriches our understanding of others. Discussions of similarities and differences result in new appreciation of the uniqueness of each ethnic group.

Expressive Culture

Three important facets of expressive culture are emphasized during the course: first, the inclusive nature of expressive culture and its value for an entire ethnic group; second, the power and force of expressive culture with its many individual voices; and third, its potential to relate to other aspects of ethnic life.

These facets are guiding principles for students and anchor their first analytic encounters with expressive culture. Once we look at a variety of images and expressive artifacts representative of an ethnic group, students quickly see how political and economic issues affect the world of art, especially in the age of mass media. They also begin to appreciate the interaction between the individual artist and the group.

Our goal is to show the distinctiveness as well as the common links revealed in the subtleties of diverse artistic expressions. Artifacts of expressive culture uniquely convey the specific, personal details essential to a person's understanding of ethnicity and ethnic identity. This understanding develops on both the conscious and subconscious levels. Rationally conceived models reflect conscious artistic decisions. But more important, the subconscious, unspoken, and experiential understanding of "who am I?" is inherently part of the artist's world.

These considerations enhance critical thinking and reflective judgment, terms we use interchangeably. Students must demonstrate skill in recognizing a problem (how identity is evidenced through artistic expression), in articulating what they know about the issue (for example, discussing media images of African American males and how particular works of art confirm or refute those images), and in making connections among ideas (examining the similarities and differences in African American and Puerto Rican views of spirituality). Students begin to understand that individual beliefs and ideas are formulated in the context of cultural experience.

The course is organized around the following sequence of questions:

1. What are the arts?
2. Who am I?
3. What do I value and why?
4. Who is the ethnic person in me?
5. How is that ethnic identity expressed in the arts as we have defined them?

This sequence of questions is addressed in several phases. In the first phase, the personal, we begin with question 1, defining and examining what constitutes the arts, using the metaphor of the ethnic arts umbrella or the ethnic arts quilt. Next, questions 2 through 4 are tackled in the Ethnic

Me assignment and class discussion. We then return to the arts and examine how ethnic identity is manifested in a variety of expressive ways. The second phase addresses the African American ethnic group. We re-ask questions 2 through 4, building a quasi-theoretical framework (an emergent, practical model), and continue on to question 5. This discussion continues for several weeks, giving us a chance to look at music, visual art, readings, and plays. Finally, the third phase addresses the Puerto Rican ethnic group, with questions 2 through 5 discussed in a similar manner.

Pervading all our discussions throughout the semester is the idea of synthesis. We ask students to reflect on their initial Ethnic Me assignment and compare and contrast that with what they learn about African Americans and Puerto Ricans. They then consider the ramifications of the negative experiences that these groups have endured, and how those experiences have been translated and molded in the world of the arts. Again and again we challenge students to comprehend the complexity of ethnicity and the world of expressive culture as forces that ultimately are positive and powerful.

WHAT HAS WORKED?

Reading and writing assignments, traditional classroom techniques to teach critical thinking and learning, have an essential role in this integrative course, but have taken a secondary place to other "learning encounters." We have spoken at length about the success of the Ethnic Me assignment. Student presentations are always educational and revealing, and overwhelmingly sincere, sometimes to the point of exuberance.

"Learning encounter" activities are designed to take students out into the community and to put them in contact with as many art venues as possible. They visit museums, theaters, and concert halls to see art collections, plays, and music and dance presentations. We also encourage other "site visits" to ethnic shops, grocery stores, restaurants, and artists, poets, storytellers, and craftspeople in the community. The guiding principles for learning encounters are: encounter, learn, and synthesize. These are a direct outgrowth of the organizing sequence of questions outlined above. We foster as much contact as possible, and many students acknowledge that they would not have sought out these encounters on their own.

Guest presentations in class are invaluable. Local storytellers, artists, and musicians literally bring the community into our classroom. We have been lucky to have access to excellent human resources who draw on their personal experiences as well as their artistic talents. Guests also give us as teachers the opportunity to respond to new ideas along with our students, a significant contribution to the breadth and depth of the course.

The "Quilt Square" assignments, introduced in spring 1997, build on the earlier umbrella metaphor for the course. The image of the quilt, especially in the material culture of African Americans, is one that students interpret with great success. Students become artists in the course by actually creating artifacts. This provides them an opportunity to present their ideas in a visual, physical mode, rather than through writing alone. A short written summary statement accompanies students' Ethnic Arts Quilt (EAQ) squares, but the focus is the visual piece, which is a new creative and interpretive activity for most. Each student creates two EAQ squares individually, at the beginning of the course for the Ethnic Me assignment and then at the end of the semester as a way of expressing synthesis. In addition, groups of students each create two squares as reaction pieces to specific African American and Puerto Rican reading assignments. At our last class meeting we display all the squares in a large open area. Faculty and students have the opportunity to review their interpretations of the issues raised during the semester and study some of the squares they might have overlooked. The results of our first run of the EAQ squares were educationally rewarding and visually stunning. Students discovered more expressive ability in themselves than they thought they had.

HOW DO YOU KEEP GOOD IDEAS FROM GOING BAD? WHAT HAS NOT WORKED?

Creating an interdisciplinary course that has integrity, that makes the desired connections, and that represents a product with which all team members feel some satisfaction is a Herculean task. As a team we feel that on occasion we fall prey to the most vociferous criticisms of interdisciplinary studies. We struggle with how not to be "a dog and pony show" and how not to rely too heavily on "splashy special events . . . and other classroom equivalents of easy listening radio" (Benson 1982, 44).

We counter this tendency by carefully choosing course materials and exercises that are useful not only for their interest and entertainment value but also for their integral connections to course concepts. As noted above, our prime directive is to teach students how to synthesize ideas. No presentation is made without analysis. Students easily fall into that "MTV-entertain-me" mode. We therefore make deliberate efforts always to come back to theoretical questions—What does it tell us about culture? What does it tell us about identity? How is that expressed through the arts? Entertainment alone accompanied by the hope that students will have an "aha!" synthesizing experience on their own has not worked.

We also find that too much teaching ("the sage on the stage") and theorizing does not work. Excessive analysis of particular arts tends to detract from the central focus on ethnic arts. Our goal is for students to make personal and meaningful connections within the broad scope of the arts.

We have found that too much theoretical background reading at any stage of the course has the potential of shifting the focus away from our work with the arts and expressive culture. To guard against this we constantly reexamine the assigned readings and assess their applicability to course goals. For example, longer essays on museums and art, or extended discussions of multiculturalism and pluralism, do not necessarily work better than more concise writings. The shorter pieces provide solid references that students can discuss and apply directly to their own experiences and reactions.

Last, we have tried short research-based group presentations in class. These have been somewhat successful on topics related to African American music and art because the information is easily accessible. But even though a range of suggested topics is always provided, students focus on the more well known "pop cult" domain with the result that less widely known figures are rarely studied. Presentations often are not especially creative and lack applicability to course concepts, often becoming an exercise in Internet surfing. Topics related to the Puerto Rican experience tend to be even less successful because available English-language sources are limited. Unless one of the group members possesses some Spanish language proficiency, song texts, titles, references—all essential information—have no real meaning. We revise this particular assignment periodically, sometimes giving more directed suggestions for topics or substituting an assignment more closely related to the readings.

CONCLUSION

Ethnic Roots and Urban Arts has invigorated the instructors and provided new challenges and learning opportunities. Our critical reassessment, reflection, and constant interaction provoke changes each semester. Concepts are frequently reconsidered and reframed. The big problem for us, as for many other interdisciplinary teams, is trying to contain our enthusiasm and desire to introduce new concepts as new insights emerge. We must regularly remind each other that the course is only one semester in duration and we have specific mandates to fulfill. We respect our commitment to the principles of the All-University Curriculum as well as to the academic content of the course.

Course evaluations are generally laudatory ("everybody should take this course"), with words of appreciation from students for exposure to the expressive cultures of new groups as well as their own. Many students seem to feel a disconnection from their own ethnic roots and acknowledge that this course has forced some real introspection. We hope students will continue to reflect on, be aware of, and appreciate the contributions of other ethnic groups to the arts. We believe that arts education is enriched through inquiry, discovery, critical thinking, and the experience of exploring new vistas.

REFERENCES

Benson, Thomas. 1982. "Five Arguments against Interdisciplinary Studies." *Issues in Integrative Studies* 1: 38–48.

Colon, Jesus. 1995. "How to Know the Puerto Ricans." In *Boricuas: Influential Puerto Rican Writings—An Anthology,* ed. Roberto Santiago. New York: Ballantine.

Cornwell, Grant H. and Eve W. Stoddard. 1994. "Things Fall Together: A Critique of Multicultural Curricular Reform." *Liberal Education* (Fall): 40–51.

Fuller, Steve. 1993. "The Position: Interdisciplinarity as Interpentration." Ch. 2 in *Philosophy, Rhetoric, and the End of Knowledge.* Madison: University of Wisconsin Press.

Newell, William H. 1998. "Professionalizing Interdisciplinarity: Literature Review and Research Agenda." In *Interdisciplinarity: Essays from the Literature,* ed. William H. Newell. New York: College Entrance Examination Board.

Prinze, Freddie. 1995. "Looking Good." In *Boricuas: Influential Puerto Rican Writings—An Anthology,* ed. Roberto Santiago. New York: Ballantine.

Riggs, Marlon. 1992. *Ethnic Notions: Black People in White People's Minds.* Berkeley, Calif.: California Newsreel.

Royce, Anya Peterson. 1982. *Ethnic Identity, Strategies of Diversity.* Bloomington: Indiana University Press.

Santiago, Roberto, ed. 1995. *Boricuas: Influential Puerto Rican Writings—An Anthology.* New York: Ballantine.

Tatum, Beverly Daniel. 1992. "Talking about Race, Learning about Racism: The Application of Racial Identity Development Theory in the Classroom." *Harvard Educational Review* 62 (1): 1–24.

West Side Story [videorecording]. 1983. Farmington Hills, Mich.: CBS/FOX Video Company.

(See the sample syllabus for recommended texts.)

ETHNIC ROOTS AND URBAN ARTS: SAMPLE SYLLABUS

This integrative course seeks to broaden students' knowledge of the diversity and richness of the artistic contributions of ethnic groups that have shaped the dynamics of the urban community. Students acquire a reference base of selected ethnic arts including visual arts, music, drama, language and literature, dance, and folkways, as well as their critical, historical, and sociological context. Students are exposed to the ethnic arts resources in the Greater Hartford area. (Emphasis on oral and written communication and values identification.)

Goals: Students will cultivate a pluralistic and inclusive view of the expressive arts of African Americans and Puerto Ricans, develop an appreciation of the artistic values of other cultures, reflect on their own individual background and heritage, and develop critical skills for evaluating the artistic contributions of diverse cultures.

Texts: Jack Agueros, "Halfway to Dick and Jane, A Puerto Rican Pilgrimage," in *The Immigrant Experience: The Anguish of Becoming American*, ed. Thomas C. Wheeler (1977); Geneva Gay, "African American Culture and Contributions in American Life," in *Educating for Diversity*, ed. Carl Grant (1995); Linda Goss and Marian E. Barnes, eds., *Talk That Talk: An Anthology of African-American Storytelling* (1989); Linda Goss and Clay Goss, eds., *Jump Up and Say! A Collection of Black Storytelling* (1995); Roberto Santiago, ed., *Boricuas: Influential Puerto Rican Writings—An Anthology* (1995).

Topics:

"Ethnic Me"—Who Am I?

Identifying the Arts and the Ethnic Arts Quilt (EAQ)

Ethnic Notions, Images of African Americans in Popular Culture—film and discussion

Weaving the Ethnic Arts Quilt—Connecting Personal and Cultural Ethnicity

African American Arts: Storytelling and Oral Tradition—The Griot

African American Customs, Beliefs, and Lifestyles

An African American Anthology—"The Whole Story" by Master Artist Walter "Rap" Bailey

African American Literature, Musical Traditions, and the Visual Arts

Ethnic Foodways

History and Culture of Puerto Rico

Latino Arts Quilt and the Puerto Rican Identity—"Who is the Puertoriqueño?"

Puerto Rican Literature, Musical Traditions, and the Visual Arts

Santeria

Beliefs and Spirituality

The Ethnic Arts Quilt—Synthesis of African American and Puerto Rican Arts

Selected Student Activities: Creation and presentation of EAQ squares for "ethnic me"; response essays on African American and Puerto Rican readings; group presentations; oral and written synthesis of course concepts and reflections; interaction with ethnic communities through museum visits and concert or theater attendance; completion of papers responding to ethnic roots, personal culture, and oral traditions; analysis and evaluation of ethnic music and art.

OUR CULTURE, THEIR CULTURE: THE INTERDISCIPLINARY PATH TO CROSS-CULTURAL STUDY

Virginia Hale

The study of cultures may be approached through many disciplines—history, philosophy, economics, sociology, art, and architecture, among others. Often when students study other cultures they learn the facts of history, something of the political and economic systems, a bit of geography, and perhaps a smattering of information about everyday life. But more and more, even in courses with a single-discipline focus, narratives, both written and visual, put a human face on a body of facts. The faculty creators of the course Literature and Film of Other Cultures represented the disciplines of literature, film studies, and cultural anthropology and, though individual team members have come and gone, the three original disciplines continue to be represented on the course team and to be the crucial players in the course. From the outset, our faculty team believed strongly in the power of written and visual literature to encourage students to get inside another culture; to experience what it is like to live in another society; to see individuals living in accordance with the customs and values of their culture, or struggling in disagreement with them.

Over the past 10 years, the team has developed units of study on China, Japan, Greece, Turkey, Brazil and Argentina, Poland and the former Soviet Union, Mexico, India and Pakistan, and South Africa. Western European countries are avoided largely because students are often reasonably familiar with them either through other course work or through personal, sometimes firsthand, experience. Moreover, a number of them have studied a Western European language—French, Spanish, or German—and had a modicum of instruction on the culture. Thus, although the course does include some Eastern European cultures, the intent is to expose students to a wider range of human experience.

Two Asian cultures, China and Japan, are selected to address some imperceptions about Orientals and to point up the differences among Asian cultures. Students need to think about the experience of living in a society dominated by religious belief, such as Pakistan and parts of Turkey. Cultures are chosen in which class or caste is a pervasive influence on the lives of the people, as in India and South Africa; the study of still other cultures allows students to contemplate limitations on freedom of expression under particular political regimes, for example in Poland and China.

Each term the team selects four cultures for study,[1] devoting three weeks to each with two weeks of introductory classes on what it means to study culture and how film and literature express cultural values. A typical semester includes an Oriental culture, an Islamic society, and a South American country among the four cultures chosen. As individual faculty members join or leave the team of instructors, the cultures reflect the interests, expertise, and even firsthand knowledge of current team members. A professor of literature who spent three years in Japan naturally wanted to include that culture as one of those to be covered. Of necessity, we select societies with a sufficiently viable film industry to produce films that are released outside each country and that have subtitles in English.

The course is organized around nine topic areas, and the literature and films are selected because they offer students a look at how the society under study treats certain of these areas. The topics are children, generations, education, gender roles, work, social stratification, patriotism, the land, and ritual. As is customary in interdisciplinary study, we search for the nexus at which the contributing disciplines merge. These nine areas guide that search.

The course has been team-taught since its inception using the lecture/section model described in the Appendix to this volume. By and large, literature and film best serve students by illustrating the cultural patterns of a society once those patterns have been identified by the methods of anthropology. For this reason, our introductory sessions on the nine areas offer detailed descriptions of how cultural anthropology approaches and defines them. A key reading in these early sessions is the introductory chapter on culture and the contemporary world in Spradley and McCurdy (1977). A portion of the first session on each culture is given over to a closer look at a particular facet of the ethnography that will be illustrated in the literature and films on that society. In full group sessions we also offer background material on a writer or a style of writing under study; instruction on and demonstration of film techniques; and guest speakers, often students, who come from the society being studied.

The team has prepared an extensive series of required readings for all sections (Hale and Stacy 1990), and all students are assigned discussion questions to be prepared for the section meetings. In that way we ensure a degree of commonality even in the section discussions. Individual sections grapple with the assigned materials, but each instructor may choose to spend time on what he or she believes is most vital to the students in that particular section. Students take a single final examination.

Our goals for the course are several. First, we want to acquaint students with a body of material totally new to them and generally not encountered in other courses. While they have read considerable literature, few, if any, have read literature from the societies included in this course. Nor is it surprising to encounter students who have never seen a foreign film or experienced the phenomenon of subtitles. Second, we want to assist students in understanding some concepts fundamental to each of the disciplines represented on the team, including the basic assumptions each team member makes and how each approaches the subject matter of the course. Third, we hope to develop a range of skills in students, especially in analysis, synthesis, and values identification.

MAKING THE CONNECTIONS

As Cornwell and Stoddard point out, "Cultures are too complex to be comprehended by any single discipline or methodology. Disciplines are lenses which bring into focus different dimensions of culture. . . . the understanding obtained through the contest and conversation of multiple disciplines is more complete and complex than that available through any single discipline" (1994, 45).

How can interdiscipinary study enhance students' skills in values identification? The following might well serve as a pattern of what happens in the course. In this case a literary form provides the starting point, but it could be a film clip or a cultural artifact, as subsequent discussion amplifies. We seek to introduce students to new material and then enable them to compare the values expressed by these forms with their own values and their own more familiar forms. One nation with a very rich body of literature and film is Japan. The Russian filmmaker Sergei Eisenstein first noted the similarity between the Japanese 17-syllable poetic form haiku and film editing. Just as the editor cuts two shots together, thereby creating a meaning that is not in them separately, the haiku poet puts two observations together to suggest an idea that is not actually stated. Appropriately enough, the word for the point at which two images are joined in haiku is *kireji*, which translates as "cutting word."

Both haiku and film use concretes to suggest abstractions. The abstractions are primarily emotional, but the concrete images are designed to give power to what is only implied. Students look at a number of examples of haiku and are asked to consider the word picture. Inevitably, because the haiku poet is striving for an emotional response, a student must work through the poem to understand the objective meaning and to examine the particular word or words that invite the subjective response. Consider, for instance, the phrase "a sunny meadow." There is nothing ambiguous here. But suppose the poet were to say "a cheerful meadow." The word cheerful is less clear and requires some interpretation on the part of the student. Words like cheerful are not to be trusted and are not used by a haiku master. This is not to say that the concept of cheerfulness cannot be conveyed in the haiku, but it is suggested rather than stated. Here is a haiku (in translation) that may serve as an example of the point:

The sea in winter
A man sitting on a rock
Waits for a fish

A man sitting by himself on a rock might be seen as a figure of patience, but because we are first presented with a winter landscape, he becomes more a figure of loneliness or hope, and a feeble hope at that. It is the joining of the two images that causes us to translate the haiku into a mood picture.

Film works the same way. Let's say that a director wants to convey the emotion of sadness. He might do what director Akiro Kurasawa does in *Ikiru*, showing an elderly man sitting alone in a playground on a child's swing, hunched over in his coat, not moving. It begins to rain.

In an article in the July 1987 *Haiku Canada Newsletter*, Findlay suggests that we consider haiku not as poetry but as a very short movie. "Certainly the beauty of the Japanese word sounds and the rhythms of the words are lost, but the beauty of the form is the idea picture rather than the words themselves" (7).

With this in mind, along with coverage in class of the technique of film editing, students write their own haiku. Once they have done so, they comment on whether the connections suggested between literature and film hold up in their products. Most of the time, they answer in the affirmative and can often visualize the way their haiku would appear on celluloid.

Finally, students consider what the exercise suggests to them about Japanese culture. They are often astounded to learn that tens of thousands of haiku are produced in Japan every month. Moreover, most Japanese children learn "classic" haiku poems by heart, just as students here learn passages from Shakespeare. But why is haiku such an important form in Japan? Students offer ideas such as the following. The Japanese language, in its written form, is pictorial, and the fact that small word pictures are at the heart of this system of expression might foster the development and persistence of the haiku art, just as it underscores implied connections with film. Moreover, the learning of written Japanese requires painstaking and careful craft, and the concentration on a single image or a few at most extends to the careful concentration on the exact images in a 17-syllable poem. Some students also note that the Japanese have always been known for their ability to do fine mechanical work.

Students often also point out that Americans frequently value the wide-open spaces—the big, the vast. The confines of an island such as Japan might urge conservation of space. The art of bonsai is, after all, making miniature. Students can call forth the sprawling poetry of Walt Whitman and compare it with the haiku, and then examine the sense of values that might be expressed by each form. Turning again to film, students readily observe that the American film—even called a blockbuster—is very rarely confined in the way that many Japanese films are.

Thus, by examining a literary form and a film technique, students gain insight into the intimate connections between language and culture and between the refinements characteristic of art and the values of the culture itself.

RESPECTING THE DISCIPLINES

As Newell points out, "Teachers have a special obligation in interdisciplinary courses to keep the logic of the course organization in front of the students. The narrower and more tightly defined the topic, the easier it is for students and teacher alike to keep track of where the course is heading" (1990, 73). Organizing the course around the nine major topic areas is vital for this purpose. Moreover, students are advised to use a grid to keep track of the specific literary and cinematic examples used in discussing each of the topics in each of the four cultures studied.

At the same time, students learn how individual disciplines function in the integrative process. Some advantage accrues from the fact that students have been exposed to the study of literature from K-12. To be sure, this is a mixed blessing, because sometimes they must reconsider assumptions they have held dear. In a similar way, though students might have little training in film theory or technique, they feel comfortable discussing film because they have grown up in a visual culture. Cultural anthropology offers them more pause, but because the overarching course "topic" is understanding other cultures, they are prepared to seize a new tool without worrying about the remaining disciplines with which they feel more secure.

One strategy that keeps interdisciplinarity in the forefront of students' consciousness is to emphasize concepts that clarify the approaches of each discipline as they try to blend them. In our discussion of the phrase "point of view," for instance, students make a mind map. To the literary critic, point of view refers to the narrative technique. Is the story or poem told in the first person, second person, or third person? Is the narrator an innocent eye (child)? Is the narrator reliable? How is point of view in drama determined? Is there one voice or many? All these questions are written on the map. Turning to film, students inscribe ways in which the filmmaker expresses point of view. Here they apply such terms as editing, camera angle, subjective/objective camera, and color. When they come to anthropology, they usually identify those broad influences that affect the way a person from a particular culture sees the world, such as religion, gender, traditions, education, family structure, and social class or caste. Students are quick to recognize that many of these coincide with our nine areas. Within each unit of the course, we attempt to clarify the rudiments of each discipline while aiming at synthesis. The mind map is one very useful technique for accomplishing that goal.

LEAPING THE BARRIERS

Teaching about other cultures holds special challenges, particularly when the course focuses on values identification. Certain biases must be overcome to reach students effectively. Four major hurdles are:

1. We think our own values (gender equality, romantic love, supremacy of the individual) are universal, and we don't consider other, perhaps conflicting, values. This is complicated by the fact that we often hold values we have never closely examined.
2. We generalize from our own experience to that of everyone else, even in our own society. So, if we are white and middle class and from the Northeast, we assume everyone's America is like our own. When approaching other cultures, we apply the same principle to what we see there. To avoid dealing with complexity, we assume a single, simple definition of "culture."
3. We believe ourselves to be models of tolerance even as we are saying "We're right and they're wrong." That way we need not question our own values.

4. We judge things as "better and worse" rather than viewing them as "different."

It would indeed be fortunate if a careful examination of students' own values could be declared a prerequisite for the course. But we find that, to move students in the direction of values clarification with respect to other cultures, they must spend time examining the values they themselves espouse. The studies of American values by Hsu (1970) and Kraemer (1973) are useful for this purpose because they alert us to some of the assumptions we can expect to encounter. Asking students to write about one value they hold and to explain how they came to espouse it is also helpful. As students discuss how their own values have been formed, they are preparing to consider views other than those of their own culture.

Students become more aware of their tendency to generalize by considering how well one part of the United States really represents America as a whole. Do New Yorkers hold the same values as folks in Nebraska or Texas? We are usually fortunate enough to have students from several states, so that the class becomes a kind of anthropological workshop with informants providing a range of viewpoints, some shared, some at great variance. This exercise readies students to question a guest speaker from Istanbul about how accurate the view of Turkey is in a film such as *Yol* (directed by Yilmaz Guney, 1983), where the plight of the Kurds is central. Students soon realize that more than one perspective may be required to gain a reliable understanding of the values of a culture.

One of the foci in the study of Argentina is the importance of the tango, Argentina's national dance. So important is it in that culture that, by law, all licensed radio stations must include two hours of tango music on the broadcast schedule each day. After exploring some of the foundations of the tango, students consider how music and dance are reflective of our culture (if indeed they are). They generate a range of ideas that stimulate an examination of our cultural values and a comparison with those of Argentina and other societies we are studying. Students are delighted to talk about music, but it quickly becomes apparent that, in the United States, there is no single national song or dance. Jazz is offered as a purely American form, but a little prodding exposes the relatively meager knowledge most students have about jazz and its roots. And so it goes with bluegrass, rhythm and blues, heavy metal, and rap. The cultural values students point to as embodied in each of these forms reveal the complexity of identifying any pervasive "American" value in our music. In the course of our discussions, the wide divergence in views among students of various ages, races, and ethnic backgrounds becomes apparent. Students then must consider whether some societies are more homogeneous than others.

In addressing hurdles three and four, we must avoid falling into cultural relativism—an easy out but not a particularly satisfying response. This is a danger inherent in interdisciplinarity itself. If there are a host of ways of looking at an issue, is it wrong to privilege any one over another? When values are the issue, indeed we must, and here we strive for "informed" judgment. In his discussion of the problem of cultural relativism, Gates (1993, 10) cites Richard Rorty's comment on the idea that one view on a topic is as good as another. Rorty says flatly that nobody holds that view except the occasional cooperative freshman. But some of our students, not always freshmen, do succumb to the easy path of the relativist. For Gates, however, the situation is grave. He says, "if relativism is right, then multiculturalism is impossible. Relativism, far from conducing to multiculturalism, would rescind its very conditions of possibility" (1993, 11).

Role playing is one device that helps students understand that all values are not necessarily equally acceptable. After students read a story and see a film about poverty in rural Brazil, they then engage in role playing to illustrate the relation between poverty and the demand for limited resources. Students take the roles of various constituencies, perhaps the mayor, a priest, an ecologist, a farmer, a social worker, an investment banker, a journalist, each with his or her own agenda. In the process of expressing the values of another, students realize the complexity of such issues, and, often, how their own values may or may not stand up well in certain circumstances.

EXAMINING CONFLICTING VALUES

Anthropology is a valuable discipline for examining conflicting values. In class, the anthropologist on the team presents students with a tradition, or a custom, and the students discuss it. Then they have the opportunity to see how it plays out in literature or in film. Take, for example, the ritual of circumcision. Many of our students are familiar with this ritual, first, because in the United States it is routinely performed soon after birth on most male children. Second, it is a religious ritual in Judaism, again performed shortly after birth, though by a mohel. In Islamic cultures, however, boys are not circumcised until they are older, usually between 8 and 12 years of age. In this instance, the ritual is related to religion, of course, and is performed by an imam, but it also has significant cultural implications as a rite of passage. In a story by Joe Pierce called "Circumcision," students read about the fears and reactions of the boy who is to be circumcised. They identify with him as his brothers and other village boys tease him with frightful stories. They watch the boy's mother and other women preparing a feast to celebrate this momentous occasion. They hear the boy's father encouraging him to be brave. In other words, literature puts a particular face on the experience. It personalizes the ritual for readers who have not themselves been a part of it. It is a short step to provocative discussion about rituals concerning coming of age, cultural ideas of masculinity, and comparative values. The topic of circumcision also offers a good vehicle for an attack on cultural relativism and the simplistic treatment of values. When we introduce the concept of female circumcision, which is practiced in a number of cultures, students react strongly against it, basing their discussion, in large part, on the different rationale offered in those cultures for the circumcision of males and females.

In South Africa, where dowry or *lobola* is paid for a bride, often with cattle as currency, romance is not a significant issue in marriage and the feelings of the bride are often not considered. Most students look askance at even the idea of an arranged marriage, which we encounter in many other cultures. In the Chinese film *Raise the Red Lantern*, they see a bride being carried to her groom whom she will see for the first time. In the South African story "Nokolunga's Wedding," students read of a girl carried off, virtually raped, and then paid for with sufficient *lobola* to content her parents. Nokolunga accepts her fate as inevitable; our students are aghast. On the other hand, the anthropologist on the team tells them that it is also customary in South Africa after one year of marriage for a woman to return to her family to report on how it is going. If she wishes to terminate the marriage, she need only return the dowry and she is free. If she wishes to continue in the relationship, the dowry is then hers and she can spend or bank it as she likes. Of course situations do differ depending on social status, and often the poor girl's dowry has been spent by her parents and she is locked into the relationship without regard for her feelings.

In discussing both circumcision and dowry, students encounter strongly differing values, and in most cases they find it impossible to take a value-free position. Thus we confront the central weakness in cultural relativism. Sir Isaiah Berlin observes:

> . . . values can clash—that is why civilizations are incompatible. They can be incompatible between cultures, or groups in the same culture, or between you and me. . . . Values may easily clash within the breast of a single individual, and it does not follow that, if they do some must be true and others false. . . . Yet [clashes] can, I believe, be minimized by promoting and preserving an uneasy equilibrium, which is constantly threatened and in need of repair—that alone, is the precondition for decent societies and morally acceptable behavior, otherwise we are bound to lose our way. (1991, 12–13; 19)

Although students are encouraged to articulate certain values that are absolute and that they will not compromise, they also see the need, at times, to tolerate a measure of ambiguity.

The cultures we study reflect a wide range of family and generational structures. China is a patrilocal society in which the woman, when she marries, goes to live with the husband's family and is subject to her mother-in-law. In Lu Xun's story and the film based on it, *The New Year's Sacrifice,* students encounter a woman known only as Xiang Lin's wife. She has sacrificed her own name and her person to her mother-in-law who, after the son's death, is free to sell his wife to another man. The mother-in-law also lays claim to all of Xiang Lin's wife's wages earned as a household servant. While modern China is disengaging from some of the more repressive of these traditional practices, particularly in urban areas, this story and film go a long way toward explaining some of the human rights issues facing women in that society. At the same time, students recognize that, if a woman bears a male child in China, she too will have her chance to rule the roost when her son marries.

The treatment of children in various societies, a topic approached through all three disciplines emphasized in the course, ranges from the pampered sons described in Chinese poetry to the child raised by an entire village in Africa. Children of the streets in India, Brazil, and Mexico are often subjects of literature and film. *Salaam Bombay, Pixote*, and *Los Olvidados* are films that illustrate the pathetic dilemma of street children in Bombay, San Paolo, and Mexico City. Each film exposes the harsh reality of poor homeless children in large cities who have been virtually abandoned to raise themselves. Students must put the values of each society in perspective while sorting out their own. In many cases, of course, students recognize that the issue is often one of class. Carefully framed discussion questions force them to engage in a dialogue about class in our own country, where daily newspapers frequently describe children who are pampered and others who are abandoned or abused.

The current extensive discourse in the media about "family values" makes these good issues on which to focus as students examine what literature and films from other cultures tell them about the subject. These issues are particularly reflective of current interdisciplinary practice as outlined by Geertz (1980) and Gunn (1992), who emphasize interpretive explanation and "the exploration of the new world of the text and the intertext" (Gunn, 253).

Reverence for elders is a Japanese tradition much admired by our students. Few of them live in multigenerational households, which were much more common in this country in the first half of the century. They understand the value of respect for the older generation. A film such as Kurasawa's *Ikiru* makes that point eloquently, portraying the younger generation struggling to balance their need for privacy with their need to show devotion to their parents. I am prompted here to add a disclaimer, because Kurasawa has been described as a director much influenced by Western ideas. In this film he is certainly suggesting that Japan is on the cusp of a change toward Western custom. More significantly, each year we find ourselves facing a conundrum with films especially, but also with literature, in that what is being produced now is less and less "a pure product." Funding, production, shipping, and distribution may now be the province of several cultures other than that of the director. Thus, a film may be made in Brazil from a Brazilian script, with a Brazilian director, but with French funding and British distribution. How much influence the global players have on the film itself is of increasing concern.

CONCLUSION

While Literature and Film of Other Cultures provides opportunities for students to examine ideas, beliefs, and practices different from their own, the pitfalls of what appears to be a broadening experience must be noted. The faculty team wants to offer students exposure to films and literature they might not otherwise encounter and to challenge them to examine the values of a range of cultures, including their own, with respect to a series of fundamental questions. The team is persuaded that students will, in the twenty-first century, have to live and work in much closer relationship to people from other cultures. At the same time, we try hard not to fall into the trap of viewing the global village as it is typically presented. Consider this excerpt from "The Stranger at the Door" by Iyer:

> The global village is one of those ideas to which almost everyone can give assent: it rhymes with all the notions with which we buoy and congratulate ourselves—the family of man, the brotherhood of souls, the replacement of walls with bridges. The global village tells us, in powerful, palpable ways, that we're all one race under the skin and that, beneath all the superficial differences of custom and fashion and tongue, the fears and fantasies of that villager in, say, Mali are not so different from our own: he, too, after all, is moved by Michael Jackson rhythms and transfixed by *Dallas* archetypes. Small wonder companies try to concoct slogans like the United Colors of Benetton: one touch of nurture makes the whole world kin. (1994, 13)

Too often, the notion of the global village imposes Western, or to go even further, American, values on other cultures. The need to guard against cultural imperialism is one of the subtextual goals of our course. The habits of mind that an interdisciplinary course provides—encouraging students to ask questions, to see things in prismatic ways, to seek an informed synthesis—are invaluable in accomplishing such a goal.

The course clearly meets the three objectives of interdisciplinary studies identified by Kavaloski. It is built on the awareness of the interconnectedness of the world, it invites "freedom of inquiry" by acknowledging the contributions of three disciplines and then transcending the limits of each of them, and it provides for "innovation"—the formation of original and unconventional insights (1979). As Davis observes in *Interdisciplinary Courses and Team Teaching*, such courses "are suited to developing the problem-solving skills most needed in today's world because they emphasize the development of comprehensive perspectives. Team teaching demonstrates how specialists work together in teams functioning some of the time as specialists, but at other times as generalists" (1995, 39).

The interdisciplinary approach offers students the enrichment that comes only from exposure to a variety of material and a variety of intellectual paths to understanding that material. The cultivation of the ability to synthesize various insights is of inestimable value to the understanding and appreciation of our culture and the cultures of others.

NOTE

1. When we first taught the course we tried to cover six cultures. We recognized the error of our ways at once and moved to four cultures in the second year. We are now thinking of moving to three cultures when we next offer the course primarily because of the access to extensive material, including foreign newspapers in English, via the Internet.

REFERENCES

Berlin, Isaiah. 1991. *The Crooked Timber of Humanity: Chapters in the History of Ideas*. New York: Knopf.

Cornwell, Grant H., and Eve W. Stoddard. 1994. "Things Fall Together: A Critique of Multicultural Curricular Reform." *Liberal Education* (Fall): 40–51.

Davis, James R. 1995. *Interdisciplinary Courses and Team Teaching: New Arrangements for Learning.* Phoenix, Ariz.: American Council on Education and Oryx.

Findlay, Seaton. 1987. "Haiku and Film." *Haiku Canada Newsletter* (July): 1–4.

Gates, Henry Louis, Jr. 1993. "Beyond the Culture Wars: Identities in Dialogue." *Profession:* 6–11.

Geertz, Clifford. 1980. "Blurred Genres: The Refiguration of Social Thought." *American Scholar* 49 (2): 165–79.

Gunn, Giles. 1992. "Interdisciplinary Studies." In *Introduction to Scholarship in Modern Language and Literature,* ed. Joseph Gibaldi. New York: Modern Language Association.

Hale, Virginia, and Paul Stacy. 1990. *Literature and Film of Other Cultures.* 2 vols. Needham, Mass.: Ginn Press.

Hsu, Francis. 1970. *Americans and Chinese: Reflections on Two Cultures and Their People.* Garden City, N.Y.: Doubleday.

Iyer, Pico. 1994. "The Stranger at the Door." *Harper's* (September).

Kavaloski, Vincent C. 1979. "Interdisciplinary Education and Humanistic Aspiration: A Critical Reflection." In *Interdisciplinarity and Higher Education,* ed. Joseph J. Kockelmans. University Park: Pennsylvania State University Press.

Kraemer, Alfred J. 1973. *Development of a Cultural Self Awareness Approach to Instruction on Intercultural Communication.* Alexandria, Va.: Human Resources Research Organization.

Newell, William H. 1990. "Interdisciplinary Curriculum Development." *Issues in Integrative Studies* 8: 69–86.

Spradley, James, and D. W. McCurdy, eds. 1977. *Conformity and Conflict.* 6th ed. Boston: Little, Brown.

LITERATURE AND FILM OF OTHER CULTURES:
SAMPLE SYLLABUS

This integrative course combines perspectives from the humanities and social sciences to broaden students' awareness of viewpoints and modes of living in other cultures. Students gain insight into the beliefs and practices, the aspirations and lifestyles, of cultures remote from their own. (Emphasis on oral and written communication and values identification.)

Goals: Students will encounter literature and films produced in other cultures; understand some fundamental concepts from the disciplines of literature, film studies, and cultural anthropology; and develop skills of analysis, synthesis, and values identification.

Texts: Virginia Hale and Paul Stacy, *Literature and Film of Other Cultures*, 2 vols. (1990); newspaper and periodical articles of current interest.

A Sample of Readings and Films:

China: Selected haiku and other short poems; LuXun, *New Year's Sacrifice;* Wang Yuanian, *An Ordinary Labourer;* Lao She, *A Brilliant Beginning;* Annie Dillard, *Encounters with Chinese Writers;* selected pieces from *China Today.*

Films: *The Blue Kite,* Zhuangzuang; *Ju Dou,* Yimou; *Iron and Silk,* Shirley Sun.

Poland: Poems of Milosz, Woityla, and Szymborska; Mrozek, *On a Journey;* Hlasko, *The Most Sacred Words of Our Life;* Choynowski, *Boarding House;* Galezyinaki, *Five Short Plays from the Little Theater of the Green Goose;* "Trying to Say 'Sex' in Polish," *Newsweek;* Konwicki, *The Polish Complex.*

Films: *Man of Marble,* Wajda; *Two Men and a Wardrobe,* Polanski; *A Year of the Quiet Sun,* Zanussi.

Argentina: Selected poetry by Lugones, Storni, de Murat, Villordo; Jose Hernandez, "Martin Fierro"; Borges, *The End;* Heker, *The Stolen Party;* Valenzuela, *The Censors;* Traba, *Conformity;* Gambarro, *Bitter Blood* (a play); Birri, *The Roots of Documentary Realism.*

Films: *Camila,* Bemberg; *The Official Story,* Puenzo; *El Muerto,* Olivera.

Topics: The study of cultures, with emphasis on ethnography, film techniques, and literary techniques as they express a national style. Nine aspects of culture are emphasized: children, generations, education, work, gender roles, patriotism, the land, social stratification, and rituals.

Selected Student Activities: Team exercise in translation; group oral report on geography, current events, or arts of a given culture; short written exercises in class (e.g., on how a story we read might be filmed); prepared written discussion questions each week; humor exercise using informant from another culture; short papers on a film or a current work of literature not on our syllabus from a culture under study.

MAKING MEANING: AN EPIC JOURNEY ACROSS CULTURAL AND DISCIPLINARY BOUNDARIES

Harald M. Sandström and Errol Duncan

INTRODUCTION

This chapter claims a double win win for interdisciplinary, team-taught world culture courses employing multiple forms of expression. We explore here two such courses in the University of Hartford's All-University Curriculum (AUC)—Cultures and Transnational Corporations (hereafter TNC) and the Caribbean Mosaic (hereafter Mosaic)—and suggest:

- how interdisciplinary and intercultural learning may be seen as an epic journey
- how such courses help students learn to make meaning
- how permeation of boundaries (Klein 1993, 1996) influences both faculty and students within and between these two courses

Specifically, students attain the following integrative skills, which together constitute the first double win:

- an integrated and enhanced understanding of world cultures
- an increased ability to integrate multiple modes of oral and written expression, enabling them to synthesize disciplinary dialects. Through such gains in linguistic synthesis, students develop a form of university language that is transportable to their majors and to courses in any discipline.[1]

Obviously, if faculty facilitate such learning experiences for students they enjoy similar benefits. Benefits for faculty include intellectual excitement, syntheses of paradigms, insights to bring to their individual disciplines (and thus professional growth), and enormous satisfaction and hope from seeing students grow and blossom. This constitutes the second double win benefit: students and faculty stimulate mutual, symbiotic growth.

Cultures and Transnational Corporations

Commerce drives us across boundaries of all kinds. Boards and operations of transnational corporations have become global. National headquarters are increasingly old-fashioned and irrelevant. TNCs, business organizations operating globally, extracting, producing, marketing, are now among the most significant international actors, without national identification and almost beyond control and regulation by national governments and international organizations.

In this course we use international business as a vehicle for studying cultures other than our own. The point is not to learn international business. It is to learn what a transnational manager needs to know to function effectively across cultural boundaries. This does not presuppose approval of what TNCs do in and to their host countries. It is based on the high probability that our students will soon find themselves working for a TNC either in the United States or abroad. It is at least equally likely that in this country they will find themselves in an increasingly diverse work force in terms of gender and ethnicity. In either case, this course helps students adjust to new cultural experiences.

The Caribbean Mosaic

The name of this course reflects the multiple ingredients of Caribbean cultures (racial-ethnic, economic, political) finding expression in wonderfully complex and, we feel, beautiful variants of literature, art, music, and dance. We view culture, one of the broadest concepts ever devised, as necessarily including social, economic, and political organization and outlook. We attempt to show how politics is flavored by the prevailing culture. Current course assignments include V. S. Naipaul's novel *Miguel Street* and a staged reading of Aimé Césaire's *The Tragedy of King Christophe*.

Boundary-Crossing and Interdisciplinarity

The foregoing illustrates that we cross boundaries broadly (van Dusseldorp and Wigboldus 1994, 93–96) or fully (Newell 1998, 533) between the humanities and the social sciences. In Mosaic we even venture into a bit of science. We study the geological formation and structure of the islands, as well as their flora and fauna, as a prelude to studying the forms of human life that evolved upon them. That human life is then analyzed from multiple vantage points within the social sciences. We study the structure of slave society—the Caribbean organization of work and social relations. We then cross into the humanities, addressing the way Jamaica's National Dance Theatre seeks to depict folk culture, for instance. We generally find it unnecessary to call attention to every boundary we cross, because too much awareness of process may distract from the task at hand. However, we discuss interdisciplinarity in the syllabus, walk students through our purpose and methods at the start of the course, occasionally ask "did you notice what we just did?" as we segue across cultural and disciplinary boundaries, and then summarize at the end of the course.

In some ways, teaching Mosaic lends itself more readily to both broad (full) and narrow interdisciplinarity than TNC. The latter covers more geographic areas and requires exposure to the historical evolution of international business. Accordingly, less time is available for deep probing of any specific culture.

TNC is one of the older courses in the AUC program and has had a longer metamorphosis. It started as a potpourri of insights and perspectives on history, political science, economics, and international marketing—the specialties of the faculty—blended more or less judiciously in a more or less equal division of labor. We learned as we went, learning also to draw each other out and to intervene politely with amplification, demurrer, and the like in what sometimes became a good-natured tug-of-war. We helped "break each other in," especially when two of the originators left and new faculty rotated in. We progressed from staying on the secure ground of our discipline and mode of teaching to venturing into previously untried topics such as literature and anthropology and modes of instruction such as group case studies. In the process, we changed both the name and the focus of the course. Multinational Corporations and Foreign Cultures became Cultures and

Transnational Corporations. We broadened the focus to include the Pacific rim, Africa, and South America.

Mosaic, only three years old, went through an easier molding process. Two of the three designers had experience in TNC (approximately 12 years between them), and the third had complementary background and was very quick to assimilate. Accordingly, we "clicked" into an interdisciplinary mode sooner.

Both TNC and Mosaic were conceived as explorations of interdisciplinarity. The creators had formal training in several disciplines and were quite aware that interdisciplinarity requires viewing the phenomena under scrutiny broadly and through multiple lenses. We were, however, largely ignorant of the professional literature. It therefore took some time before we could honestly label our courses as interdisciplinary. It has been a salutary experience to look back from a greater acquaintance with that professional discourse at what has transpired and how the courses have evolved and fructified each other. Perhaps most gratifying, our introspection and retrospection improved the courses. This may serve as a suggestion to others.

STRATEGIES

We move now into modes of instruction. We describe one strategy unique to Mosaic and two we use in both courses.

Tourist Video

With barely disguised twinkles in our eyes we launch *Video Visits to Islands of the Caribbean* (Video Travel Library MCMXC IVN) in the first Mosaic class. We watch in amusement as students try to figure out why we are running a promotional film showing white Americans diving off yachts, with nary a native in sight. An extremely well-produced video, it plays into the stereotypes many students bring to the course. The Caribbean is white sandy beaches, wonderful sun, beautiful blue waters and rain forests, and exotic food and entertainment. In the process, we get in an excellent geographic survey as the video systematically hops the islands, the students following on map handouts as well as through the maps on the video. The video also provides historic thumbnail sketches of each location, with occasional ideological editorializing, which we of course seize upon with delight as a foil for discussing biases and stereotypes.

Rather than pointing out the anomalies, we ask students to tell us what they saw and what they did not see. Invariably, students display anger at what some see as shameless exploitation of good neighbors and at the invisibility of the indigenous people of color who make the beds and cook the exotic food. Thus values clarification enters through the front door, without our having to elicit it. Students remark on the failure of tourists to experience the rich cultures and thus are primed to explore them. Later in the course, journal entries frequently betray determination to visit the Caribbean as knowledgeable and caring tourists—a goal we hope to facilitate in the future through the development of credit-bearing summer study tours of the area.

"Who Am I?": Ethics, Ethnicity, and the Vocabulary of Experiences

Relatively early in both courses (an example of TNC fructifying Mosaic because the idea was first tried in TNC), we join students in an identity discovery exercise we believe serves as a trust and community builder, an introspective eye-opener, and an aid in developing interpersonal skills. Pinderhughes (1989) developed the process and Joyce Hamilton, the University of Hartford's former director of Multicultural Programs, modified it.

We begin by filling the board with student-volunteered categories of human differences. The fuller and more varied the list becomes the better. Students usually start with gender, race, language, and religion; they then move to class or socioeconomic status, people who are physically or mentally challenged versus those who are "temporarily able-bodied," and sexual orientation. Faculty and students join in discussing the categories, linking many of them and concluding that together they reveal the rich varieties of the human race.

We then introduce ourselves in more detail. The point is to give students permission to think about and possibly volunteer relevant background information that, in retrospect, may have been formative in their self-perceptions.[2] One of us is of Jamaican origin, with some European acculturation mixed in with predominantly Jewish, East Indian, and African influences. He was born into poverty in a society deeply divided by class and shade of skin. The other is a European-American of predominantly Swedish ethnicity, with German and English influence from both parents. He, too, was born into relative poverty in a class-divided and anticlerical society (his father is a minister).

To help students understand the emotions and internal-external conversation awaiting them as they explore their ethnicity and early memories of identity formation, we model the confessional experience. Sometimes we become choked up emotionally. When this happens we explain why, and admit how vulnerable we feel. For instance, the Swede reminisces about being a teen engaged in sports, and how he became conscious of race. This consciousness surfaced when newspapers gave heavy coverage to a blatant and petty incident involving a visiting American track-and-field team. A white runner said anyone who fit a new pair of track shoes he did not want could keep them. When the "Cinderella" turned out to be a black sprinter, the white runner said he could not have them. The gross injustice of this incident disturbed the young Swede, who grew up in a homogeneous society in which he rarely saw people of color. It is abundantly evident to the class that this early encounter with racism was profoundly emotional and still results in choking back tears of anger.

After this "demo," we divide students into groups and ask them to write answers to two questions: (1) What is my ethnicity? (We ask for no other distinguishing characteristic) and (2) What is my earliest memory of messages from parents, relatives, clergy, and peers about who I am and with whom I may or may not associate? We circulate among the groups and encourage students to share their answers. It is okay to pass. After hesitant and safe beginnings, almost invariably someone will relate a self-discovery that inspires others to do the same, including those who passed earlier. It is not unusual for this group reminiscence to generate deep emotions. We ask groups to select a reporter to present a summary to the class. This process usually generates vigorous and candid discussion of formative influences in our lives.

Now, what is our rationale for putting the students through such an exercise? If we are going to study the identity of others, it behooves us first to examine our own, "warts and all." We hope this will sensitize us to the delicacy of our self-perceptions and to the imperfections with which we are all burdened. When it "clicks," and it rarely fails to, this experience engenders empathy in the study of other cultures. A secondary objective is to promote bonding among students and some appreciation of the benefit of taking an honest look inside ourselves.

This experience has at least four concrete pedagogical benefits:

- Students, through interpreting their narratives, are now open to the different narrative styles introduced in the courses.
- Students learn to be active participants in generating knowledge.
- Throughout the rest of the course, this "benchmark" of identity evolution becomes a reference point as we discuss similar processes among other people.
- We link the "Who am I?" exploration of personal identity to the shrinking world discussed below under "Permeation of Boundaries," and especially to the ethnic nationalism and conflict that threaten to destroy the global village and tear apart the delicate and beautiful mosaic of cultures in the Caribbean.

Further on Trust: The Journal

We are fully aware that crossing cultural and disciplinary borders entails risk taking and requires trust among faculty and students. We try to provide a safe outlet for venting and perspective-building through a journal. More than a travelogue, the journal contains open yet confidential "thinking aloud" about the concerns of the course and often becomes a private dialogue with the instructor. The journal also helps students cope with the multifaceted nature of the course. The many topics and methods of communication play off each other to create meaning for students in ways that enable them to organize their thoughts for the projects and examinations. The journal also helps faculty conceptualize those projects and exams. Finally, it serves as subtle (not always!) running evaluation useful for course revision. Indeed, we "sample" the journals once or twice during the semester, thereby enabling us to make midcourse corrections as warranted.

DISCOVERING THE LEITMOTIV

Reviewing our experience has made us think about what these courses are singly and together and what they can and ought to become. We looked back to their origins. We noted how they permeate each other's boundaries and how this contributed to their development and our growth. It dawned on us that we had become fellow travelers with the students as they were transformed into epic heroes and heroines, traveling mentally, discovering, conquering, because of who they were and who they became. Thus the epic journey became our leitmotiv for this chapter. It is a post hoc perspective that has already changed our approach to both courses. We now draw the attention of students to this new way of viewing their course "voyage."

Among the characteristics of the epic, the leader-hero acts with decorum on the borders or within the cultures of foreign nations, and the epic is written in a mixed narrative style. By working with multiple styles in different assignments, students at least metaphorically become epic writers. Simultaneously they become epic heroes who cross the boundaries not only of genre but also of the consciousness entailed in using these different types of text. They read literary texts and essays from multiple disciplines and attend a variety of special events; they also participate in group activities and produce group reports, write various kinds of essays, compose journals, and give their own dramatic performance.

This variety originated in our desire to introduce students to as many modes of learning and demonstrating learning as feasible. It is well-known that learners have different strengths. Accordingly, they perform at different levels in different forms of expression. Evaluations from students reveal an initial concern with the variety in the course giving way to a sense of personal victory when they participate in the activities.

Once we began viewing students and faculty as epic travelers, it became helpful to examine our subject matter through the same lens. For instance, TNCs are hardly struggling individuals like the epic heroes of mythology and literature. Yet can they not be seen as modern—and medieval—epic heroes as they routinely cross boundaries? They come, see, and conquer like Caesars, at once dictating and enabling our life styles, creating and destroying governments, indeed ruling the world, in the evocative title of a recent book, *When Corpora-tions Rule the World* (Korten 1995).

Composition theory and political economy will, in turn, shed fur-ther light on the epic journeying our courses encourage.

MAKING MEANING

To make meaning is to connect seemingly disparate phenomena or ideas in ways that generate new understanding. These ways can be both conscious and unconscious. We have explored a variety of approaches, each designed to facilitate meaning-making. Encouraging students to work in multiple genres is a key part of this process. Students negotiate various schools of meaning, digest the material, and finally create their own meaning through conversation, several different styles of writing, and in one case, acting.

A model from composition theorists Hayes and Flower lets us explore students' processes of making meaning in Mosaic and TNC and, by extension, in other interdisciplinary and intercultural courses. Hayes and Flower model the stages of a student's problem-solving responses to a writing assignment (see Figure 1). They propose that

> writing consists of three major processes: PLANNING, TRANS-LATING, and REVIEWING. The PLANNING process consists of GENERATING, ORGANIZING, and GOAL-SETTING sub-processes. The function of the PLANNING process is to take infor-mation from the task environment and from long-term memory and to use it to set goals and to establish a writing plan to guide the production of a text that will meet those goals. The plan may be drawn in part from long-term memory or may be formed anew within the PLANNING process. The TRANSLATING process acts under the guidance of the writing plan to produce language corre-sponding to information in the writer's memory. The function of the REVIEWING process, which consists of READING and EDIT-ING subprocesses, is to improve the quality of the text produced by the TRANSLATING process. It does this by detecting and cor-recting weaknesses in the text with respect to language conven-tions and accuracy of meaning, and by evaluating the extent to which the text accomplishes the writer's goals. (1980, 12)

FIGURE 1
Structure of the Writing Model

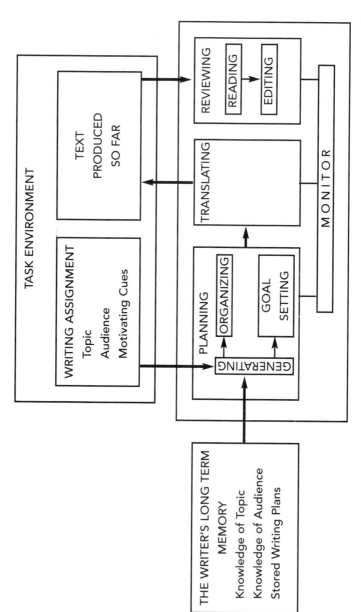

Source: Hayes and Flower (1980, 11).

Hayes and Flower note that the writer's long-term memory plays a key role in the meaning-making process. Their first subheading here is knowledge of topic. In our courses, students discuss their experiences (if any) in the geographic areas being discussed. They scan their memories for other courses with relevant culture content to use as resonance base. Students often come to our interdisciplinary courses brimming with knowledge from their departmental majors, but they generally have had little exposure to other cultures. Even those who have been to the Caribbean islands are unaware of their social variety, and know little about their geography and nothing about their history and politics. Even students from the Caribbean area often have limited knowledge. Some students in TNC have traveled or lived abroad with parents who were employed by TNCs. They offer precious firsthand experience but they often see things only from the company's perspective. Accordingly, we have to start from scratch with definitions of culture, emphasizing distinctions among general culture, business culture, and corporation-specific culture.

A second aspect of the writer's long-term memory, as described by Hayes and Flower, is knowledge of audience. Students are accustomed to writing for their instructors, but in interdisciplinary courses the speaking and writing tasks stretch them to expand their audiences. We also encourage increased awareness of the writing and thinking styles of other disciplines. For example, students in TNC read the work of an anthropologist and, when possible, hear a guest lecture by someone trained in that discipline. Students in Mosaic read a novel and a play, and are introduced to the philosophy and stylistic genre of the writer as well as the content of the writing and the way it reflects a piece of Caribbean reality. While on the face of it this "other discipline" awareness may appear to foster an additive, multidisciplinary approach rather than an integrative, interdisciplinary one, we find, in journals and group presentations and papers, that students are surprisingly adept at blending a variety of perspectives.

A third aspect of the writer's long-term memory is stored writing plans. As with knowledge of audience, students tell us they are used to just giving the faculty what they want, or to following a simplified expository essay structure. An interdisciplinary course on cultures confronts students with so much information of such variety—sometimes contradictory—that they are forced to become more active and interactive. They feel a need to comment on, evaluate, and rearrange knowledge. This process becomes especially vigorous when, partway into TNC, we introduce a segment on North American culture as a basis for comparison. With newly "objective" eyes, American students comment in class or write journal entries on how thought-provoking it is to "view themselves from afar" and to look at their values in terms of orienting themselves in a global economy.

Students must combine elements of their long-term memory with the challenges of the task environment to plan and execute their projects. Given the complexity of these challenges in interdisciplinary and intercultural courses, what we see as students' difficulties in writing may often be problems in the translating process described by Hayes and Flower. An assignment may be due, a semester may end, before they can shift from the translating mode to the editing mode. Beyond the usual problem of translating long-term memory, writing assignment, and planning into text, students face the task of translating meaning across disciplinary and cultural boundaries. Here, then, is a double translation. Ensuring that students from various disciplinary backgrounds succeed in this process represents perhaps our greatest pedagogical challenge. But we console ourselves that even when a student does not try hard enough or we do not succeed to the degree we had wished, the effort and exposure stand a good chance of yielding lasting benefit.

As students emerge from grappling with translating problems in an interdisciplinary course on world cultures, they are better able to use the symbols of world cultures. Culture mixing, increasingly common in today's interactive world, yields rich complexity. Our values meld or clash with those of other cultures with different assumptions from ours about God, work, and play. Here as elsewhere in this essay we overlap with Cornwell's and Stoddard's (1994) wonderfully thought-provoking (and titled) article on the crisscrossing of domestic and international multicultural voices.

Our challenge is to recognize the parallels between this culture blending and the multi-meaning nature of prose writing. We need to go beyond the high school requirement to write a beginning, middle, and end. We must recognize the freshness of each task and the purpose of the writer to experience a song of the self (Whitman 1855)—finding his or her voice—in the process of writing an essay. Similarly, people whose sense of themselves is challenged by the encroachments of the global economy need to retain their own voice.

Next we explore contemporary political economy as it relates to (epic) boundary crossing, nationalism, and preservation of identity.

PERMEATION OF BOUNDARIES

Boundary Permeation "Out There"

In many ways, Klein's (1993) discussion of academic boundary porosity is particularly relevant to our two courses. Indeed, it may be that the correlation between increasing academic boundary permeability and rapidly improving capabilities in transport and communication is not accidental. At any rate, analogies from political economy to Klein's analysis come readily to mind. After all, the globalization of the world economy is a major reason we attempt to alert students to the salient features of world cultures. Both TNC and Mosaic take students "abroad," and TNCs are largely responsible for the world becoming, in common parlance, a global village. The relationship between the recent evolution of the global political economy and our courses is therefore hardly surprising.

We may view the world today as shrinking in at least two dramatic ways that appear paradoxical, if not dialectically contradictory:

- Distances are becoming "smaller" due to supersonic transport and speed-of-light electronic communication, enabling production and trade to knit the world together more tightly than ever before.
- We are witnessing a near-worldwide phenomenon of growing, ethnically based nationalism that insists on boundaries that enclose smaller and smaller spaces.

Most U.S.-educated students are "geographically challenged" compared with international students. Students from other countries are more likely to be aware of at least the surrounding region because they simply have to learn about the world around them and speak the language(s) of the geographic area in which they are likely to live and work in the future. In contrast, America is physically isolated by two vast oceans, and the education system has ignored geography and deemphasized language learning.

Students entering our classroom find themselves in a dialogic situation. Like the *Star Wars* robot R2D2 with its rotating head, they are asked to develop a 360-degree perspective on the world. However, in a way R2D2 could not, we bid them to rotate those 360 degrees in a spherical, or global fashion, as if they were sitting at the epicenter of the earth looking out at the periphery. The image is obviously imperfect, because we simultaneously encourage students to "see" from within the cultures studied. Students must learn to understand the complexity of multiple perspectives, relationships, and connections, and to place themselves in unfamiliar situations. They have to view each situation in the context of the shrinking world: globalization pulling in one direction, ethnic nationalism in the other. That can be frightening. But what explorer was fearless? The epic hero conquered the fear. Likewise, both students and faculty have to conquer the fear of the vast unknown and gird their loins for a voyage of simultaneous discovery of self and of world cultures.

Inter-Course Boundary Permeation

Permeation of boundaries also occurs between TNC and Mosaic. Among the exciting by-products for the authors of coteaching the courses are the syntheses we explore across course boundaries. Commonalities emerge, even unsought, as if someone had dragged the computer icon of one course on top of the other so the insights merge. Few students take both courses, but insofar as we pass on the fruits of that permeation in each course, students benefit from the crossover.

The following is just one example of such course permeation. In Mosaic we analyze sugar plantations and their slave work forces as depicted by Mintz (1985), an anthropologist. This analysis conforms broadly to the Kentucky Fried Chicken (KFC) experience in Japan and the United States, featured in TNC (video), as well as to other TNCs, on several dimensions:

- Vertical integration in Caribbean slave production, taking sugar from planting to finished product, is mirrored in today's TNCs. Like

Kentucky Fried Chicken, they take the chicken from egg to table, or from bauxite ore in the ground to rolls of aluminum foil in our drawers. (Incidentally, Mintz contends the industrial revolution began in the Caribbean, and he makes an excellent case for this proposition.)

- In slavery (Mosaic), in industrial production (TNC)—not necessarily implying a distinction—and in forms of rule ancient and modern, we find coincidental myth generation. One myth is for the rulers, another is for the ruled, and they are mutually dependent. The rulers must rationalize their rule to themselves, but they dare not explain their rule to the ruled in the same terms lest they be found out and thwarted. Slave owners rationalized their "right" to own and brutalize slaves, and told the slaves they were inferior, nonhuman, and therefore in need of rule. TNC managers rationalize their right to pay labor less than a living wage because unemployment would be the alternative, while the workers rationalize not organizing or striking on the grounds of loyalty or probable job loss. Obviously there are exceptions to all of this.
- The term "sociality" is used by Mintz to show how African and European work ethics were synthesized on the sugar plantation to become the industrial work ethic. Put another way, sociality describes how circumstances and cultures interact to produce common types of behavior. It is like describing the motherboard of the computer hard drive of a whole culture: it integrates and coordinates all functions. Sociality therefore describes the multi-attitudes and multi-tensions contemporary humans have to cope with to survive and prosper.[3]

Thus major themes in both courses "cross over."

CONCLUSION: A DOUBLE WIN WIN

For Students

We hope we have demonstrated the benefit to students of voyaging simultaneously across cultural and disciplinary boundaries and of conceptualizing their double crossing as an epic journey. As noted at the beginning of the chapter, students attain enhanced skills in integrating and understanding world cultures and integrating multiple modes of oral and written expression.

Regarding the latter claim, we submit, following our former faculty colleague in the department of Politics and Government, Peter K. Breit, that the different disciplines of a university are dialects of one language. Undergraduates need to develop composing skills that, like the control switches on a major train line, oversee the writing styles of the diverse departments and become voices the students command. These acquired processing skills empower students to "write the academy"—to universalize, integrate, and attain greater facility in switching among the modes of expression found in the various corners of the university. This view connects at several points with the Hayes and Flower model discussed above.

Consideration of integrative skills also invokes the much discussed conundrum of whether students gain more from studying particulars (majors, fields) before they attempt to integrate knowledge. It might seem as if the logic is incontrovertible: students must have something to integrate before they seek to integrate it. It is like the child who asks for two cents' worth of mixed candy. Proprietor: "Here are two candies. You may mix them yourself."

But not so fast. We contend either way works as long as integration takes place sometime. The argument for integrating early may have a slight edge: a simultaneous introduction to multiple topics from multiple vantage points has the benefit of showing connections and relationships, thus enriching students' perspectives in particular studies. This is another way of saying that skills acquired in interdisciplinary courses are transferable to the major.

For Faculty

Students' and faculty's growth are not only parallel but symbiotic. In addition to the faculty benefits listed above—professional growth, intellectual excitement, syntheses of paradigms, "new angle" insights to bring to their disciplines, and the satisfaction of seeing students grow as boundary-crossers—we should list bonding and fellowship with colleagues as well as the opportunity to learn pedagogical styles and tricks portable back to the discipline.

Public policy analysts would call the following example an unintended consequence. Responses from the "Who am I?" exercise in TNC and Mosaic encouraged one of us to introduce it in every course he teaches in political science. What better course-eye-mind opener than exploring self-identity in a sometimes confusing and hostile, multicultural world?

This raises a question: If collective self-in-social-context discussion serves as an icebreaker and bonding mechanism in education, could it not also become a strategy in international negotiation? Perhaps that's the sort of thing former President Jimmy Carter had in mind when he asked participants in the Camp David discussions on peace in the Middle East to bring pictures of their grandchildren.

In Sum

Thus the daunting effort of learning new tricks through the AUC's courses in the "Living in a Cultural Context: Other Cultures" category brings rich dividends to both students and faculty. A former student in TNC recently walked in and said he wanted to tell current students how immensely valuable the course had been as he entered the international business work force. Needless to say, he will be a featured speaker the next time we teach the course.

Our answer, then, to the questions posed in the introduction to this volume asking whether interdisciplinary curricula, course design, and teaching are worth the bother is a resounding Yes. There is "bother" in many senses, including conquering fears of trespassing in other people's gardens and figuring out how to integrate new learning with ongoing writing and teaching agendas. But once faculty step across that boundary and begin to see the kinds of results we have described, they will find themselves enriched as pedagogues, scholars, and human beings. They will feel even more enriched if they can convince themselves, as we have done, that the sort of learning we have discussed might make a small contribution to world peace. Perhaps we should hold seats for representatives from the most troubled spots on the globe.

NOTES

1. Though it may be understood from the nature of the AUC general education structure—students take one course in each of four areas of exposure—we should stress that concrete evidence of either immediate or long-term impact on students is exceedingly hard to come by. We just do not see them again, with few exceptions. As we describe, students provide feedback in journals, course evaluations, and verbal comments about "eye-opening" and "mind-opening" experiences of identity discovery and sensitization to cultures. Much of this is privileged communication, however, prone to subjective interpretation and notoriously difficult to quantify. We are searching for models of before/after course surveys and trying to construct one of our own.

2. Biographical sketches of the authors who contributed to this chapter appear elsewhere. They show us to be quite different in ethnicity and geographic origin; we differ as well in categories invisible in the bio sketches, such as temperament, life experience, and (to some extent) ideology. Our commonalities, however, united us. Furthermore, because both of our academic odysseys spanned several disciplines, it came quite naturally for us to traverse those boundaries and to seek to integrate our knowledge and perspectives.

We met socially at the West Indian Social Club in Hartford, brought together by our common love for Jamaica and the West Indies. We found ourselves in endless discussions spanning—and connecting—innumerable topics, linking them across our disciplinary horizons. We decided to include university students in those discussions. The results have been truly exhilarating for us and, we believe, for many students.

A concluding thought concerning our bios: We are certainly not suggesting that faculty who do not match our diverse backgrounds cannot or ought not to try their hands at the kinds of courses we have developed. All we are saying is that our differences did not hurt us (except temporarily) or stop us, and our similarities, obviously, helped a great deal.

3. The reader who wishes to pursue the nature of slave society further might consult *Slavery and Social Death: A Comparative* Study, by Patterson (1982).

REFERENCES

Cornwell, Grant H., and Eve W. Stoddard. 1994. "Things Fall Together: A Critique of Multicultural Curricular Reform." *Liberal Education* (Fall): 40–51.

Hayes, John, and Linda S. Flower. 1980. "Identifying the Organization of Writing Processes." In *Cognitive Processes in Writing*, eds. Lee Gregg and Erwin Steinberg. Hillsdale, N.J.: Erlbaum.

Klein, Julie Thompson. 1993. "Blurring, Cracking, and Crossing: Permeation and the Fracturing of Disciplines." In *Knowledges: Historical and Critical Studies in Disciplinarity*, eds. Ellen Messer-Davidow, David R. Shumway, and David J. Sylvan. Charlottesville: University of Virginia Press.

Klein, Julie Thompson. 1996. *Crossing Boundaries: Knowledge, Disciplinarities, and Interdisciplinarities.* Charlottesville: University of Virginia Press.

Korten, David. 1995. *When Corporations Rule the World.* Hartford, Conn.: Kumarian and Barrett-Koehler.

Mintz, Sidney W. 1985. *Sweetness and Power: The Place of Sugar in Modern History.* New York: Penguin.

Newell, William H. 1998. "Professionalizing Interdisciplinarity: Literature Review and Research Agenda." In *Interdisciplinarity: Essays from the Literature,* ed. William H. Newell. New York: College Entrance Examination Board.

Patterson, Orlando. 1982. *Slavery and Social Death: A Comparative Study.* Cambridge, Mass.: Harvard University Press.

Pinderhughes, Elaine. 1989. *Understanding Race, Ethnicity, and Power: The Key to Efficacy in Clinical Practice.* Glencoe, Ill.: Free Press.

van Dusseldorp, Dirk, and Seerp Wigboldus. 1994. "Interdisciplinary Research for Integrated Rural Development in Developing Countries: The Role of Social Sciences." *Issues in Integrative Studies* 12: 93–138.

Whitman, Walt. [1855] 1986. "Song of Myself." *Walt Whitman's Leaves of Grass.* 1st ed. New York: Penguin.

CULTURES AND TRANSNATIONAL CORPORATIONS:
SAMPLE SYLLABUS

This integrative course is designed to expose students to the interactions between cultures and transnational corporations (TNCs) and the environments in which they operate, with special emphasis on how culture shapes values and on the tensions, good or bad, generated during cultural exchanges. (Emphasis on written and oral communication and critical thinking.)

Goals: As future workers in a rapidly integrating global economy, students need to understand sources of conflict as well as ways to achieve harmony and success. In this course they will learn to understand patterns of conflict from imperialism to neocolonialism, between Marxism and modern capitalism, between post-cold war globalization and ethnic separatism, and between host countries and transnational corporations. As members of "the global village" role-playing as TNC managers, students will develop skills needed to negotiate with people from different cultures, including listening, seeing, and reading the emotions of others. Students will learn to make connections among ideas from disciplines such as anthropology, economics, ethics, and politics, and to see the importance of continuing their quest for cultural literacy.

Texts: Vern Terpstra and Kenneth David, *The Cultural Environment of International Business* (1991); Gary Ferraro, *The Cultural Dimension of International Business* (1994); Ezra Vogel, *The Four Little Dragons* (1991).

Topics:

Introduction to "Culture" Through Cultural Anthropology

Valuing Diversity Versus Cultural Imperialism

"Who am I?" Identity Discovery Exercise

Culture Shock and Adjusting to Different Values and Lifestyles

Major World Religions and Their Impact on TNCs

History and Role of Global Companies in Shaping Colonial and Postcolonial Societies

Language and Communication: Lingua Franca, Language Hierarchy, and Conflict

Nonverbal Communication: "Don't Show Your Sole in Arabia"

Social Organization: Family, Gender Roles, and Class in Different Cultures

The Political Environment of International Business

Ethical Issues and the Social Responsibility of TNCs

Selected Student Activities: Reflecting course goals, primary emphasis is placed on a series of group activities, including two group case studies, presentations, and papers: (1) opening a campus in Africa or South America; (2) cultural aspects of success and recent failure in the Pacific Rim. Students also present news commentaries and view and offer critical commentary on the videos *The Colonel Goes to Japan*, *Kyocera* (Japanese company in the United States), and *Doing Business Internationally*.

THE CARIBBEAN MOSAIC: SAMPLE SYLLABUS

This integrative course provides an introduction to the complex and diverse Caribbean region, using readings, films, and other cross-cultural experiences. The Caribbean is culturally rich. European colonial powers (Spain, England, France, and Holland) introduced African slaves and Indian, Chinese, and Malay indentured servants. Jews and Arabs (Lebanese, Syrians) followed. All brought distinctive cultures. All made significant contributions to shaping the Caribbean. Thus the course name: The Caribbean Mosaic—an intricate pattern of colors, shades, and nuances. The variety found in Caribbean culture demonstrates that people can live in relative harmony despite diversity. The Caribbean is thus a social laboratory whose findings may have application beyond its shores. (Emphasis on written and oral communication and values identification.)

Goals: Students will gain an understanding of the struggles, conflicts, successes, and failures in the Caribbean from multiple vantage points; get beyond beaches, sun, and rum stereotypes without ignoring the impact of tourism (the abject poverty lies beyond the beaches, and students need to go there, too); ask why such contrast exists between opulence from abroad, shared by a small handful of locals, and marginal existence for the many; pursue answers at many levels, from international power relations to local attitudes; generate informed opinion about our neighbors to the south; and for many, gain a more solid grasp of their own heritage.

Texts: Selections from Sidney W. Mintz and Sally Price, eds., *Caribbean Contours* (1985); Jan Rogozinski, *A Brief History of the Caribbean* (1994); Aimé Césaire, *The Tragedy of King Christophe* (1970); V. S. Naipaul, *Miguel Street* (1984); F. C. Johnson, *Soldiers of the Soil* (1995); Michael Manley, *Politics of Change* (1990).

Topics:

Geography, Geology, and Climate of the Caribbean

Imperialism

Sugar and Slavery

European Legacies, Caribbean Adaptations

Calypso as Social Commentary

History of Steel Bands

Caribbean Literature

Contemporary Social Structure

Political Institutions

Revolutions in the Caribbean

Migration Within and From the Caribbean

Selected Student Activities: Viewing and critical commentary on tourist promotional materials; journal; oral presentations and written responses to cultural events; staged reading of *King Christophe,* a play about the Haitian revolution; visit to two Caribbean cultural events.

DISCOVERING AMERICA FOR A DECADE: A CAUTIONARY TALE

Thomas Grant

Teaching Discovering America has been an adventure in discovery and self-discovery for over a decade; but as its cocreator and the only faculty member who has taught a section every year of its existence, I think that, as an interdisciplinary contribution to the All-University Curriculum (AUC), the course has been less than wholly satisfactory. This is due primarily to the complexity of the subject; a diverse faculty, many with higher-priority commitments elsewhere in the university; and a university structure made up of separate colleges offering different, sometimes overlapping, programs in which the United States is examined. Nonetheless, our experience in teaching American civilization in a multiversity may be instructive in its own way.

BACKGROUND

At the University of Hartford in the late 1970s several professors in the Humanities division of the College of Arts and Sciences met informally to discuss the possibility of creating an American Studies major that would be housed in the college. All of us felt isolated in our own disciplines and even from each other, located as we were in departments in separate buildings. We also recognized that academic disciplines were quickly becoming more permeable as knowledge itself became increasingly interdisciplinary. American Studies programs were well established elsewhere, for example, just across town at Trinity College, and it seemed to us that Hartford was big enough to support and nourish two programs. More important, such an interdisciplinary venture fit the needs at the time of a university made up of several diverse colleges that also includes two conservatories.

Unfortunately, the American Studies initiative dissolved, primarily because the one full-time American historian involved left to take a position elsewhere, while others, many of them part-time faculty, had pressing teaching obligations in their home departments. Meanwhile, colleagues from various departments university-wide were meeting more formally to discuss interdisciplinary ventures that would be similarly broad-based, integrative, and distinctive—but also more comprehensive and ambitious. Out of these discussions emerged the AUC and an invitation to Americanists to revive the interdisciplinary study of the United States, not as a major but more modestly as a course in the "Western Heritage" division, one of five categories in the AUC. When the History department hired an Americanist who would also chair the department, we were able to reconvene as a stabilized group of predominantly tenured faculty from several disciplines. We wanted not only to introduce the interdisciplinary study of the nation to as many undergraduates as possible but to stimulate interest in other courses offered in our separate departments.

The AUC definition of the course Western Heritage: The Humanities provided us with the necessary context to begin to develop an interdisciplinary course on the United States. That AUC course sought to establish, as the 1987 proposal put it, "a common understanding of truth, art, and ethics—especially as such central questions of value and meaning are pursued by the academic disciplines which came to be called the humanities." How has this "common understanding," this "Western Heritage," been sustained, expanded, or revised in the New World? Here was the overarching question about the nation too broad and complex to be addressed adequately by any one discipline but at least approachable through interdisciplinary examination. We agreed that the answer was the political compact, born of the European Enlightenment (though not exclusively) and founded on radical ideas derived from abroad (though also home-grown)—namely, equality, the unalienable rights of the individual, and government by and for the people. So posed, the emphasis inevitably shifted so that we were exploring not the ties that bind but rather those that separate us from the Old World, that is, what makes America unique, or "exceptional," to use the term favored by the "consensus" historians dominant in the profession at the time. "America is something without precedent," said James Russell Lowell in 1864.

Of course, we would not merely celebrate America's purported uniqueness but examine it critically. Specifically, we wanted students to test the durability of the democratic compact and its political institutions by probing what decisively challenged them—most importantly, the institution of slavery and its survival in a century of racial prejudice; the rise of industrial capitalism and its social consequences; immigration and the plight of the unmeltables; and the civil rights movements among minorities and women, particularly in the post-World War II period.

We also wanted participants to challenge the exceptionalist view that we professors all pretty much embraced, perhaps too uncritically, and test whether our assumption remained a tenable proposition. Such a focus, at once precisely circumscribed yet also all-encompassing, would, we thought, attract faculty from a wide variety of disciplines well beyond the humanities. Students from the university's different colleges would be exposed to a wide variety of primary material, including social and political commentary, autobiography, literature and the arts, film, and even advertising. In the process, they would become not only critical thinkers but also better-informed citizens, one of the goals of the AUC. Such a course would be truly interdisciplinary, according to the currently accepted definition of that term: interdisciplinary studies "draws on disciplinary perspectives and integrates their insights through construction of a more comprehensive perspective" (Klein and Newell 1997, 393–94). Indeed, the political compact, announced in the Declaration of Independence and codified in the Constitution, and its testing in the crucible of history, is the topic about America that best lends itself to interdisciplinary study so defined because without the political compact the "United States" would not exist at all.

In the drafting phase, however, the course quickly fell victim to the familiar problems facing interdisciplinary initiatives—the sudden unavailability of interested full-time faculty from various disciplines due to department or college teaching obligations, and, in turn, excessive reliance on part-time (though well-qualified) personnel. Although the subject virtually mandated team teaching, recruiting personnel and ensuring a representative variety and balance among disciplines, not to mention personalities, seemed daunting under these circumstances, and, unfortunately, later hobbled our progress.

Moreover, many involved colleagues from several disciplines, including history, thought the course as proposed too similar to a conventional introductory survey in American history, such as the one offered regularly in the college's own History department, whose main goal was "coverage," that is, chronicling the building of the nation by major figures facing and resolving major crises that produced influential outcomes. Others thought the course too centered on political ideas and thus too dependent on having a political scientist on the teaching team, when we knew that none was available at the time. We had to concede that, in any case, so broad and complex a subject could not thoroughly be explored in one course; yet we wanted to remain committed to an interdisciplinary approach as originally conceived. We had, in essence, reached an impasse.

ANALYSIS

Instead of sticking to the original focus and hashing out our differences, a majority decided that we should be inclusive and also avoid protracted disagreement, amicable as it always was; it was decided that one course would be stretched out into three, presumably to do fuller justice to the complexity of the subject. After discussing variations, I drafted a conceptual framework for the new courses that was incorporated into the proposal reviewed by the AUC committee and, once passed, became the description we used in our syllabi. It read as follows:

> Discovering America is a sequence of courses which will investigate American society, culture and thought and, thus, introduce students to the distinctness of American civilization. The sequence is arranged historically and divided chronologically

into three distinct periods. In part one, American Civilization to 1865, the major themes include slavery and race relations, the nature and evolution of religious beliefs, the origins of the Revolution and of constitutional government, the impact of industrialization and westward expansion, and the significance of individualism in American life. In part two, American Civilization, 1865–1945, the major themes include the impact of capitalism and technology on American society, immigration and its social consequences, the rise of religious sectarianism, the civil rights struggles of women and minorities, the closing of the western frontier and its survival in popular myth, and the emergence of a mass consumer society. In part three, American Civilization, 1945 to Present, the major themes include the Cold War and its political consequences, the alienation of youth, the rise of information and business technologies, the fragmentation of traditional institutions, Vietnam and other foreign policy controversies, and the resurgence of the civil rights struggles among women and minorities.

Although this framework represented a practical compromise, the three-part division revealed our collective retreat from an holistic interdisciplinary study of the nation, which sought a comprehensive perspective derived from the integration of various disciplines, to the relative safety of a more teachable enterprise stressing multidisciplinary approaches and working within traditional chronological boundaries set by the History department. Such a compromise was due in part to the influence of those who wanted, quite legitimately, to stress their discipline's current commitment to studying American diversity and even opposition rather than national unity, but mainly to the fluctuating makeup of the course's ad hoc committee, most of whose more permanent members came, as is usual for such American Studies initiatives, from the History and English departments. Nonetheless, the shift in focus from the democratic compact to the more amorphous "American society, culture, and thought" seemed to open up another, perhaps less disputable approach to interdisciplinary study by highlighting the borders separating disciplines, thus encouraging an examination of how fields of knowledge are constituted and organized. Certainly, the closer study of fewer topics would seem to invite holistic interdisciplinary thinking. Klein and Newell observe: "A narrower topic leaves more time to apply diverse disciplinary perspectives and increases the likelihood that those perspectives confront the same issues instead of talking past one another. The narrower the topic, the more complex its examination can be and the more various perspectives themselves can be probed" (1997, 407). However, from committee discussions over the years and from the evidence provided in syllabi submitted for the writing of this essay, it is not apparent that anyone actually adopted an approach that seriously questioned the assumptions of the various disciplines. Nor did I, and my own reluctance is apparent in the portion of the course proposal quoted above, in which I've arbitrarily mixed neutral and value-laden phrases to describe a course that is patently Eurocentric, particularly in part one, which begins with the English colonists. I've since loosened the Eurocentric hold, and now my section, like many others, has become more multicultural, reflecting new theoretical ideas currently shaping the study of the nation at the university level. All of us would have to admit, though, that we were not prepared to venture far from the boundaries of our own disciplines, nor perhaps from our cherished assumptions about our own country.

Once passed by the AUC steering committee, Discovering America became in practice whatever individual teachers chose to emphasize given their expertise, each working within a common conceptual framework that had been rendered palatable to everyone. In the early years we at least agreed to use some common texts, such as Du Bois's *The Souls of Black Folk* or Fitzgerald's *The Great Gatsby* in part two and Moody's *Coming of Age in Mississippi* and Iacocca's *Autobiography* in part three. Some of us shared assignments designed to encourage at least cross-disciplinary if not integrated interdisciplinary thinking. For example, compare and contrast Booker T. Washington's Atlanta Exposition Address with Du Bois's response in *The Souls of Black Folk* as political, social, and rhetorical documents. Or examine *The Great Gatsby* both as a literary work of fiction and as an important document in the nativist controversy of the 1920s; how do the two approaches differ and why? But soon thereafter, common texts disappeared and faculty instead chose their own and made up their own assignments, with very little sharing—another sign that we were retreating back inside disciplinary boundaries. Although "society," "thought," and "culture" became the holy trinity, the last soon emerged in discussion and in practice as first among equals. What is American culture and how is it distinctive?

Here was an entirely new question for the ever-evolving ad hoc committee, prompted by new members from the social science disciplines, particularly sociology, and the departure, again, of the American historian for a position elsewhere. Although we were confined to the three-part historical framework insisted upon by the departed historian, many found the new focus somewhat liberating after all because "culture," however defined—we never tried to pin it down—is, as opposed to "heritage," inherently adversarial in the modern period. As Peck says, it is "contested, temporal and emergent" (1989, 179). As an object of study shared by several disciplines across the humanities, social sciences, and even the natural sciences, the complexities of a culture mandate an interdisciplinary approach:

> Cultures are too complex to be comprehended by any single discipline or methodology. Disciplines are lenses which bring into focus different dimensions of culture. No single perspective is authoritative. . . . This is an argument for syncretism, not for relativism; the understanding obtained through the contest and conversation of multiple disciplines is more complete and complex than that available through any single discipline. (Cornwell and Stoddard 1994, 45; see also Klein 1996, 152)

Studying culture so defined also warrants team teaching, but again those committed to the endeavor had teaching commitments elsewhere in the university and so no team could be recruited. Consequently, the interdisciplinary approach, such as it could be approximated, had to be developed by individual teachers working alone. From the sample syllabi submitted to me in preparation of this chapter, most still did not in practice venture very far outside their disciplines. At least on paper, an art historian taught her section of American Civilization to 1865 by dwelling on Puritan literature and nature painting but at the expense of religion and politics, while an historian taught her section comparing pre-revolution town life north and south but to the apparent exclusion of the arts. The film historian who taught a section of American Civilization, 1865–1945 did not venture far from the movie director's view of history, while the myth and symbol specialist from the Far West seldom left the Conestoga wagon train on the frontier. The criminologist's section of the same course analyzed the evolution of leisure entertainment and the subculture of crime but to the apparent neglect of other stated "themes." The sociologist who taught a section of American Civilization, 1945 to Present abandoned the stated themes to focus instead on the "everyday life" of select ethnic groups.

In my own sections of American Civilization, 1865–1945 and American Civilization, 1945 to Present, alternately taught over a 10-year period, I have tried to adhere to the conceptual framework, even though I was an advocate of the original idea for the course and strongly opposed the split into three courses. I have also attempted to examine most, if not all, of the stated themes in historical context and to ground both courses in the heritage of essential ideals out of which a new nation was formed. I've tried to play at being a polymath, and found it daunting but also exciting. Some theorists prefer solo flying anyway: "A far superior approach [than team teaching] involves a single instructor adventurous enough to undertake the task of coming to an interdisciplinary understanding of a phenomenon before entering the classroom" (Richards 1996, 127). Some colleagues outside the traditional humanities, however, use very few materials from the arts, particularly literature such as novels, feeling perhaps ill-equipped to teach them with the requisite authority. English professors, by contrast, seem to find soloing easier than others, perhaps because they are least beholden to disciplinary boundaries, customarily taking "literature" to mean anything in print, and thus they are already, as Culler puts it, "interdisciplinary from within" (1992, 213).

The only team formed in the course's first decade seemed to make the best effort to get outside and beyond the disciplines by focusing their section of American Civilization, 1945 to Present not on prevailing and familiar themes as listed in the conceptual framework but on ways of seeing the whole period—what they called four specific "frames": presidential elections, economic development and economic threats, evolving individual rights, and changes in our mass culture. By examining freshly how we perceive who we are as a postwar culture rather than depending on disciplinary methodologies, this duo found an overarching, holistic approach that is more student-oriented, drawing freely from the various disciplines but beholden to none. Student evaluations indicate that they have been successful over time, perhaps because, while holding disciplinary Ph.D.s, they are administrators who work with many departments and are compatible personalities.

Despite our individual, discipline-centered approaches to the subject, students nonetheless received practice in learning how to think across disciplinary boundaries, and in some cases, to question those very boundaries. The AUC provided necessary and helpful guidelines by stressing what are called "essential abilities," such as analytical thinking and problem solving, values analysis, and independent decision making. Students were to become active learners in a process designed to make them independent thinkers. As stated in the Discovering America proposal:

> Students will be required to analyze specific issues or problems raised by the topical readings and understand causes and effects in their historical and social contexts. They will learn how to make intelligent connections among the various sources of evidence and discover plausible and coherent solutions to their analyses and syntheses.

To accomplish this, all of us had to become extraordinarily attentive to problems of written expression, that is, become, like those of us from the English department, writing instructors as well. As stated in our proposal:

> This process in critical thinking and problem solving will be developed through regular practice in interpretive writing, under close supervision of the instructor. Students will receive guidance in making practical outlines, forming theses clearly, developing ideas persuasively, documenting sources accurately and acquiring the rudiments of a graceful and readable style. To help students improve their writing skills . . . instructors will be available for individual conferences on a regular basis to examine written

drafts and to suggest revisions of assignments. . . . Only by submitting themselves to the rigorous process of revising drafts . . . will students learn to comprehend the strength not only of their ideas but also of their values, and thus mature into independent decision makers.

Based on the sample writing assignments and exam questions submitted to me as background for this chapter, it appears that my colleagues have been imaginative and resourceful in creating original assignments that challenge students, who are drawn from the various colleges of the university, to think in an interdisciplinary mode. The most successful have been comprehensive questions framed to require integrative analysis and synthesis, drawing from a wide variety of materials. Following are some examples:

- How did the Hudson River School of painting reveal a growing disenchantment with industrialization in New England during the antebellum period?
- How did the dime novel help to justify westward territorial expansion by whites and Indian removal during the late nineteenth century?
- Why were the physical culture and popular science movements opposed to the feminist movement in the late nineteenth century?
- How would you explain why black and white readers interpreted the immensely popular Uncle Remus stories by Joel Chandler Harris very differently during the Reconstruction period?
- How did the emerging Hollywood film industry rewrite history in such popular movies as *Birth of a Nation* and *Gone with the Wind*, and why?
- How was the "cult of domesticity" movement advanced by the influence of women's magazines?
- What does the popularity of Coney Island tell us about class conflict in turn-of-the-century New York?
- How did professional baseball become "the national pastime"?
- What happened to the neighborhood tavern following World War II and why?
- What was the cultural fallout from the development of the atom bomb?

- How did the suburban mall supplant Main Street?
- How has the automobile changed our lives and what role did advertising play?

Offering satisfactory answers to such overarching questions requires students to assimilate information from many diverse sources, integrate insights from the various disciplines, and then shape their interpretation cogently, based on the evidence. Achieving this goal has been particularly challenging in practice because the classes have generally been made up, not of the freshmen and sophomores for whom the AUC was primarily designed, but of a mix of students from all four years and of various aptitudes and interests. Too many of these are seniors who regard any AUC course as at best an untimely distraction from completing their major. Yet so diverse an audience can paradoxically advance the cause of integrative learning precisely because it ranges from freshmen with few disciplinary preconceptions to seniors with too many. All the more reason to frame not only comprehensive questions that require interdisciplinary study but also assignments that exemplify the process of discovery unrestricted by disciplinary boundaries. Here are some examples of instructive assignments:

- Compare and contrast the popular "Columbus Discovering America" story over several generations. What does this reveal about the teller and his or her audience?
- Compare versions of history written by New England Puritans with those written by Native Americans.
- Create an imaginary debate among Benjamin Banneker, George Fitzhugh, and Frederick Douglass on the question: Does the Declaration of Independence contradict the institution of slavery?
- How is the society envisioned by the Gospel of Wealth advocates, such as Horatio Alger, Andrew Carnegie, and Henry George, similar to and different from our own today?
- Create an imaginary debate between Theodore Roosevelt and Charlotte Gilman on "the role of women" in the new century (the twentieth), drawing from their writings.
- What familiar contemporary social attitudes are to be found in Robert and Helen Lynd's landmark sociological study, *Middletown* (1929)?

- Account for the discrepancy between the reliable data about juvenile delinquency during the 1950s and Hollywood's exploitation of the facts in movies such as *Blackboard Jungle* (1955) and *Rebel Without a Cause* (1955).
- How was the Vietnam War conducted in Hollywood movies of the 1970s, and since?
- What is a "cultural icon" and why are these Americans regarded as such (one per student): Ernest Hemingway, Charles Lindbergh, Amelia Earhart, Humphrey Bogart, Eleanor Roosevelt, Elvis Presley, Marilyn Monroe, James Dean, Muhammad Ali, John Glenn, etc.
- Interview a member of your family who is an immigrant and show how his or her experience compares with those from the first "great wave" of immigration (1880–1912).

Assignments such as the imaginary debate invite students to get "inside" the minds of historical figures to understand how they thought and what they would say if alive today. Others that examine popular culture guide students to consider how cultural institutions, such as the movie industry, shape our attitudes, even subliminally. Still others ask students to analyze how American cultural conflicts are shaped by race, gender, and class. All such assignments, among many others, encourage students to integrate insights drawn from the various disciplines, thus making interdisciplinary thinking possible.

These assignments and questions also of course invite interaction among students working in groups—the more diverse the makeup the better. Here again, faculty unable to agree in theory about Discovering America in practice found common ground teaching their sections. Because the classes are made up of students who come from the various colleges of the university, diverse groups are easy to create. All of us who have taught sections of the course have required group projects, designed to develop not only reading comprehension and analytical and synthesizing skills but also "effective participation in group learning and oral and written presentation skills," as phrased in one sample syllabus. In my own section of American Civilization, 1865–1945, students working in groups regularly analyze the "cult of domesticity" in Victorian America, interpreting a variety of material published by both men and women and then reporting to the class. Trips are arranged to local museums and the restored homes of important figures of the time such as Harriet Beecher Stowe and Mark Twain. Students examine these restored mansions, carefully noticing how home design and room decoration, including personal effects, expressed the social attitudes and even moral assumptions of the period. In other sections of the same course, student groups have compared criminal behavior during the Great Depression as shown in Hollywood gangster movies with the documented evidence as interpreted by historians and sociologists; other groups have traced the development of an emerging mass consumer society through an analysis of ads in popular magazines, particularly during the early years of mass consumerism (1919–1929).

In American Civilization, 1945 to Present, groups of students have considered the Hollywood Blacklist of the McCarthy era from many points of view, right to left; others have explored "the feminine" and "the masculine," semiotically interpreting the cultural signs in glossy fashion magazines such as *Mademoiselle* or *Esquire;* still another group has done urban field work examining the impact of interstate highway design on neighborhoods in a small city like Hartford. Mixing male and female students of various backgrounds also reveals how interpretations are influenced by gender, race, and class. Student evaluations over the years suggest that a majority of students—ranging from lowly freshmen to jaded seniors with majors as diverse as engineering, classical piano, accounting, graphic arts, and occupational therapy— enjoyed these assignments as timely diversions from their primary studies. They particularly valued the field trips, frequently to places most admit they would not otherwise go. While all faculty have been diligent in encouraging students to develop their essential abilities, particularly writing, I am unable to say to what length colleagues have gone to meet with students in individual conferences to work on the revision process, as required in the course. I can only say that I did. The long hours in personal conferences were simply unavoidable if students were to succeed, and in some cases, merely to pass the course.

PROSPECTS

Looking back over the 10 years of the Discovering America sequence, I conclude that the course, although addressing compelling questions important to everyone as citizens in a democracy, has not been a successful example of interdisciplinary study. The subject is simply too vast and too elusive. Furthermore, teachers in a multicollege university such as ours are so much in demand in their respective colleges that they cannot give a program like the AUC concentrated attention beyond teaching sections of courses when their primary obligations permit. The program has also faced some faculty opposition, primarily from departments suffering a decline in the number of majors. The English department's long-established offerings in Greek and Roman Classics in Translation and English Romantic Literature are offered less frequently now that multiple sections of Art and Thought of Classical Greece and Romanticism in the Arts are offered under the AUC. The English department courses may in time wither away. Multiple sections of Discovering America have eclipsed the History department's own survey of American history, reducing the enrollments. The numbers of English and history majors have declined—for many reasons, but the AUC may be one. On the other hand, interdisciplinary general education programs such as the AUC may actually help these departments by providing a captive audience of potential majors (and minors) otherwise unavailable. Whether the AUC and the traditional liberal arts curriculum in the College of Arts and Sciences can have a mutually supportive and productive relationship in a university structured around nine separate colleges remains a challenge for the next decade.

REFERENCES

Cornwell, Grant H., and Eve W. Stoddard. 1994. "Things Fall Together: A Critique of Multicultural Curricular Reform." *Liberal Education* (Fall): 40–51.

Culler, Jonathan. 1992. "Literary Theory." In *Introduction to Scholarship in Modern Languages and Literatures*, ed. Joseph Gibaldi. New York: Modern Language Association.

Klein, Julie Thompson. 1996. *Crossing Boundaries: Knowledge, Disciplinarities, and Interdisciplinarities.* Charlottesville: University Press of Virginia.

Klein, Julie Thompson, and William H. Newell. 1997. "Advancing Interdisciplinary Studies." In *Handbook of the Undergraduate Curriculum,* eds. Jerry G. Gaff and James L. Ratcliff. San Francisco: Jossey-Bass.

Peck, Jeffrey. 1989. "There's No Place Like Home: Remapping the Topography of German Studies." *German Quarterly* 62:2 (Spring): 178–87.

Richards, Donald G. 1996. "The Meaning and Relevance of 'Synthesis' in Interdisciplinary Studies." *Journal of General Education* 45 (2): 114–28.

DISCOVERING AMERICA II: AMERICAN CIVILIZATION, 1865–1945: SAMPLE SYLLABUS

This integrative course examines the United States as a distinctive democratic society and focuses on core conflicts that arose after the founding of the republic, particularly the debate over slavery and the Constitution, defining "woman's sphere" in post-Civil War urban culture, and the "pursuit of happiness" under industrial capitalism in the late nineteenth and early twentieth century. Students analyze primary documents including political tracts, social essays, memoirs, and popular fiction as well as film, magazine cartoons, and advertising. (Emphasis on written communication and critical thinking.)

Goals: Students will gain an understanding of core conflicts in post-Civil War America, the impact of these conflicts today, and the ways various disciplines examine issues, interpret evidence, and draw conclusions.

Texts: Patricia Bizzell and Bruce Herzberg, ed., *Negotiating Difference* (1996); Harriet Beecher Stowe, *Uncle Tom's Cabin* (1851); Anzia Yezierska, *Breadgivers* (1925); F. Scott Fitzgerald, *The Great Gatsby* (1925); handouts; documents, photographs, etc., from the University of Hartford's Museum of Political Life.

Topics:

The Debate Over Slavery (Jefferson, Banneker, Walker, Stewart, Douglass, Fitzhugh, Christy, Stowe)

"Woman's Sphere" (Beecher, Stearns, Folsom, McCord, Grimké, Fuller, Douglass, Truth, Stanton)

Wealth, Work, and Class Conflict, including a look at the Jazz Age, the stock market crash, and the Great Depression (Alger, Carnegie, Councill, Conwell, Bellamy, Lloyd, Fitzgerald, handouts, photographs)

Selected Student Activities: Several analytical essays over the semester, using particular disciplinary approaches to evidence (revision of these essays, in consultation with the instructor, is a key part of the course); in-class presentation using the disciplinary approach of the student's major; small-group research projects on controversial issues; reports on field trips (for example, to the Harriet Beecher Stowe House in downtown Hartford). Some sections of the course meet in the Museum of Political Life, where students have access to a wealth of primary material to tap for their research projects.

AFTERWORD:

AN INTERDISCIPLINARY GENERAL EDUCATION CURRICULUM: PAST, PRESENT, AND FUTURE

Marcia Bundy Seabury and Colleagues

Whereas the preceding chapters focus on issues of interdisciplinarity arising out of particular courses, this Afterword looks across courses. For underlying the volume's framing question about how interdisciplinary courses build students' integrative skills lie other significant questions about how an interdisciplinary general education curriculum may work out as a whole. We consider here the local university site out of which the essays in this volume arose, addressing with respect to the curriculum as a whole some of the issues explored for individual courses: What goals led to the founding of the curriculum and how have they worked out in practice? What were the processes of interdisciplinary curriculum development and what are the realities after the passage of time? And what next? Thus we offer not only some nuts and bolts but also some thoughts about the future of interdisciplinary programs such as ours. In accord with the collaborative nature of this volume, this look to the future comes from several contributors who have been part of this effort for over a decade. They express ongoing belief in the kind of education made possible through programs such as the All-University Curriculum (AUC) at the University of Hartford, even as they ponder continued change.

HISTORY OF THE ALL-UNIVERSITY CURRICULUM

Curricular changes across the country during the 1980s arose from dissatisfactions within the academy that often paralleled forces outside it (see Kanter et al. 1997). Reform of general education at the University of Hartford was the result of several influences. First, the faculty of the College of Arts and Sciences, with the assistance of a three-year Andrew W. Mellon Foundation grant (1983–1986), conducted a review of its general education requirements. The faculty reaffirmed the primacy of the liberal arts and proposed that students not only in the college but across the university would benefit from a set of common requirements that would take advantage of the diversity and richness of our schools and colleges. Meanwhile, both the Council of Deans and the university's Board of Regents were discussing similar matters. The deans issued a report advocating a "curriculum for literacy," with the aim of graduating students who are both professionally proficient and liberally educated, while the regents emphasized building skills for lifelong learning. External forces were at work as well. Connecticut, followed by other states, changed its accreditation guidelines to require that one-third of all credits for the baccalaureate be a balanced distribution of courses in the humanities, arts, natural and physical sciences, mathematics, and social sciences. This change, fully in effect in 1987, postdated but reinforced the review of the general education curriculum; in and of itself, it would entail major curricular changes, for example, directing a new population of music conservatory students into required science courses.

The design and rationale of the All-University Curriculum emerged out of extensive conversations over many months at all levels of the university, including individual departments and colleges, students, the administration, and the regents. In 1985, the senior academic officer appointed a Select Committee for a university-wide general education curriculum, 75 percent of whose members were senior-level faculty. This committee proposed a 12-credit liberal education curriculum for all baccalaureate students, which would be supplemented by further general education requirements specific to the needs of a particular school or college. The goals of the curriculum, as stated in its course proposal guidelines, were:

- to provide assured breadth for baccalaureate students—to provide a sufficiently general education
- to provide a shared or common experience among students of the university, thereby increasing the interaction among students and faculty of the university
- to make clear relationships among disciplinary areas of knowledge via integrative, cross-discipline courses
- to provide a curriculum that truly takes educational advantage of the institution's collegiate structure as a comprehensive university
- to help schools and colleges to meet the new State of Connecticut regulations for breadth and balance in all baccalaureate programs

A university-wide curriculum committee would oversee the process of development and implementation of the program.

At any university, individuals and departments disagree, sometimes vehemently, on curricular structures, courses, and requirements. Amidst the controversies and turmoil that curricular revision generates, especially revision of this scope, faculty at Hartford agreed from the outset on the benefits for students of courses that push them to participate actively, think and write better, and act well upon what they have learned. Developing skills and attitudes was central for us, but not through courses focusing on those skills per se, abstracted from a specific content area. This agreement, plus the accumulating evidence of the benefits of integrative study, allowed for development of the curricular plan summarized in the introduction to this volume, linking interdisciplinary study with development of designated essential skills.

Cross-college committees focusing on the individual skills then worked to define each in ways that made sense to faculty across disciplines, offered suggestions for encouraging these skills in a variety of courses, and assembled up-to-date resources from the professional literature. Meanwhile, teams of faculty from across the disciplines and colleges came together in small groups to design the new courses, which would supplement the interdisciplinary courses recently created under the Mellon Grant for General Education to become the initial group of All-University Curriculum offerings. Each of the courses bubbled up from shared faculty interests; thus faculty assumed ownership in the process. Because all AUC courses had to be proposed by teams of faculty from across disciplines, the curriculum from the beginning involved ongoing cross-disciplinary collaboration. Faculty have commented that the process yielded lively discussions of pedagogy and epistemology and opportunities for collaboration with others who had been on the same campus for years but with whom they had not shared ideas.

At the time, the course designers did not refer to the evolving vocabulary of narrow or partial interdisciplinarity versus broad or full interdisciplinarity—in simplified terms, bringing together perspectives from disciplines within one of the traditional groupings of humanities, social sciences, or sciences versus crossing those boundaries as well. But almost all the courses that emerged, while typically based in either the humanities, social sciences, or sciences, were fairly broadly interdisciplinary, both practically in terms of which faculty were interested and available to develop them and intellectually in terms of which perspectives faculty saw as essential to include. The science and technology courses were probably most self-consciously broad in their conception: the sciences faculty, like their colleagues nationwide, wanted students to view their disciplines not as inert collections of facts but as processes related to important issues in their world. On the surface, in terms of staffing and course descriptions, the arts courses were probably the least broad, but conceptually and in practice these to varying extents have been broad as well, for example, the course on Ethnic Roots and Urban Arts.

To implement general education reform of this magnitude, strong leadership is essential. Faculty leaders were able both to articulate convincingly the goals for learning inherent in the reform proposal and to provide the energy and political skill necessary to secure the proposal's adoption. The support and leadership of the provost and president throughout the process created further momentum for the effort. The new curriculum won approval of the Faculty Senate and went into effect in fall 1987.

Gradually four to six courses would become available in each of the five breadth categories. The courses encompass traditional areas of knowledge as well as the study of contemporary issues and problems.

The criteria for courses to be accepted into the curriculum were and still are:

- Teaching and learning activities will be designed to generate active involvement on the part of students.
- Each course will integrate knowledge, methodologies, assumptions, and themes from more than one discipline or field; thus courses should be developed by teams of faculty from across disciplines and colleges. Each course team will describe the assumptions, themes, and methodologies from those disciplines that will be emphasized in the course, along with the similarities and differences that make for effective integration within the course. Teams will maintain flexibility for faculty to individualize their sections without sacrificing the central structure, content, method, and goals.
- Each course will address significant ideas and experiences needed to live fully 1) in our culture, 2) with other cultures, 3) in a social context, 4) with science and technology, or 5) with the arts; each course will be identified with one of these categories of knowledge, and
- Each course will be designed to develop student performance and competence in at least two "essential abilities." These abilities are cognitive and personal tools with which the well-educated person applies knowledge and experience. First each course must develop students' oral or written communication skill or both. Second, each course must also develop at least one of the other essential abilities: analytic thinking and problem solving, values analysis and independent decision making, social interaction, or responsibility for civic life. (From course proposal guidelines)

REALITIES MORE THAN A DECADE LATER

Now, more than 10 years after the introduction of the interdisciplinary general education curriculum at the University of Hartford, faculty participation has grown from 32 to an active roster of 80 to 90—roughly 60 full-time faculty (all on loan from their home departments), 20 adjunct faculty, and 5 teaching members of the administrative staff. Of the faculty involved in the creation of the program, all but two of those who are still at the university continue to teach in it, which speaks strongly to ongoing faculty support for the program. Within a sample three-year period (1993–1996), 9 full-time faculty left the program (because of a move, retirement, or death) while 16 joined (both faculty already teaching in the departments and new hires), demonstrating the program's ability to continue to draw new faculty. Participating faculty come from all ranks. Most teach one AUC course a semester or one a year, with a few teaching two every semester and a few others rotating in only irregularly.

We continue to offer 60 to 65 sections per semester (25 students each) of 27 different courses, plus two overseas offerings. New courses are occasionally added (most recently The Caribbean Mosaic, and Literature and Culture of Immigrant Groups in America), and a course or two has become inactive. The number of active courses has been kept relatively constant to preserve the original goals of the program, and the number of sections offered has also remained limited so that students looking for electives will more likely take upper-level courses in the disciplines. The focus on integration has fostered various curricular initiatives: for example, an AUC study-abroad program each summer in which Hartford faculty team teach across disciplines with faculty from Oxford University, and a version of Reasoning in Science on "Space Awareness Across All Ages" (supported by a Connecticut Space Consortium grant), which integrates university students with Hartford fifth and sixth graders and their parents in an historical study of scientific thinking about the sky offered at a local observatory.

In almost all cases the courses remain team taught (using the dispersed-team model described by Colarulli and McDaniel in the Appendix to this volume), with composition of the teams evolving and new teams forming. Faculty on teams that have temporarily dispersed because of faculty turnover or scheduling difficulties typically express interest in returning to that format. But the format has not been rigidly enforced. Effective structure, continuously rearticulated and actively encouraged, plus flexibility in practice works well. A team or two liked teaching together so much that they stayed together all the time. One team could not harmonize their schedules, so they taught separately but planned the course together and visited each other's sections several times each semester. Another decided to plan together, teach separately, but get together at the beginning or end of each unit for student panels, guests, and so forth. And a couple of top-notch faculty stated from the beginning, "I'd love to teach in the program [and later, "This is my favorite course to teach"] but I want my own section"; their course teams have assembled large anthologies of course materials and meet periodically to share ideas.

Faculty participation remains voluntary; most (but not all) faculty and administrators have preferred this approach to any kind of quota system. Faculty from all nine colleges participate, but the percentage has not been equally high or steady in all colleges. One positive aspect of this staffing arrangement is that underutilized faculty in some units have entered the program even as participation from other units has temporarily declined. Chairs and deans routinely consult with the AUC director on faculty development plans for new and ongoing faculty in their units. The Council of Deans and college promotion and tenure committees typically recognize AUC teaching as an important component of a candidate's portfolio, though some faculty report that particular chairs have explicitly or in practice discouraged participation on the grounds that departmental needs must come first. Job postings for new university positions now typically contain a clause referring to the "opportunity to teach in a nationally recognized interdisciplinary general education program," emphasizing that the university is seeking faculty across the disciplines who are interested in collaborative interdisciplinary work. Symbolic of the integration of the program into the university is a major new university-wide faculty award, instituted in 1994 and endowed by university regent Donald W. Davis, for outstanding contributions to the All-University Curriculum; this award joins and integrates the emphases of the traditional three awards for teaching, scholarship, and service.

An array of ongoing faculty development opportunities supports and encourages faculty to venture outside their usual territory. They are invited to sit in on a team-taught course for all or part of the semester before teaching it themselves. Each faculty member joining the AUC has a designated faculty mentor with whom to discuss the challenges of teaching interdisciplinary courses and essential skills. Funded summer workshops give newly formed and ongoing teams the opportunity for shared reading, discussion, and planning; about one-third of the faculty teams participate each year. Ongoing roundtables, sometimes in collaboration with the university's National Endowment for the Humanities-funded teaching enhancement program, bring faculty together across disciplines to discuss issues of interdisciplinary studies and student learning.

The program is administered by a three-quarter-time director and one-quarter-time associate director, both of whom are typically tenured faculty members serving rotating three-year terms. A shared administrative assistant and a student aide complete AUC office staffing. The program has finally gained a visible and stable office location in a high-traffic student area. The director has a budget that funds faculty development, workshops, travel to conferences, honoraria for guest speakers in courses, lab supplies, and so forth. The budget also provides reimbursement to the colleges, as needed, for adjunct replacement of full-time faculty who teach in the program, which helps to free them from competing departmental demands. The AUC office assembles syllabi and course materials each semester (kept on file for anyone interested), and the director distributes, collects, and reviews student course evaluations.

A faculty committee composed of representatives from each of the university's schools and colleges and from the Student Government Association meets monthly to review course proposals and oversee curriculum evolution, coherence, evaluation, and policies. Close scrutiny by this committee has ensured that faculty teams clearly articulate how a proposed course will meet the above-listed criteria. Faculty teams, in consultation with the committee, formally review their courses every five years. Committee members also contribute to faculty recruitment and development within their respective units.

Several external evaluators, including William H. Newell, Julie Thompson Klein, Zelda Gamson, Karen Spear, and Karen Schilling, have participated in the ongoing assessment of the program. These evaluators, plus other experts, have given presentations and workshops and held conversations with AUC faculty on issues in interdisciplinary and general education.

Orientation of students to the curriculum takes place not en masse in large auditoriums but in more personalized ways, with opportunities for student input, in the individual classes: via explicit statements in syllabi about interdisciplinary learning and essential skills, discussion in opening class sections, and ongoing conversation throughout the semester. To celebrate student achievement in the program, an annual AUC Award now honors a student for intellectual curiosity and motivation in areas outside his or her major, willingness to look at issues through the perspectives of multiple disciplines, and scholarly or creative accomplishment in AUC courses; in addition, a General Education Honors List recognizes students who have completed their four required AUC courses with a B+ average or better (the award and list are publicized on campus and noted on student transcripts).

The founders of the curriculum envisioned bringing students into academic conversations in the larger university community, with faculty, students, and ideas they would not otherwise have encountered. This goal continues to be realized. Virginia Hale, a contributor to this volume, recounts a representative anecdote about three of her advisees sitting on her couch at home: one turned to the others and asked not "Where are you from?" but "What AUC course are you taking?" which led to discussion of that common topic.

Are things quiet on campus? Things are never quiet, nor should they be. Probably the most frequent problem cited, familiar nationwide, is the difficulty of staffing general education courses during times of tight resources. Faculty across the disciplines continue to feel a three-way tension among the competing goals of staffing introductory courses in the major, upper-level courses, and interdisciplinary general education courses. Dissenters have remained consistent in their views over the years and vocal when the opportunity arises. As Gamson (1997) notes, many general education programs either remain or revert to cafeteria-style, a little of this and a little of that, because faculty simply do not agree on what students should study outside their majors. Some of our faculty are still convinced that general education courses are best housed within the separate departments. And the "credit crunch" also causes concern: given heavy and ever-increasing requirements for some majors (for example, students in elementary education in our state now must also declare a subject-area major for certification), space for electives may virtually disappear. (See some further concerns voiced in Thomas Grant's chapter.)

Despite the challenges of sustaining a common curriculum across the university, support for the All-University Curriculum remains strong at both administrative and faculty levels. As noted above, good faculty have remained and good new faculty have joined. Senior faculty have frequently noted that the AUC has contributed to the improvement of teaching and learning across campus because it has encouraged faculty to work together to explore a wide range of teaching techniques. AUC faculty, having broken out of their isolated classrooms and teaching methods, are spreading the culture of interdisciplinarity, collaboration, and attention to student skills. Cross-disciplinary gatherings of faculty, although difficult even to schedule amidst conflicting meetings of colleges and departments, have become a regular part of academic life. Cross-disciplinary student gatherings are familiar as well, as students across the university's varied majors work together in teams on case studies, course-related community projects, and other group activities. Thus the program continues to build a shared campus culture at the University of Hartford.

LOOKING AHEAD

What will be the future of interdisciplinary general education at our university and others as our institutions and our disciplines evolve? Because interdisciplinary general education for us has been a highly collaborative endeavor, with differing voices coming together in conversation, responses to this question likewise reflect the collaborative spirit, drawing on both spoken and written comments from key contributors to this volume.

Elizabeth McDaniel, a codesigner of the AUC and its first director, offers this overview of the ideals that have driven us and of what may lie ahead:

An interdisciplinary course

- is a learning community for students and faculty
- is an opportunity for faculty collaboration and learning

- challenges students to think in new ways, to make connections between ideas and their own lives
- offers cognitive challenges to students accustomed to fact-based education
- models the intellectual scaffolding for the undergraduate experience by demonstrating the connectedness of knowledge and the existence of multiple perspectives on every "truth"
- reconnects faculty with colleagues by focusing on their collective responsibility for the development of undergraduate students

As our institutions evolve, interdisciplinary programs such as the AUC will:

- require ongoing attention and support because traditions in higher education continue to favor the individual disciplines
- be the vehicle for facilitating creative faculty activities and innovations in educational programming
- become a keystone of undergraduate education
- require ongoing internal and external marketing to reach new audiences, to involve new faculty and students, and to reinforce their distinctiveness so they are not taken for granted by participants

As our disciplines evolve, programs such as the AUC will:

- sponsor more creative courses and involve more disciplines in existing courses
- be the outlet for further faculty interdisciplinary activities
- be supported by more research and contribute to research on interdisciplinarity

Guy C. Colarulli, another codesigner of the program, adds that whereas many of the curricular revisions across the country during the 1980s did not result in fundamental change, the more ambitious such as our own typically included attempts at integration. At least for us, regardless of whether upcoming reevaluations of general education in our various constituent colleges lead to changes in requirements or structures, "a retreat to the way things used to be simply won't happen." Indeed, Colarulli states that the current interdisciplinary curriculum remains "robust," in good part because it provides an effective structure that allows for flexibility and change (one of the principles cited in the Association of American Colleges' *Strong Foundations* report [1994]).

Is Hartford's curriculum evolving as its creators anticipated that it would? Colarulli observes:

> The long-term maintenance of a mostly team-taught, inter-disciplinary general education curriculum in a comprehensive university has proved as difficult as its adoption. We anticipated some of the problems a decade ago but others have been genuine surprises. We knew and it has proved to be true that departmental and college structures that hire, tenure, and promote faculty have first call on their services and focus. The struggle to keep full-time faculty involved, particularly as members of teams, is continual and critical. The leadership of such a curriculum, as a result, plays an indispensable role in maintaining the vitality and quality of that curriculum, more so than in a traditional department. At the University of Hartford, few of the more than 60 sections a semester offered in the AUC can be taken for granted.
>
> We did not fully understand that faculty teaching in highly specialized or professional areas are often very narrowly educated. Often they are ill-equipped, or feel themselves to be, to participate with colleagues in team teaching. It is one thing for a musician or artist, for example, to be aware of the history and culture of a work and quite another to teach such material with colleagues from the humanities and social sciences. In actuality, faculty have more to contribute than they believe they have but the time and effort involved is diversionary from their specialized or narrow focus. The result is that of a faculty more than 300 strong, a good number do not participate. The demand for classes, however, is not reduced and falls on a much smaller-than-expected group of faculty.
>
> The AUC is a 12-credit, 4-course university-wide general education requirement, accompanied by 6 required credits in writing; these 18 credits just barely fit into the highly structured professional degree programs in engineering, music, and technol-

ogy. Because students take courses in the four breadth categories least closely related to their major, they typically do not have the opportunity to take a course in the area in which they are probably best able to benefit from interdisciplinary study. Requiring another course, however, would prove difficult both because of the stringent requirements in many professional degree programs and because some faculty would consider it redundant. Thus the general education program and the majors have not yet been linked to the extent desirable, leaving ahead the challenge of optimal integration and wholeness in the undergraduate curriculum.

The AUC will continue to be a source of community for faculty across nine very different schools and colleges. It has bridged the walls of departments and colleges to encourage substantive relationships among diverse faculty. In the past, faculty from different colleges interacted, if at all, only with respect to institutional or political issues. Now, for example, a business faculty member is team teaching, with a biologist and a sociologist, a course called Living in the Environment. The AUC fosters a true university community in which ideas are the basis for interaction and discourse.

The AUC has made it more likely that students will share classes with others from across the university. It is beneficial for first-year students to come to know people who are different not only in superficial ways but who have different interests, ideas, and beliefs. In fall 1997, we piloted what elsewhere have been called FIGS (Freshman Interest Groups), in which freshmen take two or three courses organized around a theme. AUC courses now anchor a number of the FIGS. Students for example take the AUC course The Adult Journey and a linked writing course at the same time. AUC-anchored FIGS, as a result, not only integrate material from a number of disciplines but also foster further community among students. The pilot project with FIGS has led to a three-year FIPSE (Fund for the Improvement of Post-Secondary Education) grant to dramatically expand FIG offerings. The curriculum, in addition to its substantive goals, continues to bring faculty and students together who in the typical discipline-based curriculum would never talk, would never appreciate the relationships among their ideas and fields.

Thus Colarulli documents ongoing curricular evolution in which a major initiative promoting integrative education leads to further changes in that direction.

The current director of the AUC, Karen Barrett, has taught continuously in the program from the beginning and thus combines the perspectives of both faculty and administration. She emphasizes ongoing innovations and risk taking within courses as key to the future of interdisciplinary general education. For example, "responsibility for civic life" has been designated from the beginning as an essential skill to be developed in our interdisciplinary courses, and many teams have indeed created explicit opportunities for such engagement, but faculty are now working harder to encourage students to integrate interdisciplinary learning with service to their communities. Says Barrett:

> As the primary framework for general education at the University of Hartford, the All-University Curriculum will continue to play a critical role as we move into the next decade and will serve as a key locus within the university in which innovations in curriculum and teaching strategies occur. Dynamic and ever changing, the relatively young curriculum has taken on a life of its own, continually reinventing, revitalizing, and realizing its potential. Faculty will continue to be risk takers who, as experts in their respective fields, secure in their abilities as professors, are willing to go beyond conventional, traditional classroom techniques and methodologies to enhance students' educational experiences while at the same time enhancing their own professional development.
>
> While active learning via labs, debates, field trips, simulations, and so forth has been a primary facet of the curriculum, too few courses explicitly denote "responsibility for civic life" as an essential ability that should receive significant attention. If the AUC is to respond to the needs of students and society in the future, it must relate to current, real-world situations. It must encourage students to become active citizens capable of and interested in taking responsibility for themselves and those

around them. Enhancement of active learning, including service learning opportunities, is an essential direction the AUC must pursue.

Doug Dix, winner of the university's Donald Davis Award for interdisciplinary teaching, scholarship, and service, concurs:

> Hartford epitomizes disparity; it is the capital of America's wealthiest state but ranked among America's poorest cities. Its residents suffer as a consequence and the All-University Curriculum encourages service learning in part to alleviate that suffering. Because many AUC courses address disparity, the AUC is primed to mount a concerted attack on the problem. Such an attack would make the university in deed what it is in name and would enhance enthusiasm, goodwill, and the sense of purpose. Already the AUC provides faculty with exceptional opportunities to teach for intrinsic reward. I envision extending that kind of opportunity to students through increased service learning.

What next? Well, none of us ever did claim that any one curriculum structure is perfect. We were and remain believers in what we do within our departments as well as what we do across them, and, of course, teaching within our departments, like our research, has become far more interdisciplinary. Interdisciplinary general education courses, team taught when possible, are no panacea. Any program, no matter how good it looks on paper, will remain strong only to the extent that an institution's strongest faculty are willing to participate in it. That in itself bodes well, because interdisciplinary study is not for the routine-bound, the rigid, the lazy.

But we know that curricula change. Across the nation, as Gamson (1997) and others have observed, sustaining a university-wide general education program has proved notoriously difficult. Sustaining a program that cuts across the power structures of an institution can be doubly difficult. An article once linked the process of curricular change to the Myth of Sisyphus: You do what needs to be done with great effort and sweat. Then you do it again. We also know, however, that regardless of the fate of a particular curriculum, interdisciplinary teaching has changed us, both what we teach and how we teach it, whether the courses are within our departments or across. Making connections across disciplines and paying increased attention to building students' skills will remain central to us. And we have gained wonderful colleagues along the way, colleagues with whom we would not have had the opportunity to work were it not for our interdisciplinary program. This book is just one more example of the ongoing, productive collaboration that influences our scholarship as well as our teaching. Collaborative interdisciplinary work will continue to stretch us, even as it stretches our students. And perhaps "the most important thing that can happen to any mind is that it be stretched. . . . Once stretched, the mind will never retract to its original size" (Nisbet 1981, 83).

A large part of the conviction expressed in this collage is based on student responses to this process. A skim through recent course evaluation forms from even a single class (Ethnic Roots and Urban Arts in this case) reveals abundant references to sight and light: the course "opened my eyes," "awakened me," "allowed me to take the time to see things from new perspectives," "offered a lot of insight," even "brought more light into my life," according to one. This volume honors and looks to the future of those day-to-day moments of illumination for both students and faculty as they view issues from the perspectives of multiple disciplines.

REFERENCES

Association of American Colleges. 1994. *Strong Foundations: Twelve Principles for Effective General Education Programs.* Washington, D.C.: Association of American Colleges.

Gamson, Zelda F. 1997. "General Education and the Renewal of Civic Life." Presentation at the University of Hartford, 2 April, West Hartford, Conn.

Kanter, Sandra L., Zelda F. Gamson, and Howard B. London. 1997. *Revitalizing General Education in a Time of Scarcity: A Navigational Chart for Administrators and Faculty.* Boston: Allyn and Bacon.

Nisbet, Robert. 1981. "Teggart of Berkeley." In *Masters: Portraits of Great Teachers,* ed. Joseph Epstein. New York: Basic.

APPENDIX:

FOUNDATIONAL
AND FOLLOW-UP RESEARCH

Guy C. Colarulli and Elizabeth A. McDaniel;
Sheila Wright and Anne Hendershott

Colleges and universities considering interdisciplinary general education need to explore numerous curricular and administrative issues that lie outside the scope of this volume. Summaries of two such issues that University of Hartford faculty examined in detail—collaborative teaching and obtaining student input (see McDaniel and Colarulli 1997, Wright and Hendershott 1992, and Hendershott and Wright 1993)—shed light on the evolution of Hartford's interdisciplinary general education curriculum and offer ideas for other institutions to consider.

As discussed in the introduction to this volume, most of Hartford's All-University Curriculum (AUC) courses are taught by interdisciplinary teams. But while AUC faculty continue to find value in team teaching after more than 10 years, opinions in the literature are mixed. Davis (1995), for example, focuses on the many advantages that accompany the added challenges of team teaching whereas numerous others (for example, Richards 1996) are perfectly happy with or even prefer individually taught courses. One recurring consideration raised is cost. Benson cites "the relatively high cost of the typical integrative studies course" as a key argument against interdisciplinary studies; their "heavy reliance on team-teaching methods" contributes to make such programs "extravagant and cost ineffective" (1982, 46). Newell and others answer this charge by viewing team teaching either as an expensive alternative to team curriculum development or as a stage along life's way: faculty learn on the job and then are "weaned" to individually taught sections (this metaphor emphasizes the need to move on; Newell does, however, note the benefits of different sections of a course meeting together regularly).[1] The *Handbook of the Undergraduate Curriculum* in fact defines team teaching as "an expensive process" (Gaff and Ratcliff 1997; cf. Klein and Newell 1997). In the first part of this Appendix, Guy C. Colarulli and Elizabeth A. McDaniel explain the team-teaching model in place at Hartford and discuss some of the research leading to that choice. They reexamine the financial assumptions cited above by suggesting how an institution can bring faculty from different disciplines into the classroom together while containing costs.

In the second part, Sheila Wright and Anne Hendershott urge that universities include students in the conversation about their growth through interdisciplinary general education. While Davis reports the results of a questionnaire asking about students' perceptions of interdisciplinary courses, in accord with his focus, most questions probed perceptions about teaching rather than learning: the extent to which faculty have collaborated in planning, teaching, and evaluating and have integrated the subject content of the course (1995, 101, 125). In contrast, Wright and Hendershott emphasize what students understand about their own learning. The authors' work with focus groups contributes to the emerging literature on assessment options in interdisciplinary education.

I. FOUNDATIONS

Guy C. Colarulli and Elizabeth A. McDaniel

THE DISPERSED-TEAM MODEL

University of Hartford faculty designed the "dispersed-team model" to provide as much interdisciplinary and collaborative work as possible while at the same time ensuring that the university could sustain the program financially. Typical courses in the AUC meet once a week with the full faculty team and all students enrolled in the course (about 75) and once or twice a week in three sections of 25, each with one of the three faculty members. This arrangement provides opportunities for integration and interaction as the full team teaches and discusses the material together and engages students in the conversation. It also provides a small class environment with 25 or fewer students in which a faculty member can foster still more interaction and active learning as well as relate more closely to students.

The dispersed-team model is set into motion with the first in a series of collaborations among a team of faculty from different disciplines to develop a proposal for a new interdisciplinary course. The proposed course is reviewed by a committee of faculty from across the university on a number of dimensions, such as the degree of integration proposed, plans for active learning, and specification of learning outcomes including integrative skills arising from the interdisciplinary aspects of the course. After a process of comment, revision, and approval by this committee, the team of faculty sets about preparing the course in greater detail. Faculty members work together to make connections and to understand the issue or topic from a variety of disciplinary perspectives. The preparation phase is characterized by faculty learning and collaboration, which set the stage for class meetings based on the dispersed-team model. After spending months preparing a course, faculty become "master learners" ready to make connections across disciplines and to analyze the nature of those connections with students.

During the semester, faculty as a team continue to plan, implement, and evaluate the course. They are not teaching three different courses but rather one integrated, interdisciplinary course. Once a week they teach, converse, and present together. Yet in the sections they have some autonomy and a closer relationship with students than if they met only in a large group. Students reap the benefits of working with the entire faculty team and sharing in the interdisciplinary conversations as well as having small-group learning opportunities.

The model has two shortcomings: it does not offer students a pure team-taught experience, and team teaching is done in groups of 75 students, which does not offer as many opportunities for student involvement as a class of 25 would. In both cases, however, the model is not without a response. It does provide a team-taught interdisciplinary experience every week of the course and it does provide a relatively small class opportunity once or twice a week that encourages considerable interaction and active learning. It affords a mix of faculty interdependence and autonomy as well.

One of the most important secondary benefits of the dispersed-team model is that it fosters community among both faculty and students. University-wide interdisciplinary general education at Hartford has brought students from about 70 different majors together in courses designed to increase interaction and respect for different intellectual perspectives. At the same time, faculty from nine colleges of the university now interact on substantive rather than only political grounds; they enrich each other's teaching experiences and, most important, they learn from each other.

Student course evaluations reveal that many students appreciate the richness of the learning community, the multiple perspectives and voices, the integrative experiences in which they are challenged to participate. Not surprisingly, however, other students, more comfortable in traditional didactic lecture formats, struggle with the ambiguity of faculty conversations in which no right answer or one truth is communicated that they can put down in their notes. These latter are likely to be dualists, as described by Perry (1970), who complain that if a particular teacher cannot give them the truth, they want a better teacher. As Perry also emphasizes, breaking out of old ways of seeing may entail considerable discomfort. Meanwhile, faculty involved in the dispersed teams participate collectively in ongoing analysis of their work, often inviting faculty from outside the team to visit classes and evaluate their courses.

THE HIGHER EDUCATION CONTEXT

Hartford's interdisciplinary curriculum and dispersed-team model, implemented in 1987, grew out of an extensive review of the literature of the preceding decade on integrative learning, faculty collaboration, and team teaching. Of course the literature goes further back. John Henry (Cardinal) Newman (1873) advocated the development of the "integrative habit of mind," the highest of critical thinking skills, which seeks to make sense and create coherence. More recent literature continues these emphases. Critics find the undergraduate experience to be fragmented and argue for the development of greater coherence by introducing students to essential knowledge, to connections across the disciplines, and to the application of knowledge to life beyond the campus. "As students see how the content of one course relates to that of others, they begin to make connections, and in doing so gain not only a more integrated view of the knowledge, but also a more authentic view of life" (Boyer 1987, 92). According to Mark van Doren, "the connectedness of things" means giving deliberate attention to finding and making connections (Association of American Colleges 1994, 13–14).

The literature on the efficacy of team teaching at the postsecondary level was lean when we began, but is now growing. Flanagan and Ralston (1983) and Newstrom (1981) report increased student interest in course material, and Sullivan (1991) finds higher student satisfaction in team-taught courses. Lindauer reports that "although some students may find it unsettling to be confronted with alternative interpretations, the majority appreciate this more realistic view of . . . discourse" (1990, 72). Davis's survey results indicate "deep satisfaction" on the part of faculty involved in team teaching but only "a slight preference" for team-taught interdisciplinary courses on the part of students (1995, 124, 126); he urges faculty to articulate and explore with students the values of interdisciplinary team-taught courses.

As we studied the general education reforms of the 1970s and 1980s, we surveyed creative and powerful models of faculty collaboration developed to improve the quality of teaching and learning, especially integrative thinking. In traditional instructional teaching arrangements, students enroll in separate courses and whatever integration takes place is often achieved by students on their own, if at all (Davis 1995). Coming from different disciplines, faculty involved in collaborative teaching typically integrate material from various fields of knowledge into "a new, single, intellectually coherent entity" (Klein 1990, 56). Collaborative models of teaching and learning assume an "epistemological perspective that knowledge is socially constructed, created by communities rather than individuals. . . . knowledge is not poured into students but rather emerges from ongoing dialogue and social interaction among groups" (Austin and Baldwin 1991, 14–15).

MODELS OF COLLABORATION

Collaborative teaching models fall into two broad categories: those in which faculty come together only to coordinate their classes and activities and those in which faculty are engaged to the point of team teaching. Gabelnick et al. (1990) summarize many of these models in a typology of learning communities.

Models using team coordination include paired or linked courses (often a skills and a content course); courses clustered around a shared theme, period, issue, or problem (see Daniels 1984); and freshman interest groups (in which students are encouraged to enroll in a set of existing courses typically organized around a theme). These models are designed to develop greater curricular coherence, reduce the fragmentation of the curriculum, stimulate learning across disciplines, and motivate students to learn by joining together with their peers in common academic pursuits. Team coordination models entail less curricular integration, less interaction with faculty colleagues, and more faculty autonomy than models based on team teaching. Coordination models make fewer time demands and therefore have little impact on faculty load or class size because students register for separate courses. These models do not interfere with a university's existing structures but do not foster much collaboration either.

Models employing some degree of team teaching include federated learning communities (clustered courses augmented by a seminar emphasizing synthesis taught by a faculty master learner) and coordinated studies (characterized by a cohort of students and a team of faculty from different disciplines engaged in a large unit of instruction focused on a central theme and offered in an intensive block of time).

Pure team-teaching models can potentially double the cost of delivering each academic credit because two faculty members are in the classroom at the same time. These models offer greater curricular integration, faculty collaboration, interaction between faculty and students, and opportunities for the faculty to model active learning, but require more faculty collaboration and thus allow less faculty autonomy.

DIMENSIONS OF COLLABORATION

During the development of the AUC we considered the following four dimensions of the then-existing models of faculty collaboration[2] in light of our intellectual and academic goals and the realities of available resources.

Degree of Integration

The founders of the AUC sought curricular integration and opportunities to develop integrative thinking. Curricular coherence facilitates student understanding of the connectedness of knowledge. Many of the general education reforms of the 1980s viewed the development of students' ability to integrate ideas, perspectives, and discipline-based knowledge as integral to the goals of general education. When faculty participate in collaborative curricular activities, they move away from their individual areas of expertise to a broader view of their discipline and where it fits into the larger context of knowledge. Their collaboration sets the stage for the integration of student thinking. "Team teaching can be wonderful, as both faculty and students are 'surprised by joy' when they make hitherto unseen connections and experience the lovely rigor of intellectual activity" (Rinn and Weir 1984, 10). At the low end of the integration spectrum are those programs that link two or more courses for which students coregister, but in which faculty are barely or not at all jointly involved in setting goals, planning assignments, or promoting interconnections across their disciplines. At the high end, at which there is greater curricular integration, the educational experience may involve faculty members from multiple disciplines teaching an interdisciplinary course together.

Degree of Interaction

Murchland (1991) points out that it is no accident that Socrates invented the dialectic process at the same time his contemporaries were inventing democracy. Democracy is founded on the core belief in the value of everyone's participation in governance and relies on the exchange of ideas, perspectives, and values as the vehicle for achieving a better understanding, for discovering what is best, even what is true. Bringing learners, both faculty members and students, together in the same space has within it the fundamental elements of the Athenian polis. As Smith and MacGregor put it, collaboration "creates new ideas and new meaning"; conversation improves understanding (1992, 8–9). When faculty members interact with each other and with students in the classroom, the conversation is enhanced, new insights emerge, and faculty are reinvigorated (Gabelnick et al. 1990; Quinn and Kanter 1984, 1, cited in Austin and Baldwin 1991, 42).

Degree of Active Learning

This dimension is measured in terms of the degree to which students and faculty members are engaged together in thinking about the material. Students cannot be passive spectators, even if they are listening to a discussion among faculty. Joining with faculty in a struggle with ideas and perspectives encourages active learning, as students realize that their intellectual dilemmas are shared by their professors (Association of American Colleges 1994). As Bonwell and Eison note, active learning strategies involve students in more than listening, engage students in higher-order thinking and activities, place less emphasis on transmitting knowledge and more on developing students' skills, and encourage students to explore their own attitudes and values (1991, 2).

Degree of Faculty Autonomy or Interdependence

In traditional university instructional settings, faculty have virtual autonomy in the design and delivery of their courses within the parameters of an approved course description and syllabus. Except for the rare visit by a peer or academic administrator for evaluation purposes, faculty members teach unobserved and unrestrained. Across the range of collaborative models, faculty engage with their colleagues in varying degrees of discussion, planning, delivery, assessment, and evaluation. Real collaboration cannot help but create conflict, and thus it requires compromise, sharing of power and responsibility, exposure to divergent ideas and teaching styles, and loss of privacy and autonomy. But it has the potential for enhancing quality and raising expectations. The least collaborative models described in the literature have minimal effect on faculty autonomy: for example, at the extreme, courses are linked and students enroll in two courses concurrently, but faculty are not involved with each other in or out of the classroom. In the most collaborative models, faculty are engaged together in planning and delivering courses or whole blocks of courses that are team taught.

COST IMPLICATIONS

Even if faculty are sold on the overriding value and benefits of collaboration, models that do not sufficiently consider the impact on faculty load and cost are short-lived. Although collaboration has potential for the enhancement of learning, it can have a negative impact on resources, specifically class size, faculty-student ratio, and faculty time. An institution must consider multiple factors about its own institutional budgeting, traditions, and technology, as well as both short-term and long-term productivity (see McDaniel and Colarulli 1997, 28–31, for further discussion of financial considerations). The challenge is to create conditions that will result in improved learning but not dramatically increase costs. Higher education can only afford the occasional expensive pilot project or experimental curriculum; to be sustained, curricular models must balance cost and quality issues. We are, however, slowly entering a new era in which learning outcomes are increasingly the basis for consumer evaluations of colleges and universities. In this era, students and parents will focus on how much learning is accomplished and thereby will encourage institutions to support collaborative teaching as a way to improve productivity and reputation.

CONCLUSION

After consideration of the various models and dimensions of collaboration described above, in their attempt to balance both quality and cost considerations faculty at the University of Hartford designed the dispersed-team model. The model maximizes quality through team teaching and collaboration in a learning community while controlling costs by maintaining the existing faculty load and faculty-student ratio. Thus it is a model that other institutions may want to consider.

II. FOLLOW-UP

Sheila Wright and Anne Hendershott

STUDENT FOCUS GROUPS

This volume explores a teaching and learning process and the difference it makes for students: how they change, grow, see things in a new light. But what do students themselves have to say about all this? One way to evaluate the impact of an interdisciplinary curriculum on students is through focus groups. Understanding student perceptions and attitudes demands a perspective and a methodology that are themselves process-oriented. Focus groups conducted with exiting seniors can provide those students with a valuable opportunity to reflect on their cumulative experiences as undergraduates. In addition, focus groups give students another chance to be part of a working group, a team dedicated to a task, rather than an individual working in isolation without the benefit of other input. Such groups embody the emphasis on conversation that is central to our curriculum as a whole.

The hallmark of focus groups is the explicit use of group interaction to produce data and insights that might be less accessible without that interaction (Morgan 1988, 13). Because participants interact with one another and not with the moderator, the interaction provides greater accessibility to participants' points of view. The moderator maintains responsibility for keeping the discussion focused on the issue under study but still has the flexibility to digress if participants bring up other issues that are pertinent to the subject. Thus the results do not simply confirm or disprove previous assumptions but may yield new insights.

THE HIGHER EDUCATION CONTEXT

In the Harvard Assessment Seminars report, Light (1990, 81) defines assessment as a process of evaluating and improving current programs, encouraging innovations, and then evaluating the effectiveness of each innovation rather than merely testing what students have learned immediately following a course. It was in the spirit of trying to understand and encourage innovations in teaching, especially interdisciplinarity, that we chose focus group methodology.

This decision was not made in a vacuum. The same year that the University of Hartford's AUC was implemented, Boyer's seminal work *College: The Undergraduate Experience in America* (1987) was published, calling for a renewed focus on general education that would offer students a more coherent, more meaningful education. In response to Boyer's work and concerns voiced by many others, a number of innovative general education programs were initiated that would play a larger role in the undergraduate curriculum than such programs had in the past (Gaff 1991). While we recognized that developing an interdisciplinary general education program would be difficult, we also understood that evaluating its impact on students might be even more difficult but absolutely necessary.

Despite the enthusiasm for general education reform in undergraduate curricula, however, Baxter Magolda (1987) and Twombley (1990) note that not enough attention has been paid to the meaning students make of the curriculum or to the ways such a curriculum can foster change. Gaff's (1991) research also suggests that students are less affected by general education reform than they might be; he too calls for more focus on student responses.

Course evaluations do not suffice. Although Hartford faculty have found great value in the evaluations completed by each student of each interdisciplinary course, which the AUC director as well as faculty teams review in detail each semester, we wanted more understanding of meaning-making and of the perceptions and attitudes of students. Nationwide, despite a large body of literature and a number of highly reliable survey instruments, much of the yield of student course evaluations has not been helpful to those who need and want to use the results for program modification (Weimer 1991). The feedback needed to improve college teaching may not be the same as the feedback necessary to evaluate it. We were interested in evaluating the curriculum not just to judge its effectiveness but to make it more meaningful to those who are actually experiencing it.

Further, we decided that the methodology of quantifying student attitudes or behaviors as representing learning outcomes in specific courses would not provide adequate information. We wanted the opportunity to probe in an open-ended way not just student attitudes but why and how they evolved. We were looking for what Farmer has since called a "goal-free or responsive" approach to academic program assessment. With such an approach, the evaluation process is not limited to the program's stated goals: "The intent of goal-free evaluation is to discover and to judge the actual effects of the program, including its unintended or accidental effects. This approach assumes that unintended side effects of a program may be as important as its intended effects" (Farmer 1997, 597).

Although concerns have been expressed about the reliability and validity of focus groups, an article in the highly respected *Evaluation Review* (Ward, Bertrand, and Brown 1991) concludes that many applied researchers now consider focus groups an appropriate means to obtain an in-depth look at the motivations behind human behavior.[3]

A SAMPLING OF RESULTS AND THEIR IMPLICATIONS

We chose two major issues for investigation:

1. Perceptions: Students were asked a series of questions designed to determine whether any of the interdisciplinary courses they had taken had made a difference in the way they thought or challenged their thinking.
2. Behavior: Students were asked questions to explore whether any AUC course made them change their behavior in any way. They were asked whether a specific course had caused them to do something they might not have otherwise done.

Forty-eight graduating seniors first completed a questionnaire and then participated in focus groups carefully sequenced to move from general to specific questions (Figure 1; see Wright and Hendershott 1992 for further description of our methodology). One of the two project directors moderated each session.

FIGURE 1

Questions for Focus Groups

1. Looking back on the list of AUC courses you have taken during the last four years, can you give me your overall impressions of the AUC program?
   Why do you feel that way?

2. Do you see any value in taking interdisciplinary courses outside your major?
   What is your perception of interdisciplinary learning?

3. Does interdisciplinary learning take place more easily in team-taught courses or individually taught courses?
   Which do you prefer?
   Can you tell me about the advantages of each?

4. Was there any one AUC course that made an especially strong impression on you?
   How did it make an impression?

5. Did any course change the way you thought about something?
   How did this happen?

6. Did any course change anything you do, or any action or behavior?
   How did this happen?

7. Was there any one AUC course that had absolutely no impact on you?
   What do you think was lacking in the course?

8. Was there a book or reading associated with an AUC course that made a lasting impression on you?
   What was it? How did it affect you?

A few excerpts from our published results suggest the kinds of insights such research can yield. The survey provided quantitative data on issues such as which courses students felt had an impact on their thinking or behavior. Among the surprises here was that over 30 percent of our sample had taken an extra AUC course as an elective. We had suspected that students occasionally chose AUC courses as electives but did not anticipate that such a large number were doing so. In addition, we learned that the majority of graduating students had gone to art museums, musical performances, or scientific and technological sites as part of their AUC requirements and that a significant number had volunteered at soup kitchens, AIDS hospices, or food-share programs as course options.

The focus groups of course probed further. They revealed that developing new perspectives, new points of view, are important to students. Many commented that particular AUC courses requiring "new ways of thinking" offered what they had hoped and imagined would happen in college. They liked the idea of having classes that "broadened" their ideas. Many students observed that the learning experiences in the interdisciplinary courses seemed different from other courses. They reported that they had begun to realize the connectedness of the disciplines and the complexity of the issues surrounding topics from various disciplines.

According to our data, students' perceptions changed significantly as a result of taking courses in the categories "Living Responsively With the Arts" and "Living in a Scientific and Technological World." In discussions on the arts, almost all agreed that they had not wanted to take a course in this category, that they even resented it. They were convinced the arts had nothing to do with their major and little to do with their life. This finding is in accord with Astin's (1985) statistical data on incoming university students, which show they are less and less interested in learning how to "have a meaningful life" and more and more interested in developing professional and career skills. Our focus groups revealed, however, that students recognized or appreciated the value of courses in the arts category several semesters *after* they had taken these courses. They commented that now, as seniors, they saw more in the courses than they had seen while enrolled or immediately upon completion:

"I didn't like it [the art] at the time, but now that I know how to look at it I think it's pretty interesting."

"I simply had never listened to classical music before and had no idea how to analyze art. Now my parents are shocked when they hear me talk."

"I recently found myself analyzing the style of the doors and windows of a building downtown."

Such repeated comments remind us that looking for changes in attitudes, behaviors, or values immediately following an interdisciplinary course or even immediately preceding graduation may give us only partial truths.

The depth of interest nonscience majors expressed in laboratory courses such as Epidemics and AIDS and Living in the Environment was illuminating. Biology lectures and labs were at the heart of both courses, but because they were presented in a contextual framework, students overcame their apprehension about science and became involved. Over and over students expressed their shock at learning that science isn't completely objective, that the interpretation of scientific evidence is often dependent on the cultural context, that science isn't just "yes" or "no," "right" or "wrong." The interdisciplinary nature of the courses provided the catalyst for new insights. Never before, for example, had students considered that the fields of biology, government, and philosophy could be related to business problems:

"I never realized that intuition played any role in engineering or design. I guess I just assumed that discovery came from facts."

"I never thought before about the business aspect of cures for diseases."

Students' responses to these courses support the arguments of proponents of interdisciplinarity that learning in the sciences would be enhanced if the curriculum were built on areas of natural student interest, with scientific principles and procedures introduced in context (Steen 1991).

The focus group discussions indicated that students believed their behavior and the behavior of other students had changed in several ways as a result of taking certain courses. The most significant change occurred in sexual behavior as a result of taking Epidemics and AIDS. Several said they were much more cautious about practicing "safe sex" and that their friends had also changed their behavior. Students also said that they made efforts to recycle, eliminate waste, and change their living habits as a result of taking Living in the Environment. They reported volunteering for a variety of optional off-campus activities, such as working in a homeless shelter, which they found valuable.

Students in our study were divided on the value of working in groups, with many expressing strong negative views. They found it particularly difficult to work in groups if they were highly motivated but other students were not. They also discussed being confident about what they could do alone and not liking the uncertainty associated with group projects. The comments about group work that were not negative were primarily related to the lab component of courses in the science category; the benefit of "having a partner" did not seem to transfer to areas outside the sciences. The literature suggests that collaborative learning energizes students and allows them to analyze and create new perspectives (Bruffee 1984). Such learning has been shown to develop higher-level thinking skills, promote positive interdependence, and increase student retention (Cooper and Mueck 1990). Students' reactions, however, suggest the need for ongoing research in this area. Unless the use of interdisciplinary groups is carefully planned and unless students are carefully prepared for their roles, many will get discouraged before they have sufficient opportunity to recognize the value of group work.

Even though the focus group moderators consistently directed students away from discussion of specific faculty members, students returned again and again to the characteristics of the instructor. They showed remarkable agreement on the importance of enthusiasm, an historically strong predictor of teaching excellence (Feldman 1976; Goldsmid and Wilson 1980; Lowman 1984; Sherman et al. 1987). Students consistently commented that specific faculty were "really into" the content, thus motivating them to figure out why. As far back as 1968, Musella and Rusch concluded that faculty interest and enthusiastic attitude were the most important qualities for promoting thinking in students. The number of comments in the focus groups about course instructors reinforces the obvious need to enlist, retain, and reward the most highly motivated and enthusiastic faculty in interdisciplinary general education programs. In addition, course developers need to be aware of the importance of helping instructors design and translate content in ways that reflect their enthusiasm both for the material and for student learning.

FURTHER STEPS

Focus groups are useful for identifying areas that should be explored through further research and they provide an abundance of information to take back to faculty. Although faculty development efforts such as brown-bag luncheons and speaker series were embedded in the AUC from its inception, our report "from the field" led directly to additional workshops on team teaching, collaborative learning (including project evaluation), and experiential learning. The focus group results opened further discussions about the "point" of general education: What is it that we want students to know and how do we know when they know it? Is "knowing" enough or should we expect changes in attitudes and behaviors as a result of knowing? These are not new questions, nor are all the answers readily apparent; however, the focus group results gave impetus to the discussions, engaging faculty as a community of learners in a way that was not predicted. We recommend conducting focus groups with faculty as well to assess their perceptions of interdisciplinary general education courses and make comparisons possible between faculty and student opinions.

Focus groups should represent only one of a university's assessment strategies. Institutions need to employ methodological triangulation, drawing on multiple methodologies both quantitative and qualitative.[4] Many of the assumptions underlying King and Kitchener's (1994) Reflective Judgment Model emerged in our focus groups, for instance, that development is stimulated when an individual's experiences do not match his or her expectations. The Reflective Judgment Model or similar instruments might offer interdisciplinary general education programs a method of consistent longitudinal analysis of their impact on students' thinking, perceptions, and behavior.

In interdisciplinary programs—in which the goals frequently emphasize improving critical and creative thinking; encouraging reflective thinking through service learning, study abroad, and internships; and developing ethical reasoning skills and attitudes—triangulation is particularly crucial to assessment. We often are looking beyond mere mastery of content and so we must rely on instruments that are sensitive to change over time and to the many factors that contribute to change. We should probably avoid trying to "find" changes that have occurred within short periods of time (a semester or a year). But we remain convinced that focus group methodology, properly used, should be part of any effort to assess undergraduate education.

Assessment of interdisciplinary general education programs is essential for many reasons, among them:

- The public is demanding accountability from higher education.
- Employers are looking for students who can think, and who can learn how to work in fields that do not even exist today.
- Too many students continue to believe that knowledge in the major is the key to lifelong success.

Proponents of interdisciplinary general education believe it can provide students with the thinking skills and problem-solving abilities necessary for the demands of the future. We need to be able to demonstrate the value of general education to all of the above constituencies, as well as to faculty and administrators. As noted in *Strong Foundations* and elsewhere, "general education is best not seen as a finished product, but a continuing intellectual and organizational project" (Association of American Colleges 1994, 26). Focus group results support a university's vision of a "continuing intellectual and organizational project." Working with student focus groups provides faculty and administrators with an opportunity to understand the impact of the curriculum and the teaching and learning environment on students' perceptions, attitudes, and behavior. Even more important, focus group methodology creates an environment in which students can reflect both individually and collectively on critical learning experiences.

NOTES

1. See Newell (1983, 11–13; 1990, 77). Cf. Armstrong, "twice is probably enough" (1980, 61); also McFarland and Taggie's claim that "close identification of team-teaching with interdisciplinary teaching is one of the most serious impediments to the development and implementation of interdisciplinary programs," hence their university's "plan to phase out the team-teaching component" (1990, 233, 234).

2. Davis (1995, 20–21) offers a more recent analysis of continua of collaboration in interdisciplinary courses, focusing on planning, content integration, teaching, and evaluation.

3. For useful guidelines on conducting focus groups, see Kruger (1988).

4. On further options for the assessment of interdisciplinary education, see Field, Lee, and Field (1994).

REFERENCES

Armstrong, Forrest H. 1980. "Faculty Development Through Interdisciplinarity." *Journal of General Education* 32 (1): 52–63.

Association of American Colleges. 1994. *Strong Foundations: Twelve Principles for Effective General Education Programs.* Washington, D.C.: Association of American Colleges.

Astin, Alexander W. 1985. *Achieving Educational Excellence: A Critical Assessment of Priorities and Practices in Higher Education.* San Francisco: Jossey-Bass.

Austin, Ann E., and Roger G. Baldwin. 1991. *Faculty Collaboration: Enhancing the Quality of Scholarship and Teaching.* ASHE ERIC Higher Education Report No. 7. Washington, D.C.: George Washington University School of Education and Human Development.

Baxter Magolda, Marcia. 1987. "Students as the Focus of Developing, Implementing, and Evaluating Liberal Education." Paper presented at the Association for General and Liberal Studies Conference.

Benson, Thomas. 1982. "Five Arguments against Interdisciplinary Studies." *Issues in Integrative Studies* 1: 38–48.

Bonwell, Charles C., and James A. Eison. 1991. *Active Learning: Creating Excitement in the Classroom.* ASHE ERIC Higher Education Report No. 1. Washington, D.C.: George Washington University School of Education and Human Development.

Boyer, Ernest L. 1987. *College: The Undergraduate Experience in America.* New York: Harper and Row.

Bruffee, Kenneth. 1984. "Collaborative Learning and the 'Conversation of Mankind.'" *College English* 46: 83–100.

Cooper, Jim, and Randall Mueck. 1990. "Student Involvement in Learning: Cooperative Learning and College Instruction." *Journal of Excellence in College Teaching* 1: 68–76.

Daniels, Craig. 1984. "Integrated Cluster of Independent Courses: An Ideal Curricular Cluster." *Innovative Higher Education* 8: 115–23.

Davis, James R. 1995. *Interdisciplinary Courses and Team Teaching: New Arrangements for Learning.* Phoenix, Ariz.: American Council on Education and Oryx.

Farmer, Donald, and Edmund Napieralski. 1997. "Assessing Learning in Programs." In *Handbook of the Undergraduate Curriculum*, eds. Jerry G. Gaff and James L. Ratcliff. San Francisco: Jossey-Bass.

Feldman, Kenneth A. 1976. "The Superior College Teacher from the Students' View." *Research in Higher Education* 5: 243–88.

Field, Michael, Russell Lee, and Mary Lee Field. 1994. "Assessing Interdisciplinary Learning." In *Interdisciplinary Studies Today*, eds. Julie Thompson Klein and William G. Doty. San Francisco: Jossey-Bass.

Flanagan, Michael F., and David A. Ralston. 1983. "Intra-coordinated Team Teaching: Benefits for Both Students and Instructors." *Teaching of Psychology* 10 (2): 116–17.

Gabelnick, Faith, Jean MacGregor, Roberta S. Matthews, and Barbara L. Smith. 1990. *Learning Communities: Creating Connections among Students, Faculty, and Disciplines.* San Francisco: Jossey-Bass.

Gaff, Jerry G. 1991. *New Life for the College Curriculum.* San Francisco: Jossey-Bass.

Gaff, Jerry G., and James L. Ratcliff, eds. 1997. *Handbook of the Undergraduate Curriculum.* San Francisco: Jossey-Bass.

Goldsmid, Charles A., and Everett K. Wilson. 1980. *Passing on Sociology: The Teaching of a Discipline.* Belmont, Calif.: Wadsworth.

Hendershott, Anne, and Sheila Wright. 1993. "Student Focus Groups and Curricular Review." *Teaching Sociology* 21(2): 154–59.

King, Patricia, and Karen Strohm Kitchener. 1994. *Developing Reflective Judgment.* San Francisco: Jossey-Bass.

Klein, Julie Thompson. 1990. *Interdisciplinarity: History, Theory, and Practice.* Detroit, Mich.: Wayne State University Press.

Klein, Julie Thompson, and William H. Newell. 1997. "Advancing Interdisciplinary Studies." In *Handbook of the Undergraduate Curriculum*, eds. Jerry G. Gaff and James L. Ratcliff. San Francisco: Jossey-Bass.

Kruger, Richard A. 1988. *Focus Groups: A Practical Guide for Applied Research.* Newbury Park, Calif.: Sage.

Light, Richard. 1990. *The Harvard Assessment Seminars: The First Report.* Cambridge, Mass.: Harvard University Press.

Lindauer, David L. 1990. "A New Approach to Team Teaching." *Journal of Economic Education* 4 (1): 71–72.

Lowman, Joseph. 1984. *Mastering the Techniques of Teaching.* San Francisco: Jossey-Bass.

McDaniel, Elizabeth A., and Guy C. Colarulli. 1997. "Collaborative Teaching in the Face of Productivity Concerns: The Dispersed Team Model." *Innovative Higher Education* 22 (1): 19–36.

McFarland, David, and Benjamin F. Taggie. 1990. "Cutting the Gordian Knot: Secrets of Successful Curricular Integration." In *Rethinking the Curriculum: Toward an Integrated, Interdisciplinary College Education,* eds. Mary E. Clark and Sandra A. Wawrytko. New York: Greenwood.

Morgan, D. L. 1988. *Focus Groups as Qualitative Research.* Newbury Park, Calif.: Sage.

Murchland, Bernard, ed. 1991. *Higher Education and the Practice of Democratic Politics: A Political Education Reader.* Dayton, Ohio: Kettering Foundation.

Musella, D., and R. Rusch. 1968. "Student Opinion and College Teaching." *Improving College and University Teaching* 16: 137–40.

Newell, William H. 1983. "The Case for Interdisciplinary Studies: Response to Professor Benson's Five Arguments." *Issues in Integrative Studies* 2: 1–19.

Newell, William H. 1990. "Interdisciplinary Curriculum Development." *Issues in Integrative Studies* 8: 69–86.

Newman, John H. [1873] 1947. *The Idea of a University.* New York: Longmans, Green.

Newstrom, John. 1981. "The Dynamics of Effective Team Teaching." *Personnel Administrator* (July): 56–58, 64.

Perry, William G. 1970. *Forms of Intellectual and Ethical Development in the College Years.* New York: Holt, Rinehart and Winston.

Richards, Donald G. 1996. "The Meaning and Relevance of 'Synthesis' in Interdisciplinary Studies." *Journal of General Education* 45 (2): 114–28.

Rinn, Fanneil J., and Sybil B. Weir. 1984. "Yea, Team." *Improving College and University Teaching* 32 (1): 5–10.

Sherman, Thomas, L. P. Armistead, Forest Fowler, M. A. Barksdale, and Glenn Reif. 1987. "The Quest for Excellence in University Teaching." *Journal of Higher Education* 48: 66–84.

Smith, Barbara L., and Jean MacGregor. 1992. "What Is Collaborative Learning?" In *Collaborative Learning: A Sourcebook for Higher Education,* eds. A. Goodsell et al. University Park, Pa.: National Center on Postsecondary Teaching and Learning Assessment.

Steen, L. 1991. "Reaching for Science Literacy." *Change* 23: 11–20.

Sullivan, Sherry E. 1991. "Are Two Heads Better than One? An Empirical Examination of Team Teaching." *College Student Journal* 25: 308–15.

Twombley, Susan. 1990. "Preparation for Trivial Pursuit or Life? The Meaning Students Give to General Education." Unpublished paper presented at the Association for the Study of Higher Education, Portland, Ore.

Ward, Victoria, Janet Bertrand, and Lisanne F. Brown. 1991. "The Comparability of Focus Groups and Survey Results." *Evaluation Review* 15: 266–83.

Weimer, MaryEllen. 1991. *Improving College Teaching.* San Francisco: Jossey-Bass.

Wright, Sheila P., and Anne Hendershott. 1992. "Using Focus Groups to Obtain Students' Perceptions of General Education." *To Improve the Academy* 11: 87–104.

THE ALL-UNIVERSITY
CURRICULUM AT A GLANCE

CURRENT COURSES

I. Living in a Cultural Context: Western Heritage
A Western Heritage: The Humanities
Discovering America I: American Civilization to 1865
Discovering America II: American Civilization, 1865–1945
Discovering America III: American Civilization, 1945 to Present

II. Living in a Cultural Context: Other Cultures
Hunger: Problems of Scarcity and Choice
Literature and Film of Other Cultures
Native American Cultures
The Caribbean Mosaic
Literature and Culture of Immigrant Groups in America
Cultures and Transnational Corporations

III. Living Responsively with the Arts
Romanticism in the Arts: An Introduction
The Art and Thought of Classical Greece
The Italian Renaissance
Creativity: The Dynamics of Artistic Expression
Ethnic Roots and Urban Arts

IV. Living in a Social Context
Sources of Power
The Adult Journey: A Search for Meaning
Understanding the Dynamics and Environment of the World of Business
Sex, Society, and Selfhood
Discovering the News: A Critical Approach
Ethics in the Professions
Special Topics: What Is School?

V. Living in a Scientific and Technological World
Reasoning in Science
Living in the Environment
Epidemics and AIDS
Technology as a Human Affair
Seeing through Symmetry
Electricity, Electronics, and Culture

Study Abroad (Western Heritage or Arts credit)
Discovering Britain
Landmarks of Early Italy

Each course focuses on developing at least two essential abilities, including written and/or oral communication, critical thinking and problem solving, social interaction, values identification, and responsibility for civic life. And each course features opportunities for active learning. Students take at least four AUC courses, one from each of the areas farthest from their major.

For further information, for example, about courses not discussed in this volume, see the All-University Curriculum homepage, http://www.hartford.edu/AUC.

THE UNIVERSITY OF HARTFORD
AT A GLANCE

The University of Hartford, in West Hartford, Connecticut, is an independent, nonsectarian, comprehensive institution founded in 1877 and chartered in 1957 when three institutions—the Hartford Art School, Hillyer College, and the Hartt School of Music—joined together. It now consists of nine schools and colleges: the College of Arts and Sciences; the Barney School of Business; the College of Education, Nursing, and Health Professions; the Hartford Art School; the Hartt School; the College of Engineering; Ward College of Technology; Hartford College for Women (which joined the university in 1991); and Hillyer College (formerly the College of Basic Studies). Eight of these offer bachelor's degrees, while four offer associate's degrees. All students enrolled in baccalaureate programs participate in the interdisciplinary general education curriculum discussed in this volume, as do faculty from all nine colleges.

The 4,100 full-time undergraduates (75 percent living on campus), 1,200 part-time undergraduates, and 1,800 graduate students come from 44 states and 67 foreign countries. Two-thirds of the student body is from outside Connecticut. Students choose from among 78 undergraduate and 37 graduate degree programs. Ten percent of the university's undergraduates are now in programs that did not exist at the start of the decade, including physical therapy, occupational therapy, architectural engineering technology, and audio engineering technology. Students can combine studies in the various schools and colleges, for example, through such interdisciplinary programs as Acoustics and Music.

For additional information, see the university's home page, http://www.hartford.edu.